Worlds of Women

Susan M. Socolow, Samuel Candler Dobbs Professor of Latin American History, Emory University
Series Editor

The insights offered by women's studies scholarship are invaluable for exploring society, and issues of gender have therefore become a central concern in the social sciences and humanities. The Worlds of Women series addresses in detail the unique experiences of women from the vantage points of such diverse fields as history, political science, literature, law, religion, and gender theory, among others. Historical and contemporary perspectives are given, often with a cross-cultural emphasis. A selected bibliography and, when appropriate, a list of video material relating to the subject matter are included in each volume. Taken together, the series serves as a varied library of resources for the scholar as well as for the lay reader.

Volumes Published

Judy Barrett Litoff and David C. Smith, eds., *American Women in a World at War: Contemporary Accounts from World War II* (1997). Cloth ISBN 0-8420-2570-7 Paper ISBN 0-8420 2571-5

Andrea Tone, ed., *Controlling Reproduction: An American History* (1997). Cloth ISBN 0-8420-2574-X Paper ISBN 0-8420-2575-8

Mary E. Odem and Jody Clay-Warner, eds., *Confronting Rape and Sexual Assault* (1998). Cloth ISBN 0-8420-2598-7 Paper ISBN 0-8420-2599-5

Elizabeth Reis, ed., *Spellbound: Women and Witchcraft in America* (1998). Cloth ISBN 0-8420-2576-6 Paper ISBN 0-8420-2577-4

Spellbound

Spellbound

Women and Witchcraft in America

Edited by
Elizabeth Reis

A Scholarly Resources Inc. Imprint
Wilmington, Delaware

First published 1998
Printed and bound in the United States of America

Scholarly Resources Inc.
104 Greenhill Avenue
Wilmington, DE 19805-1897

Library of Congress Cataloging-in-Publication Data

Spellbound : women and witchcraft in America / edited by
Elizabeth Reis.
p. cm. — (Worlds of women ; 4)
Includes bibliographical references and index.
ISBN 0-8420-2576-6 (hardcover : alk. paper). — ISBN 0-8420-2577-4 (pbk. : alk. paper)
1. Witchcraft—Massachusetts—Salem—History.
2. Witchcraft—History. 3. Women—United States—History.
I. Reis, Elizabeth, 1958– . II. Series.
BF1576.S64 1998
133.4'3'082—dc21 97-49092
CIP

∞ The paper used in this publication meets the minimum requirements of the American National Standard for permanence of paper for printed library materials, Z39.48, 1984.

Acknowledgments

I would like to thank Susan Socolow, the series editor, and Sheryl Young and Michelle Slavin at Scholarly Resources for their guidance in editing this anthology. I also appreciate the help offered by Joan Bayliss and Irwin Noparstak. The students in my most recent Women and Witchcraft seminar at the University of Oregon deserve special mention. They read all of these essays and helped me conceptualize the introduction. Cynthia Eller, Jody Shapiro Davie, and Matthew Dennis discussed potential articles for inclusion with me, and Cynthia clarified the modern feminist spirituality movement at many points along the way. I would also like to thank the contributors to this book. Their insightful scholarship has informed my own thinking on the issues of witchcraft and witch-hunting, and I value their collegiality and friendship. My mother, Pamela Tamarkin Reis, edited a version of the introduction; she and my father, Ronald Reis, as always provided continuous support. Finally, extra thanks go to my husband, Matthew Dennis, fellow historian, parent, perceptive critic, and best friend.

About the Editor

Elizabeth Reis, author of *Damned Women: Sinners and Witches in Puritan New England* (1997), teaches history and women's studies at the University of Oregon. She is currently researching the history of angel belief in America.

Contents

Introduction

Each Halloween the most popular costuming choice among America's trick-or-treaters is the black regalia of the witch. Although some adults invariably complain that Halloween is nothing less than a dangerous neopagan ritual, its costumes and revelry approaching the practice of Satanism, most see it as harmless, indeed fun. Parents encourage the opportunity for creativity and community socializing, while children delight in scary costumes, nighttime ambling, and bags full of candy. Although few really fear the quaint, comic witches of October 31, and although the conflation of contemporary witchcraft and Satanism is flawed (its practice has nothing to do with the devil or devil worship), a connection between witchcraft and Satan nonetheless exists in the popular mind. Even today, for many, "real" witches connote the devil's presence, just as they did in seventeenth-century Massachusetts.

The Halloween debate, although pursued primarily by Christian fundamentalists on the margins of American society, raises issues that connect contemporary religious concerns with those more deeply buried in our nation's historical memory. Stereotypical notions of the witch—the old hag riding her broom to a witches' meeting at which the devil presides—are often coupled or confused with one of America's most shameful and tragic moments: the large-scale accusation and execution of "witches" during the 1692 Salem witch trials. The relationship between the colonial witches, most of whom were women, and the practitioners of witchcraft today, also predominantly female, along with the witch-hunting that has plagued them both, is the subject of this anthology.

The definition of "witch" is ambiguous and has changed over time. Thus, as these twelve essays suggest, the colonial and nineteenth- and twentieth-century perceptions of what constitutes witchcraft differ. Contemporary practitioners of Dianic Wicca or Neopagan Goddess worship deliberately call themselves witches. In so doing they claim as their spiritual ancestors the more than two hundred who were jailed on suspicion of witchcraft as well as the fourteen women executed for it at Salem.[1] And yet the accused women at Salem were not witches in this same sense. As we trace the evolving meaning of "witch" from colonial days to the present, we will also examine the effects that shifting contemporary understandings have had on later witch-hunting and witchcraft practice, as well as on the history and popular memory of Salem itself.

As the meaning of "witch" and "witchcraft" changes, so too does our understanding of women's roles in society. Standards for proper gender deportment and respectability emerge organically out of the societies that create them. They appear natural, or even, as in seventeenth-century New England, divinely ordained. Societies dominated by men, we should not be surprised to observe, institutionalize women's dependency in complex ways that are often invisible to the people living in those social worlds. Women's lives are ordered by a complicated array of disabilities and advantages, liabilities and benefits, affected also by factors like wealth, status, ethnicity, and race. Although women are not treated equally in most patriarchal orders, and some enjoy privileges denied others, such societies nonetheless subordinate and often marginalize women generally. Personhood itself is defined as generically male; women are "other." And the ultimate expression of otherness, indeed demonization, is the "witch," a label affixed preponderantly on women.

The concept of "witch" and the charge of witchcraft help to set and police the boundaries of female normality and acceptability. Women who challenge cultural notions of appropriate conduct, whether intentionally or unintentionally—even women who wholeheartedly embrace social norms—were (and still are) vulnerable to masculine apprehension and mistrust, and in extreme cases to accusations of witchcraft. With limited resources, both material and cultural, women have had limited power with which to quell or divert the consequences of popular paranoia, such as that reflected in witch-hunts. In fact, often lacking a particular female group consciousness, women themselves have participated in the persecution of other women as witches. Although witches can be either male or female, witchcraft, witch-hunting, and womanhood are inextricably linked in American history.

Accusations of witchcraft can be devastating, even deadly, yet various groups of women—African American Spiritualists, Native Americans, and contemporary followers of Wicca, for example—have pursued divination, spirit possession, and other forms of magical practice. This volume will explore some of these women and their practices, especially as they collide with the enduring legacy of Salem. Women who have pursued their own spiritual efficacy through the use of magic or witchcraft run the risk of being misunderstood, at best, or denounced as dangerous. The definition of a witch may have changed in the three hundred years since Salem, but the fear of women's power has not.

Puritan belief held that a witch was someone (in practice usually a woman) who had covenanted with the devil rather than with God, thus allowing the devil to use her shape to torment others in his war against the godly. The devil thus played a central role. In order for a woman to become a witch, Puritans believed, she was required to pledge to him her soul. Upon receipt of this promise, the devil granted the woman extraordinary powers to terrify the godly and to recruit others into the devil's service. It would be easy, but inaccurate, to characterize the Puritans simplistically as misogynists. In fact, Puritan New Englanders considered themselves to be rather more enlightened than others when it came to women's place in their society and in their theology. They did not subscribe to the prevailing European view that women were inherently more evil than men. Nevertheless, they believed that  just as women's bodies were weaker than men's, their souls, too, were less able to withstand the devil's blandishments.

Satan's direct intervention and the "witch's" explicit acceptance of his pact were necessary acts in the colonial drama. Were the accused women of seventeenth-century New England in fact practicing the black arts or worshiping Satan? There is absolutely no evidence to suggest that they worshiped the devil. Like other good Puritans, they feared the devil tremendously. Puritans worshiped God and God alone; the accused women and men were hardly exceptional in this regard. They no doubt practiced some forms of magic, but so did other colonists, even some ministers. Magic, healing, and religion coexisted uneasily in this early modern world, a world in which medical science, as we know it today, did not exist. But magical practice did not define witchcraft; witchcraft was religiously and legally defined, by both the laity and the clergy, as a pact made with Satan, and successful prosecution of a witch thus depended fundamentally on proving the commission of such a contract.

The devil had a hand in all sinful acts, according to Puritan theology, and any transgression could indicate that the sinner's soul had bonded with the devil rather than with God. A fine line existed between sinners and witches: Satan possessed the souls of all sinners alike, but witches, most of whom were assumed to be women, compounded their crime. They did not indirectly admit Satan by their sins; they sinned by directly submitting to Satan. The witch's surrender was explicit; for temporal gain she consciously vowed to promote the devil's purpose. The witch acted aggressively. Purposefully choosing the devil rather than passively waiting for Christ, she eagerly enlisted in the devil's army.

Who were the women singled out for witchcraft accusations? Carol Karlsen's work uncovers which women, in particular, were the most suspect and the most likely to attract the mistrust and loathing of their peers. Karlsen argues that marginality was a primary characteristic of suspected women. Although old age or poverty could marginalize women and render them vulnerable to witchcraft accusations, Karlsen contends that women demonized as witches were often accused because of their imminent economic power in the community. Lacking fathers, husbands, or brothers, some women had gained a measure of autonomy and, significantly, control over inheritances of land, an important form of wealth in early New England. Jealous townspeople, eager to thwart such independence and material success, used witchcraft accusations to control and subordinate these women. Karlsen's work dispels a pervasive myth about the Salem witches. They were not all decrepit, insubstantial, and disreputable women. Power, not debility, put some women at the center of malevolent resentment.

It is one thing to accuse someone of witchcraft and quite another for the entire community to believe the accusations and to act aggressively to combat the devil's onslaught. Despite a theology that suggested spiritual equality, both women and men believed women to be more vulnerable to the devil's temptations and thus more likely to become witches. In part, this discrepancy can be explained by examining women's place in early New England. According to Jane Kamensky, witchcraft accusations were a way to contain and bridle women's speech. Puritan women were enjoined to cultivate silence lest unguarded tattle lead to sin. Feminine virtue required cautious discourse, and a witch was measured, in part, by her indecorous verbal utterances, signaling the antithesis of Puritan womanhood. Ranting, slandering, mocking, cursing: Only a witch could transgress so profoundly and destructively. Accusations brought against suspected women invariably included accounts of their verbal conduct. In addition to various acts of maleficence attributed to the witch, accusers offered examples of untoward expression—shouting, cursing, telling false tales, or calling names. A disorderly tongue announced to the world a diabolical covenant, and reactions to it revealed, by their very opposition, what a virtuous woman ought to say and how she ought to say it. In the process of uncovering who had covenanted with the devil, witchcraft accusations and trials helped define and maintain gendered cultural boundaries.

During the 1692 trials, accusers, defendants, and witnesses introduced evidence that not only spoke to the existence (or absence) of a diabolical covenant but also raised questions about the deployment of maleficium by the accused. Maleficium was magic used for harmful ends, to cause sickness, to injure, or even to kill. Often testimony that a cow had taken sick or that a child had died inexplicably, shortly after the accused had walked nearby, was offered as reliable evidence of the suspected witch's guilt. Such statements—and the fact that they were accepted as reasonable proof—strike us today as outlandish, even barbaric. But although this sort of testimony added weight to the case against a defendant, even the colonial court usually sought more solid demonstration of guilt, ideally two witnesses who had seen the accused sign the devil's pact. Such evidence was exceedingly rare; presumably the devil conscripted his cohorts covertly, and few beside those who allegedly became witches themselves were available as eyewitnesses. The Salem proceedings of 1692, unlike earlier trials in New England, proved unique in the magistrates' willingness to convict based on circumstantial evidence of maleficium and on the dubious phenomenon of spectral evidence: the testimony of witnesses who claimed they had been pinched and choked by the shapes of defendants.

The accused women at Salem pleaded innocence to maleficium, even as they acknowledged the existence of magic, witches, and the devil in their world. Nevertheless, surprisingly, some confessed to witchcraft. Approximately fifty of the accused (forty women and ten men) admitted to signing the devil's book and to giving him permission to use their shapes to afflict others. What are we to make of these confessions? As Elizabeth Reis explains in her article, such admissions need to be understood not merely as statements of guilt regarding the immediate witchcraft charges at Salem, but as avowals of women's basic depravity as sinners within Puritan New England. Women who confessed to signing the devil's book were actually confessing to sinfulness in general. Because of their self-perception, women more often than men blurred the line between ordinary sin—an implicit covenant with Satan—and compacting with the devil—the explicit and damning commission of the specific, nefarious crime of witchcraft. Women could thus unwittingly (and inaccurately) represent themselves as witches.

Confession was expected and denial was not tolerated, especially from women. To deny one's identity as a witch entailed disavowing any bond with the devil. But as any good Puritan woman knew, the commission of even the most minor transgression tied one to the devil, and no one could claim freedom from all sin; indeed, to do so would have been sinful. Women were damned either way: If they confessed to the devil's pact they implicated themselves as witches, and yet, ironically, if they did so their lives were spared. If they denied the charges, on the other hand, even when they lived exemplary lives filled with Christian deeds, they could be deemed liars and witches and hanged in spite of (or, as Reis argues, because of) their denials.

That Tituba, a West Indian slave woman, confessed to witchcraft, then, should come as no surprise. Tituba's confession was the first during the trials, but what exactly she confessed to has become one of the most enduring legends surrounding the Salem trials. A slave in the Salem minister's household, Tituba allegedly started the 1692 witchcraft frenzy by introducing impressionable girls to her native sorcery, encouraging them to predict the identities of their future husbands. Bernard Rosenthal's article shows the dubious foundation of the Tituba myth. Her undeserved notoriety stems from nineteenth-century historians' efforts to discover the "cause" of the witchcraft episode. It was easier to put the onus on a single person—especially a slave woman—than to come to terms with the social, political, and religious tensions that beset the world of venerated Puritan founders. Rosenthal suggests that Tituba's unmerited reputation has a deep and enduring significance. Furthermore, our willingness to accept Tituba's culpability reflects our notions of the association of evil with the dark, dangerous, feminine "other" in American culture.

During the 1692 trials, Tituba's guilt or innocence rested on whether she had covenanted with the devil. Tituba related that she had seen the devil in the shape of a black dog or a yellow bird, and that she had made a mark with red blood in his book; her confession sealed her case. Her vivid portrayals of Satan were never questioned; indeed, throughout the trials credulity reigned when it came to the devil's physical existence and his extraordinary powers. Such conviction began to wane by the end of the trials. The trials' excesses proved embarrassing. Without dismissing the reality of Satan, for such repudiation would be tantamount to repudiating the actuality of God, Puritan lay folk and ministers gradually minimized the devil's direct intervention in the lives of believers. As the intellectual and religious world of eighteenth-century New England became more diverse and complex, the ideas of the Enlightenment gained legitimacy and Puritan orthodoxy lost its exclusive hold on the populace. In this context, the devil made few appearances. In the eighteenth century, he seemed to stay safely in hell, patiently awaiting sinners, rather than roaming abroad in the world.

If the physical Satan was an infrequent visitor to New England in the eighteenth century, he was not banished altogether, especially from the minds of religious seekers. Kenneth Minkema's article suggests that the revivals of the Great Awakening raised both the profiles of God and of the devil. As always, context was everything; in the mid-eighteenth century we see no repeat of Salem. Minkema shows that demonic visitation was no longer interpreted as evidence of witchcraft. When Martha Roberson of Boston claimed to be possessed by

Satan in 1741, after hearing the intensely moving sermons of the famous itinerant preachers George Whitefield and Gilbert Tennent, the meaning of the devil's presence became the focus of partisan debate on the impact and legitimacy of itinerancy and of religious enthusiasm itself. Opponents of revivalism construed the devil's arrival as proof of the evils attendant to Great Awakening preaching. Supporters saw his presence much less ominously and used Roberson's case to their advantage. They viewed her possession as a warning to sinners to listen to the word of God and so avoid similar Satanic intrusion. When pastoral counselors successfully routed the devil from Roberson, she became fully restored as a model of female deportment and religious piety. Roberson's "demonization" was thus temporary and superficial. Rather than being castigated as a witch and expelled from society, with the defeat of her diabolical assailant she was reintegrated into the fold. Once again, the woman other, associated here (unwillingly) with Satan, helped define appropriate womanhood. The redeemed Roberson ultimately embodied submission, not to the devil but to the religious hierarchy.

If possession cases were now seen as occasions for religious indoctrination, or increasingly as signs of mental illness, rather than as indications of witchcraft, the memory of Salem and perhaps even the practices nonetheless lingered. Matthew Dennis extends the discussion beyond New England to the Senecas of western New York during the early nineteenth century. There, too, Salem cast its long shadow, as rounds of witch-hunting accompanied native revitalization. Ironically, Seneca leaders defended this pursuit by referencing Salem, even as the events of 1692 were increasingly remembered by Euro-Americans as a distinct disgrace.

Witchcraft had been conventional among the Senecas, although it had been a gender-neutral phenomenon and had nothing to do with Christianity's Satan. *Orenda*, or power, could be utilized by men and women for good or evil; those who manipulated *orenda* to injure others were witches, whom Senecas universally feared and loathed. But as the intensifying influences of colonialism and Christianity altered Seneca life, the character of their witchcraft, not surprisingly, also changed. Coincident with the rise of the Seneca prophet Handsome Lake, in the turbulent years after the American Revolution, witchcraft accusations flourished—especially against women. In the Code of Handsome Lake, the prophet and his followers established specific guidelines for proper behavior. Witchcraft emerged in the code as a dangerous threat to Seneca well-being, and it was proscribed. While such prohibitions were consistent with tradition, Seneca witch-hunting of the early nineteenth century was not. The revitalization associated with Handsome Lake, blending tradition with elements of Christianity and Euro-American culture, conjured up an array of witches reminscent of the Salem crisis. Or, rather, the internal struggles among the Senecas as they negotiated their colonial predicament led to witch-hunting, which, as at Salem, produced witches.

The struggle to integrate Christianity with ancestrally established spirituality was not limited to Native American groups. African Americans similarly underwent a process of creative adjustment to Christianity. Beginning in the seventeenth century, they appropriated and blended the religion of their oppressors with a diverse set of non-Christian beliefs and practices from Africa, the Caribbean, and America. Nell Painter looks at one woman's efforts in nineteenth-century America to merge and balance religion in her life.

A Christian, Isabella (who later adopted the name Sojourner Truth) believed in the powers of witchcraft and magic. But as a Christian, and a newly converted Methodist at that, she resolutely placed Jesus at the center of her life. Rather than passively waiting for Christ's advances, however, Isabella tried to use Christianity as a means of empowerment. In the incident Painter describes here, however, Isabella was not averse to using any means to make her earthly existence more bearable. Ideally, Jesus helped her in times of need, but at some perilous moments she wondered if her power came from other, less commendable, sources. When Isabella placed a "curse" on the family that treated her small boy so brutally, she surprised even herself at its apparent efficacy. She did not doubt that something otherworldly had happened. Was Isabella a witch because she thought her curse had been successful? Painter's article implicitly raises this question and leads us to recognize the changing perceptions of witchcraft, magic, and women's power.

Women in America have often found their voices through religion, which in various ways has authorized their speech, even leadership, at times when women have otherwise lacked a legitimate public place and status. African American Spiritualist churches, which blend Roman Catholicism, elements of various black Protestant denominations, and, significantly, Haitian Voudon, have offered women great opportunity of expression and authority. Female congregants are empowered by their faith and by their practice of spirit possession, but they simultaneously incur a liability. In America, all churches are not created equal; churches dominated by women—and tainted by hoodoo—are perceived by outsiders as simply dens of superstition and witchcraft.

Mainstream opinion, which marginalizes Spiritualism, seems colored, not merely by fears of women's power but also by Americans' particular memory of Salem, especially of the dark, female other, the mythic instigator, Tituba. African American struggles for respectability and acceptance in a hostile world could thus militate against the spiritual leadership of black women. Indeed, in New Orleans, women were often warned against joining Spiritualist churches, as David Estes reports. Nonetheless, Estes's article shows that Spiritualism fitfully survived its reputation as it spread rapidly from Northern cities throughout the South, where it centers now in New Orleans. Women leaders of the Spiritual churches live with a striking irony, Estes argues. On the one hand, the churches' historical connection to African-Caribbean religious culture preserves traditional practice and venerates female leadership; on the other hand, it is precisely these attributes that stigmatize the faith.

Given the history of religious repression in this country, it is no wonder that African American Spiritual church leaders would seek to dissociate their rituals from the seemingly dangerous occult practice. But their conjuring of spirits, speaking in tongues, burning of candles, and use of charms are easily misunderstood by outsiders, both white and black. Estes shows that witchcraft suspicions, if not accusations and prosecutions, marginalize women Spiritualists, but that on those margins women also find ways to empower themselves. Women Spiritualists continue to strive to maintain their churches and to protect them from those who lack the ability or inclination for understanding or, at least, toleration.

Sidney Harring similarly examines religious beliefs and practices that are poorly understood and broadly stigmatized as superstitious, if not savage. He analyzes the murder trial of Lila Jimerson and Nancy Bowen, two Cayuga Iroquois women accused of killing Clothilde Marchand, whom they claimed was a witch. The article highlights issues of cultural and religious difference, the contradictions embedded in Indians' legal status, and the continued struggle by Iroquois and other Native people to live in the United States without abandoning their cultural teachings and customs. Like their Seneca relatives in an earlier time, this twentieth-century Cayuga community continued to believe in—and suffer from—the nefarious practice of witchcraft. Jimerson and Bowen, tried by the state of New York for premeditated murder, testified that their act of homicide was a necessary, justifiable attempt to rid themselves and their kinspeople of a dangerous witch. The proceedings were filled with contradictions and unanswerable questions. Whose beliefs, practices, and rules—those of New York or the Indian nation—should take precedence? Could two starkly different world views be reconciled? And what was the role of the victim's husband, a maker of Indian dioramas for local museums, in manipulating Jimerson and Bowen to commit the deed he desired done? Belief in witchcraft specifically, and Native non-Christian religious ideology and practice in general, signaled Indian "backwardness," even savagery, to outsiders and justified white racist thought and action. Yet, to the Indians, this incident, however embarrassing, served as a rallying point for the reassertion of Native solidarity, tribal autonomy, and renewed efforts to combat white racism.

Although white and even Native critics derided Jimerson's and Bowen's witchcraft as uncivilized, primitive, or pagan, magic is not something that disappeared with the advent of scientific rationalism. Magic and ritual that trace their origin to more remote pre-Christian times are practiced even today by spiritual feminists.[2] Their religion, sometimes referred to as Wicca, based on the Latin root meaning "to bend or shape," promotes personal and collective growth, transformation, and healing.

Wicca has some similarities to the magical practice of Cayugas and other Native people, but there are important differences as well. In both, modern-day practitioners use their magic as a source of power, power often denied them as marginalized people, especially as women in a patriarchal world. Cayuga traditionalists, however, would hardly call their benevolent magical practice witchcraft, which they understand as the sinister manipulation of power. Many well-meaning, benign practitioners of Wicca embrace the label of witch, which they strive to rehabilitate, and perhaps reinvent, as they attempt to link themselves with ancient and contemporary magical practice. (For contemporary Native Americans such New Age linkage can cause considerable discomfort, as we shall see in Cynthia Eller's essay.)

According to one of its leading spokespersons, Starhawk, witchcraft is a religion that began some thirty-five thousand years ago. Persecution forced witches underground to practice their craft secretly. By 1975 women had openly reclaimed the ancient title of witch. They identified with what they interpreted as the prepatriarchal goddess religion, and they began to promote a feminist interpretation of the European witch trials. Worshiping a panoply of goddesses and revering nature and women's bodies, their sacred history contends that witches have continuously battled oppression and repression, most significantly during the "burning times" in the Middle Ages. According to this controversial narrative some European witches found their way to America, where they practiced their craft, probably in Salem, Massachusetts.

Modern-day witchcraft includes a wide variety of neopagan and feminist components, as Starhawk explains in her essay. The Goddess movement has no unifying organization, written scripture, dogma, or defining ritual practice. Its witches trace their current revival to

Gerald Gardner in England in the 1940s, and individual covens, or small groups of practitioners, selectively incorporate rituals that Gardner and others have since introduced: casting circles, calling the spirits of the four directions, raising group energy, working various spells, and sharing ceremonial meals. Feminist witches see witchcraft as providing new models for women; their ritual and practice glorify women's power and affirm their bodies.

Witches form part of the larger movement of spiritual feminism. In her definition of spiritual feminists, Cynthia Eller includes women who adopt at least three of the following five characteristics: "valuing women's empowerment, practicing ritual and/or magic, revering nature, using the feminine or gender as a primary mode of religious analysis, and espousing the revisionist version of Western history favored by the movement."[3] Not all spiritual feminists call themselves witches. Indeed, some disdain the label because of its negative connotations, preferring instead to highlight their alternative religion's optimistic, beneficent world view. Borrowing from New Age spiritual practices and a host of other non-Western traditions, spiritual feminist rituals emphasize the positive. Divination, altar building, meditation, dreamwork, and curing express a feminist spirit and focus on repairing the mental and physical state of individual women and the integrity of the earth.

Issues of magical practice are controversial among spiritual feminists, whether they call themselves witches or not. They recognize magic's efficacy but realize that its use entails responsibility. Some say that any contact with the sacred is a magical transformation; others harness the power of ritual but try to distance themselves and their craft from the taint of evil doings. Modern witchcraft teaches (through new oral tradition and the writings of leaders such as Starhawk) that magic should be performed only for good. In fact, witches espouse the "threefold law" as a self-monitoring guideline: What you send returns three times over. Negative energy, practitioners believe, will revisit one who knowingly dispatches it. Despite its potential for abuse, magic is practiced, and spiritual feminists believe that, if done properly, it usually works.

Spiritual feminists also incorporate magical techniques and rituals from a variety of old and new cultures. Cynthia Eller explores witchcraft's cultural borrowings and their implications in the essay excerpted from her book, *Living in the Lap of the Goddess*. Cultural borrowings from women of color—from Goddess symbols to sweat lodges—have enriched some women's experience, while generating new debates about the ethics of cultural appropriation and domination. Some critics contend, for example, that spiritual feminists lack understanding of Native American people. Unconcerned about real, living Native people and their cultures, uninterested in learning the complex patterns of Indian lives, or unwilling to respect Native privacy, spiritual feminists are, according to these observers, too often willing to wrench ideas, practices, or ritual objects from their Native contexts and deploy them insensitively and inaccurately for their own purposes. Cultural borrowing is problematic, as Eller suggests and as some spiritual feminists recognize. It tends to caricature and even violate what it means to glorify—cultures that are complex and mutable. It turns living people into static, cultural relics, valuable only for what their heritage, real or imagined, can offer spiritual feminism.

The veneration of goddesses in ancient cultures and in African religions has been appropriated to support spiritual feminists' contention that female deities have been worshiped for millennia. But many practitioners of these pagan rituals have employed the Goddess for sexist and misogynist purposes. As Linda Jencson explains in her article, feminist goddess worshipers are not always aware of this imitation. Paradoxically, women caught up in these misogynist circles end up as victims of verbal or sexual abuse. Jencson raises important questions. Is witchcraft always feminist? What is the precise relationship between magical practice, pagan rituals, and goddess worship? How can women interested in female empowerment use their spiritual resources effectively? Must they endure association with negatively stereotyped witchcraft?

Contemporary witches contribute to public misperceptions by linking themselves (most historians would say, problematically) to the Salem witch trials. Claiming that up to two thousand self-identified witches today have chosen Salem as their home, they create a useful, shared past by appropriating the martyrology of colonial witch-hunting. Today's witches contend that the witches of Salem were practicing a form of alternative religion, which probably included nature worship, a reverence for the Goddess, and spells for healing. They see these women as scapegoats persecuted for their religious ideology, just as they feel victimized today as a result of their adherence to an alternative, non-Christian religious faith. In adopting the victims of late-seventeenth-century Salem as their witch foremothers, contemporary witches may ironically endorse the misogynist charges of those who persecuted them. The accused women were not witches, and neither the dubious judicial proceedings of three hundred years ago nor the well-meaning, if ill-informed, revisionism of today can so make them.

Salem's latter-day witches are correct about one of their claimed affinities: Those accused and executed in 1692, like themselves, did not worship Satan. Some witches deny that the popular confusion about the meaning and nature of the witch is their problem and choose to ignore the issue. Nevertheless, by assuming the label of "witch," those practicing "witchcraft" become weighted by all of the baggage associated with a term that, despite the work of some to rehabilitate it, continues to carry connotations of evil.

The excesses of the Salem witchcraft trials have certainly persisted in our nation's collective recall. Even to this day, the term "witch-hunt," applied to contemporary social problems such as the false accusation of child abuse or to political persecutions like McCarthyism, is used to invoke memories of a grim past, a time when concocted accusations were rife and innocent lives were rashly extinguished.

Women who pursue alternative feminist spirituality in today's world encounter prejudice and hostility because their belief in ritual and magic is often perceived as silly at best or as Satanic worship at worst. In this respect, modern-day witches rightly identify with the Salem witches. The persecutors of both justify their actions by alleging the women's connection to evil. This abuse is simply control of women thinly disguised as the extirpation of demons. Witches of today are derided even when their spiritual practices, per se, are not directly at issue. Arguing against Iowa's proposed Equal Rights Amendment in 1992, Pat Robertson expounded to members of the Christian Coalition that the feminist movement was "a socialist, anti-family political movement that encourages women to leave their husbands, kill their children, practice witchcraft, destroy capitalism and become lesbians."[4] Now, as in the times of our colonial ancestors, some continue to impose their particular theological beliefs to explain evil, identify sin, and subordinate women.

Notes

1. Three-fourths of those suspected of witchcraft in seventeenth-century New England were women. Carol F. Karlsen has identified 334 accusations and 35 executions in New England between the years 1620 and 1725. At Salem there were 156 accusations and 30 convictions; 14 women and 5 men were hanged; one man was pressed to death. See Carol F. Karlsen, *The Devil in the Shape of a Woman: Witchcraft in Colonial New England* (New York: Norton, 1987), 47. See also Richard Godbeer, *The Devil's Dominion: Magic and Religion in Early New England* (Cambridge: Cambridge University Press, 1992), 235–42, for useful appendixes of names and outcomes of cases before and during the Salem crisis.

2. Modern spiritual feminists should not be confused with the women of the Spiritual church in New Orleans, discussed in David C. Estes's essay.

3. Cynthia Eller, *Living in the Lap of the Goddess: The Feminist Spirituality Movement in America* (Boston: Beacon, 1995), 6.

4. Tamar Lewin, "Hers Column," *New York Times Magazine*, October 18, 1992, 24.

1

The Economic Basis of Witchcraft

~

Carol F. Karlsen

This excerpt from Carol F. Karlsen's book The Devil in the Shape of a Woman: Witchcraft in Colonial New England *contends that women were more likely to be accused, convicted, and executed for witchcraft if they did not have husbands, brothers, or sons—if as autonomous women they therefore challenged the conventional transfer of property from one generation of males to the next. Carefully reconstructing the inheritance patterns of early New England, as well as the financial and property status of accused women, Karlsen argues that while a minority of the accused women at Salem and in earlier trials were indeed quite poor, the majority of those executed were women who either had inherited property or who were about to inherit substantial amounts of land or money. As women on the margins (some may have remained poor), they were the most often suspected and, once named, the most prone to conviction and execution, despite the fact that economic matters were rarely at issue in the trial transcripts themselves. Once convicted as witches, potentially powerful women lost their property either to destruction by jealous neighbors or to the authorities, and they found themselves in a poor position to recover it, in seemingly endless legal battles, after the trials ended.*

MOST OBSERVERS NOW AGREE THAT witches in the villages and towns of late sixteenth- and early seventeenth-century England tended to be poor. They were not usually the poorest women in their communities, one historian has argued; they were the "moderately poor."

From Carol F. Karlsen, *The Devil in the Shape of a Woman: Witchcraft in Colonial New England* (New York: Norton, 1987), 77–84, 102–16, 296–300, and 305–9.

Rarely were relief recipients suspect; rather it was those just above them on the economic ladder, "like the woman who felt she ought to get poor relief, but was denied it."[1] This example brings to mind New England's Eunice Cole, who once berated Hampton selectmen for refusing her aid when, she insisted, a man no worse off than she was receiving it.[2]

Eunice Cole's experience also suggests the difficulty in evaluating the class position of the accused. Commonly used class indicators such as the amount of property owned, yearly income, occupation, and political offices held are almost useless in analyzing the positions of women during the colonial period. While early New England women surely shared in the material benefits and social status of their fathers, husbands, and even sons, most were economically dependent on the male members of their families throughout their lives. Only a small proportion of these women owned property outright, and even though they participated actively in the productive work of their communities, their labor did not translate into financial independence or economic power. Any income generated by married women belonged by law to their husbands, and because occupations open to women were few and wages meager, women alone could only rarely support themselves. Their material condition, moreover, could easily change with an alteration in their marital status. William Cole, with an estate at his death of £41 after debts, might be counted among the "moderately poor," as might Eunice Cole when he was alive. But the refusal of the authorities to recognize the earlier transfer of this estate from husband to wife ensured, among other things, that as a widow Eunice Cole was among the poorest of New England's poor.

The distinction between the economic circumstances of wife and widow here may not seem particularly significant, but in other cases the problem is more complicated. How, for instance, do we classify the witch Ann Dolliver? The daughter of prominent Salem minister John Higginson, who was well above most of his neighbors in wealth and social status, she was also the deserted wife of William Dolliver, and lived out her life without the support of a husband, dependent first on her father and then on the town for her maintenance.[3] Even if we were willing to assume that the accused shared the class position of their male relatives, the lack of information on so many of the families of witches makes it impossible to locate even the males on an economic scale.

Despite conceptual problems and sparse evidence, it is clear that poor women, both the destitute and those with access to some resources, were surely represented, and very probably overrepresented, among the New England accused. Perhaps 20 percent of accused women, including both Eunice Cole and Ann Dolliver, were either impoverished or living at a level of bare subsistence when they were accused.[4] Some, like thirty-seven-year-old Abigail Somes, worked as servants a substantial portion of their adult lives. Some supported themselves and their families with various kinds of temporary labor such as nursing infants, caring for sick neighbors, taking in washing and sewing, or harvesting crops. A few, most notably Tituba, the first person accused during the Salem outbreak, were slaves. Others, like the once-prosperous Sarah Good of Wenham and Salem, and the never-very-well-off Ruth Wilford of Haverhill, found themselves reduced to abject poverty by the death of a parent or a change in their own marital status.[5] Accused witches came before local magistrates requesting permission to sell family land in order to support themselves, to submit claims against their children or executors of their former husbands' estates for nonpayment of the widow's lawful share of the estate, or simply to ask for food and fuel from the town selectmen. Because they could not pay the costs of their trials or jail terms, several were forced to remain in prison after courts acquitted them. The familiar stereotype of the witch as an indigent woman who resorted to begging for her survival is hardly an inaccurate picture of some of New England's accused.

Still, the poor account for only a minority of the women accused. Even without precise economic indicators, it is clear that women from all levels of society were vulnerable to accusation. If witches in early modern England can accurately be described as "moderately poor," then New Englanders deviated sharply from their ancestors in their ideas about which women were witches. Wives, daughters, and widows of "middling" farmers, artisans, and mariners were regularly accused, and (although much less often) so too were women belonging to the gentry class. The accused were addressed as Goodwife (or Goody) and as the more honorific Mrs. or Mistress, as well as by their first names.[6]

Prosecution was a different matter. Unless they were single or widowed, accused women from wealthy families—families with estates valued at more than £500—could be fairly confident that the accusations would be ignored by the authorities or deflected by their husbands through suits for slander against their accusers. Even during the Salem outbreak, when several women married to wealthy men were arrested, most managed to escape to the safety of other colonies through their husbands' influence. Married women from moderately well-off families—families with estates valued at between roughly £200 and £500—did not always escape prosecution so easily, but neither do they seem, as a group, to have been as vulnerable as their less prosperous counterparts. When only married women are considered, women in families with estates worth less than £200 seem significantly overrepresented among *convicted* witches—a pattern which suggests that economic position was a more important factor to judges and juries than to the community as a whole in its role as accuser.[7]

Without a husband to act on behalf of the accused, wealth alone rarely provided women with protection against prosecution. Boston's Ann Hibbens, New Haven's Elizabeth Godman, and Wethersfield's Katherine Harrison, all women alone, were tried as witches despite sizable estates. In contrast, the accusations against women like Hannah Griswold of Saybrook, Connecticut, Elizabeth Blackleach of Hartford, and Margaret Gifford of Salem, all wives of prosperous men when they were accused, were simply not taken seriously by the courts. The most notable exception to this pattern is the obliviousness of the Salem judges to repeated accusations against Margaret Thatcher, widow of one of the richest merchants in Boston and principal heir to her father's considerable fortune. Her unusual wealth and social status may have kept her out of jail in 1692, but more likely it was her position as mother-in-law to Jonathan Corwin, one of the Salem magistrates, that accounts for her particular immunity.[8]

Economic considerations, then, do appear to have been at work in the New England witchcraft cases. But the issue was not simply the relative poverty—or wealth—of accused witches or their families. It was the special position of most accused witches vis-à-vis their society's rules for transferring wealth from one generation to another. To explain why their position was so unusual, we must turn first to New England's system of inheritance.

Inheritance is normally thought of as the transmission of property at death, but in New England, as in other agricultural societies, adult children received part of their father's accumulated estates prior to his death, usually at the time they married.[9] Thus the inheritance system included both pre-mortem endowments and post-mortem distributions. While no laws compelled fathers to settle part of their estates on their children as marriage portions, it was customary to do so. Marriages were, among other things, economic arrangements, and young people could not benefit from these arrangements unless their fathers provided them with the means to set up households and earn their livelihoods. Sons' portions tended to be land, whereas daughters commonly received movable goods and/or money. The exact value of these endowments varied according to a father's wealth and inclination, but it appears that as a general rule the father of the young woman settled on the couple roughly half as much as the father of the young man.[10]

Custom, not law, also guided the distribution of a man's property at his death, but with two important exceptions. First, a man's widow, if he left one, was legally entitled "by way of dower" to one-third part of his real property, "to have and injoy for term of her natural life." She was expected to support herself with the profits of this property, but since she held only a life interest in it, she had to see that she did not "strip or waste" it.[11] None of the immovable estate could be sold, unless necessary for her or her children's maintenance, and then only with the permission of the court. A man might will his wife more than a third of his real property—but not less. Only if the woman came before the court to renounce her dower right publicly, and then only if the court approved, could this principle be waived. In the form of her "thirds," dower was meant to provide for a woman's support in widowhood. The inviolability of dower protected the widow from the claims of her children against the estate and protected the community from the potential burden of her care.

The second way in which law determined inheritance patterns had to do specifically with intestate cases.[12] If a man died without leaving a will, several principles governed the division of his property. The widow's third, of course, was to be laid out first. Unless "just cause" could be shown for some other distribution, the other two-thirds were to be divided among the surviving children, both male and female.[13] A double portion was to go to the eldest son, and single portions to his sisters and younger brothers. If there were no sons, the law stipulated that the estate was to be shared equally by the daughters. In cases where any or all of the children had not yet come of age, their portions were to be held by their mother or by a court-appointed guardian until they reached their majorities or married.[14] What remained of the widow's thirds at her death was to be divided among the surviving children, in the same proportions as the other two-thirds.

Although bound to conform to laws concerning the widow's thirds, men who wrote wills were not legally required to follow the principles of inheritance laid out in intestate cases. Individual men had the right to decide for themselves who would ultimately inherit their property. As we shall see later, will-writers did sometimes deviate sharply from these guidelines, but the majority seem to have adhered closely (though not always precisely) to the custom of leaving a double portion to the eldest son. Beyond that, New England men seem generally to have agreed to a system of partible inheritance, with both sons and daughters inheriting.

When these rules were followed, property ownership and control generally devolved upon men. Neither the widow's dower nor, for the most part, the daughters' right to inherit signified more than *access to* property. For widows, the law was clear that dower allowed for "use" only. For inheriting daughters who were married, the separate but inheritance-related principle of coverture applied. Under English common law, "feme covert" stipulated that married women had no right to own property—indeed, upon marriage, "the very being or legal existence of the woman is suspended."[15] Personal property which a married daughter inherited from her father, either as dowry or as a post-mortem bequest, immediately became the legal possession of her husband, who could exert full powers of ownership over it. A married daughter who inherited land from her father retained title to the land, which her husband could not sell without her consent. On her husband's death such land became the property of her children, but during his life her husband was entitled to the use and profits of it, and his wife could not devise it to her children by will.[16] The property of an inheriting daughter who was single seems to have been held "for improvement" for her until she was married, when it became her dowry.[17]

This is not to say that women did not benefit when they inherited property. A sizable inheritance could provide a woman with a materially better life; if single or widowed, inheriting women enjoyed better chances for an economically advantageous marriage or remarriage. But inheritance did not normally bring women the independent economic power it brought men.

The rules of inheritance were not always followed, however. In some cases, individual men decided not to conform to customary practices; instead, they employed one of several legal devices to give much larger shares of their estates to their wives or daughters, many times for disposal at their own discretion. Occasionally, the magistrates themselves allowed the estate to be distributed in some other fashion. Or most commonly, the absence of male heirs in families made conformity impossible. In all three exceptions to inheritance customs, but most particularly the last, the women who stood to benefit economically also assumed a position of unusual vulnerability. They, and in many instances their daughters, became prime targets for witchcraft accusations. . . .

A substantial majority of New England's accused females were women without brothers, women with daughters but no sons, or women in marriages with no children at all (see table 1). Of the 267 accused females, enough is known about 158 to identify them as either having or not having brothers or sons to inherit: only sixty-two of the 158 (39 percent) did, whereas ninety-six (61 percent) did not. More striking, *once accused*, women without brothers or sons were even more likely than women with brothers or sons to be tried, convicted, and executed: women from families without male heirs made up 64 percent of the females prosecuted, 76 percent of those who were found guilty, and 89 percent of those who were executed.

These figures must be read with care, however, for two reasons. First, eighteen of the sixty-two accused females who *had* brothers or sons to inherit were themselves daughters and granddaughters of women who did not. If, as we argued earlier, these eighteen females, most of whom were young women or girls, were accused because their neighbors believed that their mothers and grandmothers passed their witchcraft on to them, then they form a somewhat ambiguous group. Since they all had brothers to inherit, it would be inaccurate to exclude them from this category in table 1; yet including them understates the extent to which inheritance-related concerns were at issue in witchcraft accusations. At the same time, the large number of cases in which the fertility and mortality patterns of witches' families are unknown (109 of the 267 accused females in New England) makes it impossible to assess precisely the proportion of women among the accused who did not have brothers or sons.[18]

Table 1. Female Witches by Presence or Absence of Brothers or Sons, New England, 1620–1725 (A)

Action	*Women without Brothers or Sons*		*Women with Brothers or Sons*		*Total*
Accused	96	(61%)	62	(39%)	158
Tried	41	(64%)	23	(36%)	64
Convicted	25	(76%)	8	(24%)	33
Executed	17	(89%)	2	(11%)	19

Table 2 helps clarify the point. It includes as a separate category the daughters and granddaughters of women without brothers or sons and incorporates the cases for which this information is unknown. Although inclusion of the unknowns renders the overall percentages meaningless, this way of representing the available information shows clearly the particular vulnerability of women without brothers or sons. Even if *all* the unknown cases involved women from families *with* male heirs—a highly unlikely possibility—women from families without males to inherit would still form a majority of convicted and executed witches. Were the complete picture visible, I suspect that it would not differ substantially from that presented earlier in table 1—which is based on data reflecting 60 percent of New England's witches and which indicates that women without brothers and sons were more vulnerable than other women at all stages of the process.

Table 2. Female Witches by Presence or Absence of Brothers or Sons, New England, 1620–1725 (B)

Action	Women without Brothers or Sons	Daughters and Grand-daughters of Women without Brothers or Sons	Women with Brothers or Sons	Unknown Cases	Total
Accused	96 (36%)	18 (7%)	44 (16%)	109 (41%)	267
Tried	41 (48%)	6 (7%)	17 (20%)	22 (26%)	86
Convicted	25 (56%)	0 (0%)	6 (13%)	12 (27%)	43
Executed	17 (61%)	0 (0%)	2 (7%)	9 (32%)	28

Numbers alone, however, do not tell the whole story. More remains to be said about what happened to these inheriting or potentially inheriting women, both before and after they were accused of witchcraft.

It was not unusual for women in families without male heirs to be accused of witchcraft shortly after the deaths of fathers, husbands, brothers, or sons. Katherine Harrison, Susanna Martin, Joan Penney, and Martha Carrier all exemplify this pattern. So too does elderly Ann Hibbens of Boston, whose execution in 1656 seems to have had a profound enough effect on some of her peers to influence the outcomes of subsequent trials for years to come.[19] Hibbens had three sons from her first marriage, all of whom lived in England; but she had no children by her husband, William Hibbens, with whom she had come to Massachusetts in the 1630s. William died in 1654; Ann was brought to trial two years later. Although her husband's will has not survived, he apparently left a substantial portion (if not all) of his property directly to her: When she wrote her own will shortly before her execution, Ann Hibbens was in full possession of a £344 estate, most of which she bequeathed to her sons in England.[20]

Similarly, less than two years elapsed between the death of Gloucester's William Vinson and the imprisonment of his widow Rachel in 1692. Two children, a son and a daughter, had been born to the marriage, but the son had died in 1675. Though William Vinson had had four sons (and three daughters) by a previous marriage, the sons were all dead by 1683. In his will, which he wrote in 1684, before he was certain that his last son had been lost at sea, William left his whole £180 estate to Rachel for her life, stipulating that she could sell part of the lands and cattle if she found herself in need of resources. After Rachel's death, "in Case" his son John "be Living and returne home agayne," William said, most of the estate was to be divided between John and their daughter Abigail. If John did not return, both shares were to be Abigail's.[21]

Bridget Oliver (later Bridget Bishop) was brought into court on witchcraft charges less than a year after the death of her husband Thomas Oliver in 1679. He had died intestate, but since the estate was worth less than £40 after debts, and since Bridget had a child to raise, the court gave her all but £3 of it during her lifetime, stipulating that she could sell a ten-acre lot "towards paying the debts and her present supply." Twenty shillings went to each of her husband's two sons by his first wife, and twenty shillings to the Olivers' twelve-year-old daughter Christian, the only child of their marriage.[22]

In other cases, many years passed between the death of the crucial male relative and the moment when a formal witchcraft complaint was filed. Twenty years had elapsed, for instance, between the death of Adam Hawkes of Lynn and the arrest of his widow and daughter. Adam had died in 1672, at the age of sixty-four, just three years after his marriage to the much-younger Sarah Hooper and less than a year after the birth of their daughter Sarah. He had died without leaving a will, but his two principal heirs—his widow and his son John from his first marriage—said they were aware of Adam's intentions concerning his £772 estate. The magistrates responsible for distributing Adam's property took their word, allowing "certain articles of agreement" between the two to form the basis of the distribution. As a result, the elder Sarah came into full possession of 188 acres of land and one-third of Adam's movable property. Her daughter was awarded £90, "to be paid five pounds every two years until forty pounds is paid, and the fifty pounds at age or marriage."[23]

It was just about the time young Sarah was due to receive her marriage portion that she and her mother, then Sarah Wardwell, were accused of witchcraft. Named with them as witches were the elder Sarah's second husband, carpenter Samuel Wardwell, their nineteen-year-old daughter, Mercy, and the mother, two sisters, and brother of Francis Johnson, the younger Sarah's husband-to-be.[24] It is not clear whether when Sarah Hawkes became Sarah Johnson she received the balance of her inheritance, but £36 of Sarah and Samuel Wardwell's property was seized by the authorities in 1692. Massachusetts passed a law at the height of the Salem outbreak providing attainder for "conjuration, witchcraft and dealing with evil and wicked spirits."[25] Attainder meant the loss of civil, inheritance, and property rights for persons like Sarah Wardwell who had been sentenced to death. Not until 1711 was restitution made to Sarah Wardwell's children.[26]

Margaret Thatcher was not formally accused of witchcraft until more than thirty years after she became an heiress. Merchant Jacob Sheaffe, Margaret's first husband, may have been the richest man in Boston when he died in 1659, leaving only his thirty-four-year-old widow and two daughters, Elizabeth and Mehitabel, to inherit.[27] What disposition was made of the estate is not clear, but the following year witnessed the death of Margaret's father, merchant Henry Webb, a man whose wealth nearly equaled that of his son-in-law, and whose highly detailed will is extant. Margaret was Webb's only child (his wife had died only months before) and he left most of his £7819 estate to her and his two granddaughters, with alternative bequests in several places in the event that Margaret had male heirs by a "second or other marriage."[28] Margaret *was* married again, to Thomas Thatcher, minister of Boston's Old South Church, but no male heirs were born.[29] Though Margaret was not named a witch until the Salem outbreak, her cousin Elizabeth Blackleach was accused in 1662, two years after Henry Webb's death.[30] Henry had left Elizabeth £140 in his will, £40 of which was to go to her then only child after Elizabeth's death.

Mary English of Salem was charged with witchcraft seven years after she came into her inheritance. Her father, merchant William Hollingworth, had been declared lost at sea in 1677, but at that time Mary's brother William was still alive. Possibly because the younger William was handling the family's interests in other colonies, or possibly because the father's estate was in debt for more than it was worth, the magistrates gave the widow Elinor Hollingworth power of attorney to salvage what she could.[31] With her "owne labor," as she put it, "but making use of other mens estates," the aggressive and outspoken Mistress Hollingworth soon had her deceased husband's debts paid and his wharf, warehouse, and tavern solvent again.[32] She had no sooner done so, however, than she was accused of witchcraft by the wife of a Gloucester mariner.[33] Though the magistrates gave little credence to the charge at the time, they may have had second thoughts later. In 1685, her son William died, and Elinor subsequently conveyed the whole Hollingworth estate over to Mary English, who was probably her only surviving child.[34]

Elinor Hollingworth had died by 1692, but Mary English was one of the women cried out upon early in the Salem outbreak. Her husband, the merchant Philip English, was accused soon after. Knowing their lives were in grave danger, the Englishes fled to the safety of New York. But as one historian of witchcraft has pointed out, flight was "the legal equivalent of conviction."[35] No sooner had they left than close to £1200 of their property was confiscated under the law providing attainder for witchcraft.[36]

Not all witches from families without male heirs were accused of conspiring with the devil *after* they had come into their inheritances. On the contrary, some were accused prior to the death of the crucial male relative, many times before it was clear who would inherit. Eunice Cole was one of these women. Another was Martha Corey of Salem, who was accused of witchcraft in 1692 while her husband was still alive. Giles Corey had been married twice before and had several daughters by the time he married the widow Martha Rich, probably in the 1680s. With no sons to inherit, Giles's substantial land holdings would, his neighbors might have assumed, be passed on to his wife and daughters. Alice Parker, who may have been Giles's daughter from a former marriage, also came before the magistrates as a witch in 1692, as did Giles himself. Martha Corey and Alice Parker maintained their innocence and were hanged. Giles Corey, in an apparently futile attempt to preserve his whole estate for his heirs, refused to respond to the indictment. To force him to enter a plea, he was tortured: Successively heavier weights were placed on his body until he was pressed to death.[37]

What seems especially significant here is that most accused witches whose husbands were still alive were, like their counterparts who were widows and spinsters, over forty years of age—and therefore unlikely if not unable to produce male heirs. Indeed, the fact that witchcraft accusations were rarely taken seriously by the community until the accused stopped bearing children takes on a special meaning when it is juxtaposed with the anomalous position of inheriting women or potentially inheriting women in New England's social structure.

Witches in families without male heirs sometimes had been dispossessed of part or all of their inheritance before—sometimes long before—they were formally charged with witchcraft. Few of these women, however, accepted disinheritance with equanimity. Rather, like Susanna Martin, they took their battles to court, casting themselves in the role of public challengers to the system of male inheritance. In most instances, the authorities sided with their antagonists.

The experience of Rachel Clinton of Ipswich is instructive. As one of five daughters in line to inherit the "above £500" estate of their father, Richard Haffield,[38] Rachel had been reduced to abject poverty at least eighteen years before she came before county magistrates in 1687 as a witch. Richard Haffield had bequeathed £30 to each of his daughters just before his death in 1639, but since Rachel was only ten at the time, and her sister Ruth only seven, he stipulated that their shares were to be paid "as they shall com to the age of sixteen yeares old."[39] While he had not made other bequests, he made his wife, Martha, executrix, and so the unencumbered portions of the estate were legally at her disposal. In 1652, since Rachel and Ruth were still unmarried (Rachel was twenty-three at the time), local magistrates ordered Martha Haffield to pay one of her sons-in-law, Richard Coy, the £60 still due Rachel and Ruth, to "improve their legacy."[40]

When Martha Haffield wrote her own will in 1662, six years before her death, she bequeathed the still-single Rachel the family farm, valued at £300, with the proviso that she share the income it produced with her sisters, Ruth (now Ruth White) and Martha Coy. The household goods were to be divided among the three. Martha had effectively disinherited her two oldest children (children of her husband's first marriage) with ten shillings apiece.[41] This will, though legal, would never be honored. In 1666, the county court put the whole Haffield estate into the hands of Ruth's husband, Thomas White, whom they named as Martha Haffield's guardian and whom they empowered to "receive and recover her estate." They declared Martha Haffield "non compos mentis."[42]

The issue that seems to have precipitated this court action was Rachel's marriage to Lawrence Clinton several months before. Lawrence was an indentured servant and fourteen years younger than his wife. Perhaps even more offensive to community standards, Rachel had purchased Lawrence's freedom for £21, with money she said her mother had given her. Once Thomas White had control of the Haffield estate, he immediately sued Lawrence's former master, Robert Cross, for return of the £21.[43]

Several issues were raised in the almost four years of litigation that followed, but arguments focused on the legality of Rachel's access to and use of the money. Never explicitly mentioned by White, but clearly more important to him than the £21, was Rachel's sizable inheritance. For Rachel, the stakes were obvious: "My brother [in-law] White . . . is a cheaten Rogue," she insisted, "and [he] goese about to undoe mee. He keeps my portion from me, and strives to git all that I have."[44] The case was complicated by a number of factors, including Lawrence Clinton's desertion of his wife.[45] White did at last gain full control of the Haffield estate, however, and retained it for the rest of his life.[46]

Martha Haffield died in 1668. Shortly before, Rachel, then thirty-nine, had been forced to petition the court for relief, "being destitute of money and friends and skill in matters of Law." The house where she and her mother had lived, she said, had been sold by White, and its contents seized. Even her marriage portion, she averred, was still withheld from her "under pretence of emprovement."[47] Giving up her attempt to claim her inheritance, she subsequently tried to make her estranged husband support her. Though the court made several half-hearted attempts to compel Lawrence to live with his wife, or at least to maintain her, by 1681 they had tired of the effort: "Rachel Clinton, desiring that her husband provide for her, was allowed 20 shillings," they declared, "she to demand no more of him." [48] No doubt Rachel's adulterous involvement with other men influenced the court's decision, although Lawrence's sexual behavior had been even more flagrant. [49] In 1677, Rachel had petitioned for, but had been denied, a divorce. [50] When she appealed again in late 1681, it was granted her. [51] From then on, she was a ward of the town. [52] In 1687, and again in 1692, she was accused of malefic witchcraft. The second time she was tried and convicted. [53]

Sarah Good's plight resembles that of Rachel Clinton, even in some of the particulars. Sarah's father, John Solart, a prosperous Wenham innkeeper, had taken his own life in 1672, leaving an estate of about £500 after debts. He left a widow, Elizabeth, and nine children—seven daughters and two sons. The court accepted testimony from three witnesses concerning an oral will he had made, and awarded the widow £165, and the eldest son, John, a double share of £84. Since two of the daughters had already received their shares as marriage portions, the other six children, including Sarah, were to receive £42 each when they came of age. [54] Sarah was then seventeen or eighteen. That same year, the widow Solart married Ezekiel Woodward, who upon this marriage came into possession of the £165 and the unpaid children's portions. [55]

More than a decade later, the surviving daughters petitioned the court for the inheritances left them by their father. By that time their mother and both of their brothers had died. After the death of their mother, they said,

> Ezekill Woodward, that maryed with our mother, did Refuse to enter into any obligation to pay our portions. Our brother Joseph, whoe would have bien of Age the last Winter, is dead, and your Honores have declared the last court at Salem, that his portion shall be devided amongst us. But except your honnours will be pleased to put us into som capacity to gitt it, we know not well how to gitt it that soe we may divid it.

Most wronged, they added, was their sister Sarah, then wife of former indentured servant Daniel Poole:

> she is 28 yers of age and she is yett without her portion. And except that she will accept of a parcell of land which our father bought at a very deare Rate for his convenience, which was well fenced, and she alow the same price for it now, the fenc is taken off, she is not like to have anything. . . .

The court responded that the daughters "could recover their right from any person withholding it," but made no provision for them to do so.[56] Twenty-three years later, litigation over the Solart estate was still going on.[57]

Sarah, at least, never did recover what she felt was rightfully hers. By 1686, the little she had was gone. Her first husband, Daniel Poole, had died sometime after the 1682 petition was filed, leaving only debts for which Sarah and her second husband, William Good, were held responsible. Two men presented testimony in court that Poole "had been his own man several years before he was married unto Sarah Solah," and that Sarah "did enjoy and dispose of [his] whole estate . . . viz. a horse, 2 cows, and all his moveable goods." Ezekiel Woodward came into court to testify that one month earlier he had delivered to William Good three acres of the Solart land—land that the Goods should have had many years before. The court ordered William and Sarah Good to satisfy Poole's creditors. When the couple could not pay, the magistrates put William Good in jail and ordered seized about £9 worth of the Goods' Wenham land. Shortly thereafter, the Goods sold the rest of their Wenham property for £5, apparently out of dire necessity.[58]

From then on Sarah and her husband were reduced to begging work, food, and shelter from their neighbors. By the time of the 1692 outbreak, they were living in Salem, where Sarah Good was one of the first witches named. Within a month, her four-year-old daughter, Dorcas, evidently her only living child, was jailed as well.[59]

As these last two cases suggest, the land and other property of witches or their families could be confiscated in ways that went beyond the 1692 attainder law. The property of women in families without male heirs was vulnerable to loss in a variety of ways, from deliberate destruction by neighbors (as Katherine Harrison experienced) to official sequestering by local magistrates. In nearly every case, the authorities themselves seem hostile or at best indifferent to the property claims of these women. One final example deserves mention here, not only because it indicates how reluctant magistrates were to leave property in the control of women, but because it shows that the property of convicted witches was liable to seizure even without the benefit of an attainder law.

Rebecca Greensmith had been widowed twice before her marriage to Nathaniel Greensmith. Her first husband, Abraham Elsen of Wethersfield, had died intestate in 1648, leaving an estate of £99. After checking the birth dates of the Elsens' two children, three-year-old Sarah and one-year-old Hannah, the court initially left the whole estate with the widow.[60] When Rebecca married Wethersfield's Jarvis

Mudge the following year, the local magistrates sequestered the house and land Abraham Elsen had left, worth £40, stating their intention to rent it out "for the Use and Benefit of the two daughters."[61] The family moved to New London shortly after, but Jarvis Mudge died in 1652 and Rebecca moved with Hannah and Sarah to Hartford. Since Rebecca was unable to support herself and her two daughters, the court allowed her to sell the small amount of land owned by her second husband (with whom she had had no children) "for the paing of debts and the Bettering the Childrens portyons."[62]

Sometime prior to 1660, Rebecca married Nathaniel Greensmith. During the Hartford outbreak, Rebecca came under suspicion of witchcraft. After Nathaniel sued his wife's accuser for slander, Nathaniel himself was named. Both husband and wife were convicted and executed.[63]

Respecting Nathaniel's £182 estate, £44 of which was claimed by the then eighteen-year-old Sarah and seventeen-year-old Hannah Elsen, the court ordered the three overseers "to preserve the estate from Waste" and to pay "any just debts," the only one recorded being the Greensmiths' jail fees. Except for allowing the overseers "to dispose of the 2 daughters," presumably to service, the magistrates postponed until the next court any decision concerning the young women's portions. First, however, they deducted £40 to go "to the Treasurer for the County."[64] No reason was given for this substantial appropriation and no record of further distribution of the estate has survived.

Aside from these many women who lived or had lived in families without male heirs, there were at least a dozen other witches who, despite the presence of brothers and sons, came into much larger shares of estates than their neighbors would have expected. In some cases, these women gained full control over the disposition of property. We know about these women because their fathers, husbands, or other relatives left wills, because the women themselves wrote wills, or because male relatives who felt cheated out of their customary shares fought in the courts for more favorable arrangements.

Grace Boulter of Hampton, one of several children of Richard Swain, is one of these women. Grace was accused of witchcraft in 1680, along with her thirty-two-year-old daughter, Mary Prescott. Twenty years earlier, in 1660, just prior to his removal to Nantucket, Grace's father had deeded a substantial portion of his Hampton property to her and her husband, Nathaniel, some of which he gave directly to her.[65]

Another witch in this group is Jane James of Marblehead, who left an estate at her death in 1669 which was valued at £85. While it is not clear how she came into possession of it, the property had not belonged to her husband, Erasmus, who had died in 1660, though it did play a significant role in a controversy between her son and son-in-law over their rightful shares of both Erasmus's and Jane's estates. Between 1650 and her death in 1669, Jane was accused of witchcraft at least three times by her Marblehead neighbors.[66]

A third woman, Margaret Scott of Rowley, had been left most of her husband Benjamin's small estate in 1671. The land and most of the cattle were hers only "dureing hir widdowhood," but approximately one-third of the estate was "to be wholy hir owne." Margaret did not remarry. By the time she was executed as a witch in 1692, twenty-one years after her husband's death, she was seventy-five years old and little remained of the estate for the next generation to inherit.[67]

In each of these last few cases, the women came into property through the decision of a father or husband. Only occasionally, however, do we find the courts putting property directly into the hands of women subsequently accused of witchcraft. Mary English's mother, Elinor Hollingworth, was one of these exceptions. In this situation, as in the others, the unusual decision of the magistrates can be attributed to the small size of the estate involved. These particular inheriting women were widows, usually with young children to support.

Looking back over the lives of these many women—most particularly those who did not have brothers or sons to inherit—we begin to understand the complexity of the economic dimension of New England witchcraft. Only rarely does the actual trial testimony indicate that economic power was even at issue. Nevertheless it is there, recurring with a telling persistence once we look beyond what was explicitly said about these women as witches. Inheritance disputes surface frequently enough in witchcraft cases, cropping up as part of the general context even when no direct link between the dispute and the charge is discernible, to suggest the fears that underlay most accusations. No matter how deeply entrenched the principle of male inheritance, no matter how carefully written the laws that protected it, it was impossible to insure that all families had male offspring. The women who stood to benefit from these demographic "accidents" account for most of New England's female witches.

The amount of property in question was not the crucial factor in the way these women were viewed or treated by their neighbors, however. Women of widely varying economic circumstances were vulnerable to accusation and even to conviction. Neither was there a direct line from accuser to material beneficiary of the accusation: Others in the community did sometimes profit personally from the losses sustained by these women (Rachel Clinton's brother-in-law, Thomas

White, comes to mind), but only rarely did the gain accrue to the accusers themselves. Indeed, occasionally there was no direct temporal connection: In some instances several decades passed between the creation of the key economic conditions and the charge of witchcraft; the charge in other cases even anticipated the development of those conditions.

Finally, inheriting or potentially inheriting women were vulnerable to witchcraft accusations not only during the Salem outbreak, but from the time of the first formal accusations in New England at least until the end of the century. Despite sketchy information on the lives of New England's early witches, it appears that Alice Young, Mary Johnson, Margaret Jones, Joan Carrington, and Mary Parsons, all of whom were executed in the late 1640s and early 1650s, were women without sons when the accusations were lodged. Elizabeth Godman, brought into court at least twice on witchcraft charges in the 1650s, had neither brothers nor sons.[68] Decade by decade, the pattern continued. Only Antinomian and Quaker women, against whom accusations never generated much support, were, as a group, exempt from it.

The Salem outbreak created only a slight wrinkle in this established fabric of suspicion. If daughters, husbands, and sons of witches were more vulnerable to danger in 1692 than they had been previously, they were mostly the daughters, husbands, and sons of inheriting or potentially inheriting women. As the outbreak spread, it drew into its orbit increasing numbers of women, "unlikely" witches in that they were married to well-off and influential men, but familiar figures to some of their neighbors nonetheless. What the impoverished Sarah Good had in common with Mary Phips, wife of Massachusetts's governor, was what Eunice Cole had in common with Katherine Harrison, and what Mehitabel Downing had in common with Ann Hibbens. However varied their backgrounds and economic positions, as women without brothers or women without sons, they stood in the way of the orderly transmission of property from one generation of males to another.

Notes

1. Alan Macfarlane, *Witchcraft in Tudor and Stuart England: A Regional and Comparative Study* (New York, 1970), 149–51; Keith Thomas, *Religion and the Decline of Magic* (New York, 1971), 457, 520–21, 560–68.

2. See Trials for Witchcraft in New England (unpaged), dated 5 September 1656 (manuscript volume, Houghton Library, Harvard University, Cambridge, Mass.).

3. On Ann Dolliver, see "Letter from Rev. John Higginson to his son Nathaniel Higginson, August 31, 1698," *Essex Institute Historical Collections* 43 (1907),

182–86; "From Rev. John Higginson of Salem, to his son Nathaniel," letter dated 20 June 1699, *Collections of the Massachusetts Historical Society*, 3rd ser., 7 (1838), 198–200; Paul Boyer and Stephen Nissenbaum, eds., *The Salem Witchcraft Papers: Verbatim Transcripts of the Legal Documents of the Salem Witchcraft Outbreak of 1692*, 3 vols. (New York, 1977), I:271–72 (hereafter cited as Witchcraft Papers); John J. Babson, *History of the Town of Gloucester, Cape Ann, Including the Town of Rockport* (Gloucester, Mass., 1860), 80–81; Sidney Perley, *The History of Salem, Massachusetts*, 3 vols. (Salem, Mass., 1924–28), I:157–58.

4. Relying on very general indicators (a married woman who worked as a servant, a widow whose husband had left an estate of £39, and so forth), I was able to make rough estimates about the economic position of 150 accused women. Twenty-nine of these women seem to have been poor. Until we have a more detailed picture of women's lives in the 17th c., however, and better ways of conceptualizing women's class experience, we cannot know the extent to which poor women were overrepresented among the accused.

5. For Abigail Somes, see *Witchcraft Papers* 3:733–37; Babson, *History of Gloucester*, 160, 211; Christine Leigh Heyrman, *Commerce and Culture: The Maritime Communities of Colonial Massachusetts, 1690–1750* (New York, 1984), 105 n., 116–17. For Tituba, see *Witchcraft Papers* 3:745–57. Documents relating to Ruth Wilford are in *Witchcraft Papers* 2:459; 3:961; *The Probate Records of Essex County, Massachusetts, 1635–1681*, 3 vols. (Salem, Mass., 1916–20), 3:93–95 (hereafter cited as *Essex Probate Records*). For Sarah Good, see below, 13–14.

6. My conclusion about the economic position of the accused is supported by John Demos's early work on New England witchcraft, which focused on the Salem outbreak. His more recent and more detailed study, however, which deals almost exclusively with the non-Salem cases, argues that prior to 1692, most of the accused came from the low ranks of New England society. (See John Demos, "Underlying Themes in the Witchcraft of Seventeenth-Century New England," *American Historical Review* 75 (June 1970): 1316–17; John Putnam Demos, *Entertaining Satan: Witchcraft and the Culture of Early New England* (New York, 1982), 84–86, 285–92. I agree that during the Salem outbreak (and, I would add, during the Hartford and Fairfield outbreaks as well), prosperous and high-ranking persons were accused more often than they had been at other times, but I find Demos's interpretation of the non-Salem cases problematic. The discrepancy in our arguments here probably has to do with our different emphases—Demos's on the rank (or status) of the accused, mine on their (or their families') economic position—and with the lack of precise measures of either rank or economic position for the colonial period, especially for women.

The difficulty of categorizing women is perhaps best illustrated by looking at accused witch Elizabeth Godman of New Haven. Although Demos does not mention her social and economic status in *Entertaining Satan*, in his earlier article he described her, much as other historians have, as "poor and perhaps a beggar." (See "Underlying Themes," 1316.) She was a widow or spinster with no household of her own, and a witness who testified against her in her 1655 witchcraft trial said that she had come to his house to beg beer. On the other hand, Godman is called "Mrs." and "Mistress" in the records (as was her only sister, who lived in England) and her possessions included books and a silk gown—indications in the colonial period of both material prosperity and status. Her estate at her death in 1660, moreover, amounted to almost £200 (a sizable estate at the time, although most of it was in the hands of New Haven's deputy governor, Stephen Goodyear, in whose household she had lived for several years). Her neighbors' remarks about her and the control of her estate by Goodyear can legitimately be seen as indications of both low status and poverty. But Godman can also be seen as a woman from a well-off if not wealthy English family who, because she was a woman alone in New England, had an anomalous status in her neighbors' eyes and was not allowed access to her own economic resources. For records concerning Godman, see *Ancient Town Records: New Haven Town Records*, ed. Franklin Bowditch Dexter (New Haven, 1917–62), 1:249–52, 256–57, 264, 462–67, 478; 2:38 (hereafter cited as *New Haven Town Records*); *Records of the Colony or Jurisdiction of New Haven, from May, 1653, to the Union*, ed. Charles J. Hoadly (Hartford, Conn., 1858), 2:29–36, 151–52, 306, 497–98 (hereafter cited as *New Haven Colony Records*).

If Demos has included Godman and other women who shared her ambiguous position in his "low rank" category, that would explain some of the difference in our interpretation. It is also possible that both his "low" and "low middle" ranks include other women—women whose fathers or husbands had estates at their deaths valued at roughly £100 to £200—many but not all of whom I see as "middling." For my own way of conceptualizing New England's economic structure, see text and n. 7, below.

7. Most families in 17th-c. New England had estates worth less than £200. However, since only a very small proportion of convicted witches who were married seem to have come from families with estates worth *more* than £200, it seems reasonable to conclude that married women from families with less than £200 estates were overrepresented among the accused. Nearly all of the convictions of married women from families with estates worth more than £200 occurred during the Salem outbreak.

In an attempt to solve the problem of inadequate records concerning the economic position of accused women, I have created three categories within which to place them: from families with estates valued at more than £500, from families with estates valued at between £200 and £500, and from families with estates worth less than £200. In the minds of many New Englanders, possession of a £200 estate distinguished a family "of quality" from other colonists and therefore seems a reasonable dividing line between the majority of colonists and their "betters." The £500 estate dividing line between the "prosperous" and the "wealthy" is more arbitrary, but it seems to fit with general colonial conceptions. Given that most people lived in families with under £200 estates, the designation "middling" overlaps the under £200 estate and the £200 to £500 estate categories.

However the economic pyramid of colonial society is drawn, in most cases placement of individuals within it is impressionistic and subject to error. Often we can locate the value of a family's estate only at the time of death of its eldest male property owner, and by that time the estate may have been substantially reduced by the transfer of property to adult children.

8. Most of the women mentioned here are discussed at greater length elsewhere in this chapter. Documentation of the accusations against Hannah Griswold and Margaret Gifford can be found in "The Records of the Court of Assistants of Connecticut, 1665–1701" (M.A. thesis, Yale University, 1937), 6–7 (hereafter cited as "Conn. Assistants Records"); *Records and Files of the Quarterly Courts of Essex County, Massachusetts*, 9 vols. (Salem, 1912–75), 7:405; 8:23 (hereafter cited as *Essex Court Records*).

9. This discussion of the inheritance system of 17th-c. New England is drawn from the following sources: *The Book of the General Lawes and Libertyes Concerning the Inhabitants of the Massachusetts*, ed. Thomas G. Barnes (facsimile from the 1648 edition, San Marino, Calif., 1975); *The Colonial Laws of Massachusetts. Reprinted from the Edition of 1672, with the Supplements through 1686*, ed. William H. Whitmore (Boston, 1887); John D. Cushing, comp., *The Laws and Liberties of Massachusetts, 1641–91: A Facsimile Edition*, 3 vols. (Wilmington, Del., 1976); *Massachusetts Province Laws, 1692–1699*, ed. John D. Cushing (Wilmington, Del., 1978); *The Earliest Laws of the New Haven and Connecticut Colonies, 1639–1673*, ed. John D. Cushing (Wilmington, Del., 1977); *Probate Records of the Province of New Hampshire, Provincial, Town, and State Papers Series*, 31, ed. Albert Stillman Batchellor (Concord, N.H., 1907) (hereafter cited as *New Hampshire Probate Records*); *Essex Probate Records*; *A Digest of the Early Connecticut Probate Records*, 1, ed. Charles W. Manwaring (Hartford, 1904) (hereafter cited as *Conn. Probate Records*); Marylynn Salmon, *Women and the Law of Property in Early America* (Chapel Hill, 1986); George L. Haskins, "The Beginnings of Partible Inheritance in the American Colonies," in *Essays in the History of American Law*, ed. David H. Flaherty (Chapel Hill, 1969); Edmund S. Morgan, *The Puritan Family: Religion and Domestic Relations in Seventeenth-Century New England* (1944; reprint New York, 1966).

10. On this point, see Morgan, *The Puritan Family*, 81–82. That there may have been varying practices here is suggested by John J. Waters, who argues that in the 18th c. at least, young men and women were expected to bring equal portions to the marriage. See "Family, Inheritance, and Migration in Colonial New England: The Evidence from Guilford, Connecticut," *William and Mary Quarterly*, 3rd ser., 39 (1982): 78–79.

11. Barnes, *The Book of the General Lawes*, 17–18. In Massachusetts, the 1647 statute concerning dower also stipulated that the widow was "to have an interest in" one-third of her deceased husband's money, goods, and other personal property. In the 1660 and 1672 editions of Massachusetts' laws, this provision was deleted. In 1692 "An Act for the Settlement and Distribution of the Estates of Intestates" was passed which gave the widow a portion of the personal estate "for ever." Although historians have generally assumed that the one-third of the personal estate was for the widow's own disposing, it is not clear to what extent this was actually the case in Massachusetts over the course of the 17th c. See Barnes, *The Book of the General Lawes*, 17–18; Cushing, *The Laws and Liberties*, 1:96, 2:268; Cushing, *Massachusetts Province Laws*, 20–21; *Essex Probate Records* 1, 2, 3, passim. See also Salmon, *Women and the Law of Property*, 147–49, for a discussion of related changes in England and Connecticut over the course of the century. In Connecticut, widows had lost whatever rights they had had to a share of their husbands' personal property by 1673. According to Salmon, in most American colonies, "dower in real property only was the rule by the beginning of the eighteenth century."

12. Since only a small proportion of men left wills during the colonial period, intestacy law played a significant role in determining inheritance practices. See Salmon, *Women and the Law of Property*, 141.

13. Barnes, *The Book of the General Lawes*, 53.

14. Young women officially came of age in New England when they reached 18; young men when they reached 21.

15. William Blackstone, *Commentaries on the Laws of England*, 4 vols. (Oxford, 1765–69), 1:433.

16. Once widowed, a woman who inherited land from her father (or who had bought land with her husband in both of their names) could make a will of her own, as could a single woman who came into possession of land. Although these were significant property rights for women, in New England few women were in a position to claim them. On this point, and other complexities of colonial women's relation to property, see Marylynn Salmon's excellent study, *Women and the Law of Property*, 144–45 and passim.

17. See below, 11–12. Although men who wrote wills and the magistrates who handled intestate cases usually stipulated that young children receive their portions "at age or time of marriage" (see, for instance, *Essex Probate Records* 1:377), the evidence suggests that in 17th-c. New England, daughters of fathers who died relatively young (and possibly most sons) did not normally come into their inheritances until they married. If daughters had received their shares when they came of age, we would expect to find probate records for single women who died before they had the opportunity to marry. Though there are many existing intestate records and wills for single men who died in early adulthood, I have located only one record involving a young, single woman.

18. It is difficult to know which of the two groups is easier to locate: women without brothers or sons or women with brothers or sons. To know whether an accused witch belongs in the former category, we often need to establish the fertility and mortality patterns for only a single generation, either her own or her parents'. To know whether an accused witch belongs in the latter category, we need to establish the patterns for both generations. This would suggest that the available figures are more likely to overstate the proportions of accused witches without brothers or sons. However, the dying out of male lines in families of witches without male heirs makes these women harder to locate in the first place, since genealogical records usually follow male rather than female lineage. The problem of even establishing these women's fertility and mortality patterns would suggest that the available figures are more likely to understate the proportions of women without brothers or sons to inherit. I suspect that these problems cancel one another out and that were we able to gather all the necessary information, the percentages provided in table 1 for 60 percent of the accused roughly approximate the percentages for all witches.

19. See Karlsen, *The Devil in the Shape of a Woman*, 24, 27–29.

20. Ann Hibbens's will is reprinted in *New England Historical and Genealogical Register* 6 (1852), 287–88.

21. See *Witchcraft Papers* 3:880–81; Babson, *History of Gloucester* 174; John J. Babson *Notes and Additions to the History of Gloucester* (Gloucester, Mass., 1876), pt. 1:83–84; Essex County Probates (Registry of Probates, Essex County Courthouse, Salem, Mass.), doc. 28612; Essex Deeds (manuscript volume, Registry of Deeds, Essex County Courthouse, Salem, Mass.), 10:62; 91:15.

22. *Salem-Village Witchcraft: A Documentary Record of Local Conflict in Colonial New England*, eds. Paul Boyer and Stephen Nissenbaum (Belmont, Calif., 1972), 155–67, esp. 156–57; *Essex Court Records* 7:237, 319, 329; Essex Deeds 5:55; 6:57–59; 10:112. For records of Bridget Bishop's 1692 trial, see *Witchcraft Papers* 1:83–109. See also Essex County Probates, doc. 20009, for the deposition of Thomas Oliver's estate after Bridget (Oliver) Bishop's execution in 1692.

23. *Essex Probate Records* 2:254–55; Ethel Farmington Smith, *Adam Hawkes of Saugus, Mass., 1605–1672* (Baltimore, 1980), 22–27. The original articles of agreement are in Essex County Probates, doc. 12899.

24. See *Witchcraft Papers* 2:387–88; 499–505, 509–12; 3:781–92, 919–20.

25. See Richard B. Morris, *Studies in the History of Early American Law* (New York, 1930), 159–60.

26. *Witchcraft Papers* 3:1006, 1010–19, 1024–25.

27. James Savage, *A Genealogical Dictionary of the First Settlers of New England* (Boston, 1860), 4:66.

28. *New England Historical and Genealogical Register* 10 (1856), 177–80.

29. Savage, *Genealogical Dictionary* 4:273–74; *Records of the Governor and Company of the Massachusetts Bay in New England*, 6 vol., ed. Nathaniel B. Shurtleff (Boston, 1853–54), 5:245 (hereafter cited as *Mass. Records*).

30. See text, above, 63.

31. *Essex Probate Records* 3:191–93; Perley, *History of Salem* 1:306.

32. *Essex Probate Records* 3:191; Perley, *History of Salem* 3:80–81.

33. *Essex Court Records* 7:238.

34. *Vital Records of Salem, Massachusetts, to the End of the Year 1849*, 6 vols. (Salem, Mass., 1916–1925), 5:337; Perley, *History of Salem* 2:355; *New England Historical and Genealogical Register* 3 (1849), 129; Essex County Probates, doc. 13569.

35. Marion L. Starkey, *The Devil in Massachusetts: A Modern Enquiry into the Salem Witch Trials* (New York, 1949), 185.

36. *Witchcraft Papers* 3:988–91. On Mary and Philip English, see also *Witchcraft Papers*1:105, 151, 313–21; 2:429, 474, 482, 693; 3:805–6, 972–73, 1043–45; Starkey, *The Devil in Massachusetts*, 146–47, 184–86, 276–77, 289–90.

37. For Martha and Giles Corey and Alice Parker, see *Witchcraft Papers* 1:239–66; 2:623–28, 632–33; 3:985–86, 1018–19; Essex County Probates, doc. 6391; Deodat Lawson, "A Brief and True Narrative of Some Remarkable Passages Relating to Sundry Persons Afflicted by Witchcraft, at Salem Village," in *Narratives of the Witchcraft Cases, 1648–1706*, ed. Charles Lincoln Burr (New York, 1914), 154–57; Robert Calef, "More Wonders of the Invisible World," in Burr, *Narratives*, 343–44, 366–67; *Vital Records of Salem* 2:138–39; Perley, *History of Salem* 2:193; 3:56, 288–93, *Essex Court Records* 6:190–91.

The Alice Parker who was executed in 1692 may or may not have been Giles Corey's daughter. Both a Mary Parker of Andover and an Alice Parker, wife of John Parker, of Salem, were hanged as witches that year. Giles (and his former wife Mary) had a daughter who was married to John Parker of Salem, but her name was usually given as Mary. Names like Mary and Alice were sometimes used interchangeably in early New England, and I suspect that the Alice Parker who was executed was in fact Giles Corey's daughter.

38. *Essex Probate Records* 2:119. The following account of Rachel Clinton's experience is heavily indebted to John Demos's chapter on her in *Entertaining Satan* (see 19–35). I am grateful to the author for sharing this chapter with me before his book was published.

39. *Essex Probate Records* 1:144–45.

40. Ibid., 144.

41. Ibid. 2:115–16. The original of Martha Haffield's will, and the inventory of her estate, is in Essex County Probates, doc. 12051.

42. *Essex Court Records* 3:321, 352; Records of the Quarterly Court, Ipswich, 1664–1674 (manuscript volume, Essex Institute, Salem, Mass.), doc. 94.

43. *Essex Court Records* 3:371–73; Essex County Quarterly Court File Papers, Works Progress Administration Transcripts, 75 vols. (Essex Institute, Salem, Mass.), 12, docs. 22–25 (hereafter cited as Essex Court File Papers).

44. Essex Court File Papers, 12:24. See also *Essex Court Records* 3:371–73.

45. *Essex Court Records* 4:14, 269. Records of the Quarterly Court, Salem, 1667–1679 (manuscript volume, Essex Institute, Salem, Mass.), doc. 34.

46. *Essex Probate Records* 2:119–20. See Demos, *Entertaining Satan*, 22–30, for a full discussion of this litigation.

47. Essex Court File Papers, 13:29; *Essex Court Records* 3:458.

48. *Essex Court Records* 4:269, 425; 5:37, 312; 6:137, 344; 7:100; 8:17. The quotation is from 8:17. See also Ipswich Deeds (manuscript volume, Registry of Deeds, Essex County Courthouse, Salem, Mass.), 4, 378; Records of the Quarterly Court, Salem, 1667–1679, doc. 34; Records of the Quarterly Court, Ipswich, 1664–1674, doc. 132; Records of the Quarterly Court, Ipswich, 1666–1682, doc. 279; Essex Court File Papers, 18: doc. 91; 21: doc. 53.

49. On Rachel Clinton, see *Essex Court Records* 3:402; 6:374–75. On Lawrence Clinton, see Ibid. 4:269; 5:267; 6:206, 278, 338; 7:181; Records of the Quarterly Court, Salem, 1667–1679, doc. 34; Records of the Quarterly Court, Ipswich, 1666–1682, docs. 283, 293, 297; Essex Court File Papers, 20: docs. 144, 148; 25: doc. 125; (Mrs.) E.J. Clinton, "The Clinton Family of Connecticut," *New England Historical and Genealogical Register* 69 (1915), 50.

50. *Essex Court Records* 6:344.

51. Massachusetts Archives (manuscript volume, Statehouse, Boston, Mass.), 9:104.

52. "Records of the Town of Ipswich from 1674 to 1696," manuscript copy, by Nathaniel Farley, 1894 (Town Clerk's Office, Ipswich, Mass.), 208, 220–22, 224, 229, 252, 273.

53. Depositions filed against Rachel Clinton in 1687 are in Suffolk Files, 2660; "Witchcraft 1687," in the manuscript collections of Cornell University Library, Ithaca, N.Y. For Clinton's 1692 trial, see *Witchcraft Papers* 1:215–19; 3:881.

54. *Essex Probate Records* 2:283–85; Boyer and Nissenbaum, *Salem-Village Witchcraft*, 139–41. The witnesses' original statements are in Essex County Probates, doc. 25861.

55. *Vital Records of Wenham, Massachusetts, to the End of the Year 1849* (Salem, Mass., 1904), 166; *Essex Court Records* 8:163–64; Essex Deeds, 15:298.

56. *Essex Court Records* 8:432–33; 9:6, 111; Boyer and Nissenbaum, *Salem-Village Witchcraft*, 141–42; Essex County Probates, doc. 25862.

57. See, for instance, Essex Deeds, 15:298.

58. Boyer and Nissenbaum, *Salem-Village Witchcraft*, 142–47; *Essex Court Records* 9:579–80; Essex Deeds, 8:147.

59. *Witchcraft Papers* 1:106, 255; 2:351–78, 612–13, 662; 3:746–47, 944, 1019–20.

60. Manwaring, *Conn. Probate Records* 1:7–8.

61. Ibid., 8.

62. *Records of the Particular Court of Connecticut, 1639–1663, Collections of the Connecticut Historical Society*, 22 (1928), 119.

63. Ibid., 258; Increase Mather, *An Essay for the Recording of Illustrious Providences* (Boston, 1684), 18–21.

64. Manwaring, *Conn. Probate Records* 1:121–22.

65. Norfolk Deeds (manuscript volume, Registry of Deeds, Essex County Courthouse, Salem, Mass.), 1:116, 154; Joseph Dow, *The History of the Town of Hampton, New Hampshire* (Salem, Mass., 1893), 1:85; 2:612–13, 928, 985–86; *Documents and Records Relating to the Province of New Hampshire, Provincial,*

Town, and State Paper Series, 1, ed. Nathaniel Bouton (Concord, N.H., 1867), 417.

66. *Essex Probate Records* 1:314–16; 2:160; *Essex Court Records* 1:199, 204, 229; 2:213; 3:292, 342, 413; 4:165, 221–22, 255; Essex Court File Papers, 12:86–87.

67. *Essex Probate Records* 2:238–39; *Witchcraft Papers* 3:727–28; Thomas Gage, *The History of Rowley, Anciently Including Bradford, Boxford, and Georgetown, from the Years 1639 to the Present Time* (Boston: F. Andrews, 1840), 170–75.

68. Although some of these women may have had sons when they were accused, the records do not indicate any. John Carrington had a son, John, as well as a daughter, Mary, but both children seem to have been the offspring of his former marriage. On the Carrington genealogy, see Demos, *Entertaining Satan*, 349, 506 n. 40.

2

Female Speech and Other Demons: Witchcraft and Wordcraft in Early New England*

~

Jane Kamensky

Jane Kamensky's essay illuminates the social power of a witch's language in Puritan New England. To the elite, her mocking and threatening words represented the potential disordering of the entire society, including an overturning of ministers' (male) authority. To common folk, the spoken malevolent words of a witch could have frighteningly concrete effects; harsh words could kill one's child or ruin one's crops. Kamensky examines the ways in which the construction of gender roles, particularly the boundaries of proper female speech, became linked with the desire to maintain social hierarchy and with the cultural definition of a witch. A woman's speech identified her as either virtuous or sinful, and most evil of all was the witch, defined as a cursing, muttering, and scolding harpy. Boundaries of acceptable male behavior were also defined but, in keeping with patriarchal authority, men ran afoul when they allowed their wives a usurping tongue, not when they spoke aggressively themselves.

"THE TONGUE IS A WITCH," Anglican minister George Webbe warned in 1619. The spoken word, he said, covertly undermined "humane Societies" by acting "*deceitfully*," through "[w]itchcraft and

*An earlier and much more compressed version of this essay was presented at the conference "Perspectives on Witchcraft: Rethinking the Seventeenth-Century New England Experience," at the Essex Institute, Salem, Massachusetts, in June 1992, and published in the *Essex Institute Historical Collections* 128:4 (October 1992).

secret poisonings." A combination of personal vigilance, neighborly watchfulness, and communal willingness to punish wrongful speakers could do much to combat what Webbe called "the faults of an euill Tongue." But, he cautioned his listeners, these faults were great and human will was a puny thing. "[T]here is no crime so capitall, no offence so heynous, but the Tongue is either principal in it, or accessary into it," Webbe lamented.[1]

Although an ocean, two generations, and a world of theological differences separated Webbe from Cotton Mather, both men would have found considerable agreement about the diabolical tendencies of wrongful speaking. In particular, they would have reached consensus on two aspects of the business of what each called "governing the tongue." First, they would have concurred that *women's* tongues were particularly prone to the kinds of evils Webbe catalogued at length. In addition, they both knew only too well that witchcraft was a crime frequently enacted by certain kinds of female speech.[2]

It was with both of these things in mind that Mather reminded the godly women of New England to attend to the psalmist's words: "I will take heed . . . that I sin not with my Tongue; I will keep my Mouth with a Bridle." In so many words, he reminded the women of his congregation that feminine virtue meant careful speech. Drawing on a long tradition that linked women's voices with disorder, Mather cautioned the "daughters of Zion" that their "Tongues are frequently not so Governed by the Fear of God, as they ought to be." To avoid this womanly vice, the pious matron needed to cultivate what Mather called a "silver tongue": speech rare and pure, free of boastful "dross." He urged: "Be careful that you don't Speak too soon. . . . And be careful that you don't Speak too much. . . . 'Tis the Whore, that is Clamorous."[3]

In fact, it was not so much the whore as the witch whose clamorousness was just then driving Mather to distraction. For in 1692, the same year Mather told Zion's daughters to mind their tongues, cataclysmic witch trials shook Massachusetts. Many observers measured the real women on trial in Salem against an ideal of modest female speech much like the one Mather invoked in his sermon. In fact, a suspect's verbal style was one ingredient of a persona that made her a likely witch and not a "daughter of Zion." Where Puritan matrons spoke softly, with tongues of silver, witches (and their possessed victims) ranted with tongues of fire.[4] Consider Mercy Short, made (in)famous as Mather's "Brand Pluck'd Out of the Burning." Like many other accusers, she had been bewitched by another woman's "ill words." After disorderly female speech brought on her "possession," Short herself quickly fell prey to a verbal sickness. Speaking as if with the devil's own voice, she was heard "railing and slandering" Mather, and became "Insolent and Abusive" to her male audience.[5] Another victim inveighed against sermons with "multiplyed Impertinencies": "hectoring," "threatening," and "mocking" the preacher.[6] Other witches announced themselves to their neighbors with "foul words" or "muttering and menacing terms."[7]

Hectoring, threatening, scolding, muttering, mocking, cursing, railing, slandering: the list reads like a handbook of verbal etiquette for witches. How far from the judicious, infrequent, and well-placed words of the silver-tongued woman! To a society that was deeply concerned with governing the verbal exchanges that constituted and enforced social hierarchy, the witch's speech revealed the full destructive potential of the female voice. The witch's cursing, the demoniac's roaring: These were the ultimate ravages of women's words left unchecked. Careful, prayerful speech was one of the comeliest "ornaments" for the "daughters of Zion." But, since the days of Anne Hutchinson, it had been clear that disorderly speech—particularly *female* speech—could be the undoing of New England's fragile social and religious order. The pressing need to regulate such "heated" speech played a pivotal role in New England witchcraft beliefs, uniting so-called elite and popular conceptions of the witch.[8] Ministers, magistrates, and common folk agreed that the witch's crime was often, at root, a crime of female speech. In turn, the charge of witchcraft offered people at all levels of society a rubric under which certain elements of female discourse could be classified, prosecuted, and held in check.

To understand early New Englanders' intense preoccupation with disorderly female speech, it is necessary to realize that speaking meant something different to Anglo-Americans in the seventeenth century than it does to us in the twentieth. We tend to regard speech—talking—as a natural part of human interaction, and therefore as something that exists outside history. But a growing body of scholarship asks us to consider spoken exchange as an aspect of daily life which—like gender, race, or class—only appears to be natural but is, in fact, cultural. Drawing on the work of sociolinguists who study the ways people in different societies create distinct kinds of "speech communities," historians have begun to explore the ways in which the meaning of speech varies historically, across time.[9] Early New England is a case in point. In colonial Massachusetts, the spoken word had a kind of power we can scarcely imagine. Speech functioned as the central arena for the definition of self. People measured their own worth by the way their neighbors, servants, trading partners, and families talked to and about them.[10]

This intense preoccupation with the power and danger of speech reached from the top to the bottom of the steeply vertical social order of early New England. Puritan elites used "conversation" as a metaphor for the human pilgrimage on earth. Minister William Hubbard, for example, explained that "Conversation" meant nothing less than "the way or course of a mans life."[11] For spiritual and secular leaders, ensuring orderly "conversation" (in the more literal sense) was a vital part of governing society. From the pulpit and from the bench, people heard constant messages about the importance of polite, well-timed, deferential speech. Ordinary people also recognized that speech falling outside the parameters of "Christian-like conversation" could wreak havoc.[12] While many of us grew up hearing that "sticks and stones can break my bones but names can never hurt me," early New Englanders were taught the opposite. The "tongue breaketh the bone" was the equivalent in seventeenth-century folk wisdom.[13] Where Puritan ideology saw heated speech as a threat to the social order, traditional beliefs cast words as potent sources of literal, physical harm.[14] Importantly, both perspectives invested speech with dramatic and fearful power.

One of the most literal manifestations of the power of speech in Puritan Massachusetts was the language of witches, a genre of verbal aggression that has largely escaped scholarly attention. Words were at their most dangerous in the theater of New England witchcraft. Recent scholarship is suggestive in this regard. We know about the importance of local gossip—what John Demos has called a "thick trail of talk"—in defining and prosecuting witches.[15] Carol Karlsen has shown that the witch was essential to the Puritan construction of womanhood, part of a dual-edged ideology that increasingly venerated female piety while clinging to elements of an older, misogynist tradition.[16] Other studies have focused on the role of witchcraft accusations in defining and maintaining social boundaries—between village and town, rich and poor, "deviant" and "normal," men and women.[17] The concern of early New Englanders with speech as a cultural force, their anxiety over the evolving roles of men and women, and their overriding attention to constructing and preserving social hierarchy came together in the prosecution of witches.

Cotton Mather once referred to himself and his fellow ministers as "Ear-witnesses" to witchcraft.[18] Like Mather, many people in seventeenth-century New England believed they could *hear* the devil's presence in the speech of a local woman before their other senses offered corroborating evidence. Their detailed recollections of the ways witches spoke allow us, at more than three hundred years' remove, also to be ear witnesses of a sort. Ministers' observations of the ravages witches inflicted upon their possessed victims, taken together with court papers documenting the verbal "crimes" witches committed in their local communities, offer rich evidence of what women said that made them sound like witches to their neighbors and their leaders in early New England.

Although Europeans had persecuted witches for centuries before the Reformation, Protestant theologians added a new wrinkle to elite conceptions of the witch.[19] Among her neighbors, the witch remained what she had always been, a source of harm, a "criminal who worked in supernatural ways."[20] But to the Protestant minister or magistrate, she became first and foremost a heretic, in league with Satan to undermine the godly society on earth. Concern with the witch's speech bridged these two levels of belief. But regardless of whether she was feared and hated for her harmfulness or her heresy—whether, that is, her audience was popular or elite—the witch announced herself and often damned herself through her disorderly tongue.

English theologian William Perkins, an authority on many subjects for New England ministers, spelled out the elite view of witchcraft. For Perkins, the witch's crime was one of heretical inversion.[21] Her covenant with the devil created an alternate set of institutions, beliefs, and allegiances by which she claimed the right to govern herself. Just as "God Hath his word and sacraments, the seals of his covenant unto believers," Perkins noted, "so the devil hath his words and certain outward signs to ratify the same to his instruments." Witches "renounced God . . . king and governor, and . . . bound [themselves] by other laws."[22] Rooting out witches was thus of vital importance to the Puritan elite, and here, too, Perkins offered help. He listed seven ways that witches might arouse suspicion, and five of these centered on the spoken word: a "common report" or "notorious defamation" of being a witch; the testimony of a fellow witch; the "mischief" that followed either from the witch's curses or her "quarreling or threatening"; and finally, the quality of her speech upon examination. Called before local authorities because her words rendered her suspicious, a witch could seal her fate at the bar by her verbal "performance." "Unconstant" or "contrary" answers, Perkins noted, "argueth a guilty mind and conscience which stoppeth the freedom of speech."[23] Hunting for witches, Perkins's definition made clear, depended in large measure on careful listening.

Perkins's formulation of the witch met with broad agreement in the seventeenth-century English-speaking world. The records of New England witchcraft confirm that religious and civil authorities on both sides of the Atlantic shared his anxiety about the verbal power of witches. Documenting their fight against Satan's minions, New England's magistrates and ministers commented in revealing detail about the threat of disorderly female language: the how, where, and what women said to sound like witches to the ears of the Puritan elite.

Verbal tone—how the witch or her possessed victim spoke—was an essential ingredient of her threat to the elite. Recall, for a moment, Mercy Short's "Insolent and Abusive" words to Cotton Mather. Samuel Willard's description of the possession of Elizabeth Knapp shows similar concern with the timbre of diabolical speech. Knapp committed an extraordinary number of verbal "transgressions."[24] Willard recounted her "shrieks" and "crying out," her "railing" and "reviling" of him. Just as these aberrations in her normal speech patterns signaled her entry into a "possessed" state, the ebbing of her "fits" meant a return to what Willard considered a more suitable tone. Where the demoniac "roared" and "screamed," yelled, bleated, and barked, the penitent girl demonstrated a more appropriate (and earthly) range of verbal skills: "sighings, sobbings," "bitter tears," "earnest profession" and "methodical declarations."[25] The witch or her victim might also be gripped by unpredictable, implacable silences. Witches and those under their influence were "seized with dumbness," their "mouths were stopped," devils "confound[ed]" their Language, rendered them "uncapable of saying anything," and so on.[26] And even this was not the greatest disruption of speech witches might effect.

The bodily process of speaking—that defining human faculty—was perverted and distorted in the most literal, material sense in the ravings of possessed girls. Dramatic physical symptoms revealed that the devil had invaded the victim's speech. One victim's tongue clung to the roof of her mouth, "not to be removed" though "some tried with their fingers to do it."[27] Others suffered as their tongues were "drawn down their Throats . . . pull'd out upon their Chins . . . their Mouths [forced] opened to such Wideness, that their Jaws went out of joint."[28] Empowered by the devil or his human emissaries, young women could rage with their mouths shut or hanging wide open, belching forth horrifying words "without the use of any of the Organs of speech."[29] The voice of the witch sounded recognizably unfeminine—even inhuman—to her ministerial audience.

But verbal style did not alone brand a witch: The "where" and "what" of her speech combined to transform a "heated" exchange into a diabolical one. The physical setting of many such "conversations" was significant. An element of public spectacle often gave a witch's heated words broader scope and amplified their danger to established authority.[30] Witches and their victims dared to spout verbal poison at elevated male targets in public settings.

Ministers victimized by these stinging words reacted with hurt and surprise. Samuel Willard noted somewhat defensively that Elizabeth Knapp had "always been observed to speak respectfully concerning" him before the devil took control of her tongue.[31] Martha Godwin, Cotton Mather recalled, addressed him with "a Sauciness that I had not been us'd to."[32] Secular authorities were no less sensitive to witches' abuse of prominent audiences. The magistrates of Salem's witch trial court often chided a suspect for her lack of deference. And the records suggest that accused witches had raised their voices against civil authorities long before Salem. John Winthrop noted in 1648, during one of the first formal witch-hunting proceedings in Massachusetts, that Margaret Jones's "behavior at her trial was very intemperate, lying notoriously, and railing upon the jury and witnesses."[33] A woman's verbal tone often signaled the presence of witchcraft. *Where* and *to whom* the suspect spoke made such strident speech impossible to overlook.

Finally, we must look at the "what" of the witch's words, for the content of her speech was arguably the most important component of its disorderly potential in the minds of the Puritan elite. Through her heated words to leading men, the witch effectively positioned herself as a dark mirror of male authority. Like a minister, she selected and interpreted texts. One afflicted girl challenged Increase Mather in open assembly to "stand up, and Name your Text." And after it was read, she said, "It is a long Text." She went on mocking him, saying, "I know no Doctrine you had. If you did name one, I have forgot it."[34] Others claimed a similar power of choice and interpretation, refusing to say what they should, too easily able to say what they should not. Cotton Mather recalled one victim who "in the Bible could . . . read [not] a word," yet when he "brought her a Quakers Book . . . that she could quietly read whole pages of." She read aloud from "a Jest-book . . . without any Disturbance. . . . A popish Book also she could endure very well." But, Mather commented (and here we glimpse her authority clashing openly with his): "It would kill her" to read from "any Book that (in my Opinion) . . . might have bin profitable and edifying for her."[35] Speaking out, stridently and publicly, challenging the sole right of male authorities (magistrates, ministers, and husbands) to speak for them: This was the essence of the witch's challenge to the elite. Witches and their possessed victims personified the danger of female verbal authority, much like Quaker women preachers, themselves often subject to prosecution as witches, much like Anne Hutchinson, who had conducted herself as a preacher and interpreter and wound up under the shadow of witchcraft.[36]

Elite reactions to witches' speech reveal the boundaries of feminine discourse in Puritan New England. Certainly "vertuous women" were granted a degree of authority by their ministers. Preachers exhorted their increasingly "feminized" congregations to read, to converse, and even to write on pious subjects.[37] But if pious matrons knew that it was their right—even their duty—to reflect and expound on sacred texts, they would also have been aware (and been kept aware by the persecution of witches, slanderers, and other mis-speakers) that certain implicit limits bounded their discourse. The witch's speech made those implicit limits manifest.

In one sense, the witch linguistically out-performed the virtuous woman. The virtuous woman was fluent in the language of the Bible, but the witch spoke in tongues—foreign and learned languages of which she was expected to know nothing.[38] The virtuous woman read, but the witch read backward. The virtuous woman knew her Scripture, but the witch could cite chapter and verse of biblical texts with facility that ministers found distinctly unsettling. Mercy Short, for example, uttered "innumerable Things . . . which would have been more Agreeable to One of a greater Elevation in Christianity," finding scriptural support for her arguments with a speed that "no man living ever" could have matched. Mather found her "Discourses . . . *incredibly beyond* what might have been expected, from one of her small education."[39] Another young woman demonstrated her bewitchment through "strains of Expression and Argument" which were "truly Extraordinary; A person of the best Education and Experience and . . . Attainments much beyond hers could not have exceeded them."[40] Any seventeenth-century listener would have recognized the implicit message: One of "small education," the recipient of the kind of learning that better suited a hearer than a preacher, was more than likely to be female. Conversely, a "person of the best Education and Experience," one who had attained significant "elevation in Christianity," was invariably male. And the woman who breached these implied gender boundaries was, as likely as not, a witch.

And yet, at other moments, the witch also fell far short of the virtuous woman in her capacity for elevated Christian speech. For all her diabolic skill when acting the part of the minister, the witch could also fail to equal the verbal proficiency of even a well-catechized child. Hence her often-demonstrated inability to recite the Lord's Prayer, and her mute rage at words like "God" and "love" and "good."[41] Such grand "failures" of speech were considered just as damning as the witch's equally florid "successes," for both claimed a linguistic authority that was inappropriate. The witch decided what she would read and what would be read to her. She chose when and what to hear, whether and how to speak, and—most dramatically—what to say. She was, in the fullest seventeenth-century sense, an author, an inventor and teller of her own story, a creator and founder of others' misery.[42] If the New England clergy was beginning to advance a version of femininity that included some verbal authority—the right to read and discourse modestly on biblical texts—the witch showed the need to limit that authority.

To elite ears, the witch's speech posed a grand threat, challenging nothing less than the hierarchical framework of Puritan society. For common folk—her neighbors and victims—her voice held a different sort of menace. The witch's words struck at the very foundation of local life: the dominion of men over their wives and farmers over their crops and livestock, the ability of parents to protect and nurture their children. But if the theater of her malice was smaller, the impact of her words in the community setting was more literal and immediate. Babies and animals dropped dead. Inanimate objects moved at will. Luck ran out.

As was true for the Puritan elite, the witch's power in the neighborhood was embodied by her fiery tongue and her effect upon the speech of others. Heated words both by and against witches were a vital part of the local matrix of witch-hunting. As a subject of slander, and as the issuer of curses and other verbal "injuries," the witch was defined and prosecuted by the spoken word.[43]

That the witch's speech to her neighbors was what some scholars have called "assaultive" is the stuff of drama and legend. Images of the witch-as-scold resonated in England and in New England.[44] One English dramatist put the question poetically: "She on whose tongue a whirlwind sits. . . . Is not that scold a witch?"[45] Although evidence of witches' scolding is impressionistic, it remains suggestive. It is important to note that the witch's words were interpreted by her neighbors as contentious and aggressive, not necessarily that they were so in any objective sense.[46] But bearing this caveat in mind, the connection between being accused of witchcraft and having a reputation for scolding appears strong in quantitative and in qualitative terms. We know, for example, that accused witches exceeded the general population (and especially the population of women) in rates of "assaultive speech," lying, and speech against authority.[47] And the testimony of neighbors in numerous cases shows that the malicious acts of a suspected witch and her heated words were often inseparable in the minds of local accusers.

Witnesses against accused witches often pointed to a contentious verbal exchange with the suspect as the incident that first tipped them off to diabolical goings-on. The neighbors of Elizabeth Garlick in East Hampton, Long Island, described her as a "duble tongued woman" who made herself suspect by having jeered and laughed at them on numerous occasions.[48] Sarah Good, executed at Salem, had spoken "in a very wicked, spitfull manner . . . with base and abusive words . . . mutring & scolding extreamly."[49] Sarah Bibber, accused Salem witch and self-described possessed victim, was also called "double tongued": "a woman of an unruly turbulent spirit . . . much given to tatling & tale Bareing . . . amongst her neighbors . . . very much given to speak bad words and would call her husband bad names." Another neighbor recalled that Goody Bibber "wood be very often spekeking [sic] againts won and [a]nother very obsa[n]ely . . . and *wichshing very bad wichchis.*"[50]

This wishing of bad wishes was one aspect of the speech of suspected witches that stood out in neighbors' ears from the deafening array of contentious speech that was a constant presence in their face-to-face communities. Only a tiny fraction of those formally accused of speech crimes in early Massachusetts were ever prosecuted as witches. But unlike the insults hurled by common slanderers and railers, the witch's words had a very literal power—power of a sort not common to women in other areas of colonial life. As "cursing" or "foretelling," a witch's words broke free of the boundaries of speech and took harmful, physical form.[51] One woman told a neighbor that he "should Repent of" his words to her "afore Seven years Came to an End," saying that she would "hold [his] noss so Closs to the grindstone as Ever it was held."[52] Some curses were more specific: that a cow would die or a child would be taken ill. Most bespoke a generic malice on the part of the "witch": that "shee would be euen with" a neighbor, or that her victim might "Rue it hereafter."[53] No matter how mundane the particular threat, the witch's cursing held out the danger of words made real. As several of her Ipswich neighbors recalled about Goody Batchelor's threats against their cattle, "As she sayde so it came to pass."[54]

And one final quality of the witch's speech as interpreted by common folk: If her words, as curses and threats, could be too trustworthy, too literal, they might also be slippery and falsely seductive. Pretended kindness or unduly "smooth words"—followed in many cases by preternatural "harm"—were as distrusted as threats. Salem "witch" Mary Parker, for example, had "fauned upon" a neighbor's wife "w'th very Smooth words," after which his child fell sick. Elizabeth Howell feared, after a heated exchange with suspected witch Elizabeth Garlick, that Garlick would "cum fauninge" to her in the morning.[55] Here we glimpse the very essence of the "double-tongued" woman: muttering and menacing at one turn, flattering and fawning at the next. Her verbal challenge came not only from the heat of her speech, but also from its unpredictability.

For common men and women, then, the witch's self-enlarging voice defined the speech of the good Christian woman in the negative. While testimony *against* suspects emphasized their clamorousness, petitions on *behalf* of the accused highlighted the decorous speech of godly wives. A "Neighbourly woman," supporters of Elizabeth How reminded the court, was "Conssiencious in her dealing[,] faithfull to her promises & Christian-like in her Conversation." She was never "heerd" to "speake badly," even when addressing her accusers. "[B]y hur discors," How's neighbors knew her to be such a woman: one "throu [thorough] in that gret work of conviktion and convertion." How could she be a witch when "hur wordes & actions wer always such as well become a good cristian"?[56] During the half century he had known accused witch Sarah Buckley, William Hubbard remarked, he had never heard "any evil in her . . . or conversation unbecomming a christian."[57] Pleading for his wife of fifty-five years, Thomas Bradbury depicted her as the very image of the good woman—that is, as the verbal antithesis of the witch. According to her husband, Mary Bradbury was "a loveing & faithfull wife" who had been "wonderfull laborious dilligent & Industryous" and content "in her place." Significantly, she was mindful of woman's ordained silence and, therefore, unlikely "to speake much for herselfe, not being so free of Speach as some others may bee."[58] The contrast was unstated but easily inferred: The woman who spoke like a goodwife *was* a good wife, while one who did not might be a witch.

Among her neighbors as before secular and clerical authorities, the witch's speech set the right order of things on its head. In her neighborhood, she bred disorder of a smaller scale than the all-out social dissolution imagined by Puritan thinkers. She attacked daily processes—cream turning to butter, calves growing into cows, children becoming adults—rather than the overarching covenant between God and humanity. But her undermining of everyday experiences represented a reversal nonetheless: a reversal wrought by female speech. The goodwife was, by definition, a follower, in deed and especially in words. She was (like Mary Bradbury) "faithful" and "industrious," cheerful "in her place" and careful not to "speak much." The witch, through her cursing, became a leader. She authored the destiny of others and, more unbecoming still, decided her own fate in the bargain. As English dramatist Thomas Heywood reminded audiences, the witch's cursing left households "turn'd topsie turvy" and families "quite upside down."[59] Her voice called to those around her: "Lets haue a turn heels over head."[60] And the world around her heeded the cry as plenty turned to want, domination to "downfall," and birth to death.

Of course, not all witches were female. Although women were, as Carol Karlsen writes, the "primary objects of witch fear" in Europe as well as in New England, men periodically joined the ranks of suspected witches. In New England, roughly 20 percent of those accused throughout the seventeenth century were men. Fully half of the few men accused, however, were "secondary" suspects, deemed witches because of family or social ties to "primary" female transgressors. When men were called before the court along with their wives, it was often "especially the woman" whom the magistrates deemed "very suspicious in point of witchcraft."[61] Moreover, once suspected, male witches faced brighter prospects than their female counterparts at every stage of the judicial process, from presentment to punishment. Only three men were formally convicted outside the Salem trials; only two of those were executed.[62] In the eyes of their peers and their clerical and secular leaders, male witches were indeed exceptional.

Because New England's male suspects were few in number and marginal to their society's definition of the witch, the documentation of their cases is, on the whole, quite sparse. Conclusions about the men who came under suspicion are thus necessarily speculative. Nonetheless, the evidence suggests that elements other than blood ties made certain men likely witches. Speech was an important aspect of this classification; male "witches" sounded wicked. What this meant, in large part, was that they failed to sound masculine.

If male witches were not the typical servants of the devil, neither were they ordinary men. Like the "daughters of Zion," New England men encountered gender-specific definitions of proper verbal deportment. With his forceful-but-governed tongue, the ideal man at once exhibited deference to his social "superiors" and reasoned authority over his family. The male "witch" failed on both counts. On the one hand, he proved unable to curb the usurping speech of his cursing witch-wife, making himself appear suspiciously—even diabolically—weak in the process. Alternatively, he personified the "brawling man" who, one contemporary proverb declared, "hath a woman's tongue in his head."[63] Being categorized as witches implicitly linked them more closely to a figure of transgressive femininity than to their male peers. Their unmanly ways of speaking made this link plausible to those around them.

The case of Hugh Parsons of Springfield, tried and acquitted in 1651–52, points up the disparity between "normal" male speech and the speech of male witches. Parsons's wife, Mary, was the first in the family to be accused. Convicted years earlier as a slanderer, she had a reputation for scolding. As if to demonstrate her diabolically unfeminine speech, Mary Parsons raised her voice against her husband, telling neighbors and local authorities that she "suspect[ed] him for a witch."[64] On his wife's insistent say-so, Hugh Parsons soon became the primary object of his neighbors' complaints to the court.

Much of the evidence against him centered on his speech: his anemic reaction to his wife's railing, his own muttering and cursing. George Colton "stood forth" to tell the court that Mary Parsons often "spake very harsh things" against her husband "before his face." If Hugh Parsons "had been innocent," Colton reasoned, "he would have blamed her for her speeches . . . he would have reproved her." But instead of "reproving" his wife, he seemed almost to welcome her domineering speech: "[I]f anybody bespeak evil of me," he answered the magistrate who informed him of his wife's charges, "she will speak as ill and as much as anybody else." Parsons, his neighbors noted with grave doubt, "said nothing for himself in way of blaming" her for having "spoken against him." All too often, folks around him noticed, Parsons remained "wholly silent" in situations where it was his right—even his duty—to speak.[65]

At home, Parsons displayed a distinctly unmanly willingness to endure his wife's unwomanly tongue. Among his neighbors, though, he was often heard to "mutter and mumble," striking out with "threatening speeches . . . uttered with much anger." Dismayed over a bargain with Rice Bedortha, for example, Parsons had cautioned Bedortha's wife that he would remember her when she did "little think on it." Such "threatening," it seemed, was Parsons's weapon of choice whenever he was "displeased." He had menaced John Mathews with a variation on "his usual speech," vowing to "be even with him." With poetic flair, Parsons had warned the victor in a civil suit against him that the judgment would rankle "as wild fire in this house and as a moth in [his] garment."[66] Accused witch William Graves had cursed his son-in-law, Samuel Dibble, in similar tones, warning that Dibble "should repent . . . long as [he] lived," and, what's more, would "live never the longer for it."[67] The consequences of these "curses" were dire; the usual litany of illness, death, and loss followed the male witch's verbal malevolence.

Such words were forceful stuff. Full of the promise of imminent harm, these threats were not lightly dismissed. Yet despite the seeming strength of cursing men like Graves and Parsons—strength measured in terms of the fear they inspired in their neighbors—male "witches" took refuge in the power of the powerless. Unwilling or unable to claim the "earthly" verbal authority permitted them as men in their society, they fought their battles through occult means. Their diabolic "power" was the ally of their social impotence. People must have wondered why, for example, Hugh Parsons habitually failed to negotiate a bargain to his satisfaction. Such transactions fell firmly within the compass of man's speaking role. And, if he felt himself unlucky in commerce, why did Parsons not seek resolution in church or in court? Why, in short, did Parsons not find appropriate ways to speak (forcefully, respectfully) in his own behalf in a culture that gave men so many opportunities to do so? In William Graves's case, neighbors must have been skeptical of the authority of a father whose expressed wishes had failed to prevent his daughter from making an undesirable marriage. Graves had not even managed to prevail in his attempts to prevent his daughter from legally claiming her portion. Only a father incapable of making himself heard in his family and then in court would resort to cursing his disobedient daughter and her progeny.

Men like Graves and Parsons puffed themselves up through their cursing. But this sort of strength merely exposed the weakness of their words, weakness that was the opposite of masculinity. For men had other means available to them, other ways to rule their families, other avenues through which to make their voices heard. Ann Hibbens's example had shown that a woman who tried to settle a score in an outspoken, officious, and self-interested manner would be counted a shrew. But decisive action and authoritative speech were *de rigueur* for men. There was a difference, neighbors knew, between verbal mastery and fearsome but cowardly threatening. Both were strong ways of speaking, certainly. But cursing was the recourse of those from whom life demanded silence. Men had other speaking parts to play.

The available evidence suggests, then, that male witches were ill-spoken men, brawlers who ranted with "women's tongues." But the converse was not true; male misspeakers weren't, by and large, considered witches. Even when neighbors deemed a man's conversation suspect, the magistrates appear to have been reluctant to agree. Consider the example of James Fuller, who had aroused the suspicions of people in Springfield by telling them that he would often "call vpon or pray to the Divil for helpe and hath . . . had familliarity wth him." Though Fuller confessed to having uttered the damning words, he admitted that he was telling tall tales. The Assistants, more than willing to give a man the benefit of the doubt, convicted him of "willfull lying" rather than witchcraft.[68] John Broadstreet of Rowley bragged to his neighbors about reading "in a book of magic," and related fantastical stories of calling on a mystical "voice" to "goe make a brige of sand ouer the sea, goe make a lader of sand up to heauen and goe to god and come downe noe more." But the magistrates labeled his untoward speech "telling a lie" rather than compacting with the devil.[69]

Gloucester's William Browne sounded more like a witch than either Fuller or Broadstreet. During the winter of 1656, he had verbally menaced Margaret Prince, then "bigg with childe," causing her (many townswomen believed) to deliver a stillborn baby. Bursting into Prince's house, Browne had proclaimed that she "would beg [her] bread before [she] dyed," an event that he predicted was not far off. He told Prince she was "very faire for the devill," and warned that "ye Devill would fetch [her] speedily." Believing Browne's prophecy that "her time Was but short," Goody Prince was "frighted" and fell to "tremblling and shaking." The ensuing stillbirth was no surprise to Prince or her neighbors, many of whom credited Browne's words with real power. One witness to the travail explained that "goody Prince was verrie Ill vppon william Brownes words." But the Ipswich magistrates were hardly convinced. In fact, they appear to have been more concerned with Browne's "speaking disgracefully" against three of the town's ministers than with what they deemed his "misdemeanor towards Goodwife Prince." Browne was fined and imprisoned for his words against authority. For his "witchcraft" (never so-called by the court), he would pay court fees to Margaret Prince's husband to defray the cost of trying the matter.[70]

Historian John Demos asserts that New England society did not make "primary" witches of men like Broadstreet, Fuller, and Browne because their offenses consisted chiefly of "reckless and boastful talk."[71] This claim, I would argue, is half right. Such men made poor witch-suspects because they were merely reckless talkers and because they were male. Intemperate bragging was more "normal," even acceptable, for men than for women. This is not to say that the authorities rewarded extravagant speech; men who blurted out such words were regularly convicted of lying, swearing, drunkenness, even of the serious crime of defaming authority. But if men were not encouraged to "publish" their discontent verbally, they were virtually never hanged for doing so. For women, in contrast, this kind of "reckless" talk was often the very essence of witchcraft or "possession." Nobody called Katherine Harrison, Elizabeth Godman, or Martha Carrier a braggart; neither Mercy Short nor Elizabeth Knapp was deemed a liar.

According to the rules of their culture they were, quite clearly, witches. The neighbors and the "governors" of these women heard the devil in their voices.

What was an early New Englander to make of a person who "set spelles & Rases the Diuell," who slandered magistrates and "ouer came" neighbors with "fayer smooth wordes," whose "cursing" and "swearing" revealed that the "devil" was "very frequent in [their] mouth"? The answer depended on the speaker's sex. These charges (and more) were leveled at Thomas Wells of Ipswich.[72] In his case, the consensus local men and women reached over time (an opinion apparently shared by the Essex County magistrates) was this: Wells was neither more nor less than "a very bad neighbor."[73] In seventeenth-century New England, female incarnations of the "very bad neighbor"—the very bad speaker—were not so lightly dismissed.

The connection between disorderly speech and the construction of womanhood figured into both elite and popular conceptions of the witch. This is not to say that speech is the key to witchcraft, for we know that many other factors—social, economic, and psychological—combined to make certain women in certain places at certain historical moments into witches. Nor is it my claim that witchcraft is the key to the Puritans' preoccupation with speech, for "governing the tongue" meant listening for all misspeaking, not only to the witch's curse. Nonetheless, reaction against disorderly female speech forged a link between elite and popular versions of the witch, a link that facilitated the prosecution of women who had transgressed so many of the boundaries their society set, including the limits of proper female discourse.[74]

When "thou speakest evill," William Perkins warned, "thy tongue is kindled by the fire of hell. . . . Cursed speaking is the divels language."[75] Both elite and common folk in early New England would have found much to agree with in Perkins's formulation. The devil, it seemed certain, entered at the mouth. But the witch's evil speech meant something different to the Puritan minister than it did to the fearful neighbor. The minister heard a version of female authorship that threatened social hierarchy and Puritan male rule. The neighbor heard words made real—words that promised not only social disruption but also physical harm. Like medieval charms, the witch's words literally embodied danger to those around her.[76]

Being able to hear a witch—to distinguish her by her manner of speaking—was a vital step on the road to disempowering her. Regulating this particular sort of women's disorderly speech was a project of central importance for both the Puritan rulers and the common folk in early New England. Witchcraft accusations offered one avenue through which to reaffirm the contours of what David Hall has called a widely shared common culture.[77] Denouncing the disorderly speech of the witch was one way to demonstrate that the Puritan elite and their subjects did, in effect, speak the same language, and that a serious break with that language would not be tolerated.

Though we now admit—and even embrace—the presence of many different voices in our society, we in the multicultural, post-modern 1990s are still wrestling with the damage words can do. Certainly the terms of the debate have changed dramatically since 1692. Since the early national period, the right of citizens to challenge authority—in speech and especially in print—has been enshrined as a defining ideal of American nationhood.[78] And we tend, at least at the level of colloquialism, to denigrate the power of words. Unlike sticks and stones, we are reminded on the schoolyard, names can never hurt us. Unlike the Puritan notion of "heated speech," with its social and even magical power, we are apt to consider someone's words as just so much hot air.

Although we might be hard pressed to acknowledge that mere speaking remains a significant act with broad social results, we continue to be engaged in our own struggles over the cultural meaning of speech. Many of these debates still center on the appropriate limits of female talk; instead of hunting witches, we construct "bitches." We also ponder, in this electronic age, just what constitutes speech. Is pornography speech? Is blocking access to a clinic a way of speaking? Which of these kinds of so-called speech merit prosecution, and which, protection?

One of the most protracted current controversies over the cultural meaning of speech is the heated debate in contemporary America about restraining hate speech—a debate that is, in essence, about the power of words. Where, we asked in 1992, as people did in 1692, does speaking end and literal, physical harm begin? Particularly on American university campuses, people are discussing the power of words with renewed vigor, and are experimenting with different definitions of verbal freedom and verbal injury. The persuasive argument against a libertarian definition of free speech is one that would have had deep resonance in seventeenth-century New England: Words are never just words. Words do things.[79]

In seventeenth-century New England, the proposition that words were capable of inflicting real damage would not have aroused debate. The ruling elite and common folks alike recognized that speech was a source of power and of danger, and that the boundaries between speaking and doing were fuzzy ones. A woman who crossed the boundaries her culture set for socially correct speech might be counted a witch by the minister whose role she usurped, or the neighbors who believed themselves harmed by her words. And the price she might pay for disrupting the social order with her speech might be as high as life itself.

Notes

1. George Webbe, *The Arraignement of an Unruly Tongue* (London, 1619), 22, 133, 16 (emphasis in original).

2. On Mather, see below. For Webbe's thoughts on female speech, see *Arraignement of an Unruly Tongue*, esp. 8, 28, 50, 75; and Webbe, *The Practise of Quietnes: Directing a Christian How to Live Quietly in this Troblesome World* (3d ed.; London, 1618), 108 ff.

On the long European tradition of female scolding, see David Underdown, "The Taming of the Scold: The Enforcement of Patriarchal Authority in Early Modern England," in *Order & Disorder in Early Modern England*, ed. Anthony Fletcher and John Stevens (Cambridge: Cambridge University Press, 1985), 116–36; Susan D. Amussen, "Gender, Family and the Social Order, 1560–1725," in *Order & Disorder*, 196–217; Lynda E. Boose, "Scolding Brides and Bridling Scolds: Taming the Woman's Unruly Member," *Shakespeare Quarterly* 42, no. 2 (Summer 1991): 179–213; and Katherine Usher Henderson and Barbara F. McManus, *Half Humankind: Contexts and Texts of the Controversy about Women in England, 1540–1640* (Urbana: University of Illinois Press, 1985).

3. Cotton Mather, *Ornaments for the Daughters of Zion* (Boston: Samuel Phillips, 1692), 49–51. It is significant that the section of this work that Mather devotes to speech is one of the longest passages on any single subject in the entire text. His image of the silver-tongued, bridled woman recalls the language of the Psalms and Proverbs. See especially Psalms 39:1; Proverbs 10:20.

So-called rules for speaking were of intense personal concern for Mather, whose own early battle with stammering left him ever thankful to God for allowing him the "free" speech so crucial to a minister's social role. See Worthington Chauncey Ford, ed., *Diary of Cotton Mather*, 2 vols. (1912, reprint New York: Frederick Ungar, 1957), I:2–3, 19–20, 35, 49–52, 55, 62, 154, 171–73, 206–7, 333–34. Mather sermons devoted to issues concerning speech include *A Golden Curb for the Mouth* (Boston: B. Green, 1709); *The Right Way to Shake Off a Viper . . . What Shall Good Men Do, When They Are Evil Spoken Of?* (Boston: S. Kneeland, 1720); and *The Good Linguist: or, Directions for Avoiding Sins of the Tongue* (Boston: Green & Allen, 1700; no extant copy). On Mather's early life see Kenneth Silverman, *The Life and Times of Cotton Mather* (New York: Columbia University Press, 1985), esp. ch. 2; and David Levin, *Cotton Mather: The Young Life of the Lord's Remembrancer, 1663–1703* (Cambridge: Harvard University Press, 1978), 32–33, 37–38.

4. Carol Karlsen argues that possessed girls (and nearly all were girls) should be treated as part of a continuum of women's involvement in witchcraft. Although they were few in number, she maintains that the possessed play a pivotal analytic role: illuminating witchcraft beliefs acting within, as well as against, New England women. See Karlsen, *The Devil in the Shape of a Woman: Witchcraft in Colonial New England* (New York: W. W. Norton, 1987), ch. 7, esp. 223–25. Because the "testimony" of these disturbed adolescent females provides some of

the fullest and most dramatic accounts of "witches' " speech, I have chosen to treat possessed girls and witches virtually interchangeably throughout this essay.

5. Cotton Mather, "A Brand Pluck'd out of the Burning" (1693), in *Narratives of the Witchcraft Cases, 1648–1706*, ed. George Lincoln Burr (New York: Charles Scribner, 1914), 272 and passim.

6. Cotton Mather, "Memorable Providences, Relating to Witchcrafts and Possessions" (1689), in Burr, *Narratives*, 119. Martha Godwin is the possessed woman in question.

7. Cotton Mather, "Wonders of the Invisible World" (1693), in Burr, *Narratives*. Mather is referring to Susannah Martin (235), Martha Carrier (243), and Bridget Bishop (226).

8. The phrase "heated speech" comes from Robert St. George's pathbreaking article " 'Heated' Speech and Literacy in Seventeenth-Century New England," in *Seventeenth-Century New England*, ed. David D. Hall and David Grayson Allen (Boston: Colonial Society of Massachusetts, 1984), 275–322.

9. On the "ethnography of speaking," see esp. the pioneering work of Dell Hymes, including *Foundations of Sociolinguistics: An Ethnographic Approach* (Philadelphia: University of Pennsylvania Press, 1974); and Hymes and John Gumperz, eds., *Directions in Sociolinguistics: The Ethnography of Communication* (New York: Holt, Reinhart, and Winston, 1972). On gender and sociolinguistics, see Dennis Baron, *Grammar and Gender* (New Haven: Yale University Press, 1986); Jennifer Coates, *Women, Men, and Language* (London: Longman, 1986); Alette Olin Hill, *Mother Tongue, Father Time: A Decade of Linguistic Revolt* (Bloomington: Indiana University Press, 1986); Cheris Kramarae, *Women and Men Speaking* (Rowley, Mass.: Newbury House, 1981); Susan U. Philips, Susan Steele, and Christine Tanz, eds., *Language, Gender, and Sex in Comparative Perspective* (Cambridge: Cambridge University Press, 1987); and Robin Lakoff, *Language and Woman's Place* (New York: Farrar, Straus & Giroux, 1976). An accessible overview of much recent work on men and women in their speech communities is Deborah Tannen's best-selling *You Just Don't Understand: Women and Men in Conversation* (New York: William Morrow and Company, 1990).

Recent works on the social history of language include Peter Burke, *The Art of Conversation* (Ithaca, NY: Cornell University Press, 1993); Burke and Roy Porter, eds., *The Social History of Language* (New York: Cambridge University Press, 1987); Richard Bauman, *Let Your Words Be Few: Symbolism of Speaking and Silence among Seventeenth-Century Quakers* (Cambridge: Cambridge University Press, 1983); History Workshop Collective, "Language and History," *History Workshop Journal*, no. 10 (Autumn 1980): 1–5 (editorial).

10. Several local studies have informed or expanded upon on St. George's notion that verbal exchange was a crucial arena for the negotiation and enforcement of social boundaries, particularly gender roles. The most sophisticated and analytically refined treatments of slander and gender in early America are Mary Beth Norton's and Cornelia Dayton's. See Cornelia H. Dayton, "Slanderous Speech in Eighteenth-Century Connecticut: Gender and the Fall from Social Grace," unpublished paper delivered at the ASLH Conference in Toronto, October 1986; Dayton, *Women before the Bar: Gender, Law and Society in Connecticut, 1639–1789* (Chapel Hill: University of North Carolina Press), esp. ch. 6; Mary Beth Norton, "Gender and Defamation in Seventeenth-Century Maryland," *William and Mary Quarterly* [hereafter *WMQ*], 3d ser., 44, no. 1 (January 1987): 3–39. Other studies of defamation include Peter N. Moogk, " 'Thieving Buggers'

and 'Stupid Sluts': Insults and Popular Culture in New France," *WMQ*, 3d ser., 36, no. 4 (October 1979): 524–47; J. A. Sharpe, *Defamation and Sexual Slander in Early Modern England: The Church Courts at York* (Borthwick Institute of Historical Research, University of York, Paper no. 58 [1980]); Lyndal Roper, "Will and Honor: Sex, Words, and Power in Augsburg Criminal Trials," *Radical History Review* 43, no. 1 (January 1989): 45–71; Helena M. Wall, *Fierce Communion: Family and Community in Early America* (Cambridge: Harvard University Press, 1990), esp. 30–48.

11. William Hubbard, *The Benefit of a Well-Ordered Conversation* (Boston: S. Green, 1684), 3. Hubbard is explicating a passage from Psalms. On conversation as a metaphor for speaking and being, see Kamensky, *Governing the Tongue: The Politics of Speech in Early New England* (New York: Oxford University Press, 1997).

12. The phrase "Christian-like conversation" appears frequently in early New England court records, particularly in petitions by neighbors defending the deportment and language of accused speech offenders. For an example from the Essex County Quarterly Courts, see William Titcombe, presentment for lying and disparaging authority, 1657, George Francis Dow, ed., *Records and Files of the Quarterly Courts of Essex County, Massachusetts* [hereafter *ECR*], 9 vols. (Salem, Mass.: Essex Institute, 1911–1978), II: 40–41; or Archie N. Frost, comp., *Verbatim Transcript of the File Papers of the Essex County Quarterly Courts, 1636–1692* [hereafter *Essex File Papers*], 75 vols. (typescript on deposit at the Essex Institute, Salem, Mass.; microfilm copy at Sterling Memorial Library, Yale University), vol. 3, docs. 116–17.

13. Hubbard, *Benefit of a Well-Ordered Conversation*, 45–46.

14. Witchcraft trials are the place where the historian can best glimpse the beliefs of common people about the power of words to inflict physical harm. The witch's curse bore the power of a medieval "charm" or "spell." See Keith Thomas, *Religion and the Decline of Magic* (New York: Charles Scribner, 1971); and Jeanne Favret-Saada, *Deadly Words: Witchcraft in the Bocage*, trans. Catherine Cullen (New York: Cambridge University Press, 1980).

15. See John Putnam Demos, *Entertaining Satan: Witchcraft and the Culture of Early New England* (New York: Oxford University Press, 1982), 246 ff. Demos also explores the connection between witchcraft and regressive "orality" in the psychological sense; see ibid., ch. 6.

16. Karlsen, *Devil in the Shape of a Woman*, passim.

17. On village and city (or "communal" versus "commercial") boundaries, see Paul Boyer and Stephen Nissenbaum, *Salem Possessed: The Social Origins of Witchcraft* (Cambridge: Harvard University Press, 1974); and Demos, *Entertaining Satan*, pt. III. On boundaries between "deviant" and "normal" behavior see Kai T. Erikson, *Wayward Puritans: A Study in the Sociology of Deviance* (New York: John Wiley & Sons, 1966); and Richard Weisman, *Witchcraft, Magic, and Religion in 17th-Century Massachusetts* (Amherst: University of Massachusetts Press, 1984). On gender boundaries, see Karlsen, *Devil in the Shape of a Woman*; and Lyle Koehler, *A Search for Power: The "Weaker Sex" in Seventeenth Century New England* (Urbana: University of Illinois Press, 1980).

18. See Mather, "Brand Pluck'd out of the Burning," in Burr, *Narratives*, 267. He was describing the rantings of the possessed Mercy Short.

19. The following discussion draws on numerous accounts. See Karlsen, *Devil in the Shape of a Woman*, esp. ch. 1, 5; Weisman, *Witchcraft, Magic, and Religion*, ch. 2, 3; and Thomas, *Religion and the Decline of Magic*, esp. ch. 14.

For an interesting exploration of the elite versus popular culture question, see Clive Holmes, "Popular Culture? Witches, Magistrates, and Divines in Early Modern England," in *Understanding Popular Culture: Europe from the Middle Ages to the Nineteenth Century*, ed. Steven L. Kaplan (New York: Mouton, 1984), 85–111.

20. Karlsen, *Devil in the Shape of a Woman*, 4.

21. On witchcraft and inversion, see Stuart Clark, "Inversion, Misrule and the Meaning of Witchcraft," *Past & Present* 87 (May 1980): 98–127, esp. 105, 110. Clark does not discuss gender role inversion.

22. William Perkins, *A Discourse of the Damned Art of Witchcraft* (ca. 1600) in *The Work of William Perkins*, ed. Ian Breward (Abingdon, England: Sutton Courtenay, 1970), quotes from 596, 600. Although Perkins notes that women were especially vulnerable to the devil's temptations (see 595–96), he uses the male pronoun to refer to witches throughout.

23. Perkins, *Discourse of the Damned Art*, 602–3. For echoes of Perkins's reasoning among the New England government and clergy, see William Jones, Deputy Governor of Connecticut, quoted in John M. Taylor, *The Witchcraft Delusion in Colonial Connecticut, 1647–1697* (New York: Grafton, 1908), 40; and Cotton Mather, "Wonders of the Invisible World," 221.

24. For a detailed account of Knapp's "diabolical distemper," see Demos, *Entertaining Satan*, 97–132.

25. Samuel Willard, "A Brief Account of a Strange and Unusual Providence of God Befallen to Elizabeth Knapp of Groton" in *Remarkable Providences, 1600–1760*, ed. John Demos (New York: George Braziller, 1972): 358–71, esp. 358–59, 363–64.

26. For "seized . . . stopped," see Cotton Mather, "Brand Pluck'd out of the Burning," 272, 279 (on Mercy Short); "confound" in Increase Mather, "An Essay for the Recording of Illustrious Providences" (1684), in Burr, *Narratives*, 18, describing Ann Cole of Hartford. [Mather's essay is hereafter referred to by its popular title, "Remarkable Providences."] "Uncapable . . . anything" in Cotton Mather, "Wonders of the Invisible World," 217.

27. Willard, "Brief Account," 361.

28. Cotton Mather, "Memorable Providences," 101. Mather is describing Martha Godwin, possessed by the widow [Mary?] Glover in 1688. Elizabeth Knapp also had her tongue drawn "out of her mouth most frightfully," see Willard, "Brief Account," 367–68.

29. Increase Mather, "Remarkable Providences," 22. The demoniac, again, is Elizabeth Knapp. Compare with Willard, "Brief Account," 370–71.

30. See, for example, Abigail Williams's interruption of a sermon at Salem meetinghouse described by the Rev. Deodat Lawson in "A Brief and True Narrative Of . . . Witchcraft, at Salem Village," in Burr, *Narratives*, 154–55.

31. Willard, "Brief Account," 371.

32. Cotton Mather, "Memorable Providences," 119.

33. Paul Boyer and Stephen Nissenbaum, eds., *The Salem Witchcraft Papers: Verbatim Transcripts of the Legal Documents of the Salem Witchcraft Outbreak of 1692* (hereafter *Salem Witchcraft Papers*), 3 vols. (New York: Da Capo Press, 1977). See, for example, the examinations of Martha Corey (I:250), Dorcas Hoar (II:390–91), Sarah Good (II:356–57, 362), Susannah Martin (II:552), and John Willard (III:827, 829). For Winthrop's description of Jones's examination, see Winthrop, *Journal: "History of New England,"* 2 vols., ed. James Kendall Hosmer (New York: Charles Scribner, 1908), II:345.

34. Abigail Williams to Increase Mather, quoted in Lawson, "Brief and True Narrative," 154.

35. Cotton Mather, "Memorable Providences," 112–13.

36. On the connections between Quakerism and witchcraft, see Christine Leigh Heyrman, "Specters of Subversion, Societies of Friends: Dissent and the Devil in Provincial Essex County, Massachusetts," in *Saints & Revolutionaries: Essays on Early American History*, ed. David Hall, John M. Murrin, and Thad W. Tate (New York: Norton, 1984), esp. 54; and Bauman, *Let Your Words be Few*.

This interpretation of Hutchinson's challenge is spelled out in Kamensky, *Governing the Tongue*, ch. 4. Strong evidence of the connection between Hutchinson's verbal "fluency," her popular appeal, and the shadow of witchcraft can be found in Edward Johnson, *The Wonder-Working Providence of Sions Saviour in New England—'History of New England' (1650/1?)*, ed. J. Franklin Jameson (1910; reprint New York: Charles Scribner, 1959), 132, 185–86; "A Report of the Trial of Mrs. Ann[e] Hutchinson before the Church in Boston, March, 1638," in *The Antinomian Controversy, 1636–1638: A Documentary History*, ed. David D. Hall (Middletown, Conn.: Wesleyan University Press, 1968), esp. 353, 365, 384; and John Winthrop, *Journal*, II:7–8.

37. Laurel Thatcher Ulrich, "Vertuous Women Found: New England Ministerial Literature, 1668–1735" in *A Heritage of Her Own*, ed. Nancy F. Cott and Elizabeth H. Pleck (New York: Simon and Schuster, 1979): 58–80. Ulrich's study of the clergy's vision of female piety is a useful corrective to writings such as Lyle Koehler's, which emphasize only the repressive constraints of Puritan gender ideology.

38. Examples of such feats under occult influence are numerous. Keith Thomas describes the phenomenon in England: see *Religion and the Decline of Magic*, 478. New England examples include the case of Ann Cole of Hartford, bewitched by Rebecca Greensmith, whose "discourse passed into a Dutch-tone." Quoted in *Increase Mather*, "Remarkable Providences," 18; and Charles J. Hoadly, "A Case of Witchcraft in Hartford," *Connecticut Magazine* 5 (1899): 557–61. Widow [Mary] Glover was fluent in her native Gaelic, and "could recite her Pater Noster in Latin very readily." See Cotton Mather, "Memorable Providences," 103.

39. Cotton Mather, "Brand Pluck'd out of the Burning," 267–68, 275, emphasis mine. See also 284.

40. Robert Calef, "More Wonders of the Invisible World" in Burr, *Narratives*, 316. Calef effectively compares his subject, Margaret Rule, to Mercy Short by calling her "Another Brand Pluck'd out of the Burning." The echoes of Anne Hutchinson here are unmistakable.

41. The prayer test is a common feature in witchcraft trials and tales. See the examination of widow Glover in Cotton Mather, "Memorable Providences," 103. For a male witch's failure under the same test, see the examination of John Willard, *Salem Witchcraft Papers*, III:829. Mercy Short is one of many witches and victims whose mouths and ears were "stop'd . . . if wee spoke any good Thing." See Cotton Mather, "Brand Pluck'd out of the Burning," 272.

42. The OED lists multiple uses of "author" as current for the period, from declarer/ sayer/ writer to father/ progenitor/ creator.

43. The loose talk of neighbors was often a critical step in the definition of a witch by her community. Nearly one-third of all non-Salem witches brought actions of slander against those whose words cast a shadow over them. This figure, derived from John Demos's work, breaks down as follows: 139 total cases, less 25 "repeaters," less an additional 15 "unknown" names, less 4 "uncertain" cases,

leaves a base of 95 known witches, of whom 26 brought actions of slander against their accusers. See *Entertaining Satan*, app. The figure certainly grossly underrepresents the weight and importance of words against witches, because it counts only official actions of slander, and those only for "witches" about whom sufficient information exists to trace their prior legal histories.

44. On England, see Thomas, *Religion and the Decline of Magic*, esp. 530; and Underdown, "Taming of the Scold," 120–21. On New England, see Karlsen, *Devil in the Shape of a Woman*, 118 ff; Demos, *Entertaining Satan*, esp. 76–79.

45. William Rowley, Thomas Dekker, John Ford, et al., "The Witch of Edmonton (1658)," in *Three Jacobean Witchcraft Plays*, ed. Peter Corbin and Douglas Sedge (Manchester, England: Manchester University Press, 1986), 188 (IV, i). Other suggestive literary evidence on the link between witchcraft and scolding is found in Thomas Heywood, "The Late Lancashire Witches (1634)," in *The Dramatic Works of Thomas Heywood* (New York: Russell & Russell, 1964), IV:167– 260.

46. See Karlsen, *Devil in the Shape of a Woman*, esp. 118. Other authors have failed to make this distinction between the witch's behavior and the social construction of that behavior; see Demos, *Entertaining Satan*, 86–88; Thomas, *Religion and the Decline of Magic*, 509.

47. Again, the figures are John Demos's, drawn from a random sampling of a variety of New England court records. See *Entertaining Satan*, 77–78. Demos combines "assaultive speech" with "theft" to support his contention that the meaning given to a witch's harsh words centered on stealing: stealing "reputation" as well as property. I would argue that it is also instructive to combine assaultive speech with other speech crimes—lying and resisting authority—to give a fuller picture of the level of verbal disorder indicated by the figures.

48. *Records of the Town of East-Hampton, Long Island, Suffolk County, New York*, 5 vols. (Sag Harbor, NY: John H. Hunt, 1905), I:132, 139, 140. For a full account of the neighborhood "gossip" element in the Garlick case, see Demos, *Entertaining Satan*, ch. 7.

49. "Examination of Sarah Good and Testimony of Sarah Gage against Good," *Salem Witchcraft Papers*, II:356–57, 362, 369.

A cursory examination of some cases from Dorsetshire, England, suggests that heated words were a potent source of suspicion on both sides of the Atlantic. See G. J. Davies, ed., *Touchying Witchcrafte and Sorcerye* (Dorset, England: Dorset Record Society Publications, no. 9, 1985), 31–32, 49–51.

50. On Bibber's "double-tongue," see depositions of Lydia Porter and Joseph Fowler, *Salem Witchcraft Papers*, I:79–80. To be heard speaking against one's husband was especially damning. See, for example, the appearance of Bridget Bishop, later executed at Salem, before the Essex County Court for "calling her husband many opprobrious names" in 1677, *ECR*, VI:386–87. Alice Parker, accused at Salem, was heard to have "called her husband all to nought" and called a deponent who took her husband's part "rogue and bid [him] to mind [his] owne business." Deposition of John West, *Salem Witchcraft Papers*, II:632–33.

On Bibber's "wishing bad wishes," see deposition of Thomas and Mary Jacobs, *Salem Witchcraft Papers*, I:80, emphasis mine.

51. On cursing, see Thomas, *Religion and the Decline of Magic*, 436–37, 502–9; St. George, " 'Heated' Speech," 301.

52. Benjamin Abbott's deposition against Martha Carrier, *Salem Witchcraft Papers*, I:192–93. See also *ECR*, III:471–72.

53. Thomas Bracy, deposition against Katherine Harrison of Wethersfield, Connecticut, reprinted in Taylor, *Witchcraft Delusion*, 50; Samuel Smith, deposition against Mary Eastwick, *Salem Witchcraft Papers*, I:301–2. For a list of other "curses," see Demos, *Entertaining Satan*, 88.

54. See testimony against the wife of Henry Batchelor by Joseph Medcalf and others, Ipswich, 1667, *Essex File Papers*, vol. 12, docs. 4–1.

It was easy for Goodwife Batchelor's threats to come true. Like a seventeenth-century version of modern-day "psychic" Jeanne Dixon, she left plenty of room for diverse outcomes to fulfill her predictions. For example, she told a cattle farmer that "such and such" of his cattle "would dye and such & such would hardly escape and some others would live." She was also heard to say that his "cattell could be much scattered in the Summer but it might be we might finde them up againe about Michaeltyde," an eventuality that would seem almost an inevitable part of the seasonal rhythms of dairying. See *Essex File Papers*, vol. 12, docs. 4–1, 6–1; *ECR*, III: 403–4.

55. Samuel Shattock, deposition against Mary Parker, *Salem Witchcraft Papers*, II:635; Elizabeth Howell described her possession by Elizabeth Garlick, *East-Hampton Town Records*, I:129.

56. Depositions of Deborah Hadley; Daniel Warner, John Warner, and Sarah Warner; and Simon and Mary Chapman for Elizabeth How, June 1692, *Salem Witchcraft Papers*, II: 440–41.

57. "William Hubbard deposition for Sarah Buckley," *Salem Witchcraft Papers*, I:146–47; see also the Rev. John Higginson's and Rev. Samuel Cheever's testimony for Buckley, *Salem Witchcraft Papers*, I:147.

58. Thomas Bradbury deposition for Mary Bradbury, *Salem Witchcraft Papers*, I:118–19. See also the petition in her behalf signed by 114 neighbors emphasizing her "curteous, & peaceable disposition & cariag" and affirming that in fifty years they had never heard of any "difference" or "falling oute" between Bradbury and her neighbors, *Salem Witchcraft Papers*, I:119–20.

A similar description of the nonwitch as nonscold is found in the case of Katherine Ellenwood, suspected for bewitching her husband into impotence. Neighbors who testified in her behalf called her "a Sevill Cariage womon, both in Word and Action," and told the court that they had "never hard [her] revele any secrets in any way nor do we think she ever wood." "Ellenwood v. Ellenwood, Salem, 1682," *Essex File Papers*, 38:15–4 (Ruth Haskins deposition); 38:16–1 (Abigail Stone and Elizabeth Hooper testimony). Verbally "publishing" the secrets of one's husband was, of course, a certain sign of scolding.

59. Heywood, *The Late Lancashire Witches*, I, i (178, 183). Interestingly, the chief symptom of the diabolic inversion of the Seeley household in Heywood's play is the perverse speech relations among members of the family:

> "The Father to the Sonne doth cry,
> The Sonne rebukes the Father old;
> The Daughter at the mother Scold,
> The wife the husband check and chide,
> But that's no wonder, through the wide
> World 'tis common." (II, i [p. 188]).

The "witch," Mrs. Generous, also demonstrates the mock penitence of the double-tongued woman, see IV, i (227–28, 236).

60. This wonderfully evocative request came from the specter of Connecticut suspect Elizabeth Clawson to her possessed victim, servant Katherine Branch. Branch fulfilled the plea by turning cartwheels in her master's parlor, see deposition of Sgt. Daniel Wescott, May 1692, Wyllys Papers/ AMBL, W-19, sheet 3. A similar image of inversion appears in Joshua Scottow's 1694 tract, *A Narrative of the Plantation of the Massachusetts Colony Anno 1628*: witches, he says, turned things "topsy turvy," as if "Heads and Heels have changed places," quoted in David D. Hall, *Worlds of Wonder, Days of Judgment: Popular Religious Belief in Early New England* (New York: Knopf, 1989), 169.

61. Presentment of Nicholas Bailey and his wife in New Haven, 1655, reprinted in *Witch-Hunting in Seventeenth-Century New England: A Documentary History, 1638–1692*, ed. David D. Hall (Boston: Northeastern University Press, 1991), 92.

Demos and Karlsen arrive at the same ratio of female to male accusers: roughly four to one. Demos identifies 22 male "witches" among the 114 people accused prior to the Salem outbreak. Of these 22, 9 were husbands of female "witches" and another 2 were "religious associates." Most of the others, he argues, became suspect in distinctly "limited" ways, *Entertaining Satan*, 57, 60–62. Karlsen uses a base figure of 75 accused men including those suspected during the Salem trials (22 percent of the 342 suspects whose sex she has been able to identify conclusively), of whom nearly half (36) were "suspect by association," *Devil in the Shape of a Woman*, 47.

62. Each of these convicted non-Salem male witches was condemned along with his wife. John Carrington of Wethersfield, Connecticut, was executed with his wife, Joan, in 1651; Nathaniel Greensmith of Hartford was executed during a local "outbreak" in 1662–63 after the confession of his wife, Rebecca; and Hugh Parsons (suspected along with his wife, Mary) had his conviction overturned in 1651. As Karlsen points out, Carrington was the only man found guilty in the "normal" course of prosecutions before 1692. "Leaving outbreaks aside," she notes, execution was "a punishment normally reserved for women," *Devil in the Shape of a Woman*, 48, see also 49–50.

Richard Godbeer argues that although women were "much more vulnerable than men to accusations of witchcraft" they were "not necessarily practicing [magic] in greater numbers," *The Devil's Dominion: Magic and Religion in Early New England* (Cambridge: Cambridge University Press, 1992), 20–21.

63. Thomas Adams, *The Taming of the Tongue*, in *The Works of Thomas Adams*, ed. Joseph Angus (1629; reprint Edinburgh: James Nichol, 1862), III:17.

64. The documents relating to Mary and Hugh Parsons's case are reprinted in Hall, *Witch-Hunting in New England*, 25–27, 29–60. Mary Parsons's conviction for slandering Widow Marshfield of Windsor, Connecticut, is described on 25–27. For Mary Parsons's suspicions of her husband, see her testimony upon examination (33, 41–42, 45–46); and the depositions of Benjamin Cooley (46), Anthony Dorchester (46), Francis Pepper (47), Mary Ashley (47), John Mathews (48), and Thomas Miller (53).

65. George Colton deposition in Hall, *Witch-Hunting in New England*, 43; Hugh and Mary Parsons examination, 41.

While Parsons's silence, especially when witches were the topic under discussion, certainly had an occult significance, it must also have served as a tacit reminder of his "feminine" verbal demeanor; see Thomas Burnham deposition, 34; and Joan Warrinar and Abigail Munn deposition, 34–35. Mary Parsons commented that her husband sometimes "gave her a naughty look but never a word," 41.

66. George and Hannah Lancton deposition, 32–33; Samuel Marshfield and Widow Marshfield depositions, 52–53; Rice and Blanche Bedortha depositions, 35, 36; John Mathews testimony, 37; see also William Branch deposition, 55; all in Hall, *Witch-Hunting in New England*.

67. Samuel Dibble deposition, 1666–67, reprinted in Hall, *Witch-Hunting in New England*, 168. Graves had also threatened his pregnant daughter, telling her "fit thyself to meet the Lord: for if thou dost not fall in labor properly: [you] would die."

68. Presentment of John Fuller, 1683, in John Noble and John F. Cronin, eds., *Records of the Court of Assistants of the Colony of Massachusetts Bay, 1630–1692*, 3 vols. (Boston: Rockwell and Churchill, 1901–1928), I:228–29.

69. Presentment of John Broadstreet, Ipswich, 1652, *Essex File Papers*, 2:46-2. Significantly, a similar claim to astrological knowledge would help condemn Katharine Harrison of Wethersfield in 1668. Witness Elizabeth Smith had heard Harrison "often speake and boast, of her greate familiaritie wth mr Lilley[,] one that tould fortunes," Elizabeth Smith deposition, September 1668, Wyllys Papers/ AMBL, W-11. After facing several trials that concluded without a certain result, Harrison was convicted by a Connecticut jury in October 1669. The magistrates reviewed the verdict and, in May 1670, declined to hang her but banished her from the colony; see Demos, *Entertaining Satan*, 362–63. Though she escaped execution, her crime was deemed significantly more serious than "telling a lie."

70. Presentment of William Browne, Ipswich, 1657, *Essex File Papers*, 3:108-113, see esp. 3:110-2 (complaint of Goodwife Prince), 3:109-3 (testimony of Deborah Skilling), and 3:113-1 (deposition of Isabel Babson, midwife). The verdict appears in *ECR*, II:36.

71. Demos, *Entertaining Satan*, 60.

72. See Brandbrook v. Wells, Ipswich, 1668, *ECR*, IV:49–50, 67, and *Essex File Papers*, 13:88-2, 88-6 through 89-1, 89-3, 89-4; Cross v. Wells, Salem, 1668, *ECR*, IV:66–67 and *Essex File Papers*, 13:104-2 through 104-4, 104-8; presentment of Wells et al., Salem, 1668, *ECR*, IV: 76–82, 99; Wells v. Nelson, Ipswich, 1669, *ECR*, IV:104–5 and *Essex File Papers*, 14:22-1 through 22-6; presentment of Wells, Ipswich, 1669, *ECR*, IV:142 and *Essex File Papers*, 14:80-1 through 80-4.

73. Brandbrook v. Wells, Ipswich, 1668, *ECR*, IV:49 (Reginald and Elizabeth Foster deposition).

74. Carol Karlsen argues that witchcraft prosecutions were "successful" only when elite and popular concerns coincided. *Devil in the Shape of a Woman*, ch. 1. See also Clive Holmes, "Popular Culture?" on this question.

75. William Perkins, *A Direction for the Government of the Tongue according to Gods word*, in Perkins, *The Works of that Famous and Worthy Minister . . . Newly Corrected* (London: John Legatt, 1635), 451. On the mouth as an "entry-point" for the devil, see St. George, " 'Heated' Speech," 281–83; Thomas, *Religion and the Decline of Magic*, 524; Rowley et al., *Witch of Edmonton*, 162.

76. See Thomas, *Religion and the Decline of Magic*, 61.

77. See David D. Hall, "The Uses of Literacy in New England, 1600–1850" in *Printing and Society in Early America*, ed. William L. Joyce, Richard D. Brown, and John B. Hench (Worcester, Mass.: American Antiquarian Society, 1983), esp. 36.

78. On the evolution of free speech doctrine, see Leonard W. Levy, *Emergence of a Free Press* [rev. ed. of *Legacy of Suppression: Freedom of Speech and Press in Early American History*] (New York: Oxford University Press, 1985); and Norman L. Rosenberg, *Protecting the Best Men: An Interpretive History of the Law of Libel* (Chapel Hill: University of North Carolina Press, 1986). The essential change in Anglo-American libel law over the last two centuries has been the movement away from the notion that words, by themselves, can harm the state or private interests.

79. Interestingly, our conception of the victims of speech has flip-flopped since colonial times. Instead of protecting authority against dissident words, our current debate centers on the need to protect members of oppressed groups against hateful or insensitive speech, often uttered by those more culturally "privileged." For a number of suggestive viewpoints on this current debate, see Paul Berman, ed., *Debating P.C.: The Controversy over Political Correctness on College Campuses* (New York: Dell, 1991).

3

Gender and the Meanings of Confession in Early New England

~

Elizabeth Reis

Elizabeth Reis's essay addresses one of the more perplexing problems of the Salem trials: Why would a woman confess to signing the devil's book in blood, thus giving the devil permission to use her shape to afflict others? Reis argues that the confessions and denials made during witchcraft trials need to be understood from within the context of Puritan religious culture, a culture in which women saw themselves as inherently vile while men more often accepted responsibility for individual sins, not for having fundamentally corrupt souls. In the volatile context of witchcraft examinations, women blurred their implicit bond with the devil forged in the commission of ordinary sin with the more explicit and egregious sin of signing the devil's book and becoming a witch; male confessors rarely linked prior sins with present witchcraft accusations. Female confessors confirmed cultural expectations about female sinners and also validated the court's procedures. Women who denied the charges, on the other hand, had to prove they were free of all sin, not merely witchcraft, an impossible task for any sinner and a poor strategy at Salem.

BY THE END OF THE seventeenth century, more and more women were becoming brides of Christ, joining their churches as full members. Yet, ironically, the avalanche of accusations and confessions at Salem seems to suggest the opposite, that women were flocking to

Satan. The outbreak at Salem is particularly vexing for historians in several ways: In addition to demonizing women, it reversed the seventeenth-century trend of acquittal for suspected witches; it witnessed women accusing other women more than had been typical in previous witch-hunting episodes; and it generated puzzling confessions from some of the accused women.[1] Bernard Rosenthal has shown that confession and strategic accusation of others were the two safest ways to avoid execution oneself.[2] Without denying the possibility of such calculations, I want to explore the causative influence of women's sense of their own depravity, and their recognition of a similar basic corruption in other women. Simply put, women were more likely than men to be convinced of their own complicity with the devil, and, given such convictions about themselves, they could more easily imagine that other women were equally damned. Although some clergy, magistrates, and laity voiced skepticism throughout the proceedings, the crisis escalated. For women as well as men, the relationship between womanhood and witchcraft was so firmly entrenched, as we shall see, that women's accusations of other women and women's confessions of their own collusion achieved at least a short-lived deadly credibility.

Women's and men's testimony against those accused was congruent with female and male notions of sinfulness. Men typically presented instances of maleficium—cows made sick or butter turned rancid—to prove a woman's witchcraft, just as they renounced specific sins to testify to conversion.[3] Women were more likely to present spectral evidence. In all the cases in which the accused were executed, there was invisible pinching and torturing of accusers during public examinations.[4] The pain they displayed seemed a clear demonstration of a consensual pact between the devil and the "witch." A witch's specter rendered explicit and immediate what the mere fact of her womanhood made only implicit and potential—her inherent unworthiness and entanglement with the devil.

After the Hartford outbreak of 1662, one might have predicted that witchcraft accusations were on the wane, vanishing with the rise in secularism, which so many Puritan ministers decried in their jeremiads. Salem's intensity seems particularly absurd, given this trend. After the Hartford crisis, in which approximately thirteen people were accused and four executed, ministers and magistrates avoided, rather than seized upon, the opportunity to prosecute those suspected of witchcraft.[5] But at Salem their doubts may have been eased (or at least temporarily suspended) because women themselves, the brides of Christ, brought forth so many clearly convincing cases, complete with the specters to prove the devil's intrigues.

Women's accusations against other women at Salem might be explained, in part, by the rage particular accusers felt toward those whom they accused, as Carol Karlsen suggests. Victims themselves of precarious economic and social circumstances, these young women perhaps feared for their future, worrying that they would end up alone, with no one to establish their marital dowries and find them husbands.[6] But I think it likely that envy and guilt mixed with rage to fuel their indictments. Many of the accusers had grown up in religious households, where they developed a strong notion of good and evil and, most important, the imminent possibility of their own damnation. Accusations of the pious, such as Rebecca Nurse, suggest not merely the rage of the disadvantaged but the envy of those who feared they would never be allowed to achieve prominence and respectability. Finally, if the accusers had doubts about their own regeneration and perhaps about the reprobation and maleficence of the pious women they indicted, they may have felt the additional guilt inherent in giving false testimony before the court and God. In such cases, could renewed, more vigorous accusation provide a measure of self-justification?[7]

The community accepted the surprising shift in the pattern of witchcraft persecution and believed the main group of accusers because the spectral evidence introduced struck them as particularly compelling and because women's vulnerability to Satan—even women who demonstrated their closeness to Christ—was even more plausible. By the end of the seventeenth century, women were joining the church at numbers equal or greater to male converts.[8] Men seemed to have been thinking less about questions of salvation and damnation; women more. Yet as increasing numbers of women became church members and seriously contemplated the meaning of conversion and their own possibility of salvation or damnation, their very faith could damn them. Some pious women found themselves accused of witchcraft by other women whose own religious anxieties allowed them to conceive and present damning evidence. Some women denied the charges; others confessed; but all suffered the disadvantage of their womanhood in facing the dangerous and disturbing accusations. We turn now to confessing and denying women and how their responses to the charges fueled the court's willingness to continue and justified its proceedings.

Why would a woman confess to witchcraft? Why would she admit to signing the devil's book and participating in a devil's baptism? Very early in the Salem witchcraft episode of 1692, the court decided not to hang those who confessed, hoping that they could be persuaded to name others involved in this wicked affair. Surely the avenue of escape this decision provided helps to account for many of the approximately fifty confessions. I am not convinced, however, that self-preservation alone explains the admissions of guilt at Salem, even though the accused faced the gallows. Furthermore, "Why did they confess?" might not be as pertinent a question to ask as "How did they confess?" Confessors' language suggests that the choice to confess or deny witchcraft charges resonated with women's and men's more general confessions in Puritan churches.

Women and men thought about sin and guilt differently, whether they were applying for church membership or trying to convince the court that they were not witches. Women were more likely to interpret their own sins, no matter how ordinary, as tacit covenants with Satan, spiritual renunciation of God, evidence of their vile natures. Men tended to focus on particular sins such as carnality or Sabbath-breaking. Women were more convinced that they had embraced the devil; men were more confident that they would be able to reform their behavior and turn to God. And so if women believed more generally that they had covenanted with the devil, it did not take much for them to be convinced that they had in fact accepted a more literal and physical invitation from Satan and become actual witches. During the Salem witchcraft trials and other episodes, the distinction between implicit sins, which bound sinners to the devil and would take them to hell, and an explicit pact with the devil, which turned sinners into witches, became blurred, particularly for women.[9]

When Alice Lake of Dorchester was about to be hanged in 1651, she insisted on her innocence, alleging she "owned nothing of the crime laid to her charge." Declaring herself innocent of witchcraft, she nonetheless believed that she deserved to be exposed as a witch because, according to the minister John Hale, "she had when a single woman play'd the harlot, and being with Child used means to destroy the fruit of her body to conceal her sin and shame." Lake believed that her sexual transgression was enough to justify her guilt as a witch. Although she had not signed an explicit compact with Satan, she still concluded—and apparently Hale concurred—that she had covenanted with him through the commission of her sin.[10]

During the witchcraft episodes, not only when the accused confessed to signing the diabolical covenant with the devil, but also when they vehemently denied any familiarity with Satan, like Alice Lake, they often conflated ordinary sins with witchcraft. Their transgressions could suggest, even to the sinners themselves, an insidious merger between regular sins and more active commitment to Satan in the form of witchcraft. At the heart of this ambiguity between sinning and witchcraft was the central idea of the covenant, which Puritans believed could bind them, individually and as a community, to God, but which, in a conflicting and darker manifestation, could chain believers to Satan.

Alice Lake's feminized denial was simultaneously a feminized confession. She disavowed witchcraft practice, yet she acknowledged her sinfulness and was hanged; her response reintegrated her into the community, but it did not exonerate her on earth. Forty years later, during the Salem witch trials, however, confession *did* save lives, although such reprieve was never articulated explicitly as policy. The biblical injunction, "Thou shalt not suffer a witch to live," prevailed in theory. But, with the scarcity of reliable witnesses and evidence, nothing was more valuable than an accused woman's confession. Admissions "proved" confessors' guilt, of course, but in practice the court sought confessions for other reasons as well. Convinced that the devil had confided in his victims, the court prolonged confessors' stays in jail so that they might name other conspirators. In some respects, then, for the court and community "witches" were more valuable alive than dead.

By September 1692, it had become clear that the court's policy of sparing confessors had encouraged (perhaps disingenuous) admissions of guilt. In an effort to stem this tide, the court decided that some confessors would stand trial, although still none were hanged.[11] The Salem episode was thus different from previous ones, in which outright confessions were rare and fatal. Nonetheless, ambiguous responses like Alice Lake's exposed the accused woman as a sinner and a "witch." Confessors at Salem, though they survived the ordeal, inculpated themselves similarly.

The confessions, denials, and accusations by the afflicted and others who testified need to be read carefully. Together this oral and written evidence can "tell us" not only about the "narrative" of the trials, but, as significant, about women, men, and the power of Puritan covenant theology. The process of cultural negotiation—between women and men; between the clergy and the magistrates; and between sources of authority and the laity—can be seen quite clearly in the trial transcripts. Admittedly, the court records of Salem and other towns have their limitations; often it is difficult to tell if they are verbatim transcripts or accounts reconstructed after the event. Sentences appear in fragments or are lost altogether, and first-person accounts often shift to the third-person, casting doubt on the proximity of the voice to that of the defendant. Some of these problems are mitigated by the sheer volume of the transcripts. Despite their deficiencies, the trial records portray a cultural and religious world that was deeply gendered.

Although women and men both understood the meanings of confession, they confessed to the charges of witchcraft or denied them in different ways. And the testimony of their neighbors—either for or against those accused—betrays a gender division as well. A confessing woman was the model of Puritan womanhood, even though she was admitting to the worst of sins, for she confirmed her society's belief in both God and the devil. She validated the court's procedures, as we shall see, and she corroborated Puritan thought concerning sin, guilt, and the devil's wily ways. Apology was critical. It was not enough to describe the devil's book and baptism. A good Puritan woman/witch needed to repent of her obvious sins. The cultural performance of confession created a paradigm of perfect redemption, and during the Salem trials the confessing woman was rewarded with her life.

In confessing these women succumbed to the unbearable pressures of their own and their community's expectations of proper female behavior. What they confessed to and the manner in which they confessed can tell modern readers about the constraints and boundaries of Puritan womanhood.[12] Denials are equally telling; women who insisted on their innocence of the crime of witchcraft often unwittingly implicated themselves because they admitted to being sinners. Ironically, those who would not confess and allow themselves to be forgiven, yet who did admit to sin, as any good Puritan should, were executed. They were unable to convince the court and their peers that their souls had not entered into a covenant with the devil; they could not wholeheartedly deny a pact with Satan when an implicit bond with him through common sin was undeniable. The sense of the depraved female self, which emerges from women's conversion narratives, merged with the community's (and each accused woman's own) expectations about the rebellious female witch.

Susannah Post's admissions, delivered at her examination in August 1692, contained the elements of a respectable confession. She acknowledged that she "had bin in the Devils snare three years: the first time I saw him he was like a Catt: he told her he was a prince: & I was to serve him I promised him to doe it the next shape was a yellow bird: it s'd I must serve him: & he s'd I should live well: the next time he appeared like a black man that time he brought a book & she touched it with a stick that was Dipt in an ink horne & it made a red mark."[13] Her description of the events was ordinary enough, paralleling and elaborating ministers' representations of the devil's powers in the context of the meetinghouse. No doubt the very ordinariness of her tales contributed to her audience's belief.

What is particularly "womanly" about Post's confession is not the detailed description of the devil's appearance or the specific information about the meeting she claimed to have attended but her admission that she had made a mistake. During her confession, "She s'd she was now willing to renownce the Devil & all his works: & she went: when bid & begged forgivnes of the afflicted & could come to them and not hurt them."[14] Despite this confession—or, I believe, because of it—the court spared Susannah Post. Her regrets and willingness to turn from the path of evil to the path of righteousness, expected of all decent Puritan women, transformed her confession from a tale of depravity and sin to a narrative of redemption.

Those confessions that were filtered through the court and written down by a court official present a certain problem of evidence for the modern reader. It is impossible to know "what really happened." Perhaps the accused did confess that the devil diverted them from praying to God, as Mary Osgood apparently did in her confession of September 8, 1692. But the possibility exists that the justice who penned her confession, John Higginson, imposed his own interpretation. We will never know if Osgood actually uttered the words inscribed in the record of her own accord, if she said them because she had learned what to say to save her own life, or if the court supplied the acceptable script for her. But if establishing the "truth" of Osgood's narrative remains impossible, its cultural significance for the community that endorsed it is undeniable. Whether heartfelt or tactical, Osgood's cultural performance helped produce or reproduce particular gender categories and arrangements, helped construct or reconstruct female subjectivity in Puritan New England.[15]

Osgood's confession contained a number of ideas about the devil and witchcraft that would have made it satisfactory to both the court and her peers. It told how the cat appeared "when she was in a melancholy state and condition," and diverted her from praying to God. "Instead thereof she prayed to the devil; about which time she made a covenant with the devil," and she consented to worship him. She renounced her former baptism, was transported through the air, and was able to name others who similarly rode a pole to a witch meeting. On the issue of afflicting others in order to coerce them into joining the devil's minions, Osgood's confession concedes she gave "consent the devil should do it in her shape, and that the devil could not do it without her consent."[16]

Consent was crucial, and mention of it in the confession validated not only Puritan theology but the court's procedures as well.[17] The clergy had expressed ambivalence about spectral evidence, ultimately advising the court that the devil had power to assume an innocent, nonconsenting person's shape. If the court had heeded the ministers' advice, it could no longer have accepted spectral evidence, inasmuch as there would be no way of telling whether a particular person had given the devil permission to use her (or his) shape. Yet the court persisted, and countless witnesses testified that they had been afflicted by particular accused witches' specters.

Osgood verified yet another element of Puritan belief concerning Satan's intrusion, thus making her confession particularly valuable as a morality tale. After describing at some length the various rewards the devil offered her in exchange for her complicity, she acknowledged that he had not delivered on a single promise. Not only did she have to reconcile herself to this disappointment, but in fact, the conditions of her life took a turn for the worse as a result of her ill-fated pact. According to the court recorder, "[H]e promised her abundance of satisfaction and quietness in her future state, but never performed any thing; and that she has lived more miserably and more discontented since, than ever before."[18] Puritans knew full well that the devil was prone to offer material or spiritual rewards but to deliver only despair.

It might be tempting to interpret these confessing women as clever manipulators of the court. Were they cognizant of their power to mock authority with their tales of the devil's misdeeds and their own collusion, followed by clever apologies comprising all the elements apparently required by the court? They knew what the court wanted to hear, especially by September 1692 when it was clear that confessors were spared. To embrace this line of analysis completely, however, would be to misread the evidence. Women (and men) came to know their parts because confession and belief in the devil were integral components of their religious world. Successful confessions confirmed cultural expectations in a number of ways: women formed a pact with the devil; women apologized; and the court was justified in convicting people based on spectral evidence.

It was the women who *denied* any collusion with Satan, or those who initially confessed but later recanted, who, by their refusal to admit complicity with the devil, displayed a measure of independence in the face of authority.[19] Women who denied guilt may have believed that they had the weight of God's witness on their side; and, indeed, many testified that their protestations of innocence would be vindicated, if not in this world, then in the next, on Judgment Day.

Such protestations unfortunately fell on deaf ears. Vehement denial and absolute refusal to confess, in effect, repudiated Puritan theology, contradicted the court's proceedings, and invalidated notions of proper female decorum.[20] Abigail Faulkner, Sr., for example, negated the court's stance on spectral evidence. When the afflicted went into fits, she announced, "It is the devill dos it in my shape," implying that he did it without her permission.[21] Though the court had accepted the "expert" testimony of Mary Osgood, which confirmed its own view, it dismissed Faulkner's claim, or at least considered it disingenuous, because Faulkner failed to admit guilt. Ironically, by denying the witchcraft accusation, Faulkner disputed the reality of witchcraft itself and by implication undermined her own expertise.

Female deniers had an especially difficult time proving their innocence because they had to prove not only that they had never signed the devil's pact, but also that they had never even implicitly covenanted with the devil through ordinary sin. Few women, however, lacked guilt and remorse for prior sins and shortcomings, and the community persistently linked former transgressions with particular accusations of witchcraft.

In testifying against a person it was important to associate unseemly conduct, particularly that which challenged gender conventions or prescriptions of ideal womanhood, with witchcraft charges. In this way women's behavior was constrained. It was not only that women who defied cultural boundaries of polite decorum, for example, were singled out and accused of witchcraft, but that the very definitions of acceptability were created and contested during the trials themselves. John Westgate testified that he was at a man's house when the accused woman, Alice Parker, arrived and "scolded att and called her husband all to nought." Westgate took the husband's side in the marital dispute, suggesting to him that "itt was an unbeseeming thing for her to come after him to the taverne and raile after thatt rate." Alice Parker then called him a rogue, and told Westgate to mind his own business. The incident might have been forgotten, except that Westgate reconstructed it for the court, adding the crucial detail that "sometime afterwards" he heard a noise and a black hog ran toward him and threatened to devour him. During the ensuing scuffle he realized the hog "was Either the Divell or some Evill thing not a Reall hog, and did then Really Judge or determine in my mind that it was either Goody parker or by her meenes, and procuring fearing that she is a Witch."[22]

The members of the court may have seen themselves as unbiased interpreters of testimony, but they, too, participated in the drama which constructed—rather than simply uncovered—evil personas. The magistrates inquired about all of her sins, not merely witchcraft, when they asked Mary Easty, "How far have you complyed w'th Satan whereby he takes this advantage ag't you?"[23] The loaded question suggested a continuum of transgression, from regular sin to the signature of a pact, the slippery slope making it all the more difficult to determine who, in fact, had surrendered. Easty replied that she was certainly "clear of this sin," that is, signing the devil's pact. In fact, she stated in a petition that, as far as she knew, she was clear "of any other scandalouse evill, or miscaryage inconsistant with Christianity."[24] The magistrates were most interested in whether or not Easty had explicitly bargained with Satan, but both Easty and the authorities appreciated the relation between sin and the devil. Through her casual sins, Mary Easty complied with the devil; how far the court believed she had actually yielded would determine her innocence or guilt in the witchcraft trials.

Testimony offered on behalf of the accused makes it clear that the witnesses and the accused knew that there was a difference between simply sinning and becoming a witch. They knew they could recognize someone who had stepped over the line, but they did not necessarily understand where that line would be drawn during the proceedings. And so, as part of their testimony, petitioners and witnesses for the accused participated in the same discourse as their foes, trying tirelessly to prove to the court not only that their defendant was not a witch, but that her life was so nearly flawless that no compact with the devil could be implied or even imagined, let alone established in court.

For a Puritan woman, good character meant carrying out one's Christian duty as daughter, wife, mother, and neighbor.[25] Nicholas Rice submitted a petition on his wife's behalf urging the court to release her from jail. In all the time they had been married, he asserted, "he never had any reason to accuse her for any Impietie or witchcraft, but the Contrary Shee lived w'th him as a good Faithfull dutifull wife and alwise had respect . . . to the ordinances of God while her Strength Remain'd."[26] Rice thus confirmed what the court and its audience already knew while attempting to mobilize that knowledge to save his wife: a witch could not possibly be a good, faithful, dutiful, and pious woman. Either one covenanted with the devil and thus clung to all one's sins, or one remained by the Lord, devoutly fulfilling earthly duties.

Some of the accused, like Mary Easty, completely disavowed any familiarity with Satan, through sin or witchcraft. But other women mused about their souls, too, and admitted that the devil had been in their hearts—in other words, that they had sinned. Their admission of his presence, at least in the context of the witchcraft trials, was used to implicate them as witches. Hannah Bromage, for example, acknowledged "that she had been under some dead nes w'h respect to the ordnances for the matter of 6 weeks." Bromage admitted nothing more than one might recount in a conversion relation. She further conceded, however, that "a sudden sugge[s]tion come into her heed sayeing I can help thee with strenth." Bromage firmly claimed that she did not succumb to Satan's devices, and she forcefully responded to the voice in her head, "Avoid satan."[27]

Though they echoed, in an unextraordinary way, the temptations the ministers often described in their sermons, Bromage's admissions were interpreted quite differently during the trials. The changed context of her testimony altered its meaning fundamentally. In contrast to confessions occurring in conversion narratives, in which prospective converts were able to follow admission with repentance for allowing Satan into their imaginations, in this volatile and mistrustful climate, Bromage's disclosure simply provoked further suspicion and investigation. The court immediately demanded to know in what shape the devil appeared. Perhaps to distance herself from any involvement with Satan's physical appearance, she replied that "she believed the devil was in her heart."[28] Bromage was later acquitted because of a lack of evidence, but the language she used to talk about the devil in her life suggests that there was indeed a very fine line between ordinary sinning and witchcraft, and that women tried to assess the states of their souls sincerely, even if doing so could expose them to the charge of witchcraft.

Rebecca Eames's confession expressly blended more typical tales of Satanic encounters with admission of a prior sin of adultery. She explained to the court that right after making a black mark with her finger, sealing the covenant, "she was then in such horror of Conscienc that she tooke a Rope to hang herselfe and a Razer to cutt her throate by Reason of her great sin in Committing adultery & by that the Divell Gained her he promiseing she should not be brought out or ever discovered."[29] Her confession displayed terrified confusion—was she horrified by the evil pact or by confrontation with her previous sin of adultery? Or did she believe she had effectively covenanted with the devil by virtue of her earlier sexual violation?

If, in their narratives of conversion, women constructed an image of themselves, not merely of their sins, as entirely retrograde, in this more dangerous context, too, we see women embrace a sense of themselves as essentially depraved, as sinners, bound to the devil. Although Rebecca Nurse, for example, denied any explicit pact with Satan, she could not say she was without sin, and, in fact, she blamed some unknown lapse for her predicament. "[W]ell as to this thing I am Innocent as the child unborne but . . . what sine hath god found out in me unrepented of that he should Lay such an Afliction upon me in my old Age."[30] Women such as Nurse, Eames, and Bromage could not help but search within themselves and sometimes confess unwittingly, convinced that they actually were in the devil's snare, that something they had thought or done had festered in their souls and would eventually be exposed.

Recantations by women who had initially confessed can provide additional clues about the feelings of guilt and reprobation women suffered and about women's place more generally. Margaret Jacobs wrote to her father from the Salem jail that she had confessed by reason of "the Magistrates Threatnings, and my own Vile and Wretched Heart."[31] Harassment seemed to have played a role; her own guilt arising from past sin—a heart absent from God and thus committed to Satan—reinforced her decision.

Recanters recognized that they now had to repent for the serious sin of lying. Margaret Jacobs related that her false confession wounded her soul, and that she retracted it because the Lord "would not let me go on in my Sins."[32] Women who took back their statements established themselves publicly as liars; clearly they were in the devil's camp with or without explicitly signing the book. The public drama of retraction further enmeshed them in the discourse of depravity, repentance, and forgiveness; as women, their lies confirmed their self-image, as well as public perceptions of them, as sinners, as essentially unworthy, and as such they endorsed their subordination not only to God but to (male) authority.

Some recognized, privately, that the court wanted to hear and believe certain things, particularly from women. Sarah Churchill's confession was motivated by three circumstances, she later told her friend, Sarah Ingersoll. She had been threatened and told "thay would put her in to the dongin," and she had persisted in her story for so long that it seemed impossible for her to back out of it. The third reason was most insightful: Churchill believed "that If she told mr Noys but ons [once] she had sat hur hand to the Book he would be leve her but If she told the truth and saied she had not seat her hand to the Book a hundred times he would not beleve hur."[33]

Churchill's apperception was more true for women than for men. Not only was it far more unusual for a man to be accused of witchcraft than a woman, but when men were accused, or when they confessed, their gender mattered as well.[34] Men's confessions and denials were different in their substance and in their reception. Men, by and large, did not confuse their own regular sinning with witchcraft. They did not enter into the particular drama of Puritan redemption and forgiveness in the same way as the women. When accused (generally because they were related to an accused woman), either they boldly confessed, weaving elaborate tales of the devil's doings, or they offered tentative and tactical admissions, or most frequently, they denied the accusation and did so audaciously. Apparently, men did not feel the need to defer to the court's procedures as did women. They were impertinent, though they sometimes paid for their insolence with their lives. In the few documented cases in which a lively exchange occurred, notions of proper male behavior were created or reinforced in the proceedings of the court. As in the trials of women, Puritan New England's social order and gender arrangements were defined, rehearsed, and endorsed.

In the case of George Burroughs, former Salem Village minister, testimony against him frequently mentioned his inappropriate behavior toward his wife.[35] John and Rebecca Putnam both observed that when the defendant lived at their house he was "a very sharp man to his wife, notwithstanding to our observation shee was a very good and dutiful wife to him."[36] Witnesses merged the two offenses—spousal abuse and witchcraft—thus gendering the witch's (and the devil's) crime. Women were likely to be taken as witches if it also could be proven that they displayed some sort of offensive carriage as wives, mothers, or daughters. Men were more likely to be considered witches if they had abandoned their duties as husbands and fathers.

John Proctor was one of five men to be executed for witchcraft; yet his attitude toward the court nonetheless reveals the efficacy men possessed. Proctor's petition to the court, declaring his innocence, was entirely different in character and tone from any petitions offered by women. Comparing the court's procedures to "Popish Cruelties," Proctor challenged the court by mentioning the barbarous torture used on three other men, Andrew and Richard Carrier and his own son, William Proctor. Proctor did not question the Puritan reality of the devil's substantial powers; in fact, he attributed the suspicion against him to "the Delusion of the Devil." But he was able, nonetheless, to transcend the world of magic, challenge the court, and demand either a change of venue or new judges; at the very least he requested that the ministers to whom he addressed his petition attend the trials. The record does not indicate the court's response to his requests.[37]

Other men also questioned the court or the accusers and addressed their shortcomings—something that women did ever so carefully, if at all. When Mary Easty dared to suggest to the court that it might isolate the afflicted people and examine them carefully to avoid fraud, she did so tactfully, and "humbly begg[ed]" the magistrates to accept her petition, "from a poor dy ing Innocent person."[38] On the contrary, when the court asked John Jackson, Sr., about his appearance at a witch meeting, he replied, with no apologies, that "these persons was not in their Right mind." George Jacobs, Sr., although he was killed, mocked the very notion of witchcraft altogether when he provoked the court, "You tax me for a wizard, you may as well tax me for a buzard I have done no harm." And later during his examination, Jacobs seemed to throw up his hands in despair, pronouncing, "Well: burn me, or hang me, I will stand in the truth of Christ, I know nothing of it."[39]

In their denials, men were able to distinguish more successfully than women their prior sins from the immediate accusation of a devil's pact. They did not conflate their sinful pasts with their alleged diabolical presents. Women's circumstances altered the nature of the cases brought against them. A woman risked being damned regardless of her response. If she embraced a sense of herself as a terrible sinner because she missed church meeting or lied or drank or committed some other common sin, then, convinced of her implicit covenant with the devil, she could easily implicate herself as a witch, though she denied that charge. If she instead steadfastly maintained her innocence, separating her prior sins from the extraordinary offense of witchcraft, the court could nonetheless convict her, convinced by her obstinancy in refusing to confess and repent. Men who denied were not hanged; a woman who dared to deny sinfulness more likely would have been.

Men also confessed in their own way, when they did so at all. Two of the ten male confessions came from thirteen-year-old boys. Stephen Johnson's, for example, is perfunctory and sounds more like a typical female confession. Some confessions were extracted by torture.[40] The court records indicate that Richard and Andrew Carrier were "Carried out to another Cambbre and there feet & hands bound." Shortly thereafter Richard was brought back in again and the court asked, "Rich'd though you have been Verry Obstinate Yett tel us how long agoe it is Since you ware taken in this Snare." At this point Richard said everything he knew—or thought the court wanted to hear—to avoid more pain. His elaborate tale included particulars about the devil's book, the baptism, how he got to the devil's meetings, and the exact manner in which he afflicted others ("I doe it by Roling up a handcherchif & Soe Imagining to be a representation of a person").[41] He told the court that the devil had his permission to afflict others.

Richard Carrier's story was believable because he followed so many of the unspoken guidelines for confession, but it was also gendered. It contained no apology, and the admissions did not follow the female model.[42] At one point Carrier wavered, indicating an ambivalence about what he admitted to doing. In an attempt to relieve himself from some of the responsibility for his actions, he announced, "The Divel Doth it Some times the Divell Sturred Me Up to hurt the Ministers Wife."[43] Richard Carrier felt compelled to acknowledge the afflictions happening before his eyes in the courtroom, and he wanted the torture to stop; but he did not want to own completely his own involvement. Woven into his story was his alibi: the devil made him do it. Even with this intricate narrative, Carrier never saw himself as the evil sinner, bonded to Satan by his own transgressive self or even for his particular transgressions.

Two other men displayed a similar divergence in their confessions. John Jackson, Jr., confessed that the devil asked him to serve him, but, significantly, he declared that he never took the ultimate, voluntary step of signing the devil's book. He did admit that the devil appeared to him in the shape of a black man, in the shape of cats, and in the shape of his Aunt How, but he "would not own that ever: the Devill babtized him nor: that ever he had signed: to the Devils book."[44] Joseph Ring, of Salisbury, was never accused of witchcraft, but his testimony against others came remarkably close to a confession. He told of how he had endured many strange happenings at the hands of the accused witches Susannah Martin and Thomas Hardy. Ring was "almost frited out of his witts" because of the noises and shapes these two presented to him, not to mention the meetings and feasts that he was forced to attend. During his ordeal, a man used to come to him, he recounted, and promised him anything he wanted, "all delectable things psons and places Imaginabl." But Ring steadfastly refused the offers. "On[e] time the book was brought," Ring recalled, "and a pen offerd him & to his aprehension ther was blod in the Ink horn but *he never toucht the pen*."[45] Like John Jackson, Jr., Ring firmly denied signing. Admission of that deed would have closed their cases; a confessed pact with Satan would have proven that the devil, rather than Christ, had taken possession of them. Yet, by admitting much less than Ring about involvement with the devil, a woman would have exposed herself to prosecution that Ring managed to escape.

Andrew Carrier, Richard's younger brother, also conceded the devil's intrusion, but his confession seems almost amusing in its ambivalence. With a hesitating stutter, he admitted that the devil had offered him a house and land in Andover. Unable to resist that tempting offer, Andrew was ready to sign the book. He saw that the ink was red, but he could not make out the rest of the names on the list; he saw the devil's seal, but he could not discern the stamp because it was nighttime; he went to the meeting and saw others there, but he had forgotten their names; he drank the wine, but did not eat the bread; and he witnessed the Lord's Supper, but did not hear the exact words used at the administration of the sacrament.[46]

Despite Andrew Carrier's irresolution and Richard Carrier's lack of apology and acknowledged distance from the devil, their confessions saved the brothers from the gallows. Neither were pressured to admit past sins, nor did they in any way associate their character with their purported deeds. Because the court, the accusers, the witnesses, and even the accused themselves all believed that women were more likely to be witches than men, women had much more difficulty establishing their innocence. In their denials, women were required to demonstrate that their souls rested with God rather than with Satan. Even in their confessions, women's cultural performance conformed to the Puritan model of depravity, redemption, and forgiveness, not only because the court and the community seemed to require this discourse, but because women themselves embraced this construction of female subjectivity. Women did not confess tentatively like Andrew Carrier; such vacillation was apparently a man's privilege. The court demanded that women's confessions include testimony to their essential sinfulness, as well as admission of past misdeeds and alliances with the devil, whether great or small, explicit or implicit.

Even a retracted confession—perhaps especially a retracted confession—constituted an archetype of Puritan womanhood. When Margaret Jacobs admitted that she had lied, she begged the court to "take pity and compassion on my young and tender years," and she promised to pray forever, "as she is bound in duty, for your honours happiness in this life and eternal felicity in the world to come." Margaret Jacobs needed to prove she was not bound in the devil's snare (she said she was not guilty of witchcraft, "nor any other sin that deserved death from man"), while at the same time she was obliged to proclaim her status as a good—that is, essentially sinful and dependent—Puritan woman.[47]

Thus during the witch trials gender arrangements that subordinated women and prescribed their behavior were culturally reaffirmed as women attested to their own sinfulness, either in their confessions or in their denials. Women constructed a sense of themselves, a female subjectivity, that was endorsed by the cultural process. If they publicly affirmed their depraved nature, their lives were spared. Those who failed to conform, those who denied and therefore hanged, cast themselves not only as witches, but as rebels against the entire order—male authority and God himself—because they would not admit that their past sinfulness had ensnared them in the devil's clutches. Puritans did not admit that women were more sinful than men and hence more likely than men to become witches. But in the process of negotiating their beliefs and ideals in practical ways, both women and men embedded womanhood in the discourse of depravity.

Notes

1. On the peculiarities of Salem, see Bernard Rosenthal, *Salem Story: Reading the Witch Trials of 1692* (Cambridge, 1993), 1–7. Carol Karlsen argues that most of the witchcraft accusations throughout the seventeenth century were made by men, but in fact her evidence demonstrates that at Hartford and at Salem the primary accusations were made by young women against older women. See

Carol F. Karlsen, *The Devil in the Shape of a Woman: Witchcraft in Colonial New England* (New York, 1987), 24–27; 222–23. In these cases, in contrast to others that Karlsen analyzes, property was much less important as an issue, and the crisis precipitated not a solitary trial but a massacre.

2. Rosenthal, *Salem Story*, esp. 48–50.

3. See Karlsen, *The Devil in the Shape of a Woman*, 40, and Rosenthal, *Salem Story*, 56–60. Richard Weisman, *Witchcraft, Magic, and Religion in 17th-Century Massachusetts* (Amherst, 1984), esp. 96–112, has interpreted the varying kinds of testimony brought against the accused as a split between elite and popular culture. He argues that the court sought to prove the signing of the devil's pact while the lay public was content with proving instances of maleficia. There was indeed a split, but it was actually a matter of gender and intimately related to the way in which men and women considered sinful acts versus sinful natures.

4. Rosenthal, *Salem Story*, 44, 68.

5. On the official restraint before and especially after the Hartford outbreak, see Karlsen, *The Devil in the Shape of a Woman*, 27, and Weisman, *Witchcraft, Magic, and Religion in 17th-Century Massachusetts*, 113–14.

6. On the persistence of the myth that the original accusations sprang from fortune-telling sessions with Tituba, see Rosenthal, *Salem Story*, 10–14.

7. My thinking on these issues has been informed by discussions with John Murrin, and I am grateful for his insight and expertise.

8. Cotton Mather confirmed that women church members far outnumbered the men. He wrote, "There are far more *Godly Women* in the World than there are *Godly Men*. . . . I have seen it without going a Mile from home, That in a Church of between *Three* and *Four* Hundred *Communicants*, there are but few more than *One* Hundred *Men*; all the Rest are *Women*." See Cotton Mather, *Ornaments for the Daughters of Zion, or the Character and Happiness of a Virtuous Woman* (Cambridge, MA, 1692), 44–45. See also Harry S. Stout and Catherine A. Brekus, "Declension, Gender, and the 'New Religious History,' " in *Belief and Behavior: Essays in the New Religious History*, ed. Philip R. Vandermeer and Robert P. Swierenga (New Brunswick, 1991), 15–37; and Gerald F. Moran, " 'Sinners Are Turned into Saints in Numbers': Puritanism and Revivalism in Colonial Connecticut," in ibid., 38–62. On the relationship between declension and male piety, see Mary Maples Dunn, "Saints and Sisters: Congregational and Quaker Women in the Early Colonial Period," *American Quarterly* 30 (Winter 1978): 582–601.

9. The confessions of the accused witches at Salem and elsewhere earlier in the seventeenth century have remained a curiosity for historians of witchcraft. In John Demos's *Entertaining Satan: Witchcraft and the Culture of Early New England* (New York, 1982), confession is not explored at great length primarily because it was an unusual feature of witchcraft episodes prior to the Salem outbreak. Chadwick Hansen, *Witchcraft at Salem* (New York, 1969), 92–95, argued that the confessors were probably, like the afflicted girls, "hysterics subject to hallucinations" (94). Paul Boyer and Stephen Nissenbaum, *Salem Possessed: The Social Origins of Witchcraft* (Cambridge, MA, 1974), 214–16, emphasized the importance of public confession as a community ritual, through which the accused witch could be reintegrated into the community. Boyer and Nissenbaum contended that the ritual was therapeutic; the confessors admitted to deeds that remained merely "unacknowledged impulses" in both the accusers and the onlookers (215). Weisman, *Witchcraft, Magic, and Religion*, 155–59, placed the confessions within the framework of covenant theology, arguing that they served

as a form of communal regeneration. Richard Godbeer, *The Devil's Dominion: Magic and Religion in Early New England* (Cambridge, 1992), 204–11, emphasized the emotional and physical torture to which the accused were subjected. Godbeer also suggested that the confessions stemmed from religious anxiety; confessors may have admitted that they sought relief from the devil, by entering his service, as a way of opting out of Christian fellowship. Karlsen, *The Devil in the Shape of a Woman*, 148, briefly suggested that in a culture that associated female discontent with witchcraft it was not surprising that some women would finally be persuaded that they had become witches. With this one statement Karlsen comes the closest to my argument; the women knew they were sinners, and so either way—implicitly or explicitly—they belonged to Satan.

10. John Hale, *A Modest Enquiry in the Nature of Witchcraft* (Boston, 1702), 18. Hale commented that although "she [Lake] did not effect it, yet she was a murderer in the sight of God for her endeavors, and showed great penitency for that sin." Quoted in David D. Hall, *Witch-hunting in Seventeenth-Century New England* (Boston, 1991), 28.

11. Rosenthal, *Salem Story*, 151–58.

12. On the relationship between apology and public execution, see Lawrence W. Towner, "True Confessions and Last Dying Warnings in Colonial New England," in *Sibley's Heir: A Volume in Memory of Clifford Kenyon Shipton*, Colonial Society of Massachusetts Publications, vol. 59 (Boston, 1982), 523–39; Ronald A. Bosco, "Lectures at the Pillory: The Early American Execution Sermon," *American Quarterly* 30, no. 2 (Summer 1979): 156–76; J. A. Sharpe, " 'Last Dying Speeches': Religion, Ideology and Public Execution in Seventeenth-Century England," *Past and Present* 107 (May 1985): 144–67; and Karen Halttunen, "Early American Murder Narratives: The Birth of Horror," in *The Power of Culture: Critical Essays in American History*, ed. Richard Wightman Fox and T. J. Jackson Lears (Chicago, 1993), 67–101. See also Emil Oberholzer, Jr., *Delinquent Saints: Disciplinary Action in the Early Congregational Churches of Massachusetts* (New York, 1955); and N. E. H. Hull, *Female Felons: Women and Serious Crime in Colonial Massachusetts* (Urbana, IL, 1987).

13. Paul Boyer and Stephen Nissenbaum, eds., *The Salem Witchcraft Papers: Verbatim Transcripts of the Legal Documents of the Salem Witchcraft Outbreak of 1692*, 3 vols. (New York, 1977), II: 647 (hereafter cited as *Salem Witchcraft Papers*).

14. Ibid. On the individual and social implications of repentance, see David D. Hall, *Worlds of Wonder, Days of Judgment: Popular Religious Belief in Early New England* (New York, 1989), 166–212; on the witchcraft confessions, esp. 192–96. For a discussion of women and repentance in eighteenth-century Connecticut, see Cornelia Hughes Dayton, "Taking the Trade: Abortion and Gender Relations in an Eighteenth-Century New England Village," *William and Mary Quarterly*, 3d ser., 48, no. 1 (January 1991): 19–50. See also Lynda E. Boose, "Scolding Brides and Bridling Scolds: Taming the Woman's Unruly Member," *Shakespeare Quarterly* 42, no. 2 (Summer 1991): 179–214. Jane Kamensky argued that women's criminal punishment usually focused on symbolic silence (wearing a sign that announced their misdeeds, for example) rather than public verbal apology. See Kamensky, " 'Saying and Unsaying': The Fine Art of Eating One's Words in Early Massachusetts," unpublished paper presented at "Possible Pasts: Critical Encounters in Early America" conference, June 1994. By contrast, during the Salem episode, verbal apology coupled with regret constituted a successful confession.

15. For a provocative analysis of similarly problematic sources, see Natalie Zemon Davis, *Fiction in the Archives: Pardon Tales and Their Tellers in Sixteenth-Century France* (Stanford, 1987).

16. *Salem Witchcraft Papers*, II: 615.

17. Bernard Rosenthal argues, "The witch-hunt became as much an affirmation of the process as a search for witches." See Rosenthal, *Salem Story*, 49.

18. *Salem Witchcraft Papers*, II: 615. Mary Lacey, Jr., also conceded that the devil did not keep his word. She said that "he [the devil] bid me to be afraid of nothing. & he would not bring me out. but he has proved a lyer from the begining." Despite her admission, the court still offered, "you may yet be deliverd if god give you repentance." See ibid., II: 520.

19. Rarely did women consistently deny other kinds of charges in church or civil proceedings. Like Goodwife Lines in New Haven in 1655, they might deny for a time but then come around to a confession. Lines "strongly denyed [stealing] at first, as she did the other things, but after confessed them." Later she "stiffly denyed sundrie times" stealing a tray from another man, "yet after confessed she stole it." On the issue of abusing her husband and calling him a devil, "she confessed the thing is true, onely she remembers not that she repeated the word deuill so often." See Franklin Bowditch Dexter, ed., *Ancient Town Records, New Haven Town Records, 1662–1684*, vol. I (New Haven, 1919), 246–47. In the Wenham, Massachusetts, congregation, when Sarah Fiske was accused of maligning her husband, Phineas, and behaving inappropriately during a Sabbath service, she denied the charges, instead blaming Phineas for "false witness bearing," not taking her side in the dispute, failing to pray for her, and acting cruelly toward her. The church concurred with Phineas's denials, found him innocent, and urged Sarah to admit her sins and apologize. Finally, months later, after reluctantly admitting publicly some "evil in these particulars whereas she should have kept secret and as the duty of a wife and as . . . her carriage at that time," the church allowed her to give her conversion relation. See Robert G. Pope, ed., *The Notebook of the Reverend John Fiske, 1664–1675* (Salem, 1974), 25–29, 32, 34, 40–47. Sarah Fiske's case is discussed in Charles Lloyd Cohen, *God's Caress: The Psychology of Puritan Religious Experience* (New York, 1986), 154–55.

20. When women steadfastly denied charges against them, like Anne Hibbon (or Hibbens) of Boston in 1640, they were considered far beyond the bounds of acceptable female behavior. The First Church of Boston excommunicated Hibbens not only for her dispute with some joiners she believed were charging exorbitant rates, but for her "obstinate Judgeing and Condemning of them [the joiners]" for lying, and perhaps most aggregiously, "She made not any humble and penitentiall acknowledgement thereof." The church records state that Hibbens condemned the church's admonition toward her and "still continued Impenitent and obstinate in these thinges, not hearkning to her husband at home; nor to the brethren and sisters in private, noe nor yet to the whole Church in Publique." See Richard D. Pierce, ed., *Publications of The Colonial Society of Massachusetts, The Records of the First Church in Boston, 1630–1868*, vol. 39 (Boston, 1961), 32–33. Hibbens apologized, in part, not for the accusations she made, but for speaking to others about it rather than taking it immediately through the proper disciplinary channels. See "Church Trial of Mistress Ann Hibbens," in *Root of Bitterness: Documents of the Social History of American Women*, ed. Nancy F. Cott (New York, 1972), 47–58. On Hibbens's unusual case, see Jane Kamensky, *Governing the Tongue: The Politics of Speaking in Early New England* (New York, 1997). Not surprisingly, in 1656, after the death of her husband, Anne

Hibbens was accused of witchcraft. See Karlsen, *The Devil in the Shape of a Woman*, 150–52.

21. *Salem Witchcraft Papers*, I: 327.

22. Ibid., II: 632. Similarly, Andrew Elliott deposed that Susannah Roots was "a bad woman" because when she lived with him and his wife Roots always absented herself from prayer, excusing herself from meeting. Immediately after he told of Roots's impiety, Elliott segued into stories of hearing mysterious voices coming from Roots's room at night, thus implicating her in the devil's deeds.

23. Ibid., I: 288.

24. Ibid., I: 303.

25. See Laurel Thatcher Ulrich, *Good Wives: Image and Reality in the Lives of Women in Northern New England, 1650–1750* (New York, 1982).

26. *Salem Witchcraft Papers*, III: 720.

27. Ibid., I: 143.

28. Ibid.

29. Ibid. I: 282.

30. Ibid., II: 594.

31. Ibid., 490.

32. Ibid., 491. Margaret Jacobs was not executed, despite her recantation. Rosenthal, *Salem Story*, 230, n. 49, suggests that authorities were not executing anyone as young as she was (thirty-eight) by the end of the trials.

33. Ibid., I, 212.

34. Unfortunately the surviving records of male examinations are scant. Instead of detailed records of conversations between the court and accused men, we are more often left only with indictments, warrants, or complaints, making it difficult to reconstruct events and their nuances.

35. In his book *Salem Story*, Bernard Rosenthal has shown how George Burroughs's trial revolved around religious dispute. It seems that George Burroughs, former Salem Village minister, was more a Baptist than a Puritan. He eschewed the Lord's Supper and refused to baptize his own children. Indeed, in the summary presentation of evidence, Burroughs was asked when he last participated in the Lord's Supper. He admitted that "it was so long since he could not tell" and that when he did attend Sabbath meetings in both Boston and Charlestown he avoided it; in the next sentence he denied that his house was haunted, and then conceded that none but his eldest child had been baptized. Massachusetts Bay prohibited execution of Baptists in 1692, but if Burroughs was proven a witch his hanging was justified. After Burroughs's examination a new script emerged, as accusers increasingly spoke of baptism by "the black man" and renounced their former baptisms—as both the devil and the Baptists required. See Rosenthal, *Salem Story*, 129–38. For the quotation, see *Salem Witchcraft Papers*, I: 153.

36. *Salem Witchcraft Papers*, I: 176. Ann Putnam, Jr.'s testimony against Burroughs linked abusive behavior with yet another serious offense found in men's trials: murder. See also John Willard's examination (ibid., III: 823), in which the court spoke of murder charges against him as well as witchcraft.

37. *Salem Witchcraft Papers*, II: 289.

38. Ibid., I: 304.

39. Ibid., II: 467, 475, 476. When Martha Corey tried to point out to the court that the clothing worn by her supposed specter did not match the clothing Corey herself actually wore, what could have been exposure of her accusers and the magistrages was interpreted as the cunning machinations of a witch. See I:

260–62. Susannah Martin's appeal to the court citing the biblical episode of Saul and the Witch of Endor as precedent for the invalidity of spectral evidence was similarly ineffectual. As we have seen, the magistrates would not budge from the insistence that consent was required before the devil would take one's shape. See II: 551.

40. We do not know if men were tortured more frequently than women. The threat of torture may have been enough for some women, convinced of their sinful natures anyway, to confess without enduring physical abuse. For a discussion of emotional and physical torture see Godbeer, *The Devil's Dominion*, 206–10.

41. *Salem Witchcraft Papers*, II: 528–29.

42. Ibid., III: 784. Neither did that of Samuel Wardwell, an accused witch who later recanted his confession but was hanged anyway. For an interesting discussion of the court's change in procedure regarding spectral evidence in Wardwell's trial, see Rosenthal, *Salem Story*, 154–56. Wardwell thought he would die whether he confessed or retracted, and later chroniclers have lauded his choice to tell the truth.

43. Ibid., II: 529.

44. Ibid., II: 469.

45. Ibid., II: 565–66. Emphasis added.

46. Ibid., II: 530.

47. Ibid., II: 492.

4

Dark Eve

Bernard Rosenthal

This excerpt from Bernard Rosenthal's book Salem Story: Reading the Witch Trials of 1692 *uncovers the myth of Tituba, the supposed "fatal spark" that ignited the 1692 Salem fiasco. In virtually all modern accounts of Salem, it is Tituba (cast either as a West Indian black or a Native woman) whose tales and rituals of witchcraft and voodoo frighten a group of impressionable young girls and make them hysterical. Without a medical explanation for their bizarre behavior, complete with fits and screaming, their parents, ministers, and doctors interpret it as the work of witches and demand to know who is afflicting them. The problem with this neat scenario is that no contemporary evidence links Tituba with these events. Tituba herself confessed to being in the devil's snare, but not to teaching sorcery to the girls. Rosenthal argues that Tituba as the dark Eve, the evil woman spoiling the Puritan Garden of Eden, has power as a cultural myth despite what we know "really happened." He explores the beginning of the trials, the fraudulent testimony, the motives of the justices, and Tituba's confession in an effort to understand how we have come to accept this myth and why it has persisted for so long.*

[Elizabeth Parris, wife of the Reverend Samuel Parris,] emerges as a good-hearted woman, simple and ineffectual, who saw her job in Salem Village as a continuing round of errands to and for the wives in the parish. But in her busy effort to bolster her husband's acceptance in the village, she absented herself more and more from home.

> Into this void, necessarily, moved Tituba, and from Tituba came the tales that excited Abigail and frightened Betty.
>
> —James F. Droney, "The Witches of Salem"[1]

IN THE BEGINNING THERE WAS Tituba: a woman who, according to the politics of the early 1960s, gained power because a working mother paid insufficient attention to her family. Although chroniclers of Salem's story vary in their explanations of her presence, Tituba appears in the overwhelming number of narrations as the central figure in the genesis of the witch trials. Her entrance onto the historical stage, in her precipitating role of beginning the witchcraft, receives its modern codification in the account by Charles W. Upham, whose *Salem Witchcraft*, published in 1867,[2] has served as the most influential work in shaping subsequent myth and history related to the Salem witch trials.

Upham offers a speculation that Tituba and her husband, John, slaves of the Reverend Samuel Parris of Salem Village, brought with them "the wild and strange superstitions prevalent among their native tribes, materials which, added to the commonly received notions on such subjects, heightened the infatuation of the times, and inflamed still more the imaginations of the credulous." He suggests that they brought with them "systems of demonology" consistent "with ideas and practices developed here." A group consisting primarily of "a circle of young girls" along with these two slaves met regularly in the Parris household, and from these meetings came the strange practices that eventually became defined as witchcraft.[3]

From Upham's association of Tituba and John with the genesis of the witchcraft accusations, a tradition grew that somewhere along the way transformed from speculation to fact. In most accounts, the role of John slips away as Tituba becomes the central, generating figure in the origins of the witch-hunt. No historical evidence supports this role assigned to Tituba, yet its tenacious hold among popularizers and even many scholars remains unshaken.

In one of the most popular modern accounts of what happened at Salem, Marion Starkey's 1949 *The Devil in Massachusetts*, Starkey writes how

> Tituba yielded to the temptation to show the children tricks and spells, fragments of something like voodoo remembered from the Barbados. . . . It is possible that history would never have heard of Abigail and Betty [the two children first afflicted] . . . had they kept Tituba to themselves. But that they could not do. Tituba's fascination was too powerful to be monopolized by two small girls. Thanks to her,

> the parsonage kitchen presently became a rendezvous for older girls in the neighborhood.

Evoking the metaphor of a "fatal spark," Starkey writes, "It was given Tituba to strike it."[4]

In the realm of major scholars, Paul Boyer and Stephen Nissenbaum similarly use the image of the "spark" in seeing Tituba as one of the precipitating agents in a cluster of causes that led to the Salem witch trials. They link Tituba's "voodoo lore" with "an intense group of adolescent girls" interested "in fortune telling and the occult."[5] Kai Erikson, in his *Wayward Puritans*, insinuates the guilt of Tituba even as he acknowledges that "no one really knows how the witchcraft hysteria began." He then proceeds to explain how

> In early 1692, several girls from the neighborhood began to spend their afternoons in the Parris kitchen with a slave named Tituba, and it was not long before a mysterious sorority of girls, aged between nine and twenty, became regular visitors to the parsonage. We can only speculate what was going on behind the kitchen door, but we know that Tituba had been brought to Massachusetts from Barbados and enjoyed a reputation in the neighborhood for her skills in the magic arts.[6]

More cautiously approaching the subject, Chadwick Hansen, in his iconoclastic *Witchcraft at Salem*, cites tradition as placing Tituba in the role of assisting in "occult experiments," but raises no questions about the tradition.[7]

We see the story again in Selma and Pamela Williams's *Riding the Night Mare*, as the authors describe how "in the dark of the night [Tituba] gave lessons in chanting and dancing to gain mysterious powers."[8] In 1983 the Essex Institute, with the best library holdings in the world on the subject, published a pamphlet entitled *The Salem Witchcraft Trials*. At first it approaches the Tituba story tentatively, suggesting it as a possibility; but soon the tale possesses the writer, and we read about "Tituba's vivid stories of sorcery and the black arts," which "*doubtless* provided an enthralling if impious outlet for the repressed adolescent feelings and imaginations of the young people" (my emphasis).[9] In present-day Danvers, Massachusetts—previously known as Salem Village, where the outbreak originally occurred—a historical marker with the following inscription stands at the excavation of the Salem Village Parsonage:

> It was in this house in 1692 that Tituba, Rev. Parris' slave , told the girls of the household stories of witchcraft which nurtured the village witchcraft hysteria. . . .[10]

The sin of Tituba is for all posterity to see.

The Tituba myth appeared on television in the PBS film *Three Sovereigns for Sarah: A True Story*,[11] and reappears fairly regularly at Halloween, as in this excerpt from a Gannett newspaper:

> It is a tale fit for a campfire. The winter of 1692 was long and cold in New England. In the Puritan settlement of Salem, townsfolk lived in icy fear, for they believed they were wresting their new lives from a land that had formerly been the devil's domain. The evil one, they believed, was manifest in the creak of a house, the howl of a wolf, the onset of disease.
>
> In that murky climate of superstition, a group of young girls passed the dreary season by the warm hearth in the house of the Rev. Mr. Samuel Parris. There Tituba, a slave from Barbados, enthralled them with stories of voodoo, of seeing the devil dance round a bonfire. She may have told their fortunes or hypnotized some of the younger girls. . . .[12]

Similarly, the story finds its way into a "Dear Steve" column in the New York *Daily News*; but Tituba's burden also crops up in more middle-brow publications, such as *Newsweek*, *Smithsonian*, and *Harvard Magazine*.[13] A recent American scholarly work carries the story as fact; in England, Tituba as teller of voodoo tales appears in a book that uses the Salem witch trials metaphorically regarding accusations of child abuse.[14] Why the continuing appeal of this fiction? Archetypally, the story works around the notion of original sin, the telling of evil stories rather than the eating of an apple or the opening of a box. In a land popularly imagined as born in religious freedom, a place of harmony where settlers and "Indians" ate turkey together, the Salem witch trials have served mythically as a national fall, as disruptive to the idyllic myth of America as is the seduction of Eve to the myth of Eden.

That the role of precipitating agent for this American fall should rest upon a woman is consistent with the archetype it perpetuates. That the woman should be dark reflects America's social engagement with the seemingly intractable problem of synthesizing a myth of national harmony with Indian wars and with slavery. The defeated groups in this war of color become merged into an ambiguously pigmented Tituba, at times "Indian" and at times "Negro."

In a valuable survey of the racial representation of Tituba, Chadwick Hansen has shown how this Indian woman emerged over the years as a half Indian, half black person, finally becoming entirely black in the hands of modern writers, from distinguished playwright to distinguished scholar.[15] Although no one race or color consistently defines her, Tituba remains in our mythology as the dark woman, the alien, who enters the Puritan world and plunges it into chaos. The myth of dark Tituba recapitulates with an American tint the myth of original sin, the archetypal tale of the woman as progenitor of evils to come.

Tituba fits easily enough into American stereotypes. On August 6, 1910, at an event memorializing one of the witch-trial victims, Carolus M. Cobb described how Tituba and John taught their knowledge of "Voodooism, or whatever name one chooses to call that form of mimetic magic which is practiced among the negroes of the south. All races of that order of intellegence [sic] originate certain forms of magic. . . ."[16] This view of Tituba, generally implicit, finds further explicit representation in Sidney Perley's standard *History of Salem Massachusetts*, published in 1924: "Like the colored race generally, and especially of the tropics, Tituba was a believer in the occult, and delighted in the exploitation of the mysterious and wonderful."[17] While contemporary perpetuators of the Tituba myth deplore such stereotypes, the unexamined roots of their representations unwittingly reside in these older beliefs.

If it remains unnecessary to belabor the racial and gender implications of Tituba as author of sin, the credibility of the actual story warrants a brief consideration in view of its persistence. Inevitably, those who believe that where there is smoke there is fire will be leery of the notion that the role of Tituba was created out of whole cloth: It was by the smoke-and-fire theory, of course, that authorities hanged people in 1692. Could it be true, however, that Tituba actually presided over a circle of girls, telling the stories she is accused of telling, and that the archetype is a coincidence, fortuitous in mythmaking about Salem? Is there a remarkable convergence of myth and history? Not if one follows reasonable rules of evidence: In the enormous quantity of data available for examining the Salem witch trials—in all the court records, in all pretrial and trial testimony (contrary to what various historians claim, some trial records did survive),[18] in all the contemporary accounts of what happened—not a single person suggests that Tituba told stories of witchcraft or voodoo. Not one person hints at it or says anything that could be misconstrued to imply it. When in 1692 Cotton Mather wrote his official version of the trials, "Wonders of the Invisible World," nothing of the tale appeared. When Robert Calef in 1700 published his response to Mather, "More Wonders of the Invisible World," nothing of this story was told. When John Hale gave his account in "A Modest Inquiry into the Nature of Witchcraft,"[19] he offered an account of fortune-telling that future mythologizers associated with Tituba; but Hale himself made no such association. When

Thomas Hutchinson published his *History of the Colony and Province of Massachusetts-Bay* in 1764,[20] the work from which the nineteenth-century accounts generally grew, he told nothing of this version of the Tituba story. Not until the nineteenth century does the story flower. At first we see phrases such as "tradition has it that Tituba . . ."; and although this qualification still appears at times, writers more often than not represent the story as true, with tradition transferred to fact.

Tituba did play a role, of course—making lurid claims about witchcraft at her examination and confessing her own guilt—but nothing she said offers a basis for the legend about her that most scholars have related as fact. Nor did her confession represent the turning point in legitimizing the witchcraft claims: This came instead from Sarah Good, the first of the three women to be interrogated in Salem Village on March 1, 1692.

The legal phase of the Salem witch trials began on February 29 with warrants for the arrest of Tituba, Sarah Osborne, and Sarah Good, all three from Salem Village. Each was accused of afflicting Betty Parris and Abigail Williams, whose behavior had evoked memories of the Goodwin children's afflictions. Added to Betty and Abigail, however, were two new names: Ann Putnam, Jr., 12, and Elizabeth Hubbard, probably 17, although sometimes described in court documents as 16 and sometimes as 18.[21] Who among them, if any, originally accused the three women remains unknown; all but Betty Parris became frequent accusers of others. The actual complaint in the warrants of February 29 came from Joseph Hutchinson, Thomas Putnam, Edward Putnam, and Thomas Preston. The men alleged that the afflictions had been occurring for the previous two months.

Elizabeth Hubbard was the niece of a physician, Dr. William Griggs, and lived in his house.[22] Thomas Putnam was the father of Ann; as the witch-hunt expanded, his name was to appear on roughly 10 percent of all warrants identifying a complainer. Edward Putnam was to offer only three other complaints, one against the child of Sarah Good. Thomas Preston made no further recorded complaints; nor did Joseph Hutchinson, although he did subsequently allege that Abigail Williams had stated her comfort with the devil, and he subsequently signed a petition on behalf of another accused woman, Rebecca Nurse. Betty Parris was a witness at the hearings held in early March for the three accused women; thereafter, she probably participated in no further judicial procedures. Ann Putnam, Abigail Williams, and Elizabeth Hubbard were to play major roles in the events that developed.

On March 1, the three accused women were examined on the charges brought against them. Sarah Good soon offered confirmation of witchcraft, since in defending herself she chose to accuse Sarah Osborne of afflicting the accusers. This decision by Sarah Good gave immediate credibility to the charges of witchcraft and set in motion a process that led to her own execution. Of the three women examined on March 1, she was the only one who would die on the gallows. Sarah Osborne died in prison on May 10 (*SWP* III:954). Tituba spent time in prison and was subsequently released.

Among the audience in the house of Nathaniel Ingersoll, where the examination of Sarah Good was held, were the four individuals named in the warrant as afflicted. The magistrates were John Hathorne and Jonathan Corwin, with Hathorne apparently asking all the questions. His first question set the tone of the examination as accusatory. In subsequent examinations, Hathorne occasionally varied from this beginning, expressing his hope that the person could prove innocence; not so with Sarah Good, nor with most of the people he questioned. "Sarah Good what evil spirit have you familiarity with[?]" Good denied that she had any or that she was in any way hurting the "poor children" who were behaving as if she were tormenting them during the examination (*SWP* II:356). Halfway through the examination there was still no substantiation from anyone that witchcraft played a role in the behavior of the "afflicted"; but Sarah Good abruptly gave the afflicted the corroboration they needed when she identified Sarah Osborne as their tormentor. The first legal testimony supporting the presence of witchcraft had been made. When Osborne took the stand, she accused no one. Tituba, however, confessed and accused them both.

Sarah Good—at the examination on March 1, in subsequent examinations, and at her trial—was named by a variety of people as an afflicting witch. Among her accusers was her daughter Dorcas. Her husband, William, while not specifically accusing her of witchcraft, offered hostile testimony against her, including an insinuation that she might have a witch mark, where the devil's familiar suckled (*SWP* II:363). The testimony against Sarah Good at her examination, as well as at her trial at the end of June, would be typical of the patterns developing in other cases. The magistrates would question the accused, and during the questioning those claiming to be afflicted would assert that the person being examined was at that very moment tormenting them. The accused would then be sent to jail and usually put in chains. Subsequently, at a grand jury hearing, or at the trial, depositions would be given against the accused. Charges here came from individuals other than the original accusers, as members of the community came forward to describe real, imagined, or fabricated offenses by the accused. Their testimony seems sometimes honest, sometimes confused, and sometimes conspiratorial.

Among those giving depositions, genuine belief in the demonic power of the accused often played a part, as it may have in the reports that Sarah Good caused cows to die, as attested by Samuel and Mary Abbey (*SWP* II:368), Thomas and Sarah Gage (*SWP* II:369), and Henry Herrick and Jonathan Batchelor (*SWP* II:375). Their testimony has no element of magic about it; that is, they report no invisible phenomena. A quarrel occurs, cows die around that time, and a correlation is drawn. Yet the dying-cow stories from the Abbeys, the Gages, and Herrick and Batchelor introduce another element that would loom large in the Salem story: They refer to events of the past. Those cows had died two or three years earlier. In some cases, testimony would be based on events happening twenty years before. Such depositions were legally accepted and suggest no particular misconduct on the part of judicial authorities in receiving them; but their unreliability helped build some of Salem's core myths.

Depositional testimony also offers instances of how people seem simply to have been duped. For example, on June 28 William Batten, William Shaw, and his wife, Deborah Shaw, testified that they had discovered 18-year-old accuser Susannah Sheldon with her hands tied. Unable to loosen the knot, they had had to cut the string that bound her. Susannah Sheldon claimed that the specters of Sarah Good and Lydia Dustin, both then in prison, had tied her up on that occasion and on others, and that when Susannah touched the string that bound her, Sarah Good would bite her. Batten and the Shaws also testified that, invisible to them, a broom had been carried out of the house and put in an apple tree, and that a shirt, a milk tube, and three poles had invisibly been removed from the house to the woods (*SWP* II:370–1). There seems no reasonable possibility to explain Susannah Sheldon's conduct other than fraud. Hysteria might make her imagine spirits attacking her, but it cannot tie her up in a knot so tight that others need a knife to free her. As for the invisible disappearances, the items had either been removed by spirits or by cooperating conspirators, whether as pranks or for more serious reasons. In this case, it appears as if there were three dupes and at least one accomplice to Susannah Sheldon.

Other kinds of lurid allegations emerged. Constable Joseph Herrick testified (with the corroboration of his wife, Mary) that, instructed to bring Sarah Good to the jail at Ipswich, he had placed her under guard in this own home. The three guards informed him in the morning that Sarah Good, barefooted and barelegged, had disappeared from them "for some time" (*SWP* II:370). Herrick was subsequently informed that on the night of March 1, with Good under guard at his house, she had tormented Elizabeth Hubbard. Samuel Sibley, the man guarding

Elizabeth Hubbard, had struck at the spectral Sarah Good, though without seeing or feeling anything: Only accusers being tormented could see their tormentors, a phenomenon called "spectral evidence." Elizabeth Hubbard, according to Herrick's testimony, had assured Sibley that he had struck Sarah Good on the arm. Moreover, Mary Herrick testified that on the morning of March 2 she saw one of Good's arms bloody from around the elbow to the wrist. As with the Susannah Sheldon episode, some combination of conspiracy and gullibility appears to explain the events.

Our choices for accounting for such testimony are fairly limited. If we exclude the possibility that an invisible Sarah Good went after Elizabeth Hubbard and took a blow from Samuel Sibley that caused her arm to bleed, and that this same invisible woman did not have the sense to get out of town, we are left with collusion of some kind or with an astonishing set of coincidences—or with the possibility that Elizabeth Hubbard somehow found out about an injury to Sarah Good's arm and staged an attack that would implicate her. Although hysteria could account for Elizabeth Hubbard seeing apparitions, it could not account for her awareness of Sarah Good's injured arm. A long tradition of popular and scholarly literature has argued for, or assumed, hysteria as offering the broadest explanation of the Salem witch trials; but too much happened that cannot be explained by hysteria.

This does not mean, however, that no hysteria occurred, and often we are forced to choose between hysteria and fraud. Yet one of the odd facts about Salem's story is that although most renditions of it evoke hysterical females reacting in court to imagined specters tormenting them, males frequently give more plausible indications of hysteria, because their behavior often occurs without evidence of the demonstrable fraud of women such as Elizabeth Hubbard or Susannah Sheldon. Such cases usually involve accounts of one-time experiences that might plausibly be explained by hysteria. Thus, on March 5 William Allen and John Hughes testify that on the night of March 1 they saw a beast transform into two or three women who they assumed to be Sarah Good, Sarah Osborne, and Tituba. Other than accusing Sarah Good, Allen's name appears in only one other instance, and this time as a petitioner on behalf of an accused woman, Mary Bradbury. John Hughes makes only one other charge, a claim that on March 2 a great white dog followed him and then disappeared, and that that night in bed he saw a great light and a cat at the foot of his bed.[23] Although this testimony appears with the materials against Sarah Good, Hughes himself makes no charge that she had anything to do with his bedtime experiences. William Allen, on the other hand, says that on March 2 Sarah Good and an unusual light appeared to him in his bedroom. Good sat on his foot, and when he tried to kick her, she and the light disappeared. If the testimony of Allen and Hughes is fraudulent, one cannot infer it clearly as one can in the case of Elizabeth Hubbard or Susannah Sheldon; thus the idea of hysteria is plausible for them in a way that it is not for the two young women.

Behavior by some women, of course, could plausibly be attributed to hysteria, as in the case of Johanna Childin. She claimed that on June 2 Sarah Good and a deceased child of Good appeared to her, with the child accusing its mother of murdering it and with Good admitting the crime and saying she gave the child to the devil. However, such a tale could also simply be a fabrication, and whether Childin's testimony represents hysteria or collusion is difficult to tell: She testified in only one other case, describing the appearance of an apparition confessing murder. Still, as the pattern would develop, men were more likely than women to be one- or two-time reporters of extraordinary phenomena.

If some testimony seems hysterically derived, and other conspiratorial, some simply leaves us guessing about inconsistencies. The testimony of the Herricks and Sarah Good's bloody arm offers the most conspicuous instance of this in the Good case. Elizabeth Hubbard's testimony is consistent with what the Herricks say about Sibley striking Good, but Sibley himself tells a slightly different story. He says that Hubbard had told him that Good was barebreasted—a sight that surely should have evoked some comment in the testimony of Hubbard or the Herricks. Moreover, Sibley says he had hit Good—according to Hubbard, since he could not see what if anything he was hitting—on the back so forcefully that he had almost killed Good: on the *back*, not the arm, as the Herricks and Elizabeth Hubbard reported. Hubbard simply did not offer consistent accounts of her encounter with the invisible world. If her inconsistency troubled others, no evidence of this survives.

What was on the mind of John Hathorne and Jonathan Corwin on March 1, 1692, can only be the subject of speculation. Assuming that they believed in witchcraft and that as honest men that sought to determine fairly whether the evidence against the accused women was sufficient to bring them to trial, what might they reasonably infer? Much of the testimony against Sarah Good would be damning if credited, although stories about the killing of cows did not come until later in the proceedings. Similarly, the inconsistency in connection with Sibley's attack on the apparition of Sarah Good appeared in subsequent depositional testimony. Still, in their presence on March 1, Betty Parris, Abigail Williams, Ann Putnam, and Elizabeth Hubbard expressed their claims of great agony, complaining that the women were torturing them.

For these two justices of the peace, assuming them fair and impartial, a moment of truth must have confronted them early in the proceedings. For this we turn to the account of John Hale, a minister whose description of the occurrences at Salem serves as one of the key documents from a contemporary and a participant in the events. Hale, who would eventually criticize the proceedings in general, nevertheless accepted the idea that witchcraft was occurring and that the "Children" were suffering. At one point he refers to "pins invisibly stuck into their flesh."[24] Hale's observation almost certainly refers to Betty Parris and Abigail Williams, whose original behavior precipitated conclusions of witchcraft. His reference is to events before the examination on March 1, but at that examination Sarah Good was accused of hurting the children in the presence of the justices as well as earlier. In other cases, clear evidence exists that accusers were claiming to be tormented by pins being stuck in them and were showing the magistrates the pins. If we may speculate that the pins also appeared in them in the presence of the justices at the examinations of March 1, or that the justices had heard about the pins earlier, Hathorne and Corwin quickly had some limited choices. Pins are visible and tangible: They are stuck in a person or not, and something puts them in the person. The justices had to choose between the accusers having inserted pins in themselves and witches having done the job. In her children's book, *The Witchcraft of Salem Village*, Shirley Jackson highlights these two alternatives and clearly points to fraud.[25] Not so the justices: They opted for witches. If we can understand the decision of Hathorne and Corwin in the context or another era, it is more difficult to understand the views of scholars who believe that the conduct of the children stemmed from hallucinations of hysteria, theories that do not plausibly account for the accusers bringing and using the pins they claimed the witches employed to attack them, as Betty Parris, Abigail Williams, and others maintained. Not having modern psychological theories to assess, Hathorne and Corwin made their decision. When Sarah Osborne's turn came, the mind-set of the judges was evident enough: They had chosen witchcraft as the only plausible alternative to fraud in the matter of pins.

Sarah Osborne came before the judges not simply accused by the four represented in the original complaint, but now by Sarah Good also. The documentation on Sarah Osborne is slim, probably because she never came to trial, dying in prison on May 10. Acknowledging the concept of witchcraft, she denied that she herself was a witch; nor did she implicate any others. Osborne raised the theological point that the devil could take the shape of others, an argument that would persist in the debate against spectral evidence. She also suggested that she herself had been attacked by the devil, a claim that failed to impress the justices.

Because Sarah Osborne was not indicted, a comparison of her case with Sarah Good's comes to a halt, except in striking similarity on two points. As in the case of Good, Osborne's husband gave damaging testimony against his wife, telling the justices that she had not been to church for a year and two months. The other similarity is this issue of church attendance, since Sarah Good also admitted to having missed church regularly. Indeed, it was this lack of church attendance more than any other factor that the women held in common—that and the use of their husbands' testimony against them. Sarah Good was 38, pregnant, and a pauper; Osborne was 60 and a woman with property, though involved in land disputes.[26]

By the time Tituba took the stand, the pattern of examination was in place: A justice would ask a hostile question, such as Why do you hurt the children?, and the accused was presumed guilty from the outset. Attempts at denial led to noisy fits and accusations by those claiming to be afflicted. Sarah Good had already given the accusers legitimacy, but without detailed accounts of how witches conducted their activities. Tituba filled this void in confessing and offering lurid tales about flying on broomsticks and other adventures with compatriot witches. As to their identity, however, she named only Good and Osborne. Nevertheless, her confession, the first in the witchcraft episode, following the claim of Sarah Good that Sarah Osborne was a witch, solidified the credibility of the accusers and their tales.

At the outset of her interrogation, Tituba flatly denied hurting the children or being a witch. Very quickly, though, she shifted her way of answering and told everything and nothing. She said four women had hurt the children, but she named only Good and Osborne. She said the night before she had been at Boston and had seen a tall man, but she named no man. She admitted hurting the children because she had been threatened if she did not, but said she would do it no more. She said a man appeared to her like a hog and a dog and told her to serve him. The dog was black. Then it turned into a man with a yellow bird. Throughout the trials and examinations, reference would be made to this yellow bird. She saw a red rat and a black rat. She said the yellow bird accompanied Sarah Good. She said she saw a thing with two legs, a head like a woman, and wings. Abigail Williams interjected that she also had seen this and had seen it turn into Sarah Osborne, a point Tituba had not made. What else had Tituba seen with Osborne? Tituba, who was giving the examiners whatever they wanted, except for new names, complied. She saw an upright hairy thing with only two legs that was like a man. Had she seen Sarah Good on Elizabeth Hubbard last Saturday? She said she saw a wolf set upon Elizabeth Hubbard. Elizabeth Hubbard then complained about a wolf. Tituba did not stop with that. She said she saw a cat with Good on another occasion. Hathorne switched away from rats and cats and wolves and dogs in search of identifying witches. What clothes does the man wear, he asked her. He wears black clothes, she said. He's a tall man with white hair. "How doth the woman go?" What woman is unclear, but Tituba had no problem with the question. She had a white hood and a black hood and a "tup knot" (*SWP* III:749). Hathorne wanted to know who was hurting the children at that very moment. Sarah Good, Tituba replied. And who hurts them now, Hathorne wanted to know. Tituba announced that she was now blind, and the questioning stopped.

A second version exists of Tituba's examination on March 1. Some of it repeats the same story, but new ingredients do appear. The night before, as she was washing the room, she had seen four witches, two of whom were Good and Osborne, hurting the children. No one asked her to explain how she had been washing the room if she had been in Boston. The witches, moreover, had threatened to take her to Boston, and had threatened the children with death. The man was with the four women. The three people whom Tituba could not identify were all from Boston. No one asked how she knew this. She saw two cats: one red, and one black and as big as a little dog. What did the cats do? Tituba did not know. Had the cats hurt or threatened her? They had scratched her. What had they wanted of her? They had wanted her to hurt the children. They had forced her to pinch the children. Did the cats suck Tituba? No, she would not let them. She went on different trips by broom with Good and Osborne to pinch Elizabeth Hubbard and Ann Putnam. Good and Osborne told her she had to kill someone, and those two wanted her to kill Ann Putnam last night.

Ann Putnam joined in to affirm Tituba's story, adding that the witches wanted her to cut her own throat, and if she did not Tituba would cut her head off. If Hathorne or Corwin wondered why Ann survived, they were silent on this. The Reverend Parris did ask for more information about the whole matter, but Tituba said she could not tell, because if she did her head would be cut off. Her interrogator asked who had made such threats. The man, Tituba says, along with Good and Osborne. Tituba changed the subject: The previous night Good had come with her yellow bird. The accusers joined in that they too had seen a yellow bird, and Tituba had seen it suck Sarah Good's right hand. Had Tituba ever practiced witchcraft in her own country?

Never. Also, Sarah Good has a cat in addition to a yellow bird. What does Osborne have? A thing that is hair all over, with a long nose, a face she cannot describe, two legs; it goes upright and is about three feet tall. Who was the wolf who appeared to Elizabeth Hubbard? Sarah Good. What clothing was the man wearing who appeared to Tituba? Sometimes black clothes and sometimes a "Searge Coat" of another color—a tall man with white hair (*SWP* III:752). What did the woman wear? Tituba did not know the color. What kind of clothes did she have? Tituba did not know the color. She was asked a third time: What kind of clothes did the woman have? She had a black silk hood with a white silk hood under it, with top knots; a woman she did not know, although she had seen her in Boston. What clothes did the little woman have? A serge coat and a white cap. The accusers were having fits, and Tituba was asked who was doing it. Sarah Good, and the accusers confirmed it—except for Elizabeth Hubbard, who was in an extreme fit and said they had blinded her.

On March 2, Tituba was examined again in prison. This time she described a green and white bird, but it never caught on: The yellow bird would prevail. She told of a man who had come to her and asked her to serve him. On a Friday morning he had showed her a book. Was it a big book or a little book? The motif of the book would continue throughout the witchcraft episode, the devil looking for a signature of alliance. Tituba did not know the size of the book. She said he would not show it to her; he had had it in his pocket. Nobody asked how he could have showed her a book that he did not show her. Did he make you write your name in the book? Not yet, said Tituba; her mistress had called her into another room. What did the man say you had to do with the book? Write my name in it. Did you? Yes, once I made a mark in the book in red blood. Did he get the blood out of your body? He said he would get it out the next time and gave a pin tied to a stick for the deed to be done later. Did you see other marks in his book? Tituba had seen many. Some red, some yellow. Did he tell you the names? Only two, Sarah Good and Sarah Osborne. How many marks were there? Nine. Did they write their names? They made marks, Tituba answered. She said Good told her she had made her mark, but Osborne would not tell. When did Good tell you? The same day I came here to prison. Did you see the man that morning? Yes, he told me the magistrates were going to examine me, that I was to tell nothing or else my head would be cut off. You say there were nine names; did he tell you the names of the others? No, but he said I would see the next time. What did you see? A man, a dog, a hog, two cats, one black and one red, and the strange monster, the hairy imp with Osborne; the man offered it to me, but I would not have it. Did he show you in the book which marks belonged to Good and Osborne? Yes. Did he tell you the names of the others? No. Did he tell you where the nine lived? Yes. Some in Boston and some in this town.

Tituba held firm. While describing a lurid world of witchcraft, she had resisted broadening the net of accusations. She would produce no new names. In 1700 Robert Calef published his "More Wonders of the Invisible World" and reported there that Tituba's confession had resulted from beatings and other abuse from her master, the Reverend Samuel Parris.[27] In 1692, a woman delegated to search her body for evidence of demonic familiars suckling her found "upon her body the marks of the Devils wounding of her."[28] No one else seems to have been suspected, and Tituba could have little hope of legal protection from abusive treatment. Instead, she would have every reason to follow the advice heard in Ann Petry's fictional depiction of her life. Here, her husband, John, tells her, "Remember, always remember, the slave must survive. No matter what happens to the master, the slave must survive."[29] Tituba was a survivor. It is hard to imagine that she felt any sense of obligation to the white society she served. She may even have used her plight to take revenge against the society that had enslaved her, as Maryse Condé writes in her stunning novel, *I, Tituba*.[30]

Whether or not she had revenge in mind, however, Tituba answered the questions with a cautious strategy: She has nothing to tell her interrogators, but she knows that she must tell them what they want to hear. So she feels her way. If they ask her something often enough, she complies. She does this in everything except in giving names. Doing so might have produced names they would not accept, and perhaps her troubles would have deepened; with Good and Osborne she was safe. They wanted more witches, she would give them more. She could hide behind the magic properties of the invisible world to play the game as safely as possible. Like Osborne, she told of her own affliction, complaining, as Hale reports, "of her fellow Witches tormenting of her" for having confessed.[31] By shrewdness or by luck, she had discovered the protection to be found in confession and in claims of her own affliction in retaliation for her cooperation. Whatever else we may guess about her, Tituba was not hysterical. Her answers were well measured in response to the questions asked of her in a room containing hostile magistrates, screaming people claiming to be afflicted, and a crowd of villagers watching the event unfold.

What should reasonable men make of such a tale in 1692? Hathorne and Corwin heard Tituba's story at a time when claims of supernatural powers for witches was a contested issue. Fifteen years earlier, John Webster in England had written a devastating critique of supposed witchcraft activity,[32] and in 1692 Shadwell's *The Lancashire Witches* had been produced in England. The play had its controversies, and the witches in it were real; but Shadwell ridiculed witchcraft and wrote scathingly in his note to the reader that if he had not depicted witches as real, he "would have been call'd Atheistical, By a prevailing party who take it that the power of the Devil should be lessened, and attribute more miracles to a silly old Woman, than ever they did to the greatest of Prophets, and by this means the Play might have been Silenced."[33] While this indeed suggests the strength of a party that believed in the powers of witches, it also makes clear the contested nature of the issue. In England enough freedom existed to express such skepticism, as shown by Webster and Shadwell. Cotton Mather would not have written so obsessively on behalf of the existence of his invisible world if some universal view of the subject had existed. So those commentators on Salem who claim that the events happened in the context of an English-speaking world that accepted without question the notion of witchcraft—and these include most of those who have written on Salem—have simply perpetuated one of the core myths about Salem: that everybody at the time believed in witchcraft or the supernatural power of witches. It was not so.

Still, it was more likely to be so in Massachusetts Bay than in England; but even in the context of their belief in the supernatural power of witches, Hathorne and Corwin had to evaluate Tituba's testimony. The conflicts in it might readily be exposing Tituba as a liar, something reasonably expected from a witch. Why not press her on the contradictions? Had she been in Boston with the witches or had she not? How could she see a book that she had not seen? Possibly the magistrates thought these details were not worth pursuing when what they wanted were names. However, a more complex possibility occurs, one that takes us to the methodological problems of recreating the core events of Salem's story: We may not be reading exactly what Hathorne and Corwin asked, or even exactly what Tituba answered.

The Salem Witchcraft Papers offers two versions of Tituba's testimony on March 1. The first was recorded by Ezekial Cheever. We do not know who recorded the second or who recorded the questioning of Tituba in prison. Possibly it was Samuel Parris, who had committed himself to witchcraft as an explanation for the difficulties in his household. Although in Tituba's case no evidence supports suspicions of fabricated testimony, there is reason for questioning transcripts in some other instances. For example, Elizabeth Hubbard's testimony against Sarah Good is signed with Hubbard's mark (*SWP* II:373), which turns out to be different from the mark given by her in her testimony against Susannah Martin (*SWP* II:575). Since people customarily had their own mark, the discrepancy is significant in suggesting that she may not have confirmed the testimony recorded in her name. As we shall see, instances occur where testimony seems simply to have been invented. Fortunately, in spite of the slipperiness of the documentation, plausible decisions as to credibility can be made.

The problem of narration manifests itself in another way. Different people, not necessarily with any attempt to mislead, simply report the events differently. Surviving documentation is often inconsistent, and conclusions often hinge on a best guess. The story of Salem Village's "witch cake" nicely illustrates the issue. Perhaps no other cake in American history has had so much written about it. This was the cake made early in the episode, before matters went to the judiciary, to determine who was bewitching the afflicted children. Generally, various versions of this story can be traced back to two differing accounts, one by the Reverend John Hale and one by Robert Calef. Calef says that a few days before March 11 "Mr. Parris's Indian Man and Woman made a Cake of Rye Meal, with the Children's Water, and Baked it in the Ashes, and as is said, gave it to the Dog" to discover witchcraft.[34] Calef, of course, was not there, and his "as is said" suggests that the whole account is removed from anyone of whom Calef himself could be sure. His chronology is demonstrably wrong, since other evidence indicates that the cake appeared before the examinations, which began on March 1.

The Reverend John Hale was in closer contact with those who would have reported the incident, such as the Reverend Samuel Parris. Hale himself went to see the afflicted girls before the judicial proceedings began. He tells us that the Indian servant and his wife baked the cake from meal and urine of the afflicted. He also tells us that Tituba confessed that she had been taught how to make the cake by her mistress "in her own country[, who] was a witch," although she herself denied being a witch.[35] At the time, of course, she had not yet been examined; the confession had not yet been elicited.

In 1857, with the publication of the Danvers Church Records, another version came to light. On March 27, the Reverend Samuel Parris, in a church service, publicly chastised a woman in the congregation, Mary Sibley, wife of the man we recall as swinging away at the invisible Sarah Good. According to Parris, the activity in connection with the witch cake unleashed the witchcraft in the community. "Nay it never broke forth to any considerable light, until Diabolical means was used, by the making of a Cake by my Indian man, who had his direction from this our sister Mary Sibley."[36] Tituba, we notice, is not even mentioned. If we proceed on the notion that Parris was most likely to know the exact details, and Calef least likely to know, Parris's testimony seems safer, particularly because it was publicly stated and easiest to contest. However, the record of this public statement is from Parris's own church records, privately written. Parris is one of the people who would write the records of testimony in the cases, one of the people whose objectivity is certainly suspect. What are we to believe? We are left with best guesses as to what we should credit. Parris was in the best position to know and, in spite of his editorial biases in transcribing testimony, there really seems no good reason for him to be inaccurate here. However, if Parris's account is accurate, Tituba lied to Hale when she said that she had been taught by her mistress in her former country; for if we believe Parris, it was her husband who had been taught, and by a woman in this country. The cuisine was not unknown in the colony. Rossell Hope Robbins writes:

> A contemporary New England almanac gives a recipe: "To cure ague, Take a cake of barley meal and mix it with children's water, bake it, and feed it to the dog. If the dog shakes, you will be cured." Mrs. Sibley may also have hoped that, alternatively, if the dog got sick, the girls would tell who or what afflicted them.[37]

Why would Tituba make up a story about learning this in the Barbados? Perhaps because she told Hale what she thought he wanted to hear. So a story that probably resolves itself as a cake made with a local recipe by John Indian, as he was known, under the direction of Mary Sibley, comes down historically as one made by Tituba using a recipe from the Barbados, with her husband rarely mentioned. As for the dog, mentioned by neither Hale nor Parris, we can only guess, although the New England recipe did call for one.

The secret of Salem will not be unlocked by determining who made the cake, nor by figuring out why the learned ministers seem not to have known a recipe that Mary Sibley knew; but the event offers a useful illustration of the extent to which uncovering what happened in the witchcraft episode becomes a textual problem—one of narration, of weighing competing narratives against each other for their reliability, at getting under the stated texts to the best versions of what might have occurred. To argue for the reliability or unreliability of every passage cited would result in a tome significantly longer than the three-volume *Salem Witchcraft Papers*. Accordingly, this study limits such analysis to selected episodes culled from a close reading of that work.

So we come back for the moment to Hathorne and Corwin hearing the testimony of Tituba, not in the dispassionate way we can analyze it now, but in the context of screaming accusers and terrified observers. Other magistrates could have been more critical, less inclined to presume guilt as Hathorne clearly was, and as Corwin may have been, although he seems to have let Hathorne do the talking. Furthermore, Hathorne was not taking the traditionally conservative New England approach: Rather than discouraging the naming of others, as Cotton Mather had in the Glover case, Hathorne encouraged it. This radical departure from traditional ways of dealing with witchcraft cases fundamentally set the course for subsequent events, as did the subsequent decision to reward confessors such as Tituba with their lives.

Historically, confession had been regarded as the most dependable and most reliable of all legal methods of finding witches. That is why in the Continental witch trials of the Middle Ages people were systematically tortured, as advocated in Europe's infamous *Malleus Maleficarum*. When one confronted the invisible world, confession offered the most trusted evidence of witchcraft.

This is one of the points made by Samuel Willard late in 1692 in *Some Miscelliny [sic] Observations On Our Present Debates Respecting Witchcrafts*. Only two legal grounds exist for conviction in witchcraft cases, Willard argues: One is a free confession by a mentally competent person; the other is testimony by two "humane witnesses"—that is, witnesses offering testimony on natural, human "Senses" as opposed to claimed divine revelation or "upon the Devils Information."[38] Within the law as it existed in 1692, Tituba's confession was "free," and severe action against her would function within the legal tradition that Willard cited, including such authorities as Perkins and Bernard.[39]

The authorities in Massachusetts Bay, however, chose to go outside their normal legal system. The authorities also chose to ignore the biblical injunction, "Thou shalt not suffer a witch to live,"[40] by keeping alive those people, such as Tituba, who confessed to witchcraft. The Salem witch trials are unique in the annals of witchcraft trials in Western civilization for their response to the issue of confession. They simply reversed the traditional rules whereby confessing witches were executed: In Salem, only those who did not confess were executed. Why this strange twist, and why the creation of a special court to handle a legal problem that English courts historically had handled?

The answer most generally given as to why the normal judicial proceedings were not used centers on the chaos of Massachusetts Bay resulting from its lack of a charter. Many explanations for the Salem witch trials have focused on this charter issue, either as creating a situation of great uncertainty that led to instability in the colony, or as creating a form of legal limbo where the authority to prosecute witches did not exist. Boyer and Nissenbaum are the most prominent recent exponents of the view that the colony lacked the legal authority to act prior to the new charter, which Increase Mather brought to the colony on May 14, 1692. According to them,

> The basic problem was that while more and more suspected witches and wizards were being arrested, not one trial had yet been held. Indeed, there could be none, for during these months Massachusetts was in the touchy position of being without a legally established government! Eight years earlier, in 1684, its original form of government had been abrogated by the English authorities, and in 1689 the administration with which the King had replaced it was overthrown in a bloodless *coup d'état.*[41]

There can be no doubt that this legal ambiguity existed. Nevertheless, judicial proceedings were occurring during the period between charters. The courts in cases not related to witchcraft had not gone out of business even though their work was certainly complicated by the ambiguity of the situation. In the witchcraft cases, although there had indeed been no trials before the new charter, there had been plenty of judicial activity. None of the authorities was taking the view that the filled jails were occupied by people put there illegally. The jailing of Tituba, as well as the numerous other arrests, offers compelling evidence that the judiciary believed in its legal authority.[42]

Indeed, when in 1689 Massachusetts Bay had found itself in the legally anomalous position of having overthrown Governor Andros and being without a charter, the government in Boston acted decisively to make sure that everyone knew that the laws and the courts would continue no matter what England thought about local authority. As David Konig points out, fourteen men were speedily condemned to death, eight more than the total number of executions between 1689 and the end of King Philip's War in 1676. Konig writes that "the sentences were unprecedented in Massachusetts judicial history. Although probably only two of the men were executed, the provisional government clearly had demonstrated its powers to all who would question them."[43] Why then the delay in 1692 of the trials' commencement until the arrival of Increase Mather?

The answer here is probably found in a conflict between the magistrates who were jailing the people—Bartholomew Gedney along with Hathorne and Corwin—and the governor, who was opposed to proceeding with indictments in the cases. In an apparent test of wills between the judiciary and the governor, Simon Bradstreet resisted bringing people to trial. Behaving in the traditional New England way, the conservative Bradstreet held the line, and he would do so until the end, until Increase Mather came not just with a new charter, but with a new governor, William Phips.

Increase Mather would emerge as one of the great voices for moderation once the trials began, so it is exquisitely ironic that he brought to power the man who tilted the balance away from the old view, who set up a special court that would have on it some of the very men who had been encouraging the arrest of people as witches.[44] Among others, Phips named to the court Jonathan Corwin, Bartholomew Gedney, and John Hathorne.[45] Thus, three of the nine men named to the court had largely precipitated the crisis by their radical treatment of the cases, and had obviously prejudged the accused. Heading the court was William Stoughton, Phips's lieutenant governor, a man who would cling to his belief in the guilt of people as witches and in the rectitude of the court even after a general consensus had been reached that the court had gone wrong. In months to come, Phips would quarrel with the methods of the court—ironically, a court created by Phips to examine matters that Bradstreet had refused to pursue—and with Stoughton in particular. From the outset, the dice were loaded, and Phips had loaded them. His motives in appointing men who knew something about the outbreak, or simply men of good reputation, may have been purely bureaucratic. If he had other motives, they are not apparent.

Tituba's fate had there been no Court of Oyer and Terminer set up by Phips must remain speculative. Under normal circumstances as a confessing witch she would almost certainly have been tried and hanged in a rare Massachusetts Bay execution for witchcraft.[46] Tituba may have been extraordinarily lucky or extraordinarily shrewd in surviving through the new way, confession. Alternatively, she may have survived simply because she was property. According to Joseph B. Felt, on June 1, 1692, at the time of the first trial, Parris sold Tituba to pay her jail fees.[47] Whether for this reason or not, Tituba survived.

With Phips's court in place, the witch trials of 1692 became almost inevitable. In a further irony, early in the proceedings Phips left the colony to deal with military affairs. This greatly decreased the power of Increase Mather, who was Phips's patron, to moderate the behavior of the court, and greatly increased that of Stoughton. With Tituba, Sarah Good, and Sarah Osborne in prison, the episode that we call the Salem witch trials had begun. Tituba, the slave who found her way to survival, slipped into mythology as the woman who by her tales brought chaos and death to the New World garden.

Notes

1. James F. Droney, "The Witches of Salem," *Boston* (Boston: Greater Chamber of Commerce, October 1963), pp. 42–6, 65, 92–3, at p. 46.

2. Charles W. Upham, *Salem Witchcraft; with An Account of Salem Village, and a History of Opinions on Witchcraft and Kindred Subjects* (1867), 2 vols.; reprinted (Williamstown, Mass.: Corner House Publ., 1971).

3. Ibid., II, pp. 2–3.

4. Marion L. Starkey, *The Devil in Massachusetts: A Modern Enquiry into the Salem Witch Trials* (New York: Alfred A. Knopf, 1949); 2nd ed. (1950), pp. 10–11, 15.

5. Paul Boyer and Stephen Nissenbaum, *Salem Possessed: The Social Origins of Witchcraft* (Cambridge, Mass.: Harvard University Press, 1974), p. 181.

6. Kai Erikson, *Wayward Puritans: A Study in the Sociology of Deviance* (New York: John Wiley and Sons, 1966), p. 141.

7. Chadwick Hansen, *Witchcraft at Salem* (New York: George Braziller, 1969), p. 31.

8. Selma R. Williams and Pamela J. Williams, *Riding the Night Mare: Women & Witchcraft* (New York: Atheneum, 1978), p. 147.

9. Katherine W. Richardson, *The Salem Witchcraft Trials* (Salem, Mass.: Essex Institute, 1983), p. 6.

10. J. W. Hanson, *History of the Town of Danvers from its Earliest Settlements to the Year 1848* (Danvers, Mass., 1848) is silent on the myth that Upham would codify.

11. *Three Sovereigns for Sarah: A True Story*, dir. Philip Leacock (PBS, 1985), 152 min.; originally presented as a three-episode series on "American Playhouse."

12. "Witch Trials Began as Prank," *Press & Sun Bulletin* (Binghamton, N.Y.), October 28, 1990, p. 140.

13. *Daily News* (New York), September 17, 1991, p. 20; *Newsweek*, August 31, 1992, p. 65; *Smithsonian*, vol. 23, no. 1 (April 1992), p. 118; *Harvard Magazine*, vol. 94, no. 4 (March–April 1992), p. 46.

14. Enders A. Robinson, *The Devil Discovered: Salem Witchcraft 1692* (New York: Hippocrene Books, 1991), p. 134; Stuart Bell, M. P., *When Salem Came to the Boro* (London: Pan Books, 1988), p. 4.

15. Chadwick Hansen, "The Metamorphosis of Tituba, or Why American Intellectuals Can't Tell an Indian Witch from a Negro," *New England Quarterly*, vol. 47, no. 1 (March 1974), pp. 3–12. For a more recent and intriguing essay on the possible origins of Tituba, see Elaine G. Breslaw, "The Salem Witch from Barbados: In Search of Tituba's Roots," *Essex Institute Historical Collections*, vol. 128 (October 1992), pp. 217–38. Breslaw speculates on a possible identification of Tituba, one that would indicate her age in 1692 as '"between twenty-five and thirty years old" (p. 224).

16. Carolus M. Cobb, "The Medical Aspect of Salem Witchcraft," typescript of talk delivered to Rebecca Nurse Memorial Association, August 6, 1910, p. 9, Essex Institute, Salem, Mass. I am grateful to the Essex Institute and to Jane E. Ward, Curator of Manuscripts, for permissions to quote from this typescript.

17. Sidney Perley, *The History of Salem Massachusetts* (Salem, Mass.: privately published, 1924), III, p. 255.

18. Regarding the issue of some *Salem Witchcraft Paper* documents being trial documents, in spite of prevailing beliefs that no trial records survive, see Chapter 7, pp. 137–8.

19. These works are reprinted to varying extents in *Narratives of the Witchcraft Cases 1648–1706*, ed. George Lincoln Burr (New York: Charles Scribner's Sons, 1914), as follows: Cotton Mather, "The Wonders of the Invisible World" (1693), pp. 203–52; Robert Calef, "More Wonders of the Invisible World" (1700), pp. 289–394. Rev. John Hale, "A Modest Inquiry into the Nature of Witchcraft" (1702), pp. 395–432.

20. Thomas Hutchinson, *The History of the Colony and Province of Massachusetts-Bay* (1764), 3 vols., ed. Laurence Shaw Mayo (Cambridge, Mass.: Harvard University Press, 1936).

21. Ann Putnam's age has variously been given by commentators as 12 or 13. I am following Deodat Lawson's indication that she was 12. Lawson "A Brief and True Narrative" (1692), in Burr, *Narratives*, p. 155.

22. More specifically, Elizabeth Hubbard was the niece of Griggs's wife, Elizabeth. See H. Minot Pitman, "Early Griggs Families of Massachusetts," *New England Historical and Genealogical Register*, vol. 123 (July 1969), p. 172.

23. In connection with the Salem witch trials, David D. Hall writes about folk legends of "shape-shifting black dogs." See *World of Wonder, Days of Judgment: Popular Religious Belief in Early New England* (New York: Alfred A. Knopf, 1989), p. 88. Perhaps the white dog is connected to this motif.

24. Hale, "A Modest Inquiry," in Burr, *Narratives*, pp. 413–14.

25. Shirley Jackson, *The Witchcraft of Salem Village* (New York: Random House, 1956), p. 87.

26. On Osborne's age, see Carol F. Karlsen, *The Devil in the Shape of a Woman* (New York: W. W. Norton, 1987), p. 243. For land disputes see Boyer and Nissenbaum, *Salem Possessed*, p. 193, which also provides details of Sarah Osborne's marriage to her servant: Various commentators have felt that this marriage made Sarah Osborne vulnerable to accusations of Witchcraft. For church attendance of Sarah Good and Sarah Osborne, see *SWP* II:360, 611.

27. Calef, "More Wonders," in Burr, *Narratives*, p. 343.

28. Hale, "A Modest Inquiry," in Burr, *Narratives*, p. 415.

29. Ann Petry, *Tituba of Salem Village* (New York: Harper Trophy, 1964), p. 12.

30. Maryse Condé, *I, Tituba, Black Witch of Salem*, trans. Richard Philcox (Charlottesville: University Press of Virginia, 1992), particularly p. 93.

31. Hale, "A Modest Inquiry," in Burr, *Narratives*, p. 415.

32. John Webster, *The Displaying of Supposed Witchcraft, Wherein is affirmed that there are many sorts of Deceivers and Imposters, and Divers persons under a passive Delusion of Melancholy and Fancy* (London, 1677). For the debate between Webster and Joseph Glanvill, an important source for defenders of the Salem episode, see Thomas Harmon Jobe, "The Devil in Restoration Science: The Glanvill-Webster Witchcraft Debate," *Isis*, vol. 72 (1981), pp. 343–56.

33. *The Complete Works of Thomas Shadwell*, vol. 4, ed. Montague Summers (London: Fortune Press, 1927), p. 101.

34. Calef, "More Wonders," in Burr, *Narratives*, p. 342.

35. Hale, "A Modest Inquiry," in Burr, *Narratives*, pp. 413–14.

36. Transcribed by William Thaddeus Harris, *New England Historical and Genealogical Register*, vol. 11 (April 1857), p. 133. For a modern printing of this episode, see *Salem-Village Witchcraft: A Documentary Record of Local Conflict in Colonial New England*, ed. Paul Boyer and Stephen Nissenbaum (Belmont, Calif.: Wadsworth Publ., 1972), p. 278. The reference to Sibley as "sister" is congregational.

37. Rossell Hope Robbins, *The Encyclopedia of Witchcraft and Demonology* (New York: Crown Publ., 1959), p. 431.

38. Samuel Willard, *Some Miscelliny Observations On Our Present Debates Respecting Witchcrafts, in a Dialogue between S & B*, pseudonymously by "P. E. and J. A." (Philadelphia, 1692), p. 7.

39. William Perkins, *A Discourse of the Damned Art of Witchcraft* (Cambridge: Perkins, 1608); Richard Bernard, *A Guide to Grand-Jury-Men . . . in Cases of Witchcraft* (London, 1627).

40. Exodus 22:18.

41. Boyer and Nissenbaum, *Salem Possessed*, p. 6

42. For a valuable discussion of Massachusetts Bay government during the period of the revoked charter, see T. H. Breen, *Puritans and Adventurers* (New York: Oxford University Press, 1980), pp. 81–105.

43. David Konig, *Law and Society in Puritan Massachusetts: Essex County, 1629–1692* (Chapel Hill: University of North Carolina Press, 1979), p. 168.

44. The view that Salem went wrong because Phips replaced Bradstreet is not an original one, but it is no less persuasive for that. See Upham, *Salem Witchcraft*, I:451.

45. For the establishment of the court see Thomas Hutchinson, *The Witchcraft Delusion of 1692*, notes by William Frederick Poole (Boston: privately printed, 1870), p. 32. Hutchinson identifies the original court members as William Stoughton, John Richards, Nathaniel Saltonstall, Wait Winthrop, Bartholomew Gedney, Samuel Sewell, John Hathorne, Jonathan Corwin, and Peter Sergeant. Burr, *Narratives*, pp. 185, 355, says that Corwin took Nathaniel Saltonstall's place when he resigned, but the original court included both. Burr seems to be following Upham, *Salem Witchcraft*, II:251.

46. In his listing of witchcraft cases in Massachusetts Bay prior to the Salem witch trials, Richard Weisman identifies four certain executions and one probable execution. See Richard Weisman, *Witchcraft, Magic, and Religion in 17th-Century Massachusetts* (Amherst: University of Massachusetts Press, 1984), pp. 191–203.

47. Joseph B. Felt, *Annals of Salem* (Salem, Mass.: W. & S. B. Ives, 1845; 2nd ed., Boston: James Munroe & Co., 1849), II:478. In a note at the end of her novel, *Tituba of Salem Village* (p. 254), Ann Petry asserts that Tituba was sold to a weaver named Samuel Conklin, who subsequently purchased John Indian. I have found no primary source to confirm either Felt or Petry. However, in his first edition of *Annals of Salem*, Felt makes no reference to the sale of Tituba. Presumably he found some evidence after the first edition and prior to the second. I can make no guess as to how good this evidence is.

5

"The Devil Will Roar in Me Anon": The Possession of Martha Roberson, Boston, 1741

~

Kenneth P. Minkema

As Kenneth P. Minkema points out, historians know little about diabolical or occult activity in the eighteenth century. Studies of religious enthusiasm have been confined to believers' more godly pursuits exemplified by the intense spiritual conversions brought about by the First Great Awakening. Minkema corrects this omission in the scholarship in his examination of Martha Roberson, a Boston woman who believed herself to be possessed by the devil. Demon possession differed from witchcraft in that the former was considered to be completely involuntary; the devil chose his victims without their consent. Possession necessitated prayer and fasting rather than persecution. In Roberson's case, the devil caused her to indulge in the most unfeminine, aggressive, and abusive speech; she returned to a more appropriately demure state only when God's presence prevailed.

But Satan was not merely Roberson's personal nemesis, Minkema argues. Both Old and New Lights (opponents and supporters of the religious revivals) used the devil's apparent machinations either to discredit or to legitimate the revivals themselves. Was this "awakening" the work of the devil or of God's spirit? New Lights saw the devil's appearance in Roberson's life as a welcome opportunity for her conversion; antirevivalist Old Lights interpreted it as the antithesis of divine law and the result of "over heated imaginations," characteristic of New Light itinerants more generally.

While visiting Boston on business in early 1741, Joseph Pitkin, a merchant from East Hartford, Connecticut, tarried longer in town than he had planned. It was "A Wonderfull Time of the Exercise of Religion there," he recalled, following visits by the great itinerant preacher George Whitefield in October 1740 and then by Gilbert Tennent, an evangelical Presbyterian minister from Pennsylvania. He "found it Proffitable to [his] soul to be there." Having delayed his departure to the last possible minute, he was suddenly urged by the wife of a local innkeeper to come to the house of "a near neighbours." There he had a long conversation with a "Young Woman" named Martha Roberson (or Robinson), who talked with him about her participation in the recent revivals. Before long, however, she told Pitkin that "the Devill is Disturbed at Your Coming he knows You are a Goodman and he hates all such and he will Roar in me anon." Taken aback, Pitkin asked what she meant. "[S]he Replyed it is now 15 weeks since the Devil Began to speak in me." Over the next two days, Pitkin had a "Conferance" with a person "Possessed with the Devil."[1]

When examining the effects of the religious revivals of the 1740s, scholars of American religious history have given little attention to reputed diabolic activity during this period of vaunted "Great Awakening."[2] Despite the impressive literature that occult practices, witchcraft, and diabolism attract for seventeenth-century British America and for early modern Europe, these topics virtually drop out of sight in accounts of eighteenth-century American religious history.[3] This dearth of information is true particularly for demon possession.

The possession of Martha Roberson, as described by Pitkin in his unpublished diary, reveals the religious, social, and personal dynamics surrounding possession in the midst of the tumultuous revivals of the early 1740s. Roberson's experience highlights changing perceptions of the devil and of human faculties. Her case also demonstrates how demonic activity became an issue in the battle between New and Old Lights over the nature and consequences of the revivals and brings into focus what each side thought about possession. As an evangelical, Pitkin approached Roberson's case without questioning its veracity; rather, he welcomed the opportunity to be an instrument of "Providence." Nevertheless, his account can be decoded to reveal categories for understanding possession, such as its public and often violent nature.

Joseph Pitkin, born in 1696, was a successful businessman, justice of the peace, sheriff, and judge of the Connecticut General Court; he was also a deacon in the East Hartford church from 1748 to his death in 1762.[4] His diary, preserved in the Connecticut State Library, is a compilation of lengthy spiritual meditations on his own conversion experience, his efforts to live a Christian life, and the benevolences of divine providence toward himself, his three wives, and many children. His account of his encounter with Martha Roberson is the last, and most dramatic, entry in the volume.

Pitkin's spiritual digest reveals him to be a thoroughgoing and earnest New Light evangelical. In what amounts to a very lengthy conversion relation, he describes his conversion during the awakenings of 1734 and 1735 in the Connecticut River Valley, and his ensuing and ongoing personal "covenant" with God. He consistently professes his own depravity, the worthlessness of his good works in meriting grace, and the total surrender of his fate into the hands of an omnipotent God.

Of Martha Roberson we know very little. She was twenty-three years old and unmarried when the events that Pitkin relates took place, and so belonged to that generation that historians have identified as experiencing unusual marital, economic, and occupational stresses compared with previous generations.[5] As fervent a New Light as Pitkin, she was "peirced by the Word" upon hearing Whitefield preach and later attended Tennent's sermons. It is Pitkin's retelling of her account that survives and renders her life so important for historians.

The Devil in the Shape of the Devil: Perceptions of Satan and Evil

After her initial statement to Pitkin, Roberson continued with her surprising narrative. However, "before she had Gone far in this Relation," Pitkin recounted, "she said several times the Devil is Greatly Disturbed and he will Roar in me anon." Then, to Pitkin's horror, she "gave a Loud shreik as Loud as her Voice would Carry it which was so surpriseing to me That I supose she saw it in my Countenance: and she Recoverd the next Breath and said pray sir Dont be surprized the Devil Endeavors to scare every Body from me that is Good."

Roberson's demon is a very real protagonist for all of the persons involved in Pitkin's account, which explains why Pitkin and others adopted an inquisitive, sympathetic approach to Roberson. From the start, those who encountered Roberson accepted without question that she was possessed; witchcraft was not even hinted at. The distinction between witchcraft and demon possession, often blurred today, was very clear then. D. P. Walker, the English historian, summarizes the distinction well: "The devil is not inside a witch's body, as he is in a demoniac's. . . . A witch has voluntarily entered into association with a devil, whereas possession is involuntary and a demoniac is not therefore responsible for her wicked actions, as is a witch."[6] The witch was to be prosecuted and persecuted; the demoniac was to be the subject of prayer and fasting.

When arrayed with the numerous and well-documented instances of presumed possessions in seventeenth- and eighteenth-century Europe, Roberson's case raises questions about the so-called "demise of Satan" set forth by scholars such as Jeffrey Burton Russell and Andrew Delbanco. In recent books, each has described the period as one in which belief in the Devil as a theological personage waned dramatically in the face of Newtonian science, Enlightenment rationalism, and clerical reactions against witchcraft persecutions and other superstitions.[7] The category of evil shifted from being personified in a diabolical being to being internalized as self-corruption or ignorance. The demonic, philosophers such as Immanuel Kant proclaimed, had no ontological status independent of the human mind.

As useful as recent studies are, they suffer from an elite orientation. As Richard Godbeer has pointed out, "Humbler folk were largely unaffected by these new intellectual currents and continued to see the world as an enchanted place, filled with occult forces."[8] A world without Satan and demons would have been absurd to Pitkin, Roberson, and the other persons involved in her episode. Thus, New England conversion narratives dating from the 1740s perpetuate an "interpsychic" view of evil rather than an "intrapsychic" one. Narrators portrayed evil as something impinging from outside their own psyches to cause wicked thoughts or actions.[9]

Pitkin's diary bears out an interpsychic world cohabited by an external, separate, and very powerful Devil. In discoursing with Roberson, Pitkin perceived himself as making "Answer" to Satan in her. His use of masculine and feminine pronouns is telling: Referring to Satan, Pitkin wrote that "*he* with great Disdain in *her* Countenance" denied Scriptural arguments; at another point, "the Devill with *her* tongue Broke forth . . . as if *he* would spit in my face."[10] This gendered language highlights the separation that Pitkin maintained between the intruding malicious presence and Roberson's "true" self and also bears out the essential innocence of the possessed person.

In keeping with the distinction that possession was involuntary, Pitkin carefully separated Roberson's personae in such a way that he portrayed her physical members—especially her tongue—as the means of Satan's expressions but preserved the integrity of her soul, which he viewed as her real self. At one point, feeling that Satan had been "dethroned" in her, he allowed that Christ still "permited him to Vent his Rage and spite with her Tongue." During the second day of interviews, Pitkin was joined by Colonel Timothy Dwight, a prominent politician whose hometown of Northampton was famous as a center of revivalism. When Dwight questioned Roberson too, "her Tongue was Interchangeably used by two different spirits."

As Roberson's case demonstrated to Pitkin, however, the Devil could do more than merely tempt converts; he could also take control of their bodies for a time. Even visible saints were not wholly immune from Satan but, as David Harley has recently shown for pre-Salem cases, were subject to obsessive possession, in which "the Devil was granted power only over the body."[11] In a sermon preached in April 1741, Joseph Sewall of the Old South Church dwelt, fittingly for the time, on the coming of the Holy Spirit. To converts he enjoined, "Do not boast as if your Work was done, and your Warfare accomplished; but rather expect to meet with Temptations, and put on the whole Armor of God, that you may be able to stand against the Wiles of the Devil."[12] Convinced by her relation that Roberson was a godly person, Pitkin "meditated Much" on "the Designe of providence in permitting satan thus to have the Command of the Tongue of the person whose soul seemd to me [to be] the Habitation of Christ by the Indwelling of the spirit." Traditionally, such an affliction would have been interpreted as a punishment for sin or as a trial of faith. Pitkin thought the latter in Roberson's case. Even more important, however, he concluded that God had arranged events so that "satan should be permitted to show openly what are his words and what his Language is, in Clear Distinction from what the spirit and Word of God speaks." The incident was not only for Roberson's edification, but for Pitkin's as well.

When Pitkin first came to Boston, he heard William Cooper deliver a prorevival lecture that included discussion of the workings of Satan. At the time there were two weekly public lectures in Boston, one on Thursday nights at the Old South Church and another, newly established in mid-1740, on Tuesday nights at Cooper's Brattle Street Church. Along with published treatises, these lectures provided the city's ministers—the ones who prayed and fasted over Roberson—with an opportunity to express their views on the revival, itinerancy, and, most important for our purposes here, evil and possession.[13]

In reviewing these materials, I have found competing attitudes about the nature of Satan and evil. Prorevivalist New Lights amply employed the devil in their depictions of the human plight, while moderates tended to blend a traditional view of the devil with progressive views of evil immanent in human nature. Antirevivalist Old Lights alone eschewed the Devil in favor of natural explanations for human behavior.

New Lights portrayed the search for conversion primarily as "overcoming Satan." In his New Year's sermon for 1741, Sewall employed the recent awakenings as proof that God's Word endured over the tumultuous powers of darkness. Nonetheless, Sewall warned, "The Old Serpent is ready still to tempt Sinners, as he did the Mother of all living." To young people he declared: "O that you may be strong to overcome the evil One, when he tempts you to delay your conversion to God!"[14] Like conversion, the godly life was for Sewall a battle against evil incursions. Satan had possession of the heart of the unregenerate sinner in the same manner as the Holy Spirit dwelt in the heart of the redeemed saint; the soul was a vessel filled either by depraved poison or by holy nectar. The Spirit of God dwelling in believers enabled them to renounce Satan's power over body and soul and to witness the destruction of Satan's kingdom by Christ.

Benjamin Colman, Cooper's senior at the Brattle Street Church, was a moderate. Although an early promoter of the revivals, he was later guarded in his optimism about their effects.[15] In speaking of the conversion of a soul, he sought a balance between the external and internal location of evil. Colman, typical of this moderate balancing, used the term "possession" to describe every unregenerate soul's enslavement to sin. In a sermon preached at the Brattle Street Church in October 1740, he declared: "The *Difficulty* of the Thing, and the *Opposition* made against it, both from within and without, increases the Wonder. The natural *Enmity* within us to God and Godliness; *indwelling Sin*, and an *evil heart of Unbelief departing from the living God*; this makes the *Wonder* in the Conversion of any. But then there are the Powers of Hell, Satan and his Hosts, in League with Flesh and blood, and a World that is *Enmity* to God."[16] By 1744, however, his search for a balanced approach led him to criticize freethinkers who dismissed the reality of an "*invisible wicked Power*." Those who doubted "whether ever there was an *Apparition* or a *Possession*" and attributed such things to "a *distempered Brain*, the Power of Melancholy, or Fitts of *Vapor*," were the victims of their own skepticism. "There is a *Medium* we shall do well to keep, that we may not be *superstitious*; but we must quarrel both with *Scripture*, *Experience* and humane Testimony, if we question the Reality of this *Fact*."[17]

For Old Lights, the possibility of diabolic powers capable of exerting themselves through human agents contradicted human autonomy and divine law. To be sure, Satan, as the personification of what was imperfect in humanity, could still use individuals as his "instruments," but never in so direct a way as possession. Their world was absent of demons (and angels) flying overhead. Instead, Satan operated through defects of the mind, "Errors in Judgment" and "overheated imaginations," as was the case with those who were worked into a frenzy by itinerant firebrands. Charles Chauncy of Old Brick Church, the major spokesman for the Old Light party, wrote that some "imagined the Devils were about them, and ready to lay hold on them, and draw them away to Hell." But the origin of such feelings he dismissed as "no other, than a *mechanical Impression* on *animal Nature*."[18]

As Chauncy's comments suggest, the difference between New and Old Light views of the devil relates to their conceptions of human psychology. All agreed that human faculties consisted of will (emotions) and understanding (reason). John Webb, the New Light pastor of the New North Church, reflected conventional wisdom when he stated that "the introductive *Faculties of the Soul* . . . are of the same Use and Importance to the Soul, that a Door is of to an House: And there are Principally the *Understanding* and *Will* . . . if the *Understanding* apprehends the Thing to be *Good*, . . . the *Will* consents to receive it, and the *Affections* embrace it."[19]

However, New and Old Lights each stressed the primacy of different faculties in conversion. New Light views of free grace placed conversion beyond human ability, while Old Lights argued for a more active human role in the process through rational perception and performance of works. For Sewall, Webb's fellow New Light, conversion was a renovation of the will through the infusion of the Holy Spirit. "In this new Birth there are holy Inclinations, and vital Principles of Grace wrought in the soul."[20] Here he used language perfected by Jonathan Edwards, the great reconciler of orthodox Calvinism and the Enlightenment, who argued that "true religion, in great part, consists in holy affections."[21] Chauncy, Edwards's opponent in a debate over the signs of grace, felt that emotions or passions had their place, but if not firmly overruled by reason they were inherently destabilizing. Through unbounded emotions, or "enthusiasm," proper order within the self was upset. For Chauncy and his allies, such spiritual confusion was best illustrated in the fanatical James Davenport and his followers, who claimed the gift of inspiration and the ability to discern grace in others. Alluding to them, Chauncy wrote, "Is it Reasonable to think that the *Divine Spirit*, in dealing with Men in a way of Grace, would give their *Passions* the *chief* sway over them? . . . One of the most *essential* Things necessary in the *new-forming* Men, is the Reduction of their *Passions* to a proper Regimen, i.e., The Government of a *sanctified Understanding*."[22]

New Light, moderate, and Old Light alike could agree that the faculty of reason made humankind the crown of creation. They also saw the danger of avoiding superstitious delusions, such as had arisen during the Salem witchcraft trials. But not all could fall in with the empiricist, rationalist mind-set that many Old Light leaders advocated. New Lights lived in a world inhabited by devils against whom they were constantly doing battle; their views of original sin, grace, redemption, and perseverance made a real satanic power necessary. When assaulted by Roberson's demon, Pitkin, like the warrior of God that he believed himself to be, stepped back "into my Tower where I then stood Undaunted." Indeed, New Lights clung to images of underworld conspiracies as a means of explaining their own world, which by the time of the Revolution translated into fears of a "ministerial" plot to undermine colonial liberties.[23]

A Work of God or of the Devil? Debating the Revivals

In *The Danger of an Unconverted Ministry* (1740), a sermon that became famous throughout the colonies, Gilbert Tennent closed with the scriptural warning that "Satan himself is transformed into an Angel of Light: Therefore it is no great Thing if his Ministers also be transformed as the Ministers of Righteousness." In so doing he associated only preachers of the New Birth with the cause of God. Tennent's sermon, which accused unconverted (that is, nonevangelical) ministers of being Satan's workers in disguise, drew the line in the sand. The devil thereby became a major figure in the revivals of the 1740s. While scholars have examined the antinomian "enthusiasm" stemming from the revivals, contemporaries were more often intent on proving or disproving that enthusiastic behavior had diabolical origins. After Whitefield's arrival, arguments abounded as to whether the revivals were "a work of the Spirit of God" or a work of the devil.

Typical of New Light polemics was that employed by William Cooper, whom Pitkin heard at the Brattle Street lecture in March 1741 when he "Vindicated the Reality of the work of Gods spirit." Though the text of the lecture is not extant, Cooper's contemporary works abundantly reveal his sentiments. In his preface to Jonathan Edwards's 1741 Yale commencement address, entitled *The Distinguishing Marks of a Work of the Spirit of God*, Cooper states: "And now, can any be at a loss to what spirit to ascribe this work? To attribute it, as some do, to the Devil, is to make the old serpent like the foolish woman who plucketh down her house with her hands (Prov. 14:1). . . . That some entertain prejudices against this work, and others revile & reproach it, does not make it look less like a work of God: it would else want one mark of its being so; for the spirit of this world, and the Spirit which is of God, are contrary the one to the other."[24] For evangelicals like Cooper, there could be no doubt that the Holy Spirit was the cause of the "work."

Following Cooper's lead, Pitkin himself defended the revivals, saying, "Lett the Pharisee and Publican stand and slur and . . . Deride it as they will; Yett Nevertheless it appears to be A wonderfull Work of God." Far from fearing that opponents of the awakenings would point to Roberson's case to prove Satan's machinations, Pitkin interpreted his encounter with her, and her eventual cure, as a sign of the legitimacy of the revivals. As Benjamin Colman pointed out, Satan was more apt to "raise those Fears and *Horrors* in some under their *first* (and but Common) Conviction."[25] In other words, Satan was most active in times of awakening because he feared losing souls; if some were deluded, that was all the more a sign that God was "pouring out" the Holy Spirit. In Pitkin's eyes, his narrative no doubt served as an indictment of those who belittled or opposed what he saw as God's work, and thereby affirmed the work.

For those Old Lights and moderates critical of the new ways of extemporaneous, emotional preaching, instances of demon possession were but manifestations of the "enthusiasm" and delusion that New Light methods and teachings threatened. In January 1742, over one hundred New England ministers met to render judgment on the late "great work." "Who can wonder," their printed verdict stated, "if at such a Time as this Satan should intermingle himself, to hinder and blemish a Work so directly contrary to the Interests of his own Kingdom?—Or, if while so much good Seed is sowing; *the Enemy should be busy to sow Tares*?" Whitefield, Tennent, and itinerants generally were branded as "false teachers" by Chauncy and other prominent Boston Congregationalists such as Samuel Mather and Mather Byles and by the Anglican Timothy Cutler. Boston newspapers, such as the *Evening Post* and the *Newsletter*, published articles that denounced the awakenings.

Roberson's case was clearly the subject of local controversy. When Pitkin first met her, she placed the beginning of her possession shortly after the time of Whitefield's visit. She received "Considerable Light and Comfort" after hearing Tennent preach when he came to town, and thereafter visited him at his lodgings. There she had a demonic fit and Tennent and his fellow ministers prayed over her. Upon his arrival in Boston, Pitkin learned that many were "Reproachfully" saying that Tennent had tried to perform exorcism on Robinson—a heretical charge among Calvinists, who held that prayer and fasting were the only means to combat possession. Later, Pitkin relates a more serious charge, that Tennent himself had "put the Devil into her and when he was Gone he would Go out again." Roberson's case was being used by those who wished to discredit the revivals and to exact revenge on "busie-bodies" such as Tennent.

Published criticisms by prominent Old Lights bear out the charges leveled against itinerants of being the means of Satan's advances. In

England, accusations of demonic possession caused by Wesley's preaching during 1740 and 1741 appeared in public prints.[26] Chauncy picked up on such accusations in his own works. In *Seasonable Thoughts on the State of Religion in New England* (1743), turning the tables on Tennent, he called itinerants "*deceitful workers*" who transformed themselves "*into the Ministers of Righteousness*, according to the Example of *Satan*, who can *transform himself into an Angel of Light*." While not possessed, such preachers were influenced by Satan. Chauncy went on to quote one authority who stated that "it is very possible . . . for Men to be really *Satan's* Instruments, animated and taught by him, to do his Work against the Interest of Christ and his Truth." And Chauncy may well have had Roberson's case in mind when he pointed out that the subjects of "*Terrors*" were often "*women* and *young* Persons." "And are not these the very Persons," Chauncy asked, "whose Passions according to *Nature*, it might be expected, would be alarmed?"[27]

In their turn, New Lights urged their opponents and listeners not to doubt the Devil's existence or to underestimate his strength. William Cooper declared, "I don't wonder that Satan rages, and shows his rage in some that are under his influence, when his kingdom is so shaken, and his subjects desert him by hundreds, I hope by thousands."[28] In his sermon on the Holy Spirit, Sewall was even more explicit. Like the Apostles, ministers were given the power "to cast out devils in the name of Jesus Christ. . . . Now it is the Spirit of God who furnisheth and sends forth . . . Ministers of Christ to show Men the miserable Bondage they are under to Satan." Applying himself directly at one point to "young women," he concluded: "Let us *try the Spirits*, and not give place to the Devil. . . . We may well expect that this malicious and subtil Adversary will be busy at such a Time as this; and should accordingly be upon our Guard, that we may not be caught in his Snare."[29] And Colman addressed the Old Light emphasis on instrumentality by stating that "the Devil needs no *Instruments* by whom to tempt: He has Access to our *Minds*, . . . to raise and move evil Thoughts in us. He *shoots* his fiery Darts, and they *enter* we know not how."[30]

Natural Causes versus Providence

The pronouncements of Cooper, Sewall, Colman, and Chauncy followed efforts among theologians both in England and in the Colonies, extending back several decades, to rehabilitate Christianity according to Enlightenment dictates. One way to take mysterious inconsistencies out of existence was to reduce it to mechanistic laws of operation. God, as the wise Creator, observed these laws in governing the universe. This move to discover a Christianity free of all irrationality in turn drew on a long history of exchanges between Puritans and Anglicans over possession and other issues going back to the late sixteenth century. Later works such as Meric Casaubon's *Treatise Concerning Enthusiasme* (1655) sought to discredit claims of possession by attributing them to "devout melancholy" or "distempers of the brain."[31]

In the early eighteenth century, English authors such as Francis Hutcheson, Thomas Woolston, and Arthur Ashley Sykes examined individual cases of possession—both biblical and otherwise—to detect impostors, while Richard Smalbroke, Zachery Pearce, and Leonard Twells sought to vindicate their reality.[32] In Massachusetts, Ebenezer Turrell wrote in 1728 concerning the alleged affliction of three girls in the town of Littleton eight years previous. He dismissed the occurrence as "the contrivance of the children of men" and the girls as playactors. To prevent such outbreaks, he advised parents to leave off superstitious practices (such as nailing up horseshoes) and unfounded beliefs. However, Turrell did not refute the possibility of possession. Such practices, he warned, gave an "invitation" to the *real* Satan. During the revivals, Rev. Mather Byles, Boston's curmudgeon, followed the investigative method Cotton Mather had used during the Salem witchcraft prosecutions of a half-century earlier. The increasing number who claimed to have holy trances and visions did not measure up under Byle's skeptical eye.[33]

For all that critics such as Chauncy, Turrell, and Byles wanted to expel arcane customs and interpretations, occult practices and beliefs persisted through the eighteenth century, as historians such as Godbeer, Jon Butler, and David D. Hall have argued.[34] Pitkin's narrative illustrates this continuity. He recorded an "illustrative" providence or omen, which to the writer's mind proved the reality of Roberson's case. During the night following the first day of interviews, Roberson and her aunt, Mrs. Silvie, "were both awake & Heard a noise Like the Bleating of A Goat . . . and somthing Came out of Capt Sheldins [where Pitkin was staying] which Drove the Goat away: and as he was Driven away there Came a violent Gust of Wind as if it would have Taken the Topp of the House off."

Pitkin's strident providentialist worldview and self-perception constructs the narrative, sometimes to the point where he is the central character and Roberson merely a mouthpiece for him to decipher. He selects from and shapes Roberson's experience to suit his purposes and assumptions, which arose from an aggressively Calvinist view of causation: The sovereign God ordered all events to serve divine purposes and to benefit the saints. In all of his conversations with Roberson, Pitkin did not seek other, secondary causes (such as physical or mental illness) for the source of Roberson's troubles, nor even witchcraft, as perhaps would have been the assumption before the Salem incident. Rather, inspired by the immediacy and urgency of revival preaching, he was quick to claim that he acted as an instrument of God in a direct confrontation with the Devil. Indeed, he takes no little amount of pride in being given this task by divine providence. From the beginning of his narrative Pitkin notes "how Providentially I was Called into the way of it." Though Roberson's initial outburst "seemd to Give the Blood a stop in my Veins for a Moment," Pitkin remarked on how "Divine strength Raised [him] to a Double Degree of Courage." Several ministers, he stated, had held a day of fasting and prayer for her to no avail; "some ministers had been almost frighted out of their witts," and "one Especially . . . Dare not Come near her nor suffer her to Come near him." Yet Pitkin boasted that "all the Mockery of satan was no more Troublesome to my soul than the Buzing of a fly." It was clear to him that God had ordered events so that he would have the opportunity "to Wrestle with Principalitys and powers."

The Psychology of Possession and Religious Revivals

Pitkin's more rationalistic contemporaries noted that alleged cases of possession, whether diabolical or divine (the latter consisting of trances, fits, visions, and prophesying), occurred more frequently at times of intense religious activity. Modern scholars too have remarked on this trend. In describing the religious environment in which possession often occurred, Keith Thomas argues that "victims were engaging in a hysterical reaction against the religious discipline and repression to which they had been subjected," and so, he concludes, it is not surprising to find possession occurring most frequently among Puritans and monastics.[35] Clarke Garrett writes that demonic possession reached "epidemic proportions" in seventeenth-century Europe and that the eighteenth century saw the greatest frequency and diversity of spirit possession since the days of the early Christian church.[36] The burgeoning of reported possessions was met with efforts to develop methods of explaining not just their physical but also their psychological origins.

When an individual exhibited the signs of possession, physicians were usually called in to rule out natural causes—indeed, physicians were often the ones who concluded a "diabolical original," as was the case with Elizabeth Knapp of Boston in 1671.[37] We do not know if Roberson's family consulted any physicians, but if they had, it is possible she would have been diagnosed as suffering from a "hystericall original," which at the time was sometimes cited as the true cause of possession behavior. Edmund Jordan's *Brief Discourse of a Disease called the Suffocation of the Mother* (1603) had sought to explain that many things commonly attributed to possession were actually caused by natural conditions such as hysteria. Hysteria was commonly described as a disturbance of the nervous system caused by uterine dysfunction, hence it was used to support the belief that women were more "impressionable" and subject to passions. The condition covered a broad range of symptoms, including epilepsy, depression, and melancholy.[38] Modern psychologists have accumulated criteria for a similar condition known as "conversion hysteria," which is thought to occur in individuals who are self-centered, sexually repressed, dependent, and exhibitionistic.[39]

Drawing on such cases, historians and psychologists have identified several important characteristics of possession cases in seventeenth- and eighteenth-century Europe.[40] In a society that emphasized that women should be submissive and resigning, possession provided an opportunity for blatant and demonstrative behavior. Individuals who were thought to be possessed were accorded much leeway in violating strict bounds of action and speech; realizing their spiritual power, they exploited their privileged status in order to get more attention. G. R. Quaife has written that "demonic possession provided an outlet for frustration and anxiety and enabled the victim to indulge safely in behaviour normally unacceptable to a Christian society, especially one in the throes of a revival."[41] Times of revivals, emotionally charged and often laying bare the tensions between conventions and ideals, were especially ripe for otherwise aberrant behavior. Critics like Chauncy feared and sought to extinguish revivalistic license that encouraged the rise of enthusiasts, including female and slave exhorters.[42]

Roberson's case verifies and extends our knowledge of the psychology of possession. Her demonic personality was characterized by violent, sexually charged outbursts. She desired to be associated with male figures vested with religious or social authority and yet was offensive to them—an expression, perhaps, of her realization that she could never attain the status she sought. When Tennent came to Boston to keep alive the spiritual fires started by Whitefield, Roberson visited him in his lodgings. She began to speak with him, "butt before he had said much to me or I to him; the Devil filld me with such Rage and spite against him That I Could have Torn him to peices and should have Torn his Cloaths off if my friends had not held me." When Pitkin, whom Roberson first took to be a minister because he visited the governor's house, was counseling her, she "Rose up with such a

Countenance of Rage and Disdain with her fist Double as if she would Come in my face." Timothy Dwight met with the same reception: "Once or twice she Rose up with her first Doubled as if she would have Gone in Col Dwights face."

Scholars of European religious history have described the theatrical nature of possession, both demonic and godly.[43] The possessed performed their roles in public settings, sometimes on their own initiative and sometimes at the instigation of others—as was the case with the celebrated Richard Dugdale, the "Surrey demoniac" of the 1690s.[44] Similarly, Roberson's most dramatic spiritual episodes occurred in front of audiences. After hearing Whitefield preach, she pushed through the crowd and "Gott near him as I Could; and Lett him know I was peirced by the word: He turned to me and said he prayed God to sett home my Conviction to saveing Conversion." When she went to speak with Tennent, she was in the company of "2 or three of my friends" and he "sitting with 4 or 5 ministers." Pitkin's interviews were conducted with several family members and neighbors present. When Timothy Dwight joined Pitkin, "a considerable number of people," no doubt hearing of the interviews through the neighborhood grapevine, were present. Even after her "cure," Roberson continued her public exhibitions. In 1744, when Whitefield again visited Boston and preached at Rev. John Webb's New North Church, Colonel John Phillips reported in his diary, "There were many cried out, Robinson's daughter and others."[45]

Language and Possession

Pitkin's reaction to Roberson's abusive language and loud tones conveys much about contemporary assumptions concerning proper female behavior.[46] As male narrator, he was intent on highlighting the inappropriate speech of his female subject. When the devil "spoke with her tongue," Roberson used idle and profane language, cried out, and screamed. But when she was "herself" she was the quiet, soft-spoken maid she was expected to be. When "the Devil has spoke in me," Roberson confessed, he "hath spoke in me all Maner of Prophane Talk all maner of Unclean Talk; all maner of follish songs: and made me Dance two Hours together . . . he has spoke in me all sorts [of] Tea Table Talk such foolish Talk as is Comonly there." After this disclosure, Roberson declared that "the Devil will Roar in me anon; and then Gave a Loud shreik as Loud as her Voice would Carry it." She regained her composure, but when Pitkin continued with his questions, "her Countenance was Changed in a Moment into the Most Dismall form of Rage and Disdain . . . the Devill with her Tongue Broke forth in the most Hideous oratory Contradicting Denying and Mocking as if he would spit in my face." With Pitkin and Dwight, distinguished representatives of two major centers of revivalism, before her, Roberson's demonic persona gave vent to the "most Disdainfull Countenance and Tone in her" and "in the Highest Degree of Derision": "Ay You Came from Hartford and he Came from North Hampton; they Tell of Conversion there Conversion, Conversion, Conversion . . . there is no such thing it is all A notion."

When it came to the issue of language, therefore, Pitkin the evangelical and Chauncy the liberal could join hands. Chauncy was outraged at the way that itinerant exhorters shouted and screamed in the pulpit, used "terrible [i.e., frightening] language" to shock their audiences, and prompted "cryings out" from their listeners. For Chauncy, the response of an audience that was appropriately engaged in a sermon was "silence and Attention." "Has not *voice* and *Action* been too often repaired to?" he objected. "Have not poor distressed Creatures been practised upon, and this by Numbers at a Time, and in Ways unfit to be mentioned, whereby their *animal Nature* has been thrown into the most horrid Confusion? I could mention a Plenty of Instances in this Kind, but I rather chuse they should be buried in perpetual Oblivion."[47]

The vulgar and boisterous language of Roberson's demonic persona, as depicted by Pitkin, contrasted strongly with the submissive aspect of her conventional one. As he proceeded to interrogate her, "the Devils Rage Grew more feirce, Interupted her, near half her time." Gradually, however, he felt he saw "Christ had Gott the Possession of her soul by his Holy spirit." When the Devil "had used her Tongue a few Breaths in Contradicting and Revileing then the spirit of God Guided her Tongue in Repeating the scriptures." Pitkin's contrast of her two personalities—the one loud, the other quiet—is punctuated by his repetition of the word "tongue," further revealing his fixation on language. "Generally," he continued, "after satan had Taken his Turn with her Tongue: she would Recover into a *Calm* Giveing her Amen and Amen to the truths of Gods word." Pitkin then asked her to pray with him. "I askd her if she Could Compose her self and *keep from Making A Noise*; she said she Could not Tell." As they prayed together, "she Continued some time *silent* but when I Came to her Case the Devil Began to *Cry aloud* with her Voice; Holld Your Tongue; Hold Your Tongue: as often and as *Loud* as she Could speak for several breaths . . . and then she would be Recoverd again and I Could hear her *softly* say Amen."[48]

Two years later, when Pitkin went back to check on Roberson's state, he found her appropriately submissive. To his satisfaction, she "walked very Humbly and Circumspectly" and "behaved very Very Decently." But he could not forget how she had spoken. "I then particularly Inquired whether she Could now say as she then Did that those Evil words which were utterd with her Tongue were the abhorrence of her soul she answerd it was Generally so. but sometimes I was almost all Devil."[49] In particular, he wanted to be assured that she would never "be Prevailed with to speak such words" again. Her conventional answer demonstrated her new conformity to accepted behavioral patterns: "No if I might have the world for it."

With her final statement, Roberson recedes into the anonymity of normality. But her episode brings us to reflect on its significance for the larger, shifting meanings of Satan and demon possession in the eighteenth century. When we join this one, as yet isolated, colonial occurrence with the large number of European cases, it seems premature to make blanket assertions about the pervasiveness of empiricist, rationalist thought in mid-eighteenth-century Euro-American society beyond a small segment of the learned elite. Whether or not the subjects were truly possessed, the number of instances shows the continuing power of possession as an explanation for a certain type of behavior.

While witchcraft accusations did continue, reaction against witch-hunts in the decades following Salem was stronger than against possession. Turn-of-the-century possession controversies such as the Surrey demoniac did not elicit the backlash that Salem did, despite the fact that, like the Salem accusers, the Surrey demoniac was widely thought to be a fraud. If by 1740 there was widespread wariness about the Devil operating through witches, the Devil was nonetheless still very real and was accorded other ways of making himself known through human "instruments." In the New England colonies, New Lights, moderates, and possibly even rank-and-file Old Lights could agree on the reality of Satan and possession.

Noticeable for its absence in Pitkin's account is witchcraft. Apart from the transparently partisan effort to blame Tennent for Roberson's possession, no mention is made of bewitchment. While Roberson's state fit seventeenth-century descriptions of obsession by the Devil of a godly person, even obsession was supposed to originate with a witch. Roberson's case suggests that in the post-Salem period obsession and possession were perceived to occur without an intermediary. In this sense, Satan was accorded more arbitrary power in mid-eighteenth-century America to afflict the godly than before.

The revivals themselves, in which both Pitkin and Roberson were eager participants, may have had a role in the re-empowering of Satan. The millennialistic fervor inspired by the awakenings brought with it anticipation for the final encounter and overthrow of Satan and his minions. In such an atmosphere, the devil became a more immediate presence.[50] Depictions of a cosmic struggle between the kingdom of God and the kingdom of Satan, particularly strong in a time of awakenings, only heightened sensitivity to perceived demonic activity. On the other hand, evangelicals like Pitkin perceived human experience—particularly revivalistic periods—as God's hand in history. Pitkin's belief in his role as an agent of God's "providence" reflected an evangelical view of causation that constructed no barrier between the natural and spiritual realms and made natural law a servant to divine purpose.

Pitkin's providentialism was central to how he interpreted Roberson's behavior. Therefore I have been careful to portray the narrative as "Pitkin's depiction" or "Pitkin's account" because it may inform us more about him than about what actually happened to Roberson. The parts that language and behavior, in particular, played in Pitkin's depiction of her case reflected an interest in perpetuating traditional gender roles, even within the newly emerging religious culture.

While the practice of witchcraft has undergone rehabilitation in our time to the extent that it is now a legitimate sectarian practice, possession can still elicit awful fascination and huge popular interest—witness movies like *The Exorcist*. There is something about possession that continues to repulse, terrify, and mystify, perhaps because of its involuntary nature. In modern Western societies, in which individual identity is so prized, possession may represent the ultimate distortion or deprivation of self. If the recent renaissance of interest in angels and guardian spirits is any indication, it seems that demons, their spirit-adversaries, will continue to be with us as well.

Notes

1. All quotes by Pitkin are taken from his diary (Connecticut State Library, MS Vault). The diary, which covers the years 1711 to 1756, is retrospective; however, he did make use of pieces he had written earlier, including, apparently, the Roberson account, which is on pages 55 to 62 of the MS.

2. Notable exceptions include Keith Thomas, *Religion and the Decline of Magic* (New York: Charles Scribner's Sons, 1971); and Jon Butler, *Awash in a Sea of Faith: Christianizing the American People* (Cambridge: Harvard University Press, 1990).

3. On witchcraft in seventeenth-century America, see Marion Starkey, *The Devil in Massachusetts: A Modern Inquiry into the Salem Witch Trials* (New York: Knopf, 1949); Chadwick Hansen, *Witchcraft at Salem* (New York: Braziller, 1966), Paul Boyer and Stephen Nissenbaum, *Salem Possessed: The Social Origins of Witchcraft* (Cambridge: Harvard University Press, 1974); Richard Weisman, *Witchcraft, Magic, and Religion in 17th-Century Massachusetts*

(Amherst: University of Massachusetts, 1984); Carol F. Karlsen, *The Devil in the Shape of a Woman: Witchcraft in Colonial New England* (New York: Norton, 1987); John Demos, *Entertaining Satan: Witchcraft and the Culture of Early New England* (New York: Oxford University Press, 1982), esp. pp. 97–131; and Richard Godbeer, *The Devil's Dominion: Magic and Religion in Early New England* (Cambridge: Cambridge University Press, 1992). On witchcraft and possession in eighteenth-century Europe, see Thomas, *Religion and the Decline of Magic*; Aldous Huxley, *The Devils of Toulon* (London: Chatto & Windus, 1952); D. P. Walker, *Unclean Spirits: Possession and Exorcism in France and England in the Late Sixteenth and Early Seventeenth Century* (Philadelphia: University of Pennsylvania, 1981); Clarke Garrett, *Spirit Possession and Popular Religion: From the Camisards to the Shakers* (Baltimore, MD: Johns Hopkins, 1987); Brian P. Levack, ed., *Articles on Witchcraft, Magic, and Demonology*, vol. 9, *Possession and Exorcism* (New York: Garland, 1992); G. R. Quaife, *Godly Zeal and Furious Rage: The Witch in Early Modern Europe* (New York: St. Martin's, 1987).

4. A. P. Pitkin, *The Pitkin Family of America* (Hartford, Conn.: Case, Lockwood and Brainerd, 1887), 14.

5. *A Report of the Record Commissioners of the City of Boston, containing Boston Births from A.D. 1700 to A.D. 1800* (Boston: Rockwell and Churchill, 1894), 124. Martha Robinson was married by Thomas Prince to Michael Mallet of Charlestown on January 6, 1746. *A Report of the Record Commissioners of the City of Boston, containing the Boston Marriages from 1700 to 1751* (Boston: Municipal Printing Office, 1898), 253. On the Great Awakening as a youthful movement, see Philip J. Greven, Jr., "Youth, Maturity, and Religious Conversion: A Note on the Ages of Converts in Andover, Massachusetts, 1711–1749," *Essex Institute Historical Collections* 108 (1972): 119–34; Gerald F. Moran, "Condition of Religious Conversion in the First Society of Norwich, Connecticut, 1718–1744," *Journal of Social History* 5 (1972): 331–43; J. M. Bumsted and John E. Van de Wetering, *What Must I Do to Be Saved? The Great Awakening in Colonial America* (Hinsdale, Ill., Dryden, 1976), ch. 7; Patricia Tracy, *Jonathan Edwards, Pastor: Religion and Society in Eighteenth-Century Northampton* (New York: Hill and Wang, 1980); Stephen R. Grossbart, "Seeking the Divine Favor: Conversion and Church Admissions in Eastern Connecticut, 1711–1832," *William and Mary Quarterly* 46 (1989): 696–740; and "Troubled Youth: Children at Risk in Early Modern England, Colonial America, and Nineteenth-Century America," in Gerald F. Moran and Maris A. Vinovskis, *Religion, Family, and the Life Course: Explorations in the Social History of Early America* (Ann Arbor: University of Michigan, 1992), 141–80.

6. Walker, *Unclean Spirits*, 10. See also David Harley, "Explaining Salem: Calvinist Psychology and the Diagnosis of Possession," *American Historical Review* 101 (April 1996): 307–30, for a discussion of historians' tendency to blur bewitchment and possession.

7. Jeffrey Burton Russell, *Mephistopheles: The Devil in the Modern World* (Ithaca, NY: Cornell, 1986), 77–78, 137–56; Andrew Delbanco, *The Death of Satan: How Americans Have Lost the Sense of Evil* (New York: Farrar, Straus, and Giroux, 1995), 57–83.

8. Godbeer, *The Devil's Dominion*, 227. On the continuity of magic and the occult in the American colonies, see Butler, *Awash in a Sea of Faith*, 67–97.

9. Murray Murphey, "The Psychodynamics of Puritan Conversion," *American Quarterly* 31 (1979): 135–47.

10. My italics.

11. Harley, "Explaining Salem," 131.

12. Sewall, *The Holy Spirit Convincing the World of Sin, of Righteousness, and of Judgment, Considered in Four Sermons: The Two Former Delivered at the Thursday-Evening Lecture in Brattle-Street, January 20th & March 3: The Other at the Old-South-Church in Boston, April 17 & 26, 1741* (Boston, 1741), 65, 113–20.

13. As an indication of how jealously lectureships were sought, Chauncy (*Seasonable Thoughts on the State of Religion in New-England* [Boston, 1743], 39) complained that when Tennent came to Boston, he not only never asked assistance of "any one of the Ministers" but also "took their *own Turns* in *Stated Lectures*."

14. Sewall, *All Flesh Is as Grass; But the Word of the Lord Endureth For Ever. A Sermon Preached at the Thursday Lecture in Boston, January 1st, 1740,1* (Boston, 1741), 7, 22.

15. For example, of the 110 clergymen who signed *The Testimony and Advice of an Assembly of Pastors of Churches in New-England, At a Meeting in Boston, July 7, 1743, Occasion'd by the Late Happy Revival of Religion in Many Parts of the Land* (Boston, 1743), Colman was among those who registered dissatisfaction with the *Testimony*'s weak stand against itinerancy. On Colman's search to strike a balance between orthodox Calvinism and natural law, see Teresa Toulouse, *The Art of Prophesying: New England Sermons and the Shaping of Belief* (Athens: University of Georgia Press, 1987), 46–74.

16. Benjamin Colman, *Souls Flying to Jesus Christ Pleasant and Adorable to Behold. A Sermon Preach'd at the Opening an Evening Lecture, in Brattle-Street, Boston, Tuesday, October 21, 1740* (Boston, 1740), 19.

17. Colman, *The Case of Satan's Fiery Darts in Blasphemous Suggestions and Hellish Annoyances* (Boston, 1744), 68.

18. Chauncy, *Seasonable Thoughts*, 71.

19. John Webb, *Christ's Suit to the Sinner, While He Stands and Knocks at the Door. A Sermon Preach'd in a Time of Great Awakening, at the Tuesday-Evening Lecture in Brattle Street, Boston, October 13, 1741* (Boston, 1741), 5–6.

20. Sewall, *All Flesh Is as Grass*, 12.

21. *The Works of Jonathan Edwards, 2, Religious Affections*, ed. John E. Smith (New Haven: Yale University Press, 1959), 95.

22. Chauncy, *Seasonable Thoughts*, 324. Similiarly, in *The Gifts of the Spirit to Ministers Consider'd in Their Diversity* (Boston, 1743), 14–15, Chauncy declared that "the *human passions* are capable of serving valuable purposes in religion, . . . always provided they are kept under the restraints of *reason*; for otherwise they will soon run wild, and may make those in whom they reign to do so too" (quoted in Charles H. Lippy, *Seasonable Revolutionary: The Mind of Charles Chauncy* [Chicago: Nelson Hall, 1981], 31). See also William Hooper, *The Apostles Neither Impostors nor Enthusiasts. A Sermon Preached at the West Church in Boston, September 1742* (Boston, 1742), which asserts that the apostles "did speak the Words of *Truth and Soberness* . . . in the full Exercise of their Reason and Understanding, and were not imposed upon by their own groundless Opinions and Fancies" (11).

23. Bernard Bailyn, *Ideological Origins of the American Revolution* (Cambridge, Mass.: Belknap, 1967), 94–159; Gordon S. Wood, *The Radicalism of the American Revolution* (New York: Vintage, 1991), 160–61, 174–75; Alan Heimert, *Religion and the American Mind: From the Great Awakening to the Revolution* (Cambridge: Harvard University Press, 1967).

24. Text taken from *The Works of Jonathan Edwards*, vol. 4, *The Great Awakening*, ed. C. C. Goen (New Haven: Yale University Press, 1972), 222.

25. Colman, *The Case of Satan's Fiery Darts*, 23.

26. Garrett, *Spirit Possession and Popular Religion*, 81–87.

27. Chauncy, *Seasonable Thoughts*, 44, 104.

28. Cooper, "Preface" to Edwards, "Distinguishing Marks of a Work of the Spirit of God," in *The Works of Jonathan Edwards*, vol. 4, *Great Awakening*, 272.

29. Sewall, *The Holy Spirit Convincing the World*, 110, 127, 132.

30. Colman, *The Case of Satan's Fiery Darts*, 13.

31. Meric Casaubon, *A Treatise concerning Enthusiasme, As It Is an Effect of Nature; But Is Mistaken by Many for Either Divine Inspiration, or Diabiolic Possession* (London, 1655). See also Julius H. Rubin, *Religious Melancholy and the Protestant Experience in America* (New York: Oxford, 1994).

32. Francis Hutcheson, *An Historical Essay concerning Witchcraft* (London, 1720); Thomas Woolston, *Discourses on the Miracles of Our Saviour* (London, 1727–1729); Arthur Ashley Sykes, *An Inquiry into the Meaning of Demoniacks in the New Testament* (London, 1737); Twells, *An Answer to the Enquiry into the Meaning of Demoniacks in the New Testament* (London, 1737); Richard Smalbroke, *A Vindication of the Miracles of Our Blessed Savior*, 2 vols. (London: James and John Knapton, 1729–1731); Zachery Pearce, *The Miracles of Jesus Vindicated* (3d ed., London, 1730).

33. Turrell, "Detection of Witchcraft," in *Collections of the Massachusetts Historical Society* 10 (1823): 6–22; for Byles, see *Proceedings of the Massachusetts Historical Society* 44 (1910–11): 685–86.

34. Butler, *Awash in a Sea of Faith*; Hall, *Worlds of Wonder, Days of Judgement: Popular Religious Beliefs in Early New England* (New York: Knopf, 1989).

35. Thomas, *Religion and the Decline of Magic*, 480.

36. Garrett, *Spirit Possession and Popular Religion*, 10.

37. On the Knapp case, see Demos, *Entertaining Satan*, 97–131.

38. Thomas, *Religion and the Decline of Magic*, 489. One such case of conversion hysteria in the British North American colonies during the revivals of the 1740s was that of Sarah Edwards, the wife of Jonathan Edwards. We know from a narrative she wrote that during the early months of 1742 she went through an intensely emotional period, characterized by "cryings out," repeated fainting and trances, and rapid emotional shifts from ecstasy to deep sadness. A surviving medical prescription from the town doctor (Beinecke Rare Book and Manuscript Library, Yale University) indicates she was diagnosed as suffering from "an Hystericall originall," which medical treatises of the day also called "Fits of the Mother" or "Hysterick Cholick" and defined as a disorder of the womb. She had given birth to children every two years since 1728, for a total of eleven. Scholars have argued that this one disruption of the cycle, in 1742, occurred because her relationship with her husband had become strained. Others see Sarah Edwards's narrative as providing for her husband an example of true piety. While Jonathan did use Sarah's narrative in a published treatise defending the awakenings, he dramatically toned it down and made it gender-neutral. But Dr. Samuel Mather's prescription, consisting of "Emplastrum Matricale" to be "applyed to her Navel and worn there for Some weeks or months together," demonstrates that even within the Edwards household she was thought to have a natural malady.

39. Juan B. Cortes and Florence M. Gattis, *The Case against Possessions and Exorcisms: A Historical, Biblical, and Psychological Analysis of Demons, Devils, and Demoniacs* (New York: Vantage, 1975), 163.

40. See Levack, *Articles on Witchcraft, Magic, and Demonology*, 63–112, 183–202, 219–50.

41. Quoted in Cortes and Gattis, *The Case against Possessions and Exorcisms*, 101.

42. Chauncy, *Enthusiasm Described and Caution'd Against* (Boston, 1742), 5, 13.

43. Garrett, *Spirit Possession and Popular Religion*, 4; Anita M. Walker and Edmund H. Dickerman, "A Woman under the Influence: A Case of Alleged Possession in Sixteenth-Century France," in Levack, *Articles on Witchcraft, Magic, and Possession*, 195.

44. Thomas Jollie, *The Surey Demoniack: Or, an Account of Satans Strange and Dreadful Actings, in and about the Body of Richard Dugdale* (London, 1697).

45. Justin Winsor, *Memorial History of Boston*, 4 vols. (Boston, 1981): II, 239n. There were two Robinson families in Boston at the time, and Martha was the only unmarried young female beyond childhood among them.

46. See Jane N. Kamensky, "Governing the Tongue: Speech and Society in Early New England" (Ph.D. diss., Yale University, 1993).

47. Chauncy, *Seasonable Thoughts*, 106, 303–4.

48. My italics.

49. Cf. Colman, *The Case of Satan's Fiery Darts*, on saints afflicted with evil thoughts: "We see 'em terrify'd and pierc'd with *hellish* Suggestions, which they abhor, and are ready to *shriek* out at: they look on 'em as *their own* wickedness, and so at themselves as *Devils* almost" (10).

50. See, for example, Christopher R. Reaske, "The Devil and Jonathan Edwards," *Journal of the History of Ideas* 33 (January–March, 1972): 123–38, which argues that the Devil became an obsession for Edwards during the revivals of 1740s.

6

Seneca Possessed: Colonialism, Witchcraft, and Gender in the Time of Handsome Lake

~

Matthew Dennis

Matthew Dennis's essay forces us to confront the ways in which definitions of witch and witchcraft are culturally constructed and gendered. In his examination of a witch-hunting episode among the Senecas in the early nineteenth century, Dennis uncovers traditional Iroquois witchcraft beliefs and traces the evolution of those beliefs in a postcolonial world, where what was traditional began to take on new meaning. Although witchcraft was traditional, it most likely had been a gender-neutral phenomenon for the Iroquois. That changed dramatically by the end of the eighteenth century, when witchcraft accusations and executions implicated women particularly. Ironically, the demonization of women encouraged by the Seneca prophet Handsome Lake—and the tentative realignment of Seneca society toward *the patriarchal arrangements of an encroaching white world—was intricately linked with Seneca revitalization.*

In a further ironic twist, Seneca leaders defended the persecution of women witches by referencing Salem, even as the events of 1692 were increasingly remembered by Euro-Americans as a distinct embarrassment. The memory of Salem was invoked by whites to help eradicate native "superstitious" practice, while it was appropriated by Seneca leaders to help protect autonomy and their right to prosecute and execute dangerous "witches."

IN THE SPRING OF 1821, on the outskirts of that rising metropolis of the West, Buffalo, New York, an unfortunate Seneca Indian "fell into a state of languishment, and died."[1] The deceased was hardly the "last of his race"; indeed, the Senecas—and other descendants of the once great Iroquois confederacy—were in the early stages of a revitalization, based on the visions and teachings of a prophet, Handsome Lake. In the first decades of the nineteenth century, "The Old Way of Handsome Lake" was young, but the prophet's codes, prescriptions, and rituals represented a creative amalgamation of traditional Iroquois culture and intrusive Euro-American ideas and technologies.[2] What had caused the untimely demise of this anonymous man among the modernizing Senecas of western New York? To his kin it was clear: witchcraft.

As William L. Stone, the nineteenth-century historian and biographer, reported melodramatically, "Nay more, the woman who had nursed him [the victim], and anxiously watched him at his bed-side, was fixed upon as the bedlam who, by aid of an evil spirit, had compassed his death."[3] Kauquatau, the "witch," fled to Canada but was apprehended, "artfully inveigled" back to the American side of the Niagara, tried by the local Seneca council, and appropriately sentenced to death. Without further delay, the "sorceress" was dispatched at Buffalo Creek by a chief named So-on-on-gise, commonly known as Tommy Jemmy, who cut her throat after another executioner had botched his bloody commission.

Of course, the Indians' shocked and horrified white neighbors saw in this "savage" execution a primitivism they believed to be ancient and traditional. In fact, this witch-hunt embodied—at least in one key aspect, that the victim was a woman—the nineteenth-century acculturation of Senecas and other Iroquois people. With the inadvertent guidance of Quaker missionaries, by the early nineteenth century Senecas had remade traditional witch-hunting, creatively incorporating a traditional Western European misogyny at odds with older Iroquois practices. The extent of Seneca transformation, on the one hand, and the firmness of their persistent commitment to tradition and autonomy, on the other, amid the changed circumstances of their lives, is suggested in the strange remarks attributed to Red Jacket, the eminent orator and leader of the Buffalo Creek Senecas, during the inconclusive trial of Tommy Jemmy for murder. As an excited editor of the *Albany Argus*, an eyewitness, reported, Red Jacket exclaimed:

> What! Do you denounce us as fools and bigots, because we still believe that which you yourselves believed two centuries ago? Your black-coats thundered this doctrine from the pulpit, your judges pronounced it from the bench, and sanctioned it with the formalities of law; and you would now punish our unfortunate brother for adher-

ing to the faith of *his* fathers and of yours! Go to Salem! Look at the records of your own government, and you will find that hundreds have been executed for the very crime which has called forth the sentence of condemnation against this woman, and drawn down upon her the arm of vengeance. What have our brothers done more than the rulers of your people have done? And what crime has this man committed, by executing, in a summary way, the laws of his country, and the command of the Great Spirit?[4]

Red Jacket's speech, in defense of "tradition" and Seneca independence, ironically appropriated a foreign history and deployed it skillfully to create space Senecas needed to survive. To a considerable degree, Red Jacket and others had little choice. They did not go out of their way to find the new historical narrative of the rising glory of America; it found them. As we will see, the Seneca orator's clever words emanated from his people's strange, colonial predicament in a "postcolonial" United States. Giving these sentiments voice was the new and more dangerous state of dependency Senecas now experienced, the dire need to accommodate and resist this new phase of an old colonialism, and the search for an effective way to conserve, or reinvent, a distinct Seneca ethnic and cultural identity in the interstices of a dominant and expanding American economy, polity, and society. The Senecas in the early national period, the era of the prophet Handsome Lake (d. 1815), confronted not only white rivals but also each other, as they struggled to find the best means to respond and adjust, and thus survive, in a rapidly changing world. Such struggles were also gendered in complex ways.

By the time of Handsome Lake, Iroquois peoples had experienced European colonialism for over two hundred years.[5] The Senecas and other Iroquois faced their colonial rivals and allies with considerable confidence in themselves and their way of life. By the mid-eighteenth century the Iroquois had endured devastating epidemics, debilitating warfare with both colonial and Native rivals, and unsettling incursions by Christian missionaries and land-hungry speculators, settlers, and squatters. Through traditional practices of amalgamation with outsiders, adoption of captives and refugees, and resourceful diplomacy and domestic politics, the People of the Longhouse had weathered the storms of the seventeenth century and emerged as powerful clients, allies, and brokers within Britain's North American empire.[6] Although much had changed in Iroquois life over the previous generations, the Iroquois people remained Iroquois, and their confederation (and its constituents) retained a considerable measure of territorial integrity, political autonomy, military strength, and diplomatic leverage.

Despite some community fragmentation and migration, Iroquois society generally continued to hew to older patterns of social life—based on localism, consensus, matrilineal kinship descent, and matrilocal residence, which offered women considerable status and authority. Their collective adjustments to colonialism had been selective and largely accomplished on their own terms.

With the American Revolution, the Iroquois, who had reluctantly fought for Britain, experienced the depressing denouement of a long colonial process. Their confederacy, which had maintained its autonomy and protected its residual power by playing one colonial power against another, was broken, and with it Iroquois unity was shattered. In Iroquoia, the Revolution was a civil war, filled with brutality, terror, indiscriminate killing of men, women, and children, and the massive expropriation of property.[7] By the spring of 1780, only two of some thirty Iroquois towns between the Mohawk River and the Ohio country survived undamaged. The rest lay in ashes or had been abandoned, with their former residents dead or dispersed into makeshift refugee camps, where they struggled against the cold, hunger, scurvy, and dysentery and contemplated their future. The demographic crisis that began with the Revolution had reduced the Iroquois population by about half by 1797, to fewer than four thousand people.[8]

The immediate post-Revolutionary period thus found the Iroquois huddled in a few small reservations, the residual properties they somehow had managed to hold, in a state of disorganization and demoralization. These communities, in the telling phrase of Anthony F. C. Wallace, were little more than "slums in the wilderness."[9] In places like Cornplanter's Town, adjacent to the Allegany Reservation, Senecas attempted to survive by employing their old ways along with any innovations that might forestall their complete demise. Change had always been a part of Seneca life, but now there was a particular urgency to their improvisation on tradition. In 1798, the first contingent of Quaker "missionaries," or technical advisers, showed up at Allegany. The Cornplanter Senecas welcomed them and appeared open to their program of technological acculturation, which the Quakers saw simply as "civilization." The Society of Friends could make a convincing case that it had no ulterior motives, would not proselytize or teach "peculiar doctrines," and did not seek economic gain, particularly through the alienation of Indian land. Their purpose was simply to introduce among the Indians "the most necessary arts of civil life" and "useful practices: to instruct the Indians in husbandry & the plain mechanical arts & manufactures directly connected with it."[10]

Though comparatively benign in its soft-peddling of Christian theology and religious practice, the Quaker mission's ultimate, ethnocentric goal, of course, was the fundamental transformation of Seneca society. At the center of all such programs was the demolition of communal ownership of property and collective patterns of work. Seneca morality too deserved attention and reform, especially their debilitating drinking habits and their unorthodox marriage customs and sexuality. In addition, the gender arrangements of Native societies, such as matrilineality and women's horticulture, marked the Indians as savage. Quakers, like other middle-class reformers emerging in the late eighteenth and early nineteenth centuries, focused particular attention on realigning Seneca gender roles to conform to Euro-American expectations and hoped to remake the Seneca's extended, maternal families into more discrete, patriarchal, nuclear units.[11]

The Quaker incentive program, offering bonuses for Seneca production of prescribed commodities, displayed their hopes for a Seneca metamorphosis. Proper men's and women's activities were distinguished from each other and encouraged. Men's production of wheat or rye, Indian corn, potatoes, and hay was rewarded with cash premiums. Women, on the other hand—offered no incentive for their customary horticultural work—were encouraged to pursue domestic occupations, like the manufacture of linen or woolen cloth, spun and woven in their own houses. This incentive plan, with its implied prescriptions about proper modes and goals of production, and its specific spatialization of this colonized Seneca landscape—placing the Seneca woman, for example, on "her husband's land" and "in her own house"—stands in large part for the entire "Friendly" program.

Yet many Quaker goals meshed with Seneca ones, which Seneca men and women differentially shared. The Indians were not averse to technological innovation and proved creative in their integration of new ideas and technologies into older patterns of life. Some were enthusiastic about acquiring facility in spoken English and the ability to read and write. And many were pleased to benefit from Quaker technical assistance and their infusion of capital for equipment and improvements, like roads, sawmills, gristmills, and blacksmith shops. Finally, some native leaders preached moral reform—especially temperance—as loudly as Quaker or competing Protestant missionaries. Bitter differences would arise among the Senecas about the proper course for accommodation with the ever-encroaching white world, but few indulged the illusion that no accommodation was necessary. That accommodation was gendered, with, for example, some men perhaps more likely than women to abandon the traditional sexual division of labor and cooperative work patterns. On the other hand, some disputes over the proper response to changing times cut across gender lines, with factions cleaving along contours of kinship or local residence, for example, dividing Seneca men and women into camps according to their relative positions on religious changes or on land controversies.

Permeating the history of Seneca negotiation of their colonial predicament in postcolonial America was the *Gaiwiio*, the "good word," or Code of Handsome Lake, which emerged in the apocalyptic visions of the Seneca prophet, beginning in 1799, and mediated the experience and accommodation of Seneca and other Iroquois people. In cooperation and conflict with outside forces, Seneca "modernization" occurred in a culturally specific way, shaped significantly by the "new religion" that became "the Old Way of Handsome Lake." The prophet of this new religion was a dissolute Seneca man named Handsome Lake. Having returned from an extended drunken binge, in which he had imbibed much and eaten little, he took to bed in the cabin of his daughter, sick and broken. On June 15, 1799, in a state of depression, bitterness, and suspicion, he apparently passed away, but within an hour or two he had revived to relate a fabulous vision.[12] Another trance occurred on August 8, and they would continue throughout the rest of the prophet's life, until his death in 1815. In his visions, Handsome Lake described the evil practices that saddened and angered the Seneca Great Spirit: They were whiskey (*One-ga*), witchcraft (*Got-gon*), compelling charms (*Gawenodus-ha*), and abortion or sterility magic (*Yondwi-nais-swa-yas*, literally, "she cuts it off by abortion").[13] The people were warned to confess, repent, and avoid sin; especially, they should be on guard against witches and the devil and "quit all kinds of frolicking and danceing except the worship dance."[14]

Those who refused to change their ways would endure a horrific Seneca Inferno. Some tortures were reserved especially for women. Handsome Lake personified the sin of witchcraft in his description of a woman who was alternately thrust into a cauldron of boiling liquid and then jerked out to freeze in the cold. "Such things happen to those who will not believe in Gaiwiio," he warned. A woman who had used love magic to attract men appeared; formerly beautiful, she was now "parched to the bone," with exfoliating flesh and writhing serpents in all the hair of her body, naked and hideous. And the prophet saw as well a woman whose delight on earth had been *gaknowe-haat* (to copulate). The Punisher "lifted up [a phallic] object from a pile and thrust it within her. Now the object was like *ha'ji-no ganaa* [a penis], and it was red hot." "You have seen the punishment of the immoral woman," the angels told Handsome Lake.[15]

Men did not escape torture from the Punisher, yet women, unlike men, were demonized for sexual transgression, now defined in ways more congruent with white prescriptions. Moreover, it is difficult to see the Punisher's brutal treatment of "immoral" women, like rape in general, as anything but the deployment of violence in the service of demeaning and disempowering women.[16]

Handsome Lake's revelations are striking in their reworking of Iroquois gender arrangements, particularly their attempt to remake Iroquois families into patriarchal units, and in their feminization of Iroquois demonology. As we have seen, the evils most reviled by the prophet emphasized female transgression, which the emerging code revised and elaborated. The specter of whiskey afflicted men and women alike,[17] but witchcraft (now more particularly feminized), use of charms, and abortion were *women's* offenses. Such female personification in Handsome Lake's grim visions heaped inordinate blame on women for the Senecas' fate, and the prophet's witch-hunts seemed to focus Seneca fear and attention on an internal and female enemy. Simultaneously, Handsome Lake's message functioned to elevate the social and political position of middle-aged men—patriarchs—and to constrain women and redefine their roles and spheres. His cult of true Seneca womanhood idealized those women who embodied, in a particular, revised Seneca fashion, the cardinal virtues of piety, purity, submissiveness, and domesticity.[18]

Women (and men) were expected to show their piety to the Creator and his prophet by faithfully performing his ceremonies and celebrating the important cycle of festivals.[19] Women's purity would be protected by avoiding drink, adultery, witchcraft or other forms of magic, and abortion. Whiskey, the prophet warned, led to all sorts of evil, especially witchcraft. Informal divorce, which traditionally had allowed Iroquois women great flexibility in ending relationships and initiating new ones, simply by excluding old partners from or inviting new partners into their houses, was rejected and defined essentially as infidelity or adultery. A woman who took up with another man while her husband was away "makes great mischief . . . and does a great wrong before the Creator." But such "infidelity" was to be tolerated and ignored by a woman similarly wronged by her spouse. The code dictated that such a woman should welcome her philandering husband home, treating him "cordially as if no trouble had occurred. . . . Be peaceful and remain silent."[20]

Purity among Seneca women, and in their households, took on a more concrete and visible form as well, especially with the advent of Quaker women at Tunesassah beginning in 1805. We do not know if Handsome Lake linked cleanliness with godliness and moral purity, but the missionary Friends certainly did, encouraging, for example, the production of soap as part of women's and girls' new home manufacturing responsibilities.

Seneca women were to learn and practice submissiveness within their households, which became increasingly limited, nuclear, and patriarchal under Handsome Lake's guidance. The Creator preferred that "the married should live together"—that is, as "man and wife" in their own separate house, not in a larger matrilineal household. Striking at maternal authority and control, the code anticipated (or described) resentment by women against men who increasingly asserted their control of the family's children; it imagined (and warned against) "the woman [who] discovers that the man, her husband, loves his child and she is very jealous and spreads evil reports of him." Ironically, as white sentimental culture was transferring responsibility for children from fathers to mothers, the prophet's syncretic prescriptions seemed to promote an older form of white patriarchy. And it sought to sever the bonds that joined daughters and mothers, formerly members of the same households, with the latter representing the strongest conservative force supporting matrilineality. Mothers were suspected of intervening in their daughters' lives "to prevent further suffering" through frequent childbirth and of encouraging daughters to induce abortions through malignant magic and charms. Allegedly jealous of their daughters' happiness under new patriarchal regimes, mothers offered their daughters evil advice to turn them against their husbands. "Says the old woman," according to the code, "My daughter, your spirits are dull, you are not bright. When I was young I was not so agreeable. I was harsh with my husband." Transforming conventional female assertiveness into harshness, and legitimate female authority into meddlesomeness, the prophet lamented "the tendency of old women to breed mischief. Such work must stop."[21]

Along with piety, purity, and submissiveness, the nature of domesticity was being renegotiated in Seneca society. Seneca women's place had always been simultaneously in the home and beyond it, as horticulturalists and gatherers, and as participants in community politics. Although Handsome Lake monopolized great amounts of power and sometimes used it to silence or defeat his political enemies locally, women remained active in public affairs, and they retained significant reserves of power. Ultimately, Seneca revitalization would be negotiated, indeed even feminized.

We are left with the question, nonetheless: Why were women singled out? Was there a conscious misogyny in Handsome Lake's teachings, reforms, and witch-hunts? Quaker missionaries were only the most recent representatives of patriarchal order, but Seneca dependency now rendered the Friends' message and program more attractive and necessary as a means of survival, at least to men like Handsome Lake. The prophet imbibed aspects of white patriarchy, which he reworked to fit his purposes. In a sense, women made likely targets, not as women qua women, but as a center of power within Seneca society that potentially or actually stood athwart Handsome Lake's program. And as vital members of rival lineages and communities, women were implicated in other aspects of the power struggle that coincided with the rise of Handsome Lake and his particular, syncretic solutions to Seneca demoralization and dependency. The complexity of this internal Seneca contest for power, reform, and survival suggests the embedded nature of gender as a vector of identity and interest, for powerful women were simultaneously members of lineages and clans and residents of particular towns and villages. The Senecas' complicated, multiple, and cross-cutting identities and social roles—not to mention the visceral distress and confusion of their predicament and the prophet's message of hope—help to account for the support Handsome Lake won while they also ensured that his program would be challenged and negotiated.

Handsome Lake did not invent patriarchy, nor was he the first to introduce misogynous witch-hunting to Iroquoia. The prophet endorsed these trends and gave them new momentum. Whether the patriarchal dimensions of his program were unself-consciously acquired from white brethren or deployed opportunistically to acquire white support and constrain the forces of tradition, especially represented by senior women, is not certain. It is clear, however, that attacks on women played a central role in the prophet's program, which largely feminized Iroquois demonology, demonized some Seneca women, and generally undermined women's social and religious status and authority.

Witches and witchcraft were not new to the Iroquois. According to the Jesuit missionary and ethnographer, Father Joseph-François Lafitau, who lived among the Iroquois early in the eighteenth century, "The men and women who cast spells [sorcerers] are regarded . . . as *agotkon* or spirits because of the traffic which people think that they have with the spirits or tutelary geniuses. . . . Those who cast spells have no other aim than to harm and work harm." These "evil ones" are "the authors of their curses and witchcraft."[22] *Agotkon, utgon,* or *otkon*, for the Iroquois, was the evil power or force that witches personified, as they mobilized *orenda*, or power, for evil rather than benevolent purposes to injure others, even their own kin. Witches—both women and men—inspired near universal fear among the Senecas and other Iroquoians, and those suspected of such maleficence were hated and avoided. Even Lafitau, who decried native shamans as *jongleurs* ("jugglers"), tricksters, and charlatans, nonetheless distinguished their efforts from those of witches, who inspired considerable antipathy among the Iroquois.[23]

Witches' afflictions threatened the mental and physical health of individuals and entire communities. Iroquois men and women struggled to discern whether the afflictions that periodically beset them were the result of natural processes or sinister magic. When natural remedies failed to produce results, and when "dream-guessing" rituals failed to have their therapeutic effect, it became clear that witchcraft lurked nearby. In a society based on consensus and the avoidance of outward expressions of conflict, witchcraft offered a covert means to assault antagonists within Iroquois communities, to indulge one's hatreds, rivalries, and jealousies in secret ways. Fear of witches certainly encouraged circumspection and repression of aggressive acts among the Iroquois; but it also bred endemic suspicion. Such was the danger of witchcraft that the Iroquois, like the Puritans, would "not suffer a witch to live." They sanctioned the execution of witches, as quickly as the act could be carried out, and they allowed witch-killing even among kin. A witch discovered among one's own lineage or clan, after all, could be more dangerous than one operating from afar—he or she could tear the heart out of one's family.[24]

Was witch-fear, diabolical sorcery, and witch-hunting gendered among the Senecas and other Iroquois in this earlier era? It is now difficult to know precisely how, but despite the inevitable silences of the documentary record, it seems clear that those suspected, accused, and executed among the Iroquois were no more apt to be women than men. It is suggestive, for example, that perhaps the most venerable witch among the Iroquois was Atotarho (or, in Onondaga, Thadodaho), the powerful male shaman and sorcerer of the Iroquois political creation myth. Likewise, Iroquois communities repeatedly accused Jesuit missionaries of committing acts of malevolence, often attributing to them the contagions that swept through Iroquoia in the seventeenth century.[25] Examples of witchcraft accusations against men could be multipled, but the point here is not to assert that such manipulation of evil was predominantly a male craft. It was not. Instead, careful reading of documentary sources, folk narratives, linguistical evidence, and archaeology suggests that Iroquois men and women believed, practiced, feared, and suffered witchcraft equally.[26]

But "traditional" witchcraft of the seventeenth and early eighteenth centuries was remade into a new "traditional" practice after Iroquois autonomy was destroyed and the Iroquois people faced their own, unprecedented Critical Period following the American Revolution. The feminization of Seneca witchcraft seems understandable only in the context of this crisis and the new state of dependency it thrust upon them. Ironically, as white Americans distanced themselves from the witch-hunts of Salem, Iroquois theology increasingly linked Seneca fathers with Puritan forefathers.

With the meteoric rise of Handsome Lake to prominence among the Allegany Senecas,[27] witch-hunting flourished. Handsome Lake's prophetic career had begun in an atmosphere of dread and foreboding over witchery. Authorized by the "frequent interviews" he claimed to have with "heavenly messengers," the prophet "succeeded in propagating a belief among the natives, that most of their bodily afflictions and disorders arose from witchcraft, and undertook to point out the individuals who had the power of inflicting these evils," according to a Quaker observer.[28] Handsome Lake's 1799 visions and prophecies precipitated the murder of one female "witch" and soon led to the implication and execution of another old woman accused of the same nefarious crime.[29]

So began Handsome Lake's campaign for reform and against "witches" who threatened his community and his new way. The prophet's purges are inscribed in the surviving documentary record, appearing in the writings of Quakers and other literate white settlers and officials and in Seneca oral traditions, religious narratives, and codes. There is much that we will never know about the Handsome Lake era witch-hunts, and conclusions about their scope and nature must remain tentative. How many were accused, and how many were executed? Which lineages, clans, and villages did they represent? How many were women and how many were men? Answers to these questions may ultimately be unanswerable. Nonetheless, Seneca traditions should not be dismissed as "mere" folktales and "superstition." As one ethnographer of the Iroquois has commented, "Most men and women were walking archives." Seneca recollections of events like the Handsome Lake witch-hunts, recorded in folk texts, deserve careful scrutiny.[30]

Witchcraft accusations, even executions, are notoriously difficult to track for historians. Mary Jemison, the famous "white woman of the Genesee," who had been captured by Indians in 1755 and subsequently adopted by Senecas (with whom she chose to live out her life), for example, claimed that "witches" "had been executed in almost every year since she [had] lived on the Genesee"; "from such trifling causes thousands have lost their lives." Independent confirmation of most of these executions is lacking, and the number is almost certainly exaggerated, but the magnitude of such an exaggeration is unknown. Analysis based on fragmentary evidence nevertheless leaves the distinct impression that those challenging community orthodoxy (whether based on "traditionalism" or new nativism) generally ran the greatest risk of witchcraft accusation. And increasingly in the late eighteenth and early nineteenth centuries it seems that women predominated among the suspected and accused.[31]

Among the most prominent and best documented events in Handsome Lake's witch-hunting campaign is the crisis initiated by witchcraft accusations in 1801, which threatened to embroil the Senecas and local Munsee Delawares, as well as their white neighbors, in war. When the prophet's niece, Jiiwi, took ill and failed to respond to treatment, Handsome Lake accused "sundry old women & men of the Delaware Nation" living near Cattaraugus, including perhaps a Munsee woman jealous of Jiiwi for having conceived a child with Silver Heels, a young chief residing at the Delaware settlement. A council at Buffalo Creek supported Handsome Lake's diagnosis, and ruled "that those persons accused of Witchcraft should be threatened with Death, in case they persisted in bewitching the People." Jiiwi's death, it was feared, would bring the execution of hostages by the Senecas and likely lead to intervention by the Delawares' western kinspeople. Quaker missionaries attempted to pacify the Senecas by assuring them that the Munsees "have no such power [of witchcraft], and we are sure it is the bad Spirit which puts such suspicions about Witchcraft into your Hearts, in order to make discord and raise War among you." Fortunately, the afflicted young woman recovered, the "witches" apparently desisted, and a major crisis was averted.[32]

According to later Quaker reports, by 1803 "very little if any improvement either in sobriety or industry [was] discoverable" among the Munsees living at Cattaraugus. It may be that the resistance of the Munsee-Delaware community to reform, nativist or Quaker, helped fuel the prophet's suspicions, especially given Handsome Lake's equation of whiskey and witchcraft. Moreover, Senecas had long suspected Munsees generally of an attachment to witchcraft and sorcery. Intriguing as well, though frankly speculative, is the possibility that these Munsee-Delawares were more readily seen as "witches" because they had been represented collectively within the Iroquois league as "women" since the mid-eighteenth century. Sometime in the 1740s the Six Nations and Delawares had settled their long-standing differences and agreed to a peaceful association in which the Delawares would be "the woman"; that is, as "women," Delawares received Iroquois protection and would eschew independent warfare, focusing instead on the cultivation of peace (especially women's responsibility among the Iroquois). While Iroquois and other Native people did not consider the relationship demeaning to the Delawares, one might wonder if the meanings or implications of gendered metaphors and symbolic language had shifted by the nineteenth century.[33]

Although by 1810 the Munsee community had moved west, Seneca tradition relates that the great witch-hunt continued. Witch-fear, and no doubt fear of witch-hunters, persisted. The terrors of the witch-hunt were coupled with the possibility of forgiveness, redemption, and reintegration into the community as the Code of Handsome Lake institutionalized confession and repentance. Did such a mechanism for rehabilitation actually encourage women terrified of being accused to own malefic acts or intentions falsely, as a means of preserving their lives? Confession—whether false or sincere—would have reduced the number of executions for witchcraft in Seneca communities, but it may well have had the additional effect of confirming the connection between womanhood and witchery.[34]

Seneca oral tradition preserved in the Code of Handsome Lake suggests that women predominated among the suspected and accused. Several cases display the feminization of Seneca witchcraft, an innovation of the prophet and, more broadly, of his times. Generalizing from the case of these two witches at Cold Spring, who were publicly and fatally whipped, Handsome Lake himself is said to have remarked, "It was natural that foolish women should have done what these did." And Handsome Lake's vision of the apocalypse associated evil with women's practice of witchcraft, predicting that "a time will come when a woman will be seen performing her witch spells in the daylight. Then will you know that the end is near. She will run through the neighborhood boasting how many she has slain by her sorcery."[35]

The less frequent witchcraft accusation leveled against a man—as against the famous Red Jacket himself, Handsome Lake's rival at Buffalo Creek—does not necessarily challenge the emerging general tendency of female witchery. But it does prod us to see Seneca witch-hunting as a complex phenomenon, gendered but also affected by matters of kinship, localism, and political rivalry. If the cast of characters is often murky in nineteenth-century Seneca witch-hunting dramas, here at least the opposing actors were clear. Red Jacket (c. 1758–1830) is often described as the most prominent "conservative" leader among the early-nineteenth-century Senecas, in contrast to Cornplanter (c. 1730s–1836), Handsome Lake's half-brother, who most successfully represented Seneca "progressivism." It is clear that Cornplanter and Handsome Lake, on the one hand, and Red Jacket, on the other, advocated different courses in Seneca accommodation to their predicament, with the former favoring adoption (at least selectively) of white customs and practices, and the latter, in increasingly more absolute terms, opposing alterations of Seneca life. As a rival source of power, Red Jacket was an obstacle to Handsome Lake's reforms; Red Jacket's oppositional position courted the prophet's ire and in 1801 precipitated a witchcraft accusation. Factionalism and political contention are crucial in explaining Handsome Lake's denunciation of, and ongoing rivalry with, Red Jacket, but they should be considered in a broader, gendered context. The Buffalo Creek chief and orator often acted as Seneca women's speaker, advocating women's interests, particularly the protection of Seneca land and its ownership by women. In this role, Red Jacket associated himself with other forces of opposition and may well have represented for Handsome Lake a gendered, feminized demon. Red Jacket managed to clear his name; Handsome Lake could not make the witchcraft charge stick. Perhaps it lacked credibility in the increasingly patriarchal climate he had helped to create.[36]

Although available sources hardly permit the sort of statistical analysis applied to seventeenth-century New England, it does seem that among early-nineteenth-century Senecas women were more often accused than men, that accusations against women were more likely to be believed, and that women "witches" were more likely to suffer execution. In a peculiarly circular manner, increasing implication of women as witches by Handsome Lake and others may have predisposed Senecas to believe charges against women and, in a related fashion, to reject those leveled against men more readily, especially men of prominence. Even if Handsome Lake's demonization of women in witch-hunts had more to do with their power than their gender, matters of gender and power are not easily distinguished, and the practical consequences of the prophet's gendered purges were significant—predominantly accusing women tended to suggest that women more than men performed witchcraft.

Handsome Lake, who, some believe, himself died at the hands of a witch, never relented in his pursuit. All hostility or opposition to his prescriptions could be explained as malevolence. The promiscuity of such accusations clearly troubled other members of the Seneca communities, both Native and white, and the reaction of Quaker missionaries and Seneca chiefs in 1809 to such violence suggests their impact. In about 1808, a "witch" (gender now unknown) was killed in front of the Cold Spring longhouse, where Handsome Lake lived. Was this an isolated case? A council between Seneca leaders and delegates of the Friends' Indian Committee, convened at least in part to deal with a witch-hunting crisis among the Allegany Senecas, suggests it was not. At the meeting Cornplanter expressed his hope that "we shall be careful in the future how we take the lives of any for witchcraft without being sure that they are Guilty, and he thought it very difficult to prove it."[37]

But, ironically, while Quakers strove to persuade Senecas that witchcraft was mere superstition and delusion, their references to "Good" and "Bad Spirits" may well have confirmed Seneca beliefs in the reality of witches, even if particular accusations lacked merit. In advocating temperance, for example, a Friend in 1802 had written that Handsome Lake "has endeavored to suppress the use of strong drink by propogating a belief amongst the Natives that whiskey is the Great Engine which the bad spirit uses to introduce Witchcraft and many other evils amongst the Indians. This *together with the advice of the Friends* has for the present had a favorable effect."[38] The Quakers' use of language similar to Handsome Lake's in their own prescriptions, and their cooperation in Native reform, seemed to signal an endorsement of sorts.

As in the witchcraft crisis in Salem, Massachusetts, in 1692, when the trials at Allegany ended, fear of witchcraft did not. New England clerical leaders like Increase Mather may have criticized the use of spectral evidence but not the belief in the manipulations of Satan; indeed, the ministers momentarily elevated conceptions of Satan's power by arguing that he could possess souls without the permission of his victims. Likewise, while the procedures used to accuse and prosecute "witches" as well as the numbers of those tried in early-nineteenth-century Seneca communities drew criticism, the fact of witches and their malefic power was apparently not rejected.[39]

The Code of Handsome Lake, if not Handsome Lake himself, came to reject the execution of witches, and opposition to apparent excesses—especially when prominent men were accused—forced the prophet to moderate his indictments, and even to leave Cold Spring for Tonawanda. But outlawing witchcraft was not the same as denying its presence. Declaring the illegitimacy of witchery in fact was nothing new; it had never been socially sanctioned. And Handsome Lake's witch-hunts themselves seemed to confirm that witchcraft—the evil, covert resistance to his nativist reform—remained a threat. In a self-fulfilling fashion, then, the prophet's assault on witchcraft itself kept witchcraft alive.

After Handsome Lake's death, another witch crisis erupted at Allegany, which again required Quaker intervention. A delegation of Friends visiting from Philadelphia in October of 1817 was beckoned to Cold Spring, where they found the chiefs in council and in "great distress." A local man had just been buried, but in his lingering sickness he had claimed to be bewitched. Worse yet, he had "charged one of their Chiefs with having some agency in it," and the deceased man's brother now threatened to take revenge. According to the Quaker chronicle of these events, the Seneca chiefs "wish'd our interference." Obligingly, the Quakers assured them that the victim's death had not been the result of witchcraft and that "it is quite time you took measures to do away [with] such notions among your people." "Brothers—you must by all means prevent one killing another for such supposed, or even real injuries," they urged. Curiously, their remarks expressed more disdain for taking justice into one's own hands than for the delusion of witchcraft that threatened to call forth the vengeance of the bereaved. Again, the Quakers seemed to emphasize that the particular case lacked merit rather than that the "supposed, or even real injuries" of witchcraft did not exist. The chiefs visited the accusing man and were able to restore him to reason, thus ending the crisis, to the great relief of the Seneca leaders. We can only speculate whether such community pressure would have been mobilized to dissuade the accuser if the object of his charges had been a woman, or whether in such a circumstance the charges would have been read as irrational expressions of feverish delirium or deep grief rather than as the legitimate diagnosis of a witch's malignancy. And we cannot know if, or to what extent, perceived excesses of earlier witch-hunts had produced a Salem-like recoil from promiscuous accusation and prosecution of "witches."[40]

Seneca women were not mere victims of Handsome Lake's reforms, any more than the Iroquois generally were, simply, passive victims of U.S. colonialism. The power of the prophet's message made it compelling, and the new religion's teachings offered a means of accommodating change while maintaining Iroquois ethnic identity and protecting some measure of autonomy. People and communities in stress often reinvent themselves in order to survive, but the new identities available to such groups are limited by imagination and constraining circumstances. Women as well as men somehow found in the new way of Handsome Lake a prospect they could imagine, and as they followed the prophet—either as devotees or, more distantly, as fellow travelers—they negotiated and renegotiated the terms of his charter and their own future.

Seneca women in particular may have found their adjustments painful—the new Seneca "traditional" world strikes us, perhaps, as much harsher and less respectful of women than the older Seneca traditional world. But the evolving, colonial situation of Senecas in postcolonial New York, while gendered, inflicted pain on men as well as women. Ironically, as the new religion became "the Old Way of Handsome Lake,"[41] it was increasingly "feminized." U.S. colonialism in general—with its destruction and alienation of hunting grounds, its conquest and then monopolization of military activity, and its reduction of native peoples to diplomatic insignificance—undermined traditional male activities—that is, hunting, warfare, and diplomacy. At the same time, despite Christianization and "civilization" programs, women's traditional activities among the Iroquois, like farming, flourished. And as a result, the rituals associated with women's social and economic contributions continued. In a sense, the patriarchal nature of Handsome Lake's Good Message might be read as a male attempt to restore a gender balance in Iroquois traditional life. Moreover, as the new way matured, women played an increasingly prominent role, as ritualists, as deaconlike "faithkeepers," and as "fortunetellers," teachers, interpreters of signs, diagnosticians, and prescribers of remedies.[42]

If we might return now to where we began, with the trial of Tommy Jemmy, we might conclude that, by the 1820s, Senecas had come a long way in their acculturation process. They had "advanced" to such a degree that their witch-hunting had begun to resemble seventeenth-century Salem. Such ironies abounded in colonial and postcolonial America. How was Seneca—the place and its people—*possessed*? Like Salem, Massachusetts, Seneca country was a site of contention, as the land was "tamed," and as new forms of economic enterprise, and ways of life, struggled to prevail. Both places—though in different ways—were colonized by outsiders, possessed in culturally specific ways. And, amid conflicts over land, modes of production, and political power, both places were "possessed" by their indigenous devils. That is, the residents of Salem and of Seneca communities struggled among themselves, as they tried to accommodate their changing worlds, control their destinies, and define the particular natures of their social, cultural, and spiritual landscapes. In the midst of their rise and fall, death and rebirth, Indian people like other Americans struggled bitterly and acted creatively as they imagined and sought alternative futures.

Finally, our story has involved the struggle to possess history. Those with the greatest degree of self-possession sought to assert their claims on "tradition" and to define their group's past as well as future. The Seneca prophet invented a "new way" that possessed a particular Iroquois past and became "the Old Way of Handsome Lake." The Seneca orator Red Jacket sought to possess even the alien history of Salem, and by playing on cultural conflicts within white society he (and Handsome Lake) found ways to conceal and protect Iroquois "traditional" life as it was being remade. On the other hand, missionaries and "civilizers" among the Senecas worked to integrate the Indians into an imperial history of human advancement. The end of Seneca history thus would occur with full assimilation.[43]

This contest, to possess history and one's self, was, like much of our story, gendered. The Seneca landscape was a doubly contested ground because, while Iroquois men and women negotiated their options, white men and women struggled too, not only to define the Indians' future but also to work out their own, particularly the organization of gender in their own new world.

Notes

1. William L. Stone, *The Life and Times of Red-Jacket, or Sa-Go-Ye-Wat-Ha; being the Sequel to the History of the Six Nations* (New York, 1841), 316; the incident is treated on pp. 316–22.

2. The classic account of Seneca revitalization is Anthony F. C. Wallace, *The Death and Rebirth of the Seneca* (New York, 1970). Elisabeth Tooker, "On the Development of the Handsome Lake Religion," *Proceedings of the American Philosophical Society* 133, no. 1 (1989): 35–50, offers some valuable correctives to Wallace.

3. Stone, *Life and Times of Red-Jacket,* 318.

4. Ibid., 320–21. At Salem during the 1692 witch crisis, twenty were executed, and four others died while in prison, most of them women. See Paul Boyer and Stephen Nissenbaum, eds., *The Salem Witchcraft Papers: Verbatim Transcripts of the Legal Documents of the Salem Witchcraft Outbreak of 1692*, 3 vols. (New York, 1977), I: 3.

5. Contact between the people of the Five Nations of the Iroquois and Europeans commenced, at least indirectly, through the European materials that filtered into Iroquoia as early as the second quarter of the sixteenth century; see James W. Bradley, *Evolution of the Onondaga Iroquois: Accommodating Change, 1500–1655* (Syracuse, N.Y., 1987), esp. 80. The advent of European people, their material culture and technologies, would precipitate greater changes in the future, but the larger pattern of assimilating foreign objects, ideas, and people on Iroquois terms would continue as long as Iroquois people retained a modicum of autonomy and power. On this theme, see Matthew Dennis, *Cultivating a Landscape of Peace: Iroquois-European Encounters in Seventeenth-Century America* (Ithaca, N.Y., 1993).

6. See Dennis, *Cultivating a Landscape of Peace*; Daniel K. Richter, *The Ordeal of the Longhouse: The Peoples of the Iroquois League in the Era of European Colonization* (Chapel Hill, N.C., 1992) and Francis Jennings, *The Ambiguous Iroquois Empire: The Covenant Chain Confederation of Indian Tribes with English Colonies from Its beginning to the Lancaster Treaty of 1744* (New York, 1984); the latter two works are especially insightful about the eighteenth-century Iroquois experience. See also Dean R. Snow, *The Iroquois* (Oxford, 1994).

7. See esp. Barbara Graymont, *The Iroquois in the American Revolution* (Syracuse, N.Y., 1972). More generally, see Colin G. Calloway, *The American Revolution in Indian Country* (Cambridge, 1995), esp. chs. 4 and 5; Calloway concludes: "The Six Nations' experience in the Revolution was one of almost total disaster" (108).

8. See Wallace, *Death and Rebirth of the Seneca*, 144, 168, 194–96; Michael N. McConnell, *A Country Between: The Upper Ohio Valley and Its Peoples, 1724–1774* (Lincoln, Neb., 1992); Dean R. Snow and Kim M. Lanphear,

"European Contact and Indian Depopulation in the Northeast: The Timing of the First Epidemics," *Ethnohistory* 35 (Winter 1988): 15–33.

9. "Slums in the Wilderness" is the title of ch. 7 in Wallace, *Death and Rebirth of the Seneca.* For a summary analysis of Seneca history and geography, see Thomas S. Abler and Elisabeth Tooker, "Seneca," in *Handbook of North American Indians: Northeast*, ed. Bruce G. Trigger (Washington, D.C., 1978), 15:505–17; see 507–13 for assessment of the postrevolutionary period through the mid-nineteenth century and for maps of the Seneca reservations. See also Tooker, "Iroquois since 1820," ibid., 449–65.

10. The Quaker program of "civilization" among the Senecas can be reconstructed from records and minutes of the Committee Appointed by the Yearly Meeting of Friends Pennsylvania, New York, &c for Promoting the Improvement and Gradual Civilization of the Indian Natives, or "Indian Committee," of the Philadelphia Yearly Meeting, housed in the Quaker Collection, Special Collections, Haverford College, Haverford, Pennsylvania. The ten boxes of diaries, reports, and correspondence (hereafter I.C. Records), as well as the ten volumes of minutes (hereafter I.C. Minutes) and other manuscripts, are also available on microfilm at the American Philosophical Society (film 824, reels 1–12), where I examined them. See also the published writings of participants, including Halliday Jackson, *Civilization of the Indian Nations; or, a brief view of the Friendly Conduct of William Penn toward them . . . and a concise narrative of the proceedings of the Yearly Meeting of Friends . . . since the year 1795, in promoting their improvement and gradual civilization* (Philadelphia, 1830); Merle H. Deardorff and George S. Snyderman, eds., "A Nineteenth-Century Journal of a Visit to the Indians of New York," *Proceedings of the American Philosophical Society* 100, no. 6 (December 1956): 582–612; George S. Snyderman, ed., "Halliday Jackson's Journal of a Visit Paid to the Indians of New York (1806)," ibid. 101, no. 6 (December 1957): 565–88; Anthony F. C. Wallace, ed., "Halliday Jackson's Journal to the Seneca Indians, 1798–1800 (Part I)," *Pennsylvania History* 19, no. 2 (April 1952): 117–47; and (Part II), ibid. 19, no. 3 (July 1952): 325–49.

11. On assimilationism in general, see Robert F. Berkhofer, Jr., *The White Man's Indian: Images of the American Indian from Columbus to the Present* (New York, 1978); see also Berkhofer, Jr., *Salvation and the Savage: An Analysis of Protestant Missions and the American Indian Response, 1787–1862* (Lexington, 1965). On the gendered nature of such assimilation campaigns, see Theda Perdue, "Southern Indians and the Cult of True Womanhood," in *The Web of Southern Social Relations: Women, Family, and Education*, ed. Walter J. Fraser, Jr., et al. (Athens, Ga., 1985), 35–51; Mary E. Young, "Women, Civilization, and the Indian Question," in *Clio Was a Woman: Studies in the History of American Women*, ed. Mabel E. Deutrich and Virginia C. Purdy (Washington, D.C., 1980), 98–110; Diane Rothenberg, "The Mothers of the Nation: Seneca Resistance to Quaker Intervention," in *Women and Colonization: Anthropological Perspectives*, ed. Mona Etienne and Eleanor Leacock (New York, 1980), 63–87; Nancy Shoemaker, ed., *Negotiators of Change: Historical Perspectives on Native American Women* (New York, 1994).

12. For Quaker relations of the event, see Wallace, ed., "Halliday Jackson's Journal," I: 146–47; [Halliday Jackson,] "The Visions of Connudiu [Handsome Lake] or Cornplanter's Brother," ibid., II: 341–44; "Henry Simmons' Version of the Visions," ibid., 345–49. The emergence of the prophet Handsome Lake is also noted in P. C. T. White, ed., *Lord Selkirk's Diary, 1803–1804* (Toronto, 1958), 245–46. The codified Seneca version appears in Arthur C. Parker, "The Code of

Handsome Lake, the Seneca Prophet," in *Parker on the Iroquois*, ed. William N. Fenton (1913; reprint, Syracuse, N.Y., 1968), esp. 21–26. These events are narrated more fully in Wallace, *Death and Rebirth of the Seneca*, chs. 8 and 9.

13. Parker, *Code*, 27–30.

14. "Visions of Connudiu," in Wallace, "Halliday Jackson's Journal," II: 342–43; "Henry Simmons' Version," ibid., 346–48. Wallace, *Death and Rebirth of the Seneca*, 242–48, provides a summary analysis of the second vision of Handsome Lake.

15. Parker, *Code*, 71–74.

16. Ibid., 72.

17. According to Mary Jemison, at least among the Senecas living along the Genesee River, "women never participated" in drunken "frolics" until after the Revolutionary War; thereafter, "spirits became common in our tribe, and has been used indiscriminately by both sexes," although intoxication remained more common among men than women (James E. Seaver, *A Narrative of the Life of Mrs. Mary Jemison* [1824; reprint, Syracuse, 1990], 127). According to Wallace, *Death and Rebirth of the Seneca*, 200, women in particular, as petty traders, obtained whiskey from whites and retailed it in their villages; women could thus be implicated in the alcohol problem even if men predominated among village drunkards.

18. Barbara Welter, "The Cult of True Womanhood, 1820–1860," *American Quarterly* 18 (Summer 1966): 151–74. Since Welter named the "cult," others have applied, extended, and modified the concept. See esp. Aileen S. Kraditor, ed., *Up from the Pedestal: Selected Writings in the History of American Feminism* (Chicago, 1968), which introduced the phrase "cult of domesticity" in the editor's introduction; Nancy F. Cott, *The Bonds of Womanhood: "Women's Sphere" in New England, 1780–1835* (New Haven, 1977). Mary P. Ryan, *Womanhood in America from Colonial Times to the Present* (New York, 1983), 113–65; Ryan, *Cradle of the Middle Class: The Family in Oneida County, New York, 1790–1865* (Cambridge, 1981); Linda K. Kerber, "Separate Spheres, Female Worlds, Woman's Place: The Rhetoric of Women's History," *Journal of American History* 75 (1988): 9–39.

19. The resident Friends' circumspection with regard to religion and their implicit encouragement of Senecas to identify their Creator, or Great Spirit, with the Quakers' "inner light" promoted the success of Handsome Lake's revised religious belief and practice. Such latitude allowed the prophet and his followers to design a way that was syncretically "progressive" but not Christian.

20. Parker, *Code*, 32–33. Of course, men were not exempt from moral prescriptions, just as middle-class white reformers were hardly willing to condone immorality among males. Nonetheless, constraints on men seem designed to ensure stable households and cultivate, not undermine, patriarchy, and among these Senecas, as among white populations, a double standard favorable to men seemed to exist. Admonitions against whiskey and against conventional Seneca sexuality and marriage practice, expressed both by Handsome Lake and Quaker missionaries, appear throughout the Quaker records.

21. Parker, *Code*, 31, 30, 32. The code's prescription that a "man and wife" should live together, establishing their own household, seemed to promote the common Quaker emphasis on a decentralized residence pattern that placed individual families in separate farmsteads. Friends praised those at Cold Spring in 1801 who began to live in such a manner, while criticizing others for "huddling together in town" in the manner of unassimilated Indians (see "Extract of a letter

from one of the Friends settled on the Alleghany River" [2/28/1801], I.C. Records, box 1). It became clear later, however, that the prophet supported residence in towns rather than on dispersed farmsteads, most likely for the same reasons that New England Puritans idealized concentrated village settlement—it promoted ritual life and knit the community together in a web of mutual support and surveillance.

22. William N. Fenton and Elizabeth Moore, eds. and trans., *Lafitau's Customs of the American Indians Compared to the Customs of Primitive Times, Publications of the Champlain Society*, no. 49, 2 vols. (1724; reprint, Toronto, 1977), I: 241.

23. The term "witchcraft" is used here to refer to all forms of malevolence (and "witch" refers to those who directed it) among the Iroquois. While the practices and practitioners designated by such terms certainly varied, especially over time and across cultural boundaries, the Iroquois themselves apparently did not divide malevolent acts or distinguish terminologically between, say, those of "witches" and those of "sorcerers." See Annemarie Shimony, "Iroquois Witchcraft at Six Nations," in *Systems of Witchcraft and Sorcery*, ed. Deward E. Walker, Jr. (Moscow, Idaho, 1970), 239–65, esp. 242–43. On Iroquois notions of *otkon* and *orenda* and witchcraft beliefs and practices see Lafitau, *Customs of the American Indians*, I: 240–41; Wallace, *Death and Rebirth of the Seneca*, 84; Ake Hultkrantz, *The Religions of the American Indians*, trans. Monica Setterwall (Berkeley, 1979), 12; Richter, *Ordeal of the Longhouse*, 24–25; Snow, *The Iroquois*, 54, 96, 98; Dennis, *Cultivating a Landscape of Peace*, 90–94. See also George S. Snyderman, "Witches, Witchcraft, and Allegany Seneca Medicine," *Proceedings of the American Philosophical Society* 127, no. 4 (1983): 263–77; David Blanchard, "Who or What's a Witch? Iroquois Persons of Power," *American Indian Quarterly* 6, no. 3–4 (1982): 218–37; DeCost Smith, "Witchcraft and Demonism of the Modern Iroquois," *Journal of American Folk-Lore* 1, no. 3 (1888): 184–93; Smith, "Onondaga Customs," ibid., 195–98; Smith, "Additional Notes on Onondaga Witchcraft and Hon-do-i," ibid. 2, no. 7 (1889): 277–81; Lewis Henry Morgan, *The League of the Ho-de-no-sau-nee, Iroquois*, ed., William N. Fenton (1851; reprint, Secaucus, N.J., 1962), 164–65; Annemarie Anrod Shimony, *Conservatism among the Iroquois at the Six Nations Reserve, Yale University Publications in Anthropology* 65 (New Haven, 1961), esp. 261–88; Bruce G. Trigger, *The Children of Aataentsic: A History of the Huron People to 1660*, 2 vols. (Montreal, 1976), I: 66–67, 81, 424–25, 500, 534–44, 589–601, 646, 657, 696, 708, 715–19; Elisabeth Tooker, *An Ethnography of the Huron Indians, 1615–1649, Bureau of American Ethnology Bulletin* 190 (Washington, D.C., 1964), 117–20. The latter two works focus on the culturally similar Iroquoians, the Hurons; most scholars of the seventeenth-century Iroquois, facing gaps in the documentary record, accept generalizations about Iroquois culture that draw on evidence from other related Iroquoians, especially the Hurons.

The secondary works listed above base their discussion of Iroquoian witchcraft belief and practice in the seventeenth and eighteenth centuries on extensive contemporary references to such native belief and practice. See esp. Reuben Gold Thwaites, trans. and ed., *The Jesuit Relations and Allied Documents*, 73 vols. (Cleveland, 1896–1901).

24. See esp. Wallace, *Death and Rebirth of the Seneca*, 76–77, 84; Shimony, *Conservatism among the Iroquois*, 261–62. Father Francesco Giuseppe Bressani's relation of 1653, based on his missionary work primarily among the Hurons, reported that "the confidence of the Savages in the multiplicity of spells and

witchcraft went so far, that upon mere suspicion they often killed and burned even their fellow-countrymen, without any other accuser or judge than a dying man, who said that he had been bewitched by such a one, who was killing him" (Thwaites, *Jesuit Relations*, 39: 27).

25. The epic of the Peacemaker exists in numerous full and fragmentary versions. For a description and analysis of the epic see William N. Fenton's introduction to Arthur C. Parker, *Parker on the Iroquois*, ed. William N. Fenton (Syracuse, N.Y., 1968), 38–46. A convenient summary version is Paul A. W. Wallace, *The White Roots of Peace* (Philadelphia, 1946). See also the discussion in Dennis, *Cultivating a Landscape of Peace*, esp. 91, 93–94. For an example of a Jesuit executed as a "witch" see Thwaites, *Jesuit Relations*, 30:229; 31:73–75.

26. Scholars of Iroquois culture and history agree almost uniformly that Iroquois "witches" could be women *or* men; scholars have not argued for any gender imbalance in such accusations. See, for example, Snow, *The Iroquois*, 98: "Witches, it was believed, could be either male or female"; or Shimony, "Iroquois Witchcraft at Six Nations," 243: "The belief in witches, both male and female, is a well-documented indigenous trait."

27. According to Halliday Jackson, *Civilization of the American Natives*, 42, by 1801 Handsome Lake had "acquired considerable influence in the nation, so as to be appointed high priest and chief Sachem in things civil and religious"; see also ibid., 47, 50.

28. Ibid., 42.

29. Wallace, *Death and Rebirth of the Seneca*, 261–62.

30. On the processes and powers of Iroquois memory, see William N. Fenton, "Structure, Continuity, and Change in the Process of Iroquois Treaty Making," in *The History and Culture of Iroquois Diplomacy: An Interdisciplinary Guide to the Treaties of the Six Nations and Their League*, ed. Francis Jennings et al. (Syracuse, N.Y., 1985), 13, 34 n. 28. See Walter J. Ong on *Orality and Literacy: The Technologizing of the Word* (London, 1982), esp. 57–68, on oral memorization; James Axtell, *The Invasion Within: The Contest of Cultures in Colonial North America* (New York, 1985), 14–15, discusses the implications of orality in the face-to-face worlds of American Indians in the colonial period.

31. See James E. Seaver, *Narrative of the Life of Mary Jemison*, 128, on the accusation against Jemison; on the accusation against the woman cousin of Big Tree, see 159–60; here, certainly gender and kinship as well as other factors combined to render the women vulnerable to accusation of witchcraft.

32. On the Seneca-Munsẹe witch crisis see Halliday Jackson, *Civilization of the Indian Natives*, 42–43; "Joseph Ellicott's Letter Books," *Publications of the Buffalo Historical Society* (1926): 122–23 (quotation: "sundry old women . . ."); "A Message from the People called Quakers of Pennsylvania To Corn-planter and the other Chiefs of the Seneca Nation settled on the Allegeny River" (5/n.d./1801), I.C. Records, box 1 (quotation of Quaker advice); Henry Drinker, Nichlas Waln, Thos. Stewardson to "Friend" (n.d.), I.C. Records, box 1; "A Message from the People called Quakers of Pennsylvania, the children of Onas, to the Muncey Tribe of Indians settled at Cataragus" (5/23/1801), I.C. Records, box 1; William Wallace and Henry Baldwin to Thomas McKean, governor of Pennsylvania (April 14, 1801), I.C. Records, box 1; Jonathan Thomas, Joel Swaine, Jacob Taylor to the Committee (6/28/1801 and 8/3/1801), I.C. Records, box 1. See also "To David Mead and other Friends, from the 2 Principal Chiefs of Muncy and others" (April 11, 1801), I.C. Records, box 1.

33. Report of committee visiting the Seneca missions [12/14/1803], I.C. Records, box 2. On Seneca suspicions of Munsees as predisposed toward witchcraft, see Deardorff and Snyderman, eds., intro. to "A Nineteenth-Century Journal" (1806), 592; and see Wallace, *Death and Rebirth of the Seneca*, 256. On the complex meaning of the symbolic transformation of Delawares into "women," see Dennis, *Cultivating a Landscape of Peace*, 108–10, esp. 109 n. 79.

34. Benjamin Cope et al. to the Committee from Cattaraugus (8/12/1810), I.C. Records, box 2. On the institutionalization of confession and repentance, see Parker, *Code*, 69.

35. Parker, *Code*, 46, 27–29 n. 3, 58.

36. See Wallace, *Death and Rebirth of the Seneca*, 202–6, 259–60; Stone, *Life and Times of Red-Jacket*, 166–67; it should be noted that Red Jacket himself was a believer in witchcraft and caused the execution of at least one (female) victim; we have already seen his role in the defense of Tommy Jemmy, the witch-killer in 1821. Handsome Lake's accusation against Red Jacket is embedded in the *Code*, 68.

37. The 1808 execution is mentioned in a footnote, Deardorff and Snyderman, "Nineteenth Century Journal [1806]," 598 n. 18; Cornplanter's speech appears in Report to the Indian Committee (10/19/1809), I.C. Records, box 2.

38. "One of the Friends in Seneca Country," January 1802, quoted from the Logan Papers, Historical Society of Pennsylvania, in Snyderman, "Witchcraft and Allegany Seneca Medicine," 276 n. 21. On good and bad spirits, see also Jackson, *Civilization of the Indian Natives*, 65: "Brothers, we are sensible that there are two spirits at work in the minds of men. The one produces in us a disposition of love and good will toward all men, and is a comforter for all good actions. The other excites the evil thoughts and desires, and influences to bad action."

39. On continuing belief in the devil's power, which accompanied the rejection of spectral evidence at Salem, see Elizabeth Reis, *Damned Women: Sinners and Witches in Puritan New England* (Ithaca, N.Y., 1997), ch. 2. In the long run, however, Reis argues that Satan became a less proximate force in the daily lives of New England Puritans after the Salem crisis.

40. Thomas Stewardson et al., report on visit to Senecas to the Indian Committee (10/16/1817), I.C. Records, box 3.

41. Tooker, "Development of Handsome Lake Religion," observes that support for Handsome Lake was hardly universal, that his teachings continued to be controversial after his death in 1815, and that the path to institutionalization was not smooth. She dates the revivals of Handsome Lake's teachings to the 1820s and especially the 1860s, in contrast to Wallace, *Death and Rebirth of the Seneca*, who dates the renaissance to the 1840s.

42. See Annemarie Shimony, "Iroquois Religion and Women in Historical Perspective," in *Women, Religion, and Social Change*, ed. Yvonne Yazbeck Haddad and Ellison Banks Findly (Albany, N.Y., 1985), 397–418.

43. It is likely that my own "possession" of this history would be contested by those who claim exclusive ownership, especially contemporary adherents to the Longhouse Religion.

7

Sojourner Truth's Religion in Her Moment of Pentecostalism and Witchcraft

~

*Nell Irvin Painter**

Was Sojourner Truth (a.k.a. Isabella) a witch? It depends on the definition of "witch." As Nell Painter argues in this essay, historians' understanding of religious culture and identity needs to be far more expansive, particularly when it comes to African-American spirituality. Isabella's religion blended magical elements (that is, using God's power to get what she wanted) with Methodism, African spirituality, American folk culture, and the Calvinist Dutch Reformed Church. Her personal beliefs incorporated a little bit of the various religions she had encountered, and over the course of her lifetime her beliefs evolved. As a free woman, Isabella embraced a perfectionist strand of Methodism, which encouraged abstinence, simple living, and the presence of the Holy Spirit. Isabella was transformed by an overwhelming conversion experience and felt a new means of power with Jesus' love. But despite her new-found faith, according to Painter, Isabella never relinquished her traditional ways of relating to the world.

Inspired by her desire to regain her son from enslavement and retaliate against his owners/torturers, Isabella felt tremendous spiritual power; and she was amazed, and a little frightened, when her "magic" (and God's will) actually seemed to work. Did she consider herself a "witch"? Not in the seventeenth-century sense

*I would like to acknowledge the generous assistance and support that Richard Newman of the Du Bois Institute at Harvard has given me over the course of my work on Sojourner Truth.

of the word, to be sure. But if a witch is one with the power to effect good or evil magically—a definition embraced by modern witches—then Isabella may well have put herself in that category, at least in terms of this one episode. Her wrath and her will, she believed, were so strong that anything was possible.

Over her lifetime, Sojourner Truth followed a religious trajectory: Like many Americans, her religious convictions were never set in stone, and she altered her beliefs across the fifty-five years of her adulthood. In 1827–28, however, she was still known by her birth name of Isabella, and she was making the complex transformation from slavery to freedom. Over the course of her thirty or so years of life, she had spent more time in the household of her former owners, John and Sally Dumont, than she had with her parents, out of whose household she had been sold when she was ten. Her religious beliefs were as complex and contradictory as her psychological history.

As is always the case, Isabella's family (in the larger sense of the word), cultural, and psychological circumstances exerted crucial influences on her religion. The larger lesson of her life is that historians and biographers need to attend carefully to their subjects' communities and their impact on religion. In Sojourner Truth's case, this means focusing not only on what her mother, Elizabeth, taught her—the Pater Noster, or Lord's Prayer—but also how her master, John Dumont, supplied her metaphor for God's means of tracking people's behavior.

Sojourner Truth's religious history upsets many symbolic constructions that are common in the study of black life and religion. Ordinarily, scholars speak in the singular and merge the categories, so that historic black religion becomes the same thing as "the" black church, which is Protestant, and both black religion and "the" black church are automatically situated in the plantation South. But paying close attention to the experience and the beliefs and the religious communities of Sojourner Truth disrupts these assumptions. The discrepancies are instructive, and they can help us investigate the meanings of nineteenth-century black religion with sensitivity. Sojourner Truth's religion questions theories about the balance between Africanity and what, for shorthand purposes, will be called Methodism, between blackness and American-ness. Asking about Sojourner Truth immediately relocates the investigation from the Southern slave community—always assumed to be a plantation society—to places where African Americans lived surrounded by whites.

The figure we know as Sojourner Truth was born Isabella in Ulster County, New York, in the Hudson River Valley in about 1797. Although she lived with her parents until she was about ten years old, she was a slave until 1827. During her years of enslavement she lived with white families, mostly Dutch speaking, and Dutch was her first language. She was about forty-six when she became Sojourner Truth, over fifty when she bought her first house, and nearly sixty when she began to live with other black people, her daughters. Her experience as a worker and as a Christian occurred mainly in white settings.

That was the experience of most antebellum black Northerners (particularly if they lived outside large cities) and of half of antebellum black Southerners. Plantations—in which more than one black family lived and worked—were exceedingly rare north of Virginia. Black workers toiled on farms and households more among whites than blacks. Sojourner Truth's experience was that of more than one-half of her black contemporaries, a statistic that African American historiography does not reflect.

African American historiography also tends to stress continuities, preferably from Africa, rather than change within and over generations, as though the most essential characteristics of black religious practices were stable and traceable only to Africa. Sojourner Truth's religious history, again, does not conform to that mythic pattern, for although her religion may have owed some of its expressive form to Africa, her communities and her beliefs were also rooted in the magic of rural Ulster County, Dutch Calvinism, Methodist Perfectionism, millenarianism, and spiritualism, all of which she shared with a few black and many white friends and coreligionists. Her religion evolved over the course of her lifetime, a psychological phenomenon that is not unusual. Yet African American history accommodates individual growth uneasily.

Sojourner Truth's religious itinerary will not be traced in this essay. Instead, the focus will be on the complexity of her convictions at one moment in the late 1820s, when she was becoming free—both legally and psychologically. Her history is drawn from the single primary source for her life at that time, the *Narrative of Sojourner Truth*, first published in 1850. Her religious beliefs at the time were intricate, drawing upon the power both of Pentecostalism and witchcraft. Because this was 1827–28, fifteen years before she became Sojourner Truth, she will be referred to by the name she was known by then, Isabella. Purists, please bear with the importation of a twentieth-century word, "Pentecostalism," and seventeenth-century word, "witchcraft," into the early nineteenth century.

Isabella's religious sensibility in 1827 was syncretic—which is the very essence of African-American culture—and also very much in flux at the time. Her original concept of God was distant, familiar, and magical: He was a "great man" who, unlike Isabella, was literate and kept track of what should not be forgotten in a "great book." [1] God and her longtime master, John Dumont, had ways of knowing and habits of recall in common. With Dumont, as with God, Isabella sought to strike deals in order to get what she wanted. Before becoming a Methodist in 1827, Isabella was one of thousands of rural Americans who sought to control and manipulate the world and the people in it in various ways, including through using God's power to her own ends. [2] As she became a Methodist, however, she began to see worship as an end in itself, not part of a deal.

Not only was Isabella's religious culture one that blended beliefs and habits from animist West Africa, American folk culture, the Calvinist Dutch Reformed Church, and the Arminian Methodists, she was also formulating her own notions of religion in the midst of the Second Great Awakening, when even Calvinists were susceptible to the unusual enthusiasms of the revival associated with the people called Methodists. Her concept of religion was moving away from the magical, and her idea of the deity was changing from the distant, judgmental, Calvinist God to whom her mother had taught her to pray. She was coming to believe in the closer, more caring God she was encountering with the Methodists she had met more recently.

During 1827 Isabella was leaving the Afro-Dutch Reformed Calvinism and magic of her slave years for a Pentecostal perfectionism that she embraced of her own volition and to which she adhered for several decades. Holiness was her religion of freedom, and it meant living one's life in a holy way by avoiding alcohol, ostentatious dress or furnishings, dancing, and profanity. Such a style of living came easily to someone like Isabella, whose material possessions were few and who herself was poor. Isaac and Maria Van Wagenen, with whom she spent her last year in bondage in Ulster County, also held holiness values. Isabella was one of the founders of the Kingston, New York, Methodist Church in 1827, and her very inclusion indicates that it belonged to the democratic, enthusiastic, perfectionist strand of Methodism, a kind of religion that in the twentieth century would be called "Pentecostalist."

As Pentecostalists, Isabella and the Methodists with whom she worshiped laid great emphasis on the Holy Spirit, or, as they said often, simply "the Spirit." The moment they concentrated on most was Pentecost, the holiday fifty days after Easter commemorating the day after Jesus' resurrection, when the Holy Spirit filled the Apostles. The Apostles spoke in tongues (glossolalia), a practice that has distinguished many Pentecostalists since the time of the Apostles. Isabella, however, does not mention glossolalia, nor is it prominently associated with those to whom she was close. Rather than speaking in tongues, antebellum holiness people used a variety of phrases that evoked the Pentecost: "Pentecostal outpourings of the Holy Spirit," "outpouring of the Spirit," "effusions of the Holy Spirit," "a return of apostolic days," and "Pentecostal revival."[3]

The significance of Pentecost in 1827 in the context of Isabella's Methodist perfectionism was amplified by the many cultural meanings of Pinkster. "Pinkster" is Dutch for Pentecost, but Pinkster in early-nineteenth-century New York was not merely the Dutch celebration of the Pentecost or, hence, of the Holy Spirit. Pinkster had also become the only moment in which black New Yorkers came together and celebrated as a people. Before Isabella became a Methodist, she would not have had second thoughts looking forward to Pinkster as a great good time. But for a Methodist committed to living a holy life and resisting worldly temptations, the anticipation of Pinkster represented a spiritual rebuke. For this black New Yorker, the revels of Pinkster became a consummate symbol for backsliding that was saturated with racial and religious significance.

In 1827 Pinkster came on the fourth of June, exactly one month before general emancipation, a coincidence that would have endowed the holiday with added significance. At this point Isabella had been living with the Van Wagenens for several months, but their virtue proved no match for the prospect of Pinkster in the year of freedom. Isabella "looked back into Egypt" and imagined carousing among her black friends back at the Dumonts' at Pinkster. The thought of "their wonted convivialities" whetted her appetite for more rambunctious amusements than came with her life with the quiet, pious, and perhaps boring Van Wagenens.[4]

With an intensity that the more abstract notion of slavery was too pervasive to embody, Pinkster in 1827 bore a bundle of meanings for Isabella: slavery and blackness, freedom and apprehension, hope and vice and pleasure, and commitment to a life of religious purity—the old world and the new order all at once. Isabella faced Pinkster with a holiness that was new to her, and these abstemious convictions were still fragile enough to be vulnerable to the attraction to the holiday of a lifetime. Isabella's near relapse into celebrating freedom with the pleasures of the flesh provoked a crisis that led to her rebirth.

Isabella nursed her anticipation in secret, until one morning she told Maria Van Wagenen that she had an intimation that John Dumont would come fetch her. Isabella said that she would go back with him. In the course of that very day, Dumont appeared.

As a middle-aged Sojourner Truth retold it twenty years later, the interchange between Isabella and Dumont was playful, like family, like lovers. She does not explain why he said he came by or stopped at the Van Wagenens' house, but she says that she told him she was going home with him. She thought "his manner contradicted his words" because he was smiling at her when he said he would not take her back after she had run away from him. Yet he waited—or so she thought—while she got herself and her baby ready to leave. As Sojourner Truth dictated the scene in her *Narrative*, Dumont sat himself in his open carriage, and Isabella was about to join him. But before she could climb into the back of the vehicle, "God revealed himself to her, with all the suddenness of a flash of lightning, showing her, 'in the twinkling of an eye, that he was *all over*'—that he pervaded the universe—'and that there was no place where God was not.' "[5] Isabella feared certain, awful annihilation should she receive "another such 'a look,' " but the second look did not come.

When Isabella regained consciousness of the world around her, Dumont was gone. She walked into the Van Wagenens' house to resume her work, but work lost out to the travail of conversion. After tremendous spiritual turmoil came blessed relief. She felt that a friend had come to shield her from the "burning sun" of God's wrath.

In the peaceful aftermath of torment, she found an ally. "Who *are* you?" she asked of the vision that beamed "with the beauty of holiness, and radiant with love." Evoking images of light and asking a version of Paul's emblematic question, "Who art thou?" Isabella was, like countless evangelicals before her, re-enacting Paul's conversion on the road to Damascus.[6] Her vision was of Jesus, who loved her, who had always loved her, who would stand between Isabella and God's fury. "When he came," she recalled, "she should go and dwell with him, as with a dear friend." As African Americans, especially women, have discovered and rediscovered generation after generation, the liberating presence of Jesus eased Isabella's pain.[7]

As she would say later, Isabella had been baptized in the Holy Spirit. She experienced a second birth of entire sanctification and had been born again with an assurance of salvation that gave her the self-confidence to oppose the rich and powerful of this world. As a vulnerable woman who had been deprived of her parents, overworked, neglected, beaten, and sexually abused, she had approached this world with a vivid sense of her worthlessness, convinced that insuperable barriers separated her from the prominent people for whom she worked. But now she had a friend in Jesus, whom she sometimes likened to "a soul-protecting fortress," sometimes to a power that raised her "above the battlements of fear." The assurance of her sanctification and God's constant support released Isabella from the crippling conviction that she was nothing. She discovered a new means of power, what holiness people called the power of the Spirit, that redressed the balance between someone who was poor and black and female and the rich white people who enslaved, overworked, and abused her.[8]

Before this dramatic conversion, Isabella had identified God with the behaviors she associated with her earthly master, John Dumont. Then she was born again into an egalitarian relationship with Jesus, who cared for her as a friend, as an equal. In her earlier conception of God, he had been powerful and judgmental, but she could dissemble before him. Her Jesus was powerful and loving, and he could look into her heart. The old God belonged to her religion of slavery. Her new religion suited her rebirth into freedom.[9]

Isabella's faith buttressed her in a desperate struggle for her son, Peter, after his illegal sale to the South, but in the struggle she found Methodism inadequate and returned to older ways of relating to the world.[10] Isabella first discovered that Peter had been sold away from Dumont's place (where she had left Peter when she ran away from Dumont in late 1826) while she was working for the Van Wagenens and learning to be a Methodist. Just after she left, her master, John Dumont, had sold Peter to one of his in-laws, a Dr. Gedney, who was his wife's (Sally Dumont's) cousin. Gedney took Peter to New York City, evidently intending to take him to England. But Peter, who was only five or six years old at the time, was too young to perform the tasks that Gedney had in mind. Peter's youth did not protect him from the trauma of multiple sales and removals. Gedney sold Peter to his brother, Solomon Gedney, who then resold the boy to his brother-in-law, an Alabama planter named Fowler, who had married Solomon Gedney's sister, Eliza, who was Sally Dumont's second cousin.

Although New York state law prohibited the sale of New York slaves into places where slavery would continue to be legal after 1827, the law was subject to routine and massive contravention. Peter was only one of thousands of black New Yorkers, like the former slave narrator, Solomon Northup, who was illegally sold into perpetual bondage in the South.[11]

Isabella felt hopeful that her God would help her recover her son. She called first at the Dumonts', where Sally Dumont scoffed: "*Ugh*! a *fine* fuss to make about a little *nigger*!" Dumont expressed surprise at "such a halloo-balloo about the neighborhood; and all for a paltry nigger!!!" To which Isabella replied, with immense determination, "*I'll have my child again*." Isabella had no money, but, she said, "God has enough" or even better, the power to regain her son. She felt, she recalled much later, "so *tall within*—I felt as if the *power of a nation* was within me!" [12]

Isabella then went to Mrs. Gedney—the mother of Solomon Gedney, mother-in-law of Fowler, and the aunt of Sally Dumont. Gedney's response was self-pitying. She missed her daughter Eliza and scoffed at Isabella's reminder that her son, unlike Gedney's daughter, was too young to be so far from his mother. Finding the Dumont-Gedney-Waring family utterly unsympathetic, Isabella did not despair. "Oh, God, you know I have no money, but you can make the people do for me, and you must make the people do for me," she said to her ally. "Oh, God, make the people hear me—don't let them turn me off, without hearing and helping me." [13] She sought and received advice and money for legal fees from prominent Dutch lawyers with whom she would live and work in 1828. [14]

The process of getting Peter back took about a year, but by the spring of 1828 Peter returned to Kingston. His actions and appearance nearly broke his mother's heart. Peter shrieked piteously and refused to go to her. Regarding his mother as though she were a monster, he clung to his "dear master," with whom he begged to stay. Isabella was utterly disconcerted. She knew she had run afoul of a prominent family by going to court, and here, at the culmination of her efforts, her boy was hysterically denying her. She could lose her child and her year's efforts through his refusal to acknowledge her as his mother.

Several adults soothed Peter and convinced him that Isabella was, indeed, his own mother. Once he was mollified, Isabella got a good look at him, and again, her spirits fell: "Oh, Lord Jesus, Look! see my poor child!" Peter was covered with scars from head to toe, and his lacerated back was as rough as a washboard. Isabella discovered that Fowler had whipped, kicked, and beaten Peter, even though the boy was less than seven years old. Seeing her child's tortured body overwhelmed Isabella with sorrow—"Oh my God! Pete, how *did* you bear it?"—and with anger.

In this moment of anguish, Isabella forgot her Methodism, forgot the faith that does not seek retaliation. She returned to the magic of the rural culture in which she had grown up and sought vengeance in an act of everyday witchcraft. Cursing Fowler and his family, she called upon her God to "render unto them double" for what they had done to Peter. [15] The curse expressed a mother's anguish rather than the Methodist ideal of meek submission and sprang from the world of folk religion in which Isabella and the masses of early Americans had come of age. As the curse of one who was poor and afflicted, her malediction was doubly likely to work. [16]

Isabella remained in touch with the Dumont-Gedney-Waring family even after Peter's return, living and working for various branches in a seeming act of forgiveness that astonished even John Dumont. She told her old master that she hoped her efforts would lessen Solomon Gedney's anger toward her, which had nearly caused her to lose a job with his cousins. Then, one day, when she was working in the home of Frederick Waring, Solomon Gedney's and Sally Dumont's uncle, one of his daughters rushed up to her with shocking news. The same Fowler who had abused Peter so brutally had beaten Eliza Gedney Fowler to death.

Isabella said that her feelings were contradictory. She said that she mourned Eliza and grieved for Eliza's family, even for her mother, who had laughed when Isabella had appealed to her for assistance in rescuing Peter. Nonetheless, Isabella recognized—as the Gedneys had not—that a man who would abuse a black child so cruelly as Fowler had abused Peter could murder someone white, even his own wife.

The coincidences were remarkable. Isabella was only once in her life in the house of Frederick Waring, on the very day when the news of Eliza's murder arrived. Twenty years later, Sojourner Truth was convinced that "a special providence of God" was at work, that the Gedneys' anguish was an act of "retributive justice" that was God's answer to her curse. Eliza's mother lost her mind and spent her days pacing about, crying Eliza's name; one of Eliza Fowler's children was chronically depressed. In 1828 and perhaps also in 1848, Isabella inwardly remarked, "Oh, my God! that's too much—I did not mean quite so much, God!"[17]

The Methodist perfectionist that Isabella became in the late 1820s would not ordinarily have used witchcraft, but in a moment of extreme provocation a mother who had only recently been born again into the assurance of Jesus' love had uttered a curse that would bear more bitter fruit than she might ever have imagined. After the recovery of her son and the death of Eliza Gedney Fowler, Isabella may never again have turned to witchcraft, but she never lost that force of character.

In sum, we are not used to thinking of Sojourner Truth as a witch, but at the moment when she was becoming free and finding herself as a Pentecostalist, the rural Afro-Dutch culture in which she had spent her entire life re-exerted itself. Isabella's malediction may have had its African roots, but witchcraft was also native to Ulster County, New York, as it was native to seventeenth-century New England. The coexistence of Pentecostalism and witchcraft in Isabella's life in 1828 demands a closer and more careful look at all the manifestations of what we call black religion in the early nineteenth century and demands a closer and more careful look at the blackness of American religion at the same time.[18]

Such an examination, I suspect, will show the extraordinary difficulty of drawing lines of race and ethnicity in rural folk life, in which people of Native American, African, and European descent grew up, lived, and worked so closely together. This multifaceted cultural demographic context provides the psychological foundation for much of African American religious history.

Notes

1. See also Benjamin E. Mays, *The Negro's God as Reflected in His Literature* (Boston: Chapman and Grimes, 1938), 14.

2. See David D. Hall, *Worlds of Wonder, Days of Judgment: Popular Religious Belief in Early New England* (New York: Knopf, 1989), 5–7, 100.

3. Richard Wheatley, *The Life and Letters of Mrs. Phoebe Palmer* (New York: W. C. Palmer, 1881), 302, 264, 341–42.

4. [Olive Gilbert and Frances Titus], *Narrative of Sojourner Truth; A Bondswoman of Olden Time, Emancipated by the New York Legislature in the Early Part of the Present Century; With a History of Her Labors and Correspondence Drawn From Her "Book of Life"* (1878; reprint, Salem, NH: Ayer, 1990), 63–64.

5. *Narrative of Sojourner Truth*, 65.

6. See Christian R. Davis, "The Rhetoric of Nineteenth-Century American Evangelical Autobiography" (Ph.D. diss., Pennsylvania State University, 1985), 25.

7. *Narrative of Sojourner Truth*, 66–68; and James H. Cone, *God of the Oppressed* (San Francisco: Harper, 1975), 31–32, 35, 105, 139.

8. Arthur A. Stone et al., "Coping with Stressful Events: Coping Dimensions and Issues," in *Life Events and Psychological Functioning: Theoretical and Methodological Issues*, ed. Lawrence H. Cohen (Newbury Park, Calif.: Sage, 1988), 187.

9. Jacquelyn Grant, *White Women's Christ and Black Women's Jesus: Feminist Christology and Womanist Response* (Atlanta, Ga.: Scholars Press, 1989), 104, 144, 215.

10. Gayraud S. Wilmore, *Black Religion and Black Radicalism: An Interpretation of the Religious History of Afro-American People*, 2nd ed. (Maryknoll, N.Y.: Orbis, 1983), 12–14, 57–60.

11. See Solomon Northup, *Twelve Years a Slave*, ed. Sue Eakin and Joseph Logsdon (1853; reprint, Baton Rouge: Louisiana State University Press, 1968).

12. *Narrative of Sojourner Truth*, 44–45.

13. *Narrative of Sojourner Truth*, 70.

14. G.[ilbert] Vale, *Fanaticism; Its Source and Influence, Illustrated by the Simple Narrative of Isabella in the case of Matthias, Mr. and Mrs. B. Folger, Mr. Pierson, Mr. Mills, Catherine, Isabella, &c. &c A Reply to W. L. Stone, with Descriptive Portraits of All the Parties, While at Sing-Sing and at Third Street.—Containing the Whole Truth—and Nothing But the Truth* (New York: G. Vale,

1835), I; 11. The New York Manumission Society, which flourished at the turn of the century, helped recover New York slaves illegally sold South, but it had been most active in New York City.

15. *Narrative of Sojourner Truth*, 52–54.

16. Jon Butler explains that in seventeenth-century England and early America witches were thought to have dealt ordinarily in *maleficium*, which harmed other people. Witchcraft was usually a curse aimed at a neighbor who had refused a favor or given an insult, as in Isabella's case. See Butler, *Religion and Witchcraft in Early American Society* (St. Charles, Mo.: Forum, 1974), 2; and Keith Thomas, *Religion and the Decline of Magic: Studies in Popular Beliefs in Sixteenth and Seventeenth Century England* (London: Weidenfeld and Nicholson, 1971), 264–67, 502–7. See also Henry H. Mitchell, *Black Belief: Folk Beliefs of Blacks in America and West Africa* (New York: Harper & Row, 1975), 112; and Eugen Weber, *Peasants into Frenchmen: The Modernization of Rural France, 1870–1914* (Stanford: Stanford University Press, 1976), 26.

17. *Narrative of Sojourner Truth*, 55–58.

18. See Albert J. Raboteau, *Slave Religion: The "Invisible Institution" in the Antebellum South* (New York: Oxford University Press, 1978), 131–37, 147–149; and Russell E. Richey, *Early American Methodism* (Bloomington: Indiana University Press, 1991), 60–64.

8

"Hoodoo? God Do": African American Women and Contested Spirituality in the Spiritual Churches of New Orleans

~

David C. Estes

Spiritual power (sometimes derided as witchcraft) and female strength have been inextricably coupled throughout American history, at times enabling women, but in other instances rendering them suspect. In early twentieth century African American Spiritual churches, prospective church members feared the label of "witch" and sought to distance themselves from any suggestions of occult practice. Yet their religious behavior did (and still does) come under suspicion because of its emphasis "on the manipulation of one's present condition through magico-religious rituals and esoteric knowledge." Members of the Spiritual church, most of whom have been and still are women, believe in the power of mediums to communicate with spirits. To believers the spirits bring messages from beyond this world; spirits are invoked during special rituals and have the gift of prophecy. Does this avowed ability make Spiritual women "witches"?

David Estes suggests that it is the Spiritual church's connection to Haitian Vodoun that makes their religious practices suspect. Despite the church's acknowledged syncretic blend of many religions, including Catholic, Baptist, Methodist, Pentecostal, nineteenth-century Spiritualist as well as Haitian Vodoun, Spiritual ministers continually repudiate hoodoo practices, suggesting that it is the devil's work and that such associations demean the Spiritual church and undermine its success.

The popular misconception of hoodoo as evil sorcery is one reason Spiritual woman distance themselves from this element of their religious heritage; the popular devaluation of female leadership is another. Folk legends and oral histories of the New Orleans Spiritual church's founder, Mother Anderson, betray the gender, racial, and religious discrimination believers have experienced. As a result, members honor Anderson and women's leadership roles more generally by finding sanctions in the lives of prominent biblical women rather than in their more immediate history of female leadership in African Caribbean religions. Respectability is important to African American Spiritual church women—indeed, failure to cultivate respectability can be dangerous to African Americans in a racist world—and reactions against a faith seen as dominated by powerful women popularly linked with sorcery threatens to undermine what these believers have created.

A RECENT POEM by Brenda Marie Osbey, "Mother Catherine," imaginatively narrates the reception this charismatic New Orleans healer and Spiritual minister (c.1874–1930) received upon arriving in heaven. Osbey's brief narrative commands attention because it draws on local history to depict the gender and racial discrimination that has oppressed African American female Spiritual leaders in general in that city. The poem opens with a series of straightforward statements verging on heresy from the perspective of orthodox Christianity: "My name is catherine. / some call me mother / some saint."[1] Thus Catherine Seal, standing before God, introduces herself to heaven's assembled white residents, who have gathered to witness her arrival and public trial. Charged with "sainthood," as if it were a crime, she replies, perceptively yet dismissively, "Is this your idea, my child, / of the evil in me?" Her followers' belief in her sainthood is all the more disturbing because they are the black masses, whose "dancing in the chapel" is "the work of the very devil," according to God himself. Although Mother Catherine cannot be banished from heaven, she is consigned to toiling in its laundry. Thus God hopes to prevent "her followers / forever banging at the gates of heaven crying for justice. / they are negroes, remember." Nevertheless, Mother Catherine does not accept her fate quietly. She still speaks to those on earth who can hear in the thunder's rumbling "mother catherine / washing the robes of the blessed congress of the saints / and showering down her blessings on her people." Seemingly only a domestic servant in the mansions of heaven, Mother Catherine becomes the true saint, and her ultimate sanctification is a revolutionary protest against the attempts of white male Christians to discredit the spiritual power of African American women.

Osbey's poem succinctly dramatizes what is a dominant pattern in the history of religious expression in her native New Orleans. Spiritually powerful women of African descent have been prominent in the city's religious life. As a result of prevailing ideologies of race and gender, these religious figures have been received in contradictory ways—revered by some while dismissed as irreligious, if not manifestly evil, by others, who might nonetheless still fear them. This pattern, apparent already in the Voodoo that arose during the French and Spanish colonial period, continues to shape ways in which women clergy and members of the Spiritual churches, founded in the 1920s by Leafy Anderson, publicly enact their identity in worship rituals.

Spiritualism is not simply a twentieth-century name for Voodoo, as is generally assumed by many of the New Orleanians who have heard of this small but culturally significant church.[2] The beliefs and rituals of each contain identifiable African and Christian religious traditions, yet in quite different proportions. Marked contrasts in institutional structure, despite the correspondences of some particular features, also suggest that Spiritualism is not simply Voodoo with a new name. Nevertheless, the historical presence of Voodoo profoundly shaped the urban cultural matrix in which women formed and still maintain Spiritual churches. Today, the term "Voodoo" connotes paganism and black magic in a wide range of popular discourses. When called "voodoos" by family members or neighbors, Spiritual ministers therefore rise to the challenge by proclaiming their Christianity and denying any connection to Voodoo. To understand Spiritualism on its own terms requires acknowledging the absoluteness of their distinction. Yet, situated historically within the same urban geography, Spiritualism and Voodoo share many features. Recognizing these similarities confirms the longevity of the public performance of spirituality by African American women in New Orleans.

In a recent study of New Orleans Voodoo, Ina Fandrich argues that it was "a women's religion whose membership and leaders were women, mainly free women of color, but enslaved African and Afro-Creole and some white women also joined their circles."[3] Its preeminent priestess was Marie Laveau (1783–1881), who can be considered the legendary foremother of all spiritually powerful women of African heritage in New Orleans. Upon her death, one local paper eulogized her for tending cholera and yellow fever victims and for visiting inmates on death row in the parish prison. Another claimed that in her old age she had renounced all supernatural powers and joined the Catholic church. A third refused to consider her a saint and denounced her as "the prime mover and soul of the indecent orgies of the ignoble Voudous; and to her influence may be attributed the fall of many a virtuous woman."[4] Over the years, Marie Laveau has continued to be remembered with such divergent feelings of respect and horror. For example, Robert Tallant opens his fictionalized version of her biography by claiming simply that "Marie Laveau was the last great American witch."[5] Yet in his similarly sensationalistic *Voodoo in New Orleans*, Tallant quotes an informant whose words suggest that not all New Orleanians sought to demonize her: " 'Marie Laveau?' said an ancient Negress, still cooking for a family in the French Quarter. 'Sure I heard of her. I don't know if she was good or bad; folks says both ways. But I know this: she was a *powerful* woman."[6]

Barbara Rosendale has perceptively examined the cultural processes at work in Euro-American accounts of Voodoo ceremonies. They are typically classified as orgies rather than as authentic worship rituals. Outside observers depict Voodoo women as erotic objects and overlook their dynamic spirituality: "The characterization of New Orleans Voodoo as a matriarchy did not stand as a positive example of the creative potential of womanhood. It framed yet another abomination to the eyes of God, further extending the gulf between Us [Euro-American observers] and Them [black participants]."[7] Laveau herself is a deeply disturbing figure in New Orleans history because she embodies "the full range of possibilities inherent in the feminine principle the major Western religious traditions have reduced to simple oppositions. Marie's reputation reflects these perceived contradictions, holding her not only to be an evil temptress and sorcerer, but a saintly nurse during yellow fever epidemics and a ministering angel bringing last solace to condemned prisoners."[8] Rosendale repossesses Laveau as the misunderstood Other, threateningly subversive, spiritual, and successful. As such a person, she is the prototype of Mother Catherine Seal and other twentieth-century ministers in New Orleans's indigenous Spiritual churches. Even though these women disavow practicing Voodoo, they confront similar biases against African-based religious practices and women's spiritual authority, and they celebrate a positive self-image in defiance of persistent public disparagement.

Leafy Anderson (c. 1887–1927) founded the Spiritual church in New Orleans shortly after moving there in 1920. She had opened her first Spiritual church approximately seven years earlier in either Chicago or Pittsburgh. From this beginning, she went on to become the founder and president of an association called the Eternal Life Christian Spiritualist Churches.[9] E.L.C.S. Church Number 12, located in a racially mixed New Orleans neighborhood, was flourishing at the time of her sudden death in 1927. Zora Neale Hurston published the only contemporary report of this congregation by a trained anthropologist. She arrived in New Orleans in 1928, unfortunately eight months after

Mother Anderson's death. Hurston was intent on documenting "hoodoo," an African American term denoting conjuration and the loosely organized belief system that is Voodoo's twentieth-century legacy. Her remarks are significant because they confirm the presence of hoodoo, and therefore a historical link to African religions, in the early years of New Orleans Spiritualism. Aware of the creative creolization of independent cultures that meet in a new geographic location, Hurston explained that nineteenth-century American Spiritualism, "as a technique for communication with the dead, has a ready appeal to the black, and is often closely combined with hoodoo practices. There are many advantages to a hoodoo doctor in embracing spiritualism. Hoodooism is in disrepute, and certain of its practices forbidden by law. A spiritualistic name protects the congregation, and is a useful devise [*sic*] of protective coloration."[10]

Rather surprisingly, Hurston concluded that Mother Anderson had no affiliation with hoodoo, thus missing her seminal role in the perpetuation of authentic African American religious culture.[11] Her congregation was "apparently free of hoodoo," although "a strong aroma of hoodoo clings about the other eleven" Spiritual congregations in the city. Her followers claimed that she "was not a hoodoo doctor" and that the other churches were " 'stolen' by hoodoo worshipers." Following the lead of these self-proclaimed legitimate inheritors, Hurston portrayed Mother Anderson as working within the widespread practices of American Spiritualists, or spirit mediums, who claimed an ability to communicate with the dead on behalf of the living.[12] Evidence of such practices during Hurston's research trip included a Monday night "meeting presided over by a woman, which the spirit of Mother Anderson (now deceased) attends." Hurston incompletely assessed the roots of Mother Anderson's spirituality by ignoring the principle she herself enunciated, that "a spiritualistic name . . . is a useful devise [*sic*] of protective coloration." Mother Anderson's "legitimate" heirs were apparently more savvy than was Hurston to the riskiness of displaying African American female spirituality to an outsider, regardless of her race and gender. Yet Hurston, probably unwittingly, recorded a telling disparity between their words and their deeds. Even while disavowing any connection to hoodoo, at the Monday meeting Mother Anderson's followers sold vials of "Spirit oil" for fifty cents. It was used, according to Hurston, "to anoint one's body against various illnesses and troubles." Had this custom's resemblance to hoodoo practices stimulated Hurston to question what the believers said, she might have perceived these women's acute sense that their spirituality endangers them and that their self-expression depends on "protective coloration."

Roman Catholicism, dominant in New Orleans since the colonial period, has been a second important source of such cultural camouflage in Spiritual churches. The sacramentals of Catholicism—saints' images, holy water and oils, candles, and incense, for example—its liturgical style, and its priestly vestments and titles have all been adapted by Spiritual leaders to convey their own spirituality. They have also drawn from black Baptist, Pentecostal, and Holiness denominations in creating a religion that followers reared in a wide array of churches find meaningful. The presence of images, rituals, customs, and beliefs from such heterogeneous origins distinguishes the style and content of Spiritualism in New Orleans, making that city the "Mecca of the Spiritual movement."[13]

The elaborateness with which religious practices have creolized in New Orleans Spiritualism was intrinsic in the manner that spirituality was initially expressed by Leafy Anderson, Catherine Seal, and the other women who established churches in the formative period of the 1920s and early 1930s. Creolization was more than a self-conscious defensive tactic, as Hurston noted, protecting believers from denunciation and possible ostracism for their African-based practices. Creolization of religious practices occurred because women found that the process offered them an opportunity for self-expression through the improvisatory recombination of existent cultural forms and artifacts. Although in 1934 the first male leader to emerge, Reverend Thomas Watson, made organizational unity his goal, the legacy of his female predecessors is a response to a continuing need quite different from his. They created what has been recognized as "almost exclusively a women's movement under women's leadership."[14] Primarily African Americans, these women were intent on publicly repossessing the spirituality that ideologies of race and gender withheld from them.

The founders of these churches succeeded by being sufficiently self-confident to pursue their goal in the characteristically expressive style traditional among African Americans. These women fragmented diverse, socially accepted ways of exhibiting spirituality and then reassembled the pieces into devotional forms rich with meaning and aesthetic pleasure within the boundaries of black expressive culture. This process can be seen in the following discussions of special worship services honoring deceased leaders and saints and also of chanted sermons. Spiritualism has remained a vital women's movement in New Orleans because it nurtures a distinct religious identity that society at large stigmatizes as deviant. Still today, women lead more than half of the fifty or so Spiritual congregations and prayer rooms in existence; their assistants—ordained to the ranks of missionary, evangelist, minister, or even bishop—are generally women, and the members are almost exclusively women.

Despite the predominant influence of women in the origin and development of New Orleans Spiritualism, gender discrimination is a problem within the denomination today. As one senior woman minister, who is widely respected in the city, told me: "We have people right in our denomination that don't care nothing about women preachers. They'll tell us that women don't have no business in the pulpit. . . . A lot of the male ministers would rather you don't come in their pulpit. . . . I'll stay out on the floor with everybody else" rather than sit with the ordained ministers in the rostrum behind the pulpit.[15] The practice of consecrating women as bishops has proved divisive, and only one of the two national associations of Spiritual churches based in New Orleans allows them to hold this office. In response to this intragroup discrimination, the well-respected minister's nonconfrontational approach is fairly typical: "You don't have to push yourself. That's what I believe in, not pushing my way on people. If they receive me, good. If they don't, well, I accept their rejection and pray for them."

Contemporary members readily acknowledge the satisfaction that they enjoy by being Spiritual, even though they must withstand scorn and even rejection for practicing this religion. One woman, who was reared a Catholic but is now a Spiritual minister along with her husband, explained to me in an interview that she first sought advice from Archbishop Lydia Gilford because of a domestic problem: She "taught me that I can talk to the Lord for myself [instead of having to go to a priest]. . . . I didn't know I had a spirit. I didn't know I was a spirit. I learned that I have a spirit and . . . it made me feel alive. . . . It made me feel like I was somebody. It made me feel like I had a voice that someone was gonna hear me."[16] Observing other women's behavior during services at Infant Jesus of Prague Spiritual Church enhanced her nascent self-esteem: "I was happy in the Spiritual church. I was happy to see the people singing and I was happy to see the women wearing the beautiful robes and I liked the way they could talk and I didn't know a woman could do all that. I was amazed." She now praises Spiritualism for giving "a woman so many opportunities to express her ideals and the way the Lord has spoken to her."

During the six years she attended services before joining the church, a memorable dream offered a new understanding of her own potential: "I saw the Lord's supper—Last Supper—and he put his right hand out of the picture. In the dream, you know, and he said, 'Heal my people.' Just like that. . . . I kneeled down and I took his hand and he took my hand." Thinking at first that she was going to die, she bought a life insurance policy, a reaction that now makes her laugh at her youthful ignorance. Becoming Spiritual meant a complete break from her family. The rift between herself and her mother never healed before the older woman's death. Yet a dream in which the deceased mother's spirit appeared to her has provided comforting assurance that acceptance has finally come. Despite being classified as a hoodooist by those closest to her, she never doubted herself: "I didn't understand [them]. I say I'm still serving the Lord. I stopped doing everything I used to do and I was happy."

This woman's personal growth conforms to the pattern described by Carol Lois Haywood in a study of white women mediums in contemporary Spiritualist groups in Indiana: "The self-concept in the traditional woman's role is demonstrably passive as well as deferential and self-effacing. While gender expectations are basic to personality, especially to self-concept, women can reject *some* aspects of the role for a more religious and, at the same time, more active concept of the self. . . . A clearer, more active self-concept provides some basis for resisting social identity."[17]

In choosing to become Spiritual, the woman mentioned above and others like her in New Orleans resist more than the passivity and deference demanded of women. They must also withstand being considered "hoodoos" by other African Americans, among whom rumors circulate associating Spiritual churches with the practice of conjuring spirits with malign intentions. This negative stereotyping does not come from white New Orleanians. Indeed, very few of them know of the Spiritual churches, which are located generally in poorer black sections. Yet many residents in these neighborhoods have heard ominous warnings, and even children can often identify an otherwise unexceptional house where a reverend mother holds services and gives spiritual readings in her prayer room. African Americans who denounce the Spiritual church for occultism have some of the same fears that led whites to condemn Voodoo in the last century. Suspicions are aroused by claims of familiarity with spirits and the occurrence of possession during worship. In addition, Spiritual leaders are reputedly able to heal illness and manipulate events by performing magico-religious rituals to which they are privy. The fact that women are empowered by means of such spirituality and use of charms makes the Spiritual church an intimidating hex sign for African Americans who, along with whites, perpetuate an ideology of gender that denies women's spirituality.

The experiences of the former Catholic discussed above illustrate the dread of the Spiritual church felt by African Americans who equate it with malevolent aspects of Voodoo and hoodoo. As children, she says, "We heard so many things about Marie Laveau. . . . It was like they'll [Spiritual believers] burn a light on you. They gonna do you this and do you that and it always had a fear about the Spiritual religion." Burning candles, an accepted sacramental in Roman Catholicism, is similarly prominent in Spiritual rituals. Yet outsiders overlook this connection in favor of emphasizing similarities to Voodoo charms. This woman was also taught that it was "a background religion" for "low people"—that is, for "people that want to hurt you." Spiritualism was portrayed to her as heathen: "I didn't hear God. I didn't hear his name mentioned. All I heard is, don't go there. Don't get into this. They will hurt you. They will misuse you. They will trample you and I was afraid."

"Voodoo queen" is the slang term most frequently used to sum up disapproval of Spiritual women. The woman above expresses the emotional pain that the label caused her after she joined the church: "All my relatives look like they went haywire and left me alone and thought I was a Voodoo queen or something like that. . . . They thought I had gone crazy." The term originated with outside, white observers of New Orleans Voodoo in the nineteenth century. Still today, their understanding of Voodoo's organization persists. Supposedly, rival queens vied with each other in displaying their powers in order to attract followers. Although the queen might be assisted by a man, he never assumed the title of king. Thus, as a "Voodoo queen" the Spiritual woman not only perpetuates paganism but also uses it as a means of upsetting the traditional gender hierarchy. She is the solitary monarch who finds completeness within herself and needs no king. The derogatory tone with which "Voodoo queen" is typically spoken indicates the animosity that her unconventional spirituality arouses.

To refute the disgraceful charges of hoodooism and to claim honorable status within the community, Spiritual believers assert their Christianity. The punning maxim "Hoodoo? God do" frequently punctuates testimonies and sermons. Speakers then proceed to proclaim their acceptance of the Bible and of the divinity of Jesus. Most important in terms of this analysis, they explain their belief in spirits and the practice of possession as within the bounds of Christian orthodoxy. That assertion is, however, more a rhetorical construction than doctrinal fact, as the following discussion demonstrates.

One bishop instructed the congregation thus in her testimony: "We don't care if they call us hoodoo. We don't care if they call us voodoo. . . . Let them know you learn the Bible in our church. Let them know that you're taught to pray until the Holy Ghost comes upon you. And then you know you can't do nothing without the Holy Ghost, and when you get the Holy Ghost, you can do all things, because he has done what? He has strengthened your body to be able to let men and women know that you are a child of the King."[18] Here she counters censure by the rhetorical strategies of oversimplification and renaming. All the various spirits that worshipers name and invoke in their rituals are fused into the Holy Ghost. Thus she deflects accusations of occultism by emphasizing that the Spiritual church accepts the Christian doctrine of the Trinity. Her approach is commonly used. For example, the Bible passage quoted most frequently in testimonies and sermons is "God is a spirit, and they that worship him must worship him in spirit and in truth" (John 4:24). At the same service, another female bishop similarly explained her association with spirits in a way congruent with Catholic beliefs: "People are afraid of us [because] I dare to call the saints. All you got to do is get into oneness with God, call on the angels of heaven. God will dispatch the one you need."

In actual practice, the term "spirit" is not used as restrictively as allusions to the Christian doctrine of the Trinity imply. For example, the bishop's remarks quoted above were made during a memorial service for Leafy Anderson, a ceremony during which the spirit of this deceased leader is invoked through song and dance. She introduced the concept of the "spirit guide" from American Spiritualism, in which it denotes one of the two categories of spirit "helpers." Whereas "loved ones," the first group of helpers, are the souls of deceased relatives or close friends, spirit guides can be complete strangers, including historical figures.[19] Over the course of a career, the medium may have several different spirit guides, each serving a different role. Historically, common guides have included a little girl and an American Indian, both of whom protected the medium from unwanted spirits.[20] According to one of the Spiritual archbishops in New Orleans, everyone has a spirit guide, whether its presence is recognized or not.[21] These spirits are actively interested in benefiting the believer's earthly life and are not solely concerned with preparing her for the afterlife. Although it originated in American Spiritualism, the notion of spirit guides has become thoroughly integrated into New Orleans Spiritualism, with the understanding that hoodoo and Christianity are in contention. For example, Archbishop Lydia Gilford told documentary photographer Michael P. Smith that "there is a lot of Hoodooing going around": " 'They do it by trying to take control of your spirit guides.' For that reason she won't tell anyone who her spirit guides are, because she doesn't want to be 'brought down or made sick. . . . The Lord can always raise you up,' she maintains, 'but I don't want to be worried about it.' "[22]

Leafy Anderson claimed White Hawk as a spirit guide during her years in Chicago, but she did not continue to rely on him in New Orleans. During her ministry there, she worked with three spirit guides, two of whom are still widely known. The most popular spirit in New Orleans Spiritualism is Black Hawk. In 1832 he led the Sauk and Fox tribes of the upper Mississippi Valley in an armed uprising against the United States. Special services known as "feasts" are celebrated in many churches to honor him. Queen Esther of the Hebrew Bible is another of Mother Anderson's guides, and the spirit of Father John, the third of her guides, may be based on the legendary Voodoo priest Doctor John, a contemporary of Marie Laveau. Father John is no longer widely honored. Today, many Catholic saints are recognized as spirit guides. Among the more popular are Saint Joseph, the Blessed Mother (Mary), and Saint Anthony. Elaborate temporary altars visually dominate the annual feasts for these saints, and churches are typically filled with visitors from other congregations for these services.[23]

"Entertaining spirits" is important in Spiritual worship services, and it is not unusual for at least a few of the participants to "fall out" or "shout," as the trance state is called. They say that "the spirit was high" if a larger than usual number of worshipers experience trance. As Felicitas D. Goodman has explained, the religious state of altered consciousness is normal human behavior "when it is a *ritualized action*, capable of being called forth and terminated on a given cue or signal."[24] In Spiritual services, the rituals that induce trance include singing, clapping, and dancing. Shouting typically occurs at well-defined points in the traditional order of the service, generally during the chanted sermon or the extended period of singing and dancing following it. However, Spiritual leaders always remain open to the spirit and will quickly improvise the structure of the service if worshipers start to "get happy" and begin to shout at other points. Those experiencing trance exhibit distinctive physical characteristics including heavy breathing, sweating, and trembling. Other behavior includes glossolalia, twirling in place, pacing the aisles, and rapid dancing. Ushers try to circle the shouter, holding hands with each other to prevent her from hurting herself in a fall. Clergy as well as members of the congregation may fall into trance. Generally, it is attributed simply to the presence of "spirit" (in the singular). On rare occasions, the complicated steps of the dancer are a sign of the particular spirit possessing the person. Although the testimonies of Spiritual followers reveal their belief in a dualistic universe that contains invisible forces of good and evil, the spirits manifesting themselves during worship services are always beneficent.[25] Worshipers often whisper emphatically, "Thank you, kind spirit" upon emerging from trance. This sentence acknowledges the profound contentment they find in being possessed.

Worshipers value moments of altered consciousness for providing deep spiritual satisfaction, but not all are comfortable with the same intensity of ecstasy in public worship. Some leaders encourage more restraint during their services than do others. Worshipers drawn to the Spiritual church for the opportunities it affords for shouting form affiliations where they feel freest to invoke the spirit. Spiritual people enjoy talking about possession experiences at social gatherings after services. Informally, they tease each other about their appearance while in the spirit. Their laughter is double-edged. In pointing to behavior that outsiders may see as grotesque or irreligious, they seem to be sharing that point of view. Actually, the joke turns on the outsiders, whose limited vision makes them incapable of discerning the presence of spirit within the physical body.

Another type of possession is also widespread, but it is limited almost exclusively to the clergy. Spirits may appear with messages or prophecies that the possessed minister then delivers to the appropriate individuals in the congregation, either in a private whisper or out loud for all to hear. Some churches regularly hold "bless" services for healing and prophecy on weekday evenings. In the final portion of the service, when the lights may be lowered, robed ministers take their stations in front of the altar to anoint with oil those who come forward. These same ministers, or other clergy members assisting them, then become possessed and deliver prophesies. Meanwhile, the seated congregation contributes to the heightened spiritual tension by singing. Usually, "spirit," with no further specification, is recognized as present. Sometimes, however, one of the aforementioned spirits or a deceased minister is acknowledged by name. Messages typically refer to a problem confronting the individual. Any predictions tend to be of favorable events, but on one occasion I heard a bishop publicly prophesy the death of a member's spouse. Messages generally conclude with an injunction to perform a particular ritual, generally involving candles, water, prayers, or Bible passages. Ministers do not ask for money in exchange for delivering messages from the spirits at a worship service. Candles and other ritual paraphernalia may, however, be offered for sale at its conclusion.

Human contact with spirits regularly occurs outside of public worship as well. They are invoked, for example, when leaders meet privately with "clients" who seek assistance in dealing with a variety of personal problems. For such consultations, the spiritual adviser expects a cash "donation," which in some cases the client places on the open pages of a Bible before leaving. Many believers have home altars at which they seek contact with their personal spirit guides during private devotional rituals. Spirits of saints, historical figures, and relatives all may appear spontaneously without being ritually solicited, and these memorable occurrences are sometimes shared publicly in the testimonies that precede the sermon in a regular worship service. These narratives not only convey the quality of the speaker's own spirituality but also instruct believers in the characteristics and powers that distinguish one spirit from another.

The spirits of deceased religious leaders form a distinct category in the Spiritual church. They continue to offer valued guidance to members, and special memorial services are held to solicit messages from them. Occasionally, these services are called "séances."[26] The term itself suggests the influence of American Spiritualism, but in the New Orleans churches the séance has been recontextualized as a worship ritual in the characteristically expressive style of traditional African American culture. Mother Anderson may have encouraged the development of services honoring deceased leaders by telling believers before her death, "I am going away but I shall come back and you shall know that I am here."[27] Similarly, one of Mother Catherine's followers said of her leader: "She will return—by resurrection, reincarnation, spirit communications or any other means Jehovy will permit."[28] Today, a few individual churches memorialize deceased founders in special worship services. For the past several years, the largest church has held a service honoring all deceased leaders on the Sunday afternoon closest to December 12, the date of Mother Anderson's death.

The most enduring of these memorial services is the one conducted by Bishop Inez Adams at Queen Esther Divine Spiritual Temple of Christ, which she founded in 1957. Bishop Adams was ordained as a minister in 1952 and was consecrated as a bishop in 1970.[29] She feels a particularly strong connection to Mother Anderson because she ordained Dora Tyson, who in turn became Bishop Adams's leader. Over the years, Mother Dora correctly prophesied that Bishop Adams's husband would find work; she also healed her child of seizures and interpreted her visions as revelations of the spiritual work to which she was being called. Thus, Bishop Adams feels that she has benefited from the spiritual power of Mother Anderson as continued in the ministry of Mother Dora.

Bishop Adams annually honors Mother Anderson on the anniversary of her death. The tribute varies from year to year. Sometimes it is a single service, and other years it is a series held on as many as four consecutive nights. The founder's framed photo usually sits on a special table in front of the altar, along with white flowers and candles. Sometimes a Bible alongside it is opened to John 14, one of her favorite chapters. It begins, "Let not your heart be troubled," a fitting saying for a service designed to invoke the consoling power of her spirit.

Bishop Adams is quite clear about the reason for this service with its special altar and ceremonies: "We not worshiping her. We just thank the Lord for she came here and taught us the way. She's called in our development class [an occasional midweek series for spiritual growth] our spirit teacher. She is a good teacher, and I declare if you want to learn, you seek God, that spirit will help you."[30]

Many people speak at these services about Mother Anderson's life as well as her ongoing spiritual presence. Worshipers may testify about ways she has assisted them, as in court cases and in childbirth. Leaders, on the other hand, refer not only to her intervention in their affairs but also to events during her life in New Orleans. These stories, which may be recounted at regular services as well, emphasize the racial, sexual, and religious discrimination that she fearlessly confronted. At one service, Bishop Adams emphasized the connections to their own experiences: "Children, she came here and suffered for us, and all they did, they called her everything. Called her Beelzebub. They say she was a man disguised as a woman. She was a hoodoo. She was two heads [a conjuror]. Oh bless God, children. They be saying all that about you. They say it about me."[31] The legendary crisis in Mother Anderson's ministry came when she was arrested, according to many, for leading a band of marchers, barefoot and carrying candles, through the streets of the city without a permit. Others say she was preaching outdoors. One female bishop even blames the arrest on "Baptist ministers who wanted her run out of town."[32] When brought before the judge, she prophesied that his child at home was gravely sick. After finding this warning to be correct, he dismissed the charges and, out of gratitude, helped her to obtain a state ministerial license.[33] As is characteristic of legends that have been passed on orally over the years, details vary from person to person. Yet in every case, Mother Anderson's prophesy about the child is a sign of her compassion. Her clairvoyance convinces the judge that she is not practicing Voodoo and thus deserves to be licensed as a Christian minister. Bishop Adams's interpretation of this trial foregrounds the dynamics of race in the confrontation: "[Mother Anderson] came into this land—this terror-ridden and segregated land—and stood up in the courthouse and prophesied to the Caucasian judge. When Negroes were saying, Guess what? Get ready. Oh praise God! She came in and told him."[34]

At the memorial service for Mother Anderson, Bishop Adams always invites worshipers to come forward to light candles on the special altar. Then follows a period of singing and dancing. Frequently, the song is the quietly hypnotic "In the Spirit World." Each stanza is composed of the repetition of a simple line, such as "She's in the spirit world," "We're gonna meet up again," or "Mother Anderson's here."

Robed ministers, moved by her spirit, will prophesy to worshipers as the singing continues. The mood is tranquil, as opposed to the frenzy that accompanies the arrival of the spirit on most other occasions.

As mentioned above, Spiritual churches celebrate a cycle of feasts to honor various saints.[35] The displays of female spirituality are particularly vibrant at the series of services in which Bishop Adams honors Queen Esther, one of her spirit guides. This biblical figure was also one of Leafy Anderson's spirit guides, although she is not as popular today as is Black Hawk. There is no written record of Mother Anderson's particular association with Queen Esther or the ceremonies devoted to her during the early years of the Spiritual church. Bishop Adams is the only leader who regularly feasts Queen Esther today.

The book of the Bible bearing her name tells how Esther used her position as wife of the Persian king Ahasuerus to inform him of the plot to annihilate her fellow Jews. Spiritual women acknowledge Esther's great beauty and testify that she empowers them to be physically attractive. Even more important, however, is the courage she displayed in pleading her case without the required invitation to enter the king's court. This action is a model that women find relevant to their own lives, as one minister testified: "Truly I'm just so proud . . . for the many years that I have known her [Esther] and known that she was bold and courageous. She stood up for what was right. Truly tonight this is what we come for. To ask the Lord to give us boldness so that we might be able to stand up to our foes because when you are on the Lord's side, Satan is going to strike on every hand, but if we continue to do as Queen Esther, just stand up, stand tall and be bold, I know that everything is going to be all right."[36] Another woman, now a bishop, testified that Queen Esther's spirit empowered her to become a minister. Therefore, Queen Esther had been invoked at her ordination: "I came from under the spirit of Queen Esther. I was ordained under the spirit of Queen Esther in '61 on the second day of April on the Easter Sunday night, and I thank God that the Lord have abled me to come and enjoy Esther's meeting 'cause I asked her a favor, and the work is already done, and I will give you a token for her table from me and my family."[37] The novena provided this woman a public opportunity to recollect the roots of her spirituality in a female spirit force.

Around Queen Esther's feast day on March 15, Bishop Adams conducts a series of services visually dominated by an elaborate temporary altar built for the occasion. It stretches across the rostrum on which ministers typically sit and extends out to the front pew. Covered with white cloth, the altar is filled with cakes, candy, fruit, and flowers arranged symmetrically. The T-shape is the traditional design for all feast altars, but the bows and tall seven-day candles in pink, Queen Esther's color, mark it as dedicated to her. A framed lithograph of Esther taken from a devotional book always stands on one of the three tiers at the back of the altar. One year, her picture rested beneath a statue of Saint Joseph, whose day is March 19 and for whom Bishop Adams frequently erects a similar altar.

Bishop Adams typically prepares worshipers for this elaborate ceremonial display by holding "Queen Esther novenas" every Friday night beginning in January. Their format is similar to the bless service described above. Typically a dozen women attend, in contrast to the crowds of one hundred or more that fill the church at the time of the feast. All of the services in this complex series are led by the same minister, a woman called "the Instrument" who "represents" Queen Esther. Bishop Adams formerly assumed this role herself, but in the mid-1980s her assistant, Minister Geraldine Coleman, some twenty years younger than the bishop, began to perform the duties. Her striking rhinestone tiara, scepter, and pink robe lend a theatricality to the event that contrasts with the demanding spiritual work required of her as the Instrument. To prepare, she fasts the day of each service, following Queen Esther's example before she went to the king. After testimonies have been spoken, a period of singing helps Minister Coleman to get in contact with the spirit of Queen Esther. She dances counterclockwise around the congregation, often purifying the church with incense. Depending on the dictates of the spirit, she prophesies to members of the congregation or invites them to kneel before her to be blessed. These rituals vary, but each week she relies on the spirit of Queen Esther in order to respond to each worshiper as an individual. Minister Coleman acknowledges that she is more subdued than many others when in the trance state. She does not manifest Queen Esther's presence by shouting or falling out. Rather, a quiet intensity marks her style as an intermediary to the spirit world.

Bishop Adams, on the other hand, behaves much more exuberantly when filled with the spirit of Queen Esther. At one novena, she got up from her seat after the testimonies, went into her living quarters behind the sanctuary, and changed from her ordinary white robe into a pink vestment and high heels. She returned to dance along with Minister Coleman and invoke the spirit of Queen Esther. Immediately before concluding the service, Bishop Adams explained to the congregation: "I come to tell you all tonight Esther's not a dead spirit. She's a live one. She believe in praising God. . . . I sat there in my seat. She just kept on a pushing me. You know one thing? I know what it is to be whipped by spirit. It didn't take me long to go up there and put this pink robe on. O thank you, Jesus. Praise God. We come tonight to say to you that the channel of blessing is open. When you represent a spirit, and when you dealing with a spirit, you gonna do like that spirit do. . . . When you get in harmony with the spirit, then spirit gonna get in harmony with you."[38] When she told her congregation about this incident during regular worship the next Sunday, she added a detail that illuminates why the spirit was moved to whip her: "Friday morning in the spirit I was dancing with my pink robe on. And then I had the nerve to come in here Friday and sit down with a little white choir robe on, and the spirit kept shaking me. And I said, Lord, what's wrong?" This remark suggests that private moments of communication with spirits are not considered sufficient of themselves. They are understood as preparatory for public displays of possession that open "the channel of blessing" for worshipers. In this case, Bishop Adams pointed out the contradictions in her own behavior in order to demonstrate how strongly Queen Esther desired people to be able to observe her spirit's presence.

Another contrast complicates the dynamics of this event: the two women's different styles of manifesting Queen Esther. Bishop Adams's participation came not only as an acknowledgment of her own errors, but also as a critique of her minister's imperfect conduct as the Instrument. Bishop Adams underscored this judgment at the close of the novena: "Esther don't sing all them dead, dry songs. The forces that uses us and dwells in here do not come all the time with dead, dry songs. You might sing something slow sometime, but not every Friday night. Dragging, dragging. I don't mean to criticize you, but I want you to get in harmony with the spirit." Because Queen Esther is a spirit guide of Bishop Adams, she was responsible for reproving Minister Coleman publicly so that participants could experience Queen Esther's spirit fully and genuinely. Failure to correct the error could have led to further whipping. Minister Coleman remained silent, accepting her bishop's admonition. At the previous year's culminating Queen Esther feast, Bishop Adams had announced her wish that Minister Coleman be her successor as leader of Queen Esther Temple. The relationship between the two women is, in many ways, like that between teacher and pupil, and public worship in the Spiritual tradition is an acceptable time for instruction to be given about spirit possession.

Events at this novena demonstrate women's empowerment through possession by a female spirit. But mediumship has exacting requirements. Leaders perform rituals with a high level of self-consciousness and have the responsibility to critique inappropriate trance behavior publicly. The hierarchical Spiritual clergy is responsible for maintaining traditional standards by teaching, primarily through demonstration, appropriate techniques for invoking spirits. Believers do not share the dismissive view of outsiders who consider possession to be an unconscious and uncontrollable frenzy. Trance is actually a loss of self-control for which one prepares through fasting, prayer, and other devotional rituals. Trance behavior can be evaluated by those with spiritual knowledge, and the devotee can modify her preparations for possession in order to manifest the spirit more authentically. As exemplified in the Queen Esther novena described above, ritual possession occurs between a self-consciously patterned preparatory stage and a period of critical reflection after the return to normal consciousness. Bishop Adams's observations at the close of the novena have a function quite similar to that of the comments, discussed previously, that worshipers exchange informally about their trance behavior, even though her rhetoric does not employ humor. The traditions of the Spiritual church encourage such communal self-reflection in a range of voices because believers want at least some rational understanding of the altered consciousness that figures prominently in their worship. The store of traditional knowledge about spirits exchanged in various modes of ordinary discourse can, in turn, play an important role in making trance an event that enhances the status of the possessed devotee as a spiritually powerful woman in her community.

Like prophesies, sermons are a traditional genre of inspired speech through which women communicate spiritual truths. The chanted sermon is a focal point in African American Protestant worship, and Spiritual churches similarly foreground this traditional genre of inspired discourse in regular Sunday worship and many other occasions such as anniversaries and conventions, although not at the bless and novena services.[39] In the history of African American religion, preaching has been restricted almost exclusively to men on the basis of a literal interpretation of New Testament teachings about the role of women. Spiritual believers, on the other hand, consider preaching a spiritual gift and encourage women to deliver the word. There is no written or oral record of Mother Anderson's oratorical powers. Yet New Orleans Spiritualism has become notable—or notorious, according to many outsiders—for allowing African American women to be inspired in the pulpit. Like their male counterparts, they authenticate their ministry by recounting emotionally powerful dream visions in which they received a personal call from God.

One of the most accomplished New Orleans Spiritual preachers in the traditional chanted style was Archbishop Lydia Gilford, who passed away in 1989. She was raised a Catholic but was first taken to a Spiritual church by her mother, who advised her to burn candles there to resolve her marital discord. Lydia Gilford joined the Spiritual church in 1945. She was active in the choir before being ordained. In 1966, during an illness, she was called by the spirit in a vision to stop working full-time as a beautician and open the Infant Jesus of Prague Spiritual Church. Confronting discrimination against women bishops in the Spiritual associations, she founded her own conference, which included churches in Texas as well as New Orleans. The ministers and bishops under her direction wore distinctive hand-made miters decorated with ribbons and sequins. She was a disruptive presence in African American religious circles in New Orleans because of her outspokenness against gender discrimination, and public oratory was a weapon she used skillfully.[40]

The traditional African American sermon is a highly patterned, extemporaneous event that is frequently a precursor to trance for many in the congregation. The preacher's rhythmic, musical delivery, known as chanting, elicits increasingly louder and more passionate responses from those in the pews. Archbishop Gilford considered chanting as confirmation that the preacher's language is divinely inspired: "The Spirit comes in. You leave self. . . . You leave yourself, and that other self comes out and goes doin' what the Lord wants you to do. . . . You got to ask God to strip yourself. Use your body as a living sacrifice, you see. When he does this, then you commence to get out of self. Then you commence to deliver and do what he wants you to do."[41] While preaching, she experienced the amnesia that accompanies trance in some religious traditions:[42] "Half of the things they tell me I done did, I don't know anything about it." Archbishop Gilford generally taped her sermons in order to find out what the spirit inspired her to say, and she also learned about what happened from informal conversation with members during meals in the church kitchen after the service. According to her, "When I preach, they come and reminisce over it."

Gender discrimination had a direct influence on Archbishop Gilford's sermons. They were not only a product of her personal spirituality; they were also an important means by which she exhorted her followers, predominantly women, to persevere in claiming fully the spiritual life that God intended for humans, without any respect to gender. One Sunday she visited the Baptist church across from her own on Religious Street for an appreciation service honoring the organist who played for both congregations, but she left her offering and quickly returned to Infant Jesus to join the service there. In remarks preceding her sermon, she informed her congregation that the Baptists refused to recognize her as an ordained minister by seating her in the rostrum with the other clergy: "When I went over to Good Shepherd today, I know'd my place. I know'd my place was not in the pew. . . . I know'd I was supposed to be in the rostrum, and if you don't like me in the rostrum, hit the door."[43] The unsettling experience moved her to attack male ministers directly: "The men that don't want women in their pulpit is very much afraid. They're afraid that the women are gonna shake 'em up." Having come up against such men repeatedly during her ministry, Archbishop Gilford considered Infant Jesus a refuge from gender discrimination. Yet, unlike many male ministers, she had to raise the money herself to keep the church open in order to be able to express her spirituality publicly. At this point in her life, she was holding services in a small building in a fairly isolated warehouse district near the Mississippi River, having lost the large following that allowed her to rent the Carver Theater building in the heart of a lower-income black neighborhood. Yet she could still declare: "I can preach in this building when I can't preach nowhere else." That day the spirit filled her with a sermon befitting the occasion, and the loudspeaker above the front door broadcast her defiant, inspired words toward the Baptist church where she had been humiliated. She began by reading her text:

It [the occurrence at Good Shepherd] made me know
what my subject was today
And I'm coming to you very briefly
As briefly as the spirit of the Lord let me
From the sixth chapter of Ephesians
Starting in the tenth verse
Reading as far as the spirit of the Lord give utterance
Cause it's truly in me as I'm giving it to you today
Finally my brethren be strong in the Lord
And in the power of his mind
Put on the whole armor of God
And ye may be able to stand against the wiles of the devil
For we wrestle not against flesh and blood
But against principalities
Against power and against the ruler of the darkness of this world
Against spiritual wickedness in high places.[44]

Drawing on the military imagery in Ephesians later in this sermon, she spoke to her largely female congregation about the battle for equality in the Lord's service:

We getting ready to let men and women know of
the Lord and Savior Jesus Christ
We finally got to tell our brother what to do
'Cause some of us is so weak

But we got to let 'em know that we strong in the Lord
Huh?
And in his power and his might . . .
But we still weak by the wayside
We still trembling by the wayside
The Lord want a bold soldier
He don't want no coward soldier
He want you to put on the whole armor of faith
He want you to dress yourself up
Good God almighty
Yes sir[45]

In another sermon, entitled "A Wonderful Counsellor," Archbishop Gilford charged male ministers with full responsibility for gender discrimination in the church. According to the divine plan, men and women of all ages are equally capable of being inspired with the power of prophetic speech:

Woman had to bring man here first
I ain't seen a man have a baby yet
Huh?
I ain't seen a man him have none yet
He made male and female
A woman is a wonderful thing
A woman is a wonderful thing
For people to get up and discriminate
The discrimination is between the preachers
It's between the reverends talking about the different ministries
The ministry got to get straight first
If the head is wrong the body gonna be wrong
You straighten the ministry out then you'll be all right
Don't care who delivering the word
Come out of the mouth of babes and sucklings
The eighth division of Psalms tells it to us
That baby there can tell me thus say the Lord[46]

Discrimination against women is even more reprehensible because men know that women speak the truth, according to Archbishop Gilford. In the following passage from "A Wonderful Counsellor," there is an implied correspondence between Jesus the counselor and plain-speaking women. Silencing them is thus a cowardly act to avoid inspired truths.

'Cause we got a counsellor that will lead us and
direct us which way to go
And you find you'll come out successful
So many of us today we don't want that

We want sugar coat
That's why they don't want the women in the pulpit
The women gonna tell it like it is
Tell it like it is[47]

Archbishop Gilford's pulpit oratory was successful, in part, because she used language creatively within the traditional aesthetics of African American sermonic discourse. She creatively reworked traditional images and themes from her feminist point of view. Yet unlike many women preachers, she was comfortable chanting in the same style used by many men. Even when her message was not overtly feminist, her sermons challenged gender discrimination simply because she asserted that her words were divinely inspired. She never spoke from notes, trusting the spirit to guide her thoughts and tongue. Irrefutable proof of her belief that God does not discriminate was the protracted trance state into which many in her congregation entered when her sermons reached their climax. Her inspired words provided the appropriate ritual context for many others, particularly women, to touch the source of their own spiritual power and to celebrate through ecstasy.

Spiritual churches continue to be vibrant centers of women's spirituality in New Orleans neighborhoods seventy-five years after Leafy Anderson opened Eternal Life Christian Spiritualist Church Number 12. Today's leaders revere Mother Anderson and invoke her spirit, but they do not try to imitate her in every detail. For example, over time they have come to call themselves "Spiritual" rather than "Spiritualist" in order to avoid being mistaken, according to them, for fortune-tellers. Even more significantly, the name of Jesus is spoken in these churches even though Mother Anderson did not allow her followers to do so. Under the influence of American Spiritualism, she held "that Jesus as a man was not important—he was merely the earthly body of a nameless 'Spirit' by which name the deity is always addressed."[48] New Orleans Spiritualism remains true to its heritage not by perpetuating its founder's personal expressions of spirituality. Instead, it survives because leaders encourage members—both groups predominantly women—to accept and unveil their spiritual nature. Churches and prayer rooms are sites of rituals continually being improvised on the basis of traditional practices. Worship is a dynamic encounter of present and past. This creative spirituality is all the more remarkable since it continues in defiance of intense community resistance to Spiritualism as an institution. Women who frequently suffer emotionally from rejection by close friends and family are able to resist censure by forming a positive self-consciousness in these churches.

New Orleans Spiritualism has encouraged the development of women's spirituality, in large measure, because members do not ignore outsiders' persistence in equating the church with Voodoo. The theology and rituals of Spiritualism provide all members, but particularly women, with effective strategies for resisting such demonization without compromising their spirituality.

Notes

1. Brenda Marie Osbey, "Mother Catherine," *Southern Review* 30 (1994): 833. For a contemporaneous account of this religious leader see the 1934 essay "Mother Catherine," reprinted in *Zora Neale Hurston: Folklore, Memoirs, and Other Writings* (New York: Library of America, 1995), 854–60. See also the entry on Catherine Seal by Edward B. McDonald in *Notable Black American Women, Book II*, ed. Jessie Carney Smith (New York: Gale Research, 1996), 581–86.

2. Claude F. Jacobs and Andrew J. Kaslow provide the most complete introduction to the churches under discussion here in *The Spiritual Churches of New Orleans: Origins, Beliefs, and Rituals of an African-American Religion* (Knoxville: University of Tennessee Press, 1991). See also Hans Baer, *The Black Spiritual Movement: A Religious Response to Racism* (Knoxville: University of Tennessee Press, 1984); and Michael P. Smith, *Spirit World: Pattern in the Expressive Folk Culture of Afro-American New Orleans* (New Orleans: New Orleans Urban Folklife Society, 1984). There is no census of Spiritual church membership in New Orleans. My fieldwork over the past decade confirms the estimate of approximately fifty individual churches and prayer rooms, many with a small number of members, made by Jacobs and Kaslow. They found evidence of more than one hundred other Spiritual worship places that existed in the past. For an inclusive list of the churches, unfortunately with no indication of those that are inactive, see Kaslow and Jacobs's *Prophecy, Healing, and Power: The Afro-American Spiritual Churches of New Orleans*, Cultural Resources Management Study for the Jean Lafitte National Historical Park and the National Park Service (New Orleans: Department of Anthropology and Geography, University of New Orleans, 1981), 105–18.

3. Ina Johanna Fandrich, "The Mysterious Voodoo Queen Marie Laveaux: A Study of Power and Female Leadership in Nineteenth-Century New Orleans" (Ph.D. diss., Temple University, 1994), 167. She acknowledges that the high status accorded women in Voodoo is attributable, in part, to their roles as priestesses, mediums, and healers in West African societies. Also influential were "the sociopolitical, economic, and demographic dynamics prevailing" in New Orleans (179). For example, enslaved and free women of color outnumbered men in their respective social categories by two to one. Liaisons between women of color and white men were further encouraged because of the small number of white women citizens. Fandrich contends that free women of color "found social protection in Roman Catholicism, and many of them sought spiritual guidance and sisterhood in the Voodoo houses" (180). Free men of color, on the other hand, found social prestige and brotherhood by joining Freemason lodges, the free colored militia, and the military.

4. "A Sainted Woman," *New Orleans Democrat*, June 18, 1881. The obituaries mentioned here are excerpted by Fandrich, *Mysterious Voodoo Queen*, 263–

67. She offers the most careful assessment to date of biographical data regarding Marie Laveau. It is important to note that at some unspecifiable time she passed her position of leadership on to her daughter Marie Héloïse Glapion (1827–1881). Because the daughter assumed her mother's name, the Marie Laveau of legend tends to be a composite figure based on the lives of both women, who coincidentally died in the same year.

5. Robert Tallant, *The Voodoo Queen* (1956; reprint, Gretna, LA: Pelican, 1983), 1.

6. Robert Tallant, *Voodoo in New Orleans* (New York: Macmillan, 1946), 47.

7. Barbara Rosendale, "Marie Laveau: The Voodoo Queen Repossessed," *Folklore and Mythology Studies* 15 (1991): 48.

8. Ibid., 53.

9. The only reference to a Pittsburgh church appears in "Pay Last Respects to Mother Anderson," *Pittsburgh Courier*, December 24, 1927. A published report on the E.L.C.S.A. convention lists sixteen member congregations and missions, founded either by Anderson or her associates, located in Chicago, Indian Harbor (Indiana), Little Rock, Mariana (Arkansas), Memphis, Pensacola, Tallahassee, Century (Florida), Houston, Biloxi, and New Orleans (*Louisiana Weekly*, December 4, 1926). For further biographical information see the entry on Leafy Anderson written by Robert L. Johns in *Notable Black American Women, Book II*, ed. Jessie Carney Smith (New York: Gale Research, 1996), 9–11; and Jacobs and Kaslow, *The Spiritual Churches*, 32–37.

10. Zora Neale Hurston, "Hoodoo in America," *Journal of American Folklore* 44 (1931): 319.

11. In "Mother Catherine," written four years later, Hurston admires this leader for perpetuating Africanisms but does not suggest she is a hoodooist. The contrasts between Anderson and Seals in these two texts demonstrate the significant development during the early 1930s in Hurston's understanding of African American female spirituality, a change similarly suggested by the ways she revised "Hoodoo in America" prior to excerpting it in *Mules and Men* (1935).

12. For information about Spiritualism's influence on New Orleans Spiritualism see Jacobs and Kaslow, *The Spiritual Churches*, 73–82, 129.

13. Baer, *Black Spiritual Movement*, 22. For a thorough discussion of the influences on the Spiritual belief system from Roman Catholicism, Pentecostalism, Spiritualism, and Voodoo see Jacobs and Kaslow, *The Spiritual Churches*, 49–95.

14. Jacobs and Kaslow, *The Spiritual Churches*, 183. Although these scholars acknowledge the seminal leadership of women in the early years of the church, their discussion of Spiritualism's development as an institution privileges the work of men to the exclusion of women. Jean M. Humez has noted a similar male bias in historical accounts of the African Methodist Episcopal (AME) church. The institutional records on which historians typically rely do not adequately preserve the contributions of women "in creating and supporting the grass-roots organizational units of African Methodism." Through autobiographies, however, Humez has discovered that AME women were interested in a more ecstatic expression of spirituality and in the recognition of women preachers, just as were their twentieth-century Spiritual sisters in New Orleans. See " 'My Spirit Eye': Some Functions of Spiritual and Visionary Experience in the Lives of Five Black Women Preachers, 1810–1880," *Women and the Structure of Society: Selected Research from the Fifth Berkshire Conference on the History of Women*, ed. Bar-

bara J. Harris and JoAnn K. McNamara (Durham: Duke University Press, 1984), 129–43.

15. Personal interview, June 9, 1989.

16. Personal interview, February 23, 1989.

17. Carol Lois Haywood, "The Authority and Empowerment of Women among Spiritualist Groups," *Journal for the Scientific Study of Religion* 22 (1983): 164.

18. Testimony at Queen Esther Spiritual Temple of Christ, December 11, 1988.

19. Irving I. Zaretsky, "In the Beginning Was the Word: The Relationship of Language to Social Organization in Spiritualist Churches," *Religious Movements in Contemporary America*, ed. Irving I. Zaretsky and Mark P. Leone (Princeton: Princeton University Press, 1974), 211.

20. J. Stillson Judah, *The History and Philosophy of the Metaphysical Movements in America* (Philadelphia: Westminster, 1967), 69–70.

21. Jacobs and Kaslow, *The Spiritual Churches*, 127–28.

22. Smith, *Spirit Worlds*, 57.

23. For information on the devotion to these spirits, see Jacobs and Kaslow, *The Spiritual Churches*, 125–48; Jason Berry, *The Spirit of Black Hawk: A Mystery of Africans and Indians* (Jacksonville: University Press of Mississippi, 1995); and David C. Estes, "Across Ethnic Boundaries: St. Joseph's Day in a New Orleans Afro-American Spiritual Church," *Mississippi Folklore Register* 21 (1987): 9–22.

24. Felicitas D. Goodman, *Ecstasy, Ritual, and Alternate Reality: Religion in a Pluralistic World* (Bloomington: Indiana University Press, 1988), 36.

25. Similarly, in American Spiritualism "the possessing entities are disposed kindly toward their human hosts" and only the demons have been "dispossessed," according to Felicitas Goodman, *How about Demons? Possession and Exorcism in the Modern World* (Bloomington: Indiana University Press, 1988), 27.

26. The term "séance" refers to contacting departed spirits either during worship or during private consultations. Despite Mother Anderson's custom of holding séances, the term is seldom used by Spiritual followers today. Not all believers feel that the living should try to communicate with deceased relatives and friends (Jacobs and Kaslow, *The Spiritual Churches*, 141, 208).

27. " 'Mother' Anderson Dies, Followers Await Her Spirit," *New Orleans Morning Tribune*, December 15, 1927.

28. "Mother Catherine Will Rise from Her Grave, Negroes Say," *New Orleans Morning Tribune*, August 15, 1930.

29. Bishop Adams aroused controversy in 1970 when she was consecrated a bishop by a leader not affiliated with the organization of Spiritual churches to which she belonged. To quiet the dissension, she agreed to be reconsecrated: "After that I had the privilege to tell them, I say now you all may not know it but consecrating me over you've set me up over every bishop in this organization, giving me a second consecration. I said that should make me an archbishop if I wanted to be that" (Personal interview, June 9, 1989).

30. Mother Anderson Memorial Service, Queen Esther Divine Spiritual Temple of Christ, December 11, 1988. For a fuller discussion of this service see David C. Estes, "Ritual Validations of Clergywomen's Authority in the African American Spiritual Churches of New Orleans," *Women's Leadership in Marginal Religions: Explorations outside the Mainstream*, ed. Catherine Wessinger (Urbana: University of Illinois Press, 1993), 149–71.

31. Mother Anderson Memorial Service, December 11, 1988.

32. Personal interview, April 29, 1989.

33. I have been unable to locate this incident in extant precinct arrest books or in the records of the night court. The following newspaper account of another arrest, however, verifies that legal obstacles interfered with Spiritual worship rituals in the early years: "Neighbors said they heard 'all kinds of noises' coming from 1239 Desire Street, the home of Mr. and Mrs. Antonio Vega. So Corporal Rosch and Patrolmen Blancher and Smith raided. They found Lethe Anderson, 200-pound negress, 'raving around.' The permit was issued for a 'fish fry' but the police say it became a voodoo meeting. Twenty negroes, the Vegas, and several white men were arrested" ("Fish Fry Ends in Voodoo Revel, Police Charge," *New Orleans Times-Picayune*, April 17, 1925).

34. Mother Anderson Memorial Service, December 11, 1988.

35. Saint Joseph feasts have received more scholarly attention than have others. See David C. Estes, "St. Joseph's Day in a New Orleans Afro-American Spiritual Church." *Mississippi Folklore Register* 21 (1987): 9–21; and Andrew J. Kaslow, "The Afro-American Celebration of St. Joseph's Day in New Orleans," *Perspectives on Ethnicity in New Orleans*, ed. John Cooke and Mackie J-V Blanton (New Orleans: Committee on Ethnicity in New Orleans, 1979), 48–52. Jason Barry describes Black Hawk feasts in *Spirit of Black Hawk*, 1–9, 125–37.

36. Queen Esther Novena, 1989.

37. Testimony at Queen Esther Novena, January 19, 1990.

38. Queen Esther Novena, February 16, 1990.

39. For discussions of the traditional African American sermon, see Gerald L. Davis, *"I Got the Word in Me and I Can Sing It, You Know": A Study of the Performed African-American Sermon* (Philadelphia: University of Pennsylvania Press, 1985); and Bruce A. Rosenberg, *Can These Bones Live? The Art of the American Folk Preacher*, rev. ed. (Chicago: University of Chicago Press, 1988). For information on women and the traditional sermon, see Elaine J. Lawless, *Handmaidens of the Lord: Pentecostal Women Preachers and Traditional Religion* (Philadelphia: University of Pennsylvania Press, 1988); and Catherine Louise Peck, "Your Daughters Shall Prophesy: Women in the Afro-American Preaching Tradition" (M.A. thesis, University of North Carolina at Chapel Hill, 1983).

40. For a fuller discussion of Archbishop Gilford see David C. Estes, "Preaching in an Afro-American Spiritual Church: Archbishop Lydia Gilford and the Traditional Chanted Sermon," *Cultural Perspectives on the American South*, vol. 5, *Religion*, ed. Charles Reagan Wilson (New York: Gordon and Breach, 1991), 79–102; and Smith, *Spirit World*, 50–60.

41. Personal interview, February 21, 1989.

42. Goodman writes that "whether people remember the content of the ecstasy is not left to individual choice, but rather depends on what is expected in their religious community. . . . Amnesia will set in only if there is an express instruction demanding it" (*Ecstasy*, 39–40).

43. "Put on the Whole Armor of God," Infant Jesus of Prague Spiritual Church, July 13, 1986.

44 . Ibid.

45. Ibid.

46. "A Wonderful Counsellor," Infant Jesus of Prague Spiritual Church, January 11, 1987.

47. Ibid.

48. Hurston, "Hoodoo," 319.

9

Red Lilac of the Cayugas: Traditional Indian Laws and Culture Conflict in a Witchcraft Trial in Buffalo, New York, 1930

~

Sidney L. Harring

The witch murder trial of two Cayuga women in New York bears many similarities to the trial of Tommy Jemmy, described by Matthew Dennis in "Seneca Possessed," this volume. In both cases, the issue of jurisdiction arose; who had the authority to make decisions about Indian affairs: the tribe or the state? The two scenarios also throw into relief the persistence of traditional Native beliefs and the contradictions of assimilation.

In the case presented by Sidney Harring, ironies abound as both sides embraced and denied witchcraft. In her confession, for example, one of the accused women named the murder victim as a "white witch" who used magic to kill the Indian people. The defendant, in turn, claimed to have recruited a woman well versed in traditional spiritual medicine to kill the "witch." When their efforts failed, the two Cayuga women used a gag and a hammer instead. The case turned into nothing less than an examination of Iroquois assimilation. White New Yorkers were shocked to learn that their "civilized" Indian neighbors still clung to such "savagery."

From Sidney L. Harring, "Red Lilac of the Cayugas: Traditional Indian Laws and Culture Conflict in a Witchcraft Trial in Buffalo, New York, 1930," *New York History* 73, no. 1 (January 1992): 65–94. Reprinted by permission of the New York State Historical Association.

Harring's article pushes us to confront the enduring differences between Native American and white religious belief, and among Iroquois people themselves, even into the twentieth century. Indian religion could be tolerated by white New Yorkers to the extent that it embraced values compatible with Christianity—for example, a tradition of sharing or a belief in the "great spirit." Witchcraft did not fall under that rubric. And like black Spiritualists and other marginalized people, the Cayugas were concerned about respectability and survival; many sought to deny any connection between the practice of witchcraft and traditional longhouse religion. For them, the case was an embarrassment and a liability. But if some wanted to distance themselves from these two women, the majority defended them against racist white justice, which equated Indian spirituality with superstition and violence and saw Indians generally as sexually immoral and criminal. Once demeaned, Indian religious and cultural belief could be rejected as irrelevant to the proceedings, and the defendants could be tried in a legalized, ethnocentric fashion. But Cayuga resistance, and the ambiguities of Indians' legal status, led to a less predictable outcome. Harring's essay highlights questions not only about stereotypes and justice but also about the definition of "witch," which often turns on the complex, imagined relationship between women and evil, in this case Native American women who (at least since Tituba) have been particularly vulnerable to these racist charges.

NATIVE AMERICAN LAW IS LARGELY the history of government policy toward Indians. Native Americans have struggled, however, to shape that law. While their struggle can be chronicled, it is not reflected in the evolution of legal doctrine: The issues that move people are not necessarily the same issues that move courts.

Assimilation has been the dominant governmental policy in Indian law since the 1880s. But the revival of a strong traditional Indian culture in the late 1960s reflected an undercurrent of traditional Indian life surviving and growing on Indian reservations.[1] The Iroquois of New York State are a good source for a revised history of Native American law. The Iroquois were among the first Native Americans relegated to reservations and were often distinguished from Native Americans in the West. Justice Cuthbert Pound of the New York State Court of Appeals said of them:

> They have in varying degrees adopted the arts and institutions of civilization, and, except in an international sense, they may not fairly be called a "feeble remnant," nor may it be said of them that "their

> fiery tempers" or "their nomadic habits" show a total want of capacity for self government ranking them with the uncivilized Indians of the west. Farms and orchards abound and dwelling houses and barns are found that compare not unfavorably with those of the neighboring communities. Churches and schools are maintained and modest accumulations of wealth arc not unusual.[2]

These images were brought under public scrutiny in Buffalo in 1930 and 1931 when Lila Jimerson, whom the press called the "Red Lilac of the Cayugas," and Nancy Bowen, an old Cayuga traditional healer, from the nearby Cattaraugus reservation, were charged with the "witch murder" of a white woman. In this important trial the Iroquois proved themselves articulate strategists for their own interests, at odds with state and federal Indian policy and the image of assimilated Natives. The witch murder trial went to the heart of the deep cultural differences between Iroquois and white America, underscoring the fundamental fallacy of the assimilationist model.

The question of individual guilt or innocence is usually the heart of any murder trial. But in the present case, the social context is of particular importance. Briefly, these are the facts: Henri Marchand, Jr., a twelve-year-old, returned from school on March 7, 1930, to a gruesome scene: The body of his mother, Clothilde, was

> lieing [*sic*] at the foot of the stairs. . .beneath a heavy cabinet containing a radio loudspeaker. . . . The corner of the room was spattered with blood. An electric floor lamp had been overturned. The remnants of a vase which had been standing on the cabinet . . . were scattered about the floor.

Terrified, the boy ran a short distance to the Buffalo Museum of Science to bring back his father and brother Paul. Henri Marchand, Sr., summoned a doctor from nearby Deaconness Hospital who announced that the woman had been dead about two hours.[3]

Three police officers, including two detectives, arrived shortly on the scene. Foul play was suspected because the body was severely lacerated. The autopsy showed that a tightly bound paper wad soaked in chloroform had been stuffed down Clothilde Marchand's throat while she was still alive. There was no other evidence. But a neighbor reported seeing two Indian women walking "up and down the block and every time they passed the place they would pause, appearing to be examining it." By ten o'clock the police arrested Lila Jimerson at the house of her father, Anson, in a remote area of the Cattaraugus reservation, twenty-five miles from Buffalo. Once in police custody in Buffalo, Lila named Nancy Bowen, whom the police arrested on the reservation and brought back to Buffalo early the next morning.[4]

Within a few hours of their arrests, both women confessed to the murder. Lila Jimerson had known the Marchands for nearly ten years. It must, in fact, have been Henri Marchand who identified Lila as one of the two women and gave police precise directions to her father's house. Henri had often come to the Cattaraugus reservation to vacation and to work on dioramas of Iroquois life that he sculpted for the New York State Museum in Albany and the Buffalo Museum of Science. He had built a life-sized replica of an Indian "cabin," Jimerson's house, and had posed Lila, nude above the waist, in "Iroquois village" scenes. During this interaction, Lila became infatuated with Marchand, and resolved to kill Clothilde Marchand in order to marry Henri.

Lila allegedly recruited Nancy Bowen to this endeavor. Mrs. Bowen, a sixty-six-year-old Cayuga widow—a curer and herbalist—lived on a farm nearby. She was deeply grieving the recent death of her husband, "Sassafras Charlie," who had also practiced traditional medicine. Nancy belonged to a community of Iroquois who shared a strong traditional belief in spirits. According to the confessions, Lila had convinced Nancy that Clothilde Marchand was a "white witch" who used magic to kill off the Cayuga and Seneca people, including Nancy's husband. For six months, Lila and Nancy has resorted to traditional Iroquois witchcraft to kill Clothilde, but had failed.[5]

On March 6, Lila and Nancy walked five miles across the reservation to the trolley line that ran from Dunkirk to Buffalo, and took a streetcar to downtown Buffalo. Nancy carried a bottle of chloroform that Lila had purchased in a village near the reservation, and a tightly wadded paper ball. Then they walked to Jefferson Street, where Lila bought a "ten-cent" hammer. Lila led Nancy to the Marchand house and left her nearby. From a phone booth, she called Henri Marchand at the museum and asked him to take her for a ride in his car. Henri complied, allegedly because "Indians loved to go for automobile rides." They drove around Buffalo from 2:00 to 3:00 P.M., when Henry dropped off Lila to "meet [her] friend."

At virtually the same time, Nancy knocked on Clothilde Marchand's door, was recognized as Lila's friend, and admitted into the house. In poor English, Nancy asked Marchand: "You, witch?" Clothilde laughed and appeared to answer "yes." Nancy hit her on the head with the hammer, which had been concealed in her bag. Clothilde struggled violently and was hit several more times. Nancy then forced the chloroformed wad of paper down her throat and left the house. Lila and Nancy met on Jefferson Avenue at about 3:30 P.M. and returned to Cattaraugus[6]

District Attorney Guy Moore did everything he could to emphasize the sensational nature of the case. He moved the case with unusual speed to a jury trial. He announced that he would seek the death penalty for both women, and he engaged in deliberate racism, emphasizing the murder as an "Indian" crime. The trial of Jimerson and Bowen became a trial of the Iroquois people in general, and of the traditional Iroquois in particular.

The case against the women was ready in two weeks, faster than any previous capital case in Buffalo. New revelations fell into two categories: first, the nature and extent of witchcraft practices within the Iroquois community; and second, the details of Henri Marchand's relationship with Lila Jimerson. It was the state that decided to delve more deeply into witchcraft. They unearthed the body of Sassafras Charlie Bowen to dispel a rumor that Nancy had shot him accidentally as she shot at "demons," although the connection to Clothilde's murder was at best tangential.[7]

Similarly, the state was obsessed with searching the reservation for evidence, most specifically the hammer used in the murder. According to the confession, Nancy had thrown it into a creek near Jimerson's house. After a week, when the police could not find it, they used its disappearance as an excuse for warrantless and indiscriminate searches. Traditional Seneca and Cayuga societies were exposed to the unrestricted prying of dozens of police agents. Seneca Chief Ray Jimerson protested unsuccessfully this trespassing on Seneca land.[8]

In contrast, it was nine days before District Attorney Moore's attention turned to whites. On March 15, Moore finally arrested Henri Marchand as a material witness. He was compelled to make this move when the Buffalo *Times* printed four love letters Marchand had written to Lila Jimerson, letters that revealed an affair of at least two years' duration.[9] These letters exposed two things about Marchand: He had a motive to kill his wife, and he had repeatedly lied to the police. Furthermore, their anonymous appearance in the newspaper illustrates how alienated the Senecas were from white legal procedure—Lila's family had given the letters to the press, rather than to the police.

Jury selection began on March 19. It proceeded slowly owing to prejudicial pretrial publicity and the fact that many prospective jurors asserted they would not vote to execute a woman.[10] The trial began the following Monday, but was soon interrupted when United States Attorney Richard Templeton entered the courtroom. At the request of the Bureau of Indian Affairs, the United States Attorney General had ordered Templeton to participate in the Indians' defense. State Judge F. Bret Thorne and District Attorney Moore were outraged at this unprecedented federal intervention in New York State affairs, and Thorne delayed the trial only four hours while Templeton familiarized himself with the case. Moore attributed federal intervention to Indian "troublemakers" opposed to the "republican form of government."[11] In truth, the Iroquois community had been working hard to save Jimerson and Bowen from a legalized lynching.

When the trial resumed and Moore put Nancy Bowen on the witness stand, Templeton objected to swearing her in "until he could consult with the Attorney General of the United States to determine her status." Templeton was raising the issue as to whether the State of New York had any right to try an Iroquois. He was overruled and the trial proceeded. Nancy gave five hours of powerful testimony. She spoke in Seneca, the language in which she understood the world. The interpretations into English were at issue, so the defense retained their own interpreter to make sure that what Nancy said was accurately translated for the jury.[12]

When Bowen testified, she introduced new factual information. She had received instructions to kill Mrs. Marchand in three letters sent by an unknown "Mrs. Dooley," postmarked from Buffalo and Cleveland. A quote from one letter indicates their purpose:

> I know something Secret. I decided that I'd better tell you and help you out. What I can. This is what I know Charlie Bowen is killed by a witch in this City of Buffalo. It was from a French woman. . . . She killed Charlie because he have good medicine to sell in the city. Her witchcraft didn't work so good so she decided to kill him. . . .
>
> She kill many, many that way, indians & white. But let me tell you more. She said she fixed another doll the same this doll is his wife Nancy.

The letters provided a complete plan for Nancy's murder.[13] District Attorney Moore missed their significance: for if Lila had influenced Nancy so strongly, why did Nancy operate from instructions given in letters?

But Nancy's testimony was sensationally upstaged by that of Henri Marchand. Henri's behavior toward Lila emerged as more complex, manipulative, and sordid. Indian women, he said, were naturally shy, and would not pose for him nude above the waist unless he made love to them. Because he needed accurate representation of their breasts for his dioramas, he made love to them out of "professional necessity." In two days on the stand, Henri claimed so many love affairs that he could not count them. Lila was one of them, but he did not love her. Because Marchand was a free-loving French artist, whose wife knew all about his affairs, he had no motive to kill her.

The case for the defense required less than a day. An expert testified that the handwriting on the "Mrs. Dooley" letters was not Lila

Jimerson's, thereby implicating an unknown additional party and undermining Moore's "jealous lover" theory because it is hard to recruit collaborators for such schemes. The defense's major effort was to save Lila from the death penalty. Nancy Bowen did not face such a risk. She was sixty-six years old and, as the defense portrayed her, the unwilling tool of unknown parties, distraught at the death of her husband, sincerely engaged in Iroquois witchcraft, and lacking a *mens rea* for murder—that is, the required mental element, the specific intent to kill. The defense recalled Henri Marchand to the stand, to discredit him again about lying to and using Lila and to remind the jury what a venal person he was.[14]

On Tuesday, April 1, as both sides were ready to do their summaries, Lila Jimerson collapsed from a lung hemorrhage. At first the reports from the hospital were that her condition was not serious and she would return to trial. But on Wednesday afternoon, Judge Thorne declared a mistrial and discharged the jurors. Immediately there were rumors of a plea bargain, and the next day Lila weakly pleaded guilty to the reduced charge of second-degree murder. Although both her family and Iroquois leaders protested, Lila had been worn down and did not want to face another trial.[15]

But the case was not to be disposed of so easily. Within two weeks, the state was ready to retry Nancy Bowen, who had not pleaded guilty. Lila Jimerson soon expressed a desire to withdraw her plea and stand trial again. Sympathizers, including the president of the Seneca Nation, approached the famous attorney Clarence Darrow, who agreed to enter the case if "it would not be too long a trial," but eventually declined because "no principle of law was involved."[16]

Cattaraugus Reservation Senecas and Cayugas, who had not testified in the trial, agreed to "tell what they know" in the retrial. Lila, strengthened by the support of her people, prevailed in her determination to stand trial again. In the process, she dismissed her original lawyers and hired a new one, John McGovern. District Attorney Moore did not oppose her motion to withdraw her plea, either because he still wanted a capital conviction, or because he did not think a death-bed guilty plea would hold up on appeal.[17]

It was not until March 1931 that the state retried Lila Jimerson separately from Nancy Bowen. The defense was straightforward: Lila testified that she had had an affair with Henri Marchand, but denied killing Clothilde or inducing Nancy to kill her. She fully implicated Marchand when she stated that he had tried to hire numerous Iroquois to kill his wife because he was "tired of her." Although Henri, who by then had a new, eighteen-year-old wife, stayed away from the trial and was not called to testify, it is likely that the all-male jury believed he was responsible for the murder. It acquitted Lila in less than an evening of deliberation. One week after Lila's acquittal, Nancy pleaded guilty to second-degree manslaughter and was sentenced to the time that she had already served.[18] The return of the two women to Cattaraugus represented a stunning victory for an Iroquois defense faced with a hostile and racist white court.

What did witchcraft mean to the Iroquois in upstate New York in 1930? What is the significance of the witchcraft issue in the Buffalo trial? Anthropologists have devoted a great deal of effort to understanding the social meaning of witchcraft.[19] Students of comparative law know that when preliterate peoples are conquered, their legal systems are pushed aside and foreign law imposed on them. Such impositions create resentment as well as injustice. When questions are formulated around what problems conquest creates for the new dominant legal form, the cultural integrity of a people as it is embodied in their own law is denied. For example, the forced assimilation of tribal peoples creates problems for Anglo-American law in proving *mens rea*, the required mental element of a crime. Criminal intent can be impossible to demonstrate cross-culturally because Western notions of intent do not apply to many of the complex behavior systems existing in other societies.[20] Nancy Bowen's innocence of mind was apparent to all who heard her testify to killing, as a matter of course, a witch who repeatedly killed Iroquois people.

The presence of witchcraft within Iroquois culture after 130 years of reservation life was totally inconsistent with popular views that the Iroquois were assimilated or that New York State's Indians were different from "savages" out west. Because they were deeply rooted in an Iroquois tradition misperceived by whites, Lila Jimerson and Nancy Bowen, who were descended from the most traditional, conservative, and antagonistic Seneca, were beyond the understanding of the dominant alien culture.[21]

Their trial focused a great deal of popular attention on New York Iroquois. For a month, Buffalo's three newspapers were full of stories about their society, religion, education, legal status, and witchcraft. The slant of the Buffalo *Times* suggested that the Iroquois were being rapidly assimilated. The *Courier Express* ran a Sunday magazine feature of photographs of Henri Marchand's Buffalo Museum of Science dioramas under the title "The Iroquois Indian Lives Again in Buffalo." The pictures illustrated strong and handsome Indian figures going about daily chores, and included a half-naked figure of Lila Jimerson.[22] The text was as racist and romanticized as the dioramas.

The Iroquois had indeed returned to Buffalo, but not as museum models. They were living participants in the Jimerson and Bowen trials. Every day the courthouse hallway was filled with Iroquois men and women—Seneca, Cayuga, Tuscarora. They arose by 4:00 A.M., walked many miles, rode trolleys, and waited in the hall to observe, to confer with each other, and to discuss strategy. They were treated rudely by bailiffs and ridiculed in the local papers. The Iroquois were seldom allowed into the courtroom, which was full of newspaper reporters from all over the country, and also armed security men.[23] This security was unheard of in Buffalo courts of that day. Given that no threats were made during the trial, these security measures reflect an unrealistic racist fear of Iroquois "violence."

Religion, culture, and race were major concerns during the trial. The manner in which Lila and Nancy were portrayed offers insights into the nature of those concerns. Physical descriptions of Lila were unflattering. She "look[ed] like nothing in the world but the happy berry picker who comes to the back door of a hotel." Her coloring was the subject of considerable discussion; Lila's mother was Cayuga, her father was part Seneca and part white. The press tried to explain her involvement in the murder racially: The savagery came from her Indian blood; the careful planning and cunning avoidance of blame, from her white blood.[24]

Lila Jimerson's social background was as ordinary for the Cattaraugus reservation of that time as were her coloring and racial stock. She lived neatly and simply in the more isolated part of the reservation, always with her father and aunt, her mother having died when she was very young. She had never held a regular job, but was a fast and efficient grape picker. Despite her education (she could read and write, and play the piano) and some acceptance of Christianity, in many ways Lila had chosen to participate in customary Iroquois life.

Nancy Bowen was among the most traditional residents of the reservation: Short and stocky, she did not speak English very well, dressed only in plain black dresses, and "had never owned a hat." She farmed and gathered herbs and bark in the forests for use doing healing rituals. Together with her husband, Charlie, she was at the center of traditional Iroquois medicine on the Cattaraugus reservation and deeply involved in the world of Iroquois religion.[25]

The press was substantially concerned about the extent to which traditional religion was practiced by the Iroquois. Such "paganism" was seen by whites as an impediment to assimilation and a contributing factor in the murder of Clothilde Marchand. The traditional "longhouse" religion of the Iroquois included dances, sacred laws, a system of morality, the tradition of sharing, and belief in the "great spirit," who was "like the Christian god." It did not include witchcraft.[26]

Witchcraft was well established, however, in the original Seneca belief systems. Historical literature on the Seneca describes both witchcraft and the tribally authorized execution of witches. In the spring of 1799, the Seneca Chief Cornplanter ordered three of his sons to kill a woman who he thought had been responsible for killing his daughter. When they found her working in an open field, they stabbed her to death and buried her. The killing upset the village, so a chief's council was called to deliberate the slaying. The council decided that "justice had been done and in order to put away evil from the people, those of familiar Spirits must be driven out of the land."[27] In an 1822 case, the Seneca Chief Red Jacket personally defended Tommy Jemmy, who was accused by a white court of carrying out a tribally ordered witch killing. At issue was Seneca sovereignty as represented by the Seneca Nation's right to apply its own customary laws.[28]

Lewis Henry Morgan wrote in 1851 that the killing of witches was "frequent among the Senecas in the past fifty years." Morgan went on to describe something of the context of the belief system:

> A belief in witches is to this day, and always has been, one of the most deeply-seated notions in the minds of the Iroquois. The popular belief on this subject rose to the most extravagant degree of the marvellous, and the supernatural. . . . [Witches] were imbued with the power of doing evil, and were wholly bent upon deeds of wickedness. . . . Such was the universal terror of witches, that their lives were forfeited by the laws of the Iroquois. Any one who discovered the act might not only destroy the witch, but could take to himself the dangerous power of deciding who it was. To this day it is next to impossible, by any process of reasoning, to divest the mind of a Seneca of his deep-seated belief in witches.[29]

Witchcraft was the heart of Lila's and Nancy's defense. The witch killing of Marchand was regrettable but nonetheless appropriate. This was testified to by the leading Seneca expert of the day, Arthur C. Parker. Among other activities, he was the author of more than 100 scholarly works on the Iroquois. According to Parker:

> Only confessed witches could be punished for their witchery. . . . According to the belief a witch is under the control of the Great Spirit, and has an order to tell the truth when questioned. Thus, it is the belief that when a witch is asked the question, 'Are you a witch?', she cannot deny it. . . . The hammer used in the case was the proper instrument with which to expel the witch supposed to be inhabiting

> Mrs. Marchand's frail frame. The blows on the forehead and crown were properly struck. . .in order to banish the evil spirit.[30]

Another strategy of the defense was to take the press on a walk around the reservation's graveyards and witchcraft sites where all-night vigils had been held to call upon the spirits of dead warriors to kill the witch Clothilde Marchand. The locations contained, among other items, simple paper dolls, cut from Marchand's letters to Lila.[31] This tour was a bold stroke on the part of the attorneys, but it was also controversial. On one hand, it clearly showed that Lila's and Nancy's beliefs were well established, traditional, and genuine; they were not manufactured as a way to escape criminal responsibility. Every means of exorcising the witchcraft had been tried and had failed before Clothilde Marchand was killed. On the other hand, the continuing existence of witchcraft embarrassed many Iroquois when those beliefs were equated with the traditional longhouse religion.

It can be seen how deeply rooted in the culture witchcraft practices were from their appearance in many contexts. When a chicken had "gone crazy" on the morning of the murder, Nancy was convinced that "witches were working" and that the "Mrs. Dooley" letters were accurate. A tragic sequence of traditional questions formulated to expose the witch had sealed Clothilde's fate. While Nancy was in jail, Lila's aunt complained that Nancy was "witching" her. Nancy herself asked the jailors for medicine to banish the witches that were giving her headaches.[32]

At this point it is useful to place witchcraft in its social context. Anthropologists have explained the phenomenon as an "adaptive and adjustment" mechanism serving a variety of functions in a society undergoing rapid social change.[33] Kluckhohn's study of witchcraft among the Navajo suggests that it flourished as Indian traditions were increasingly destroyed by white society. To fully encompass witchcraft practices is difficult, however, because of their secretive, specialized nature. Furthermore, in the confusion of conquest, many Native populations are divided among themselves. For instance, some Iroquois, embarrassed that the witchcraft issue suggested that they were backward and violent, encouraged their people to renounce Lila and Nancy and leave them to the mercy of white justice.

But the majority of the Iroquois people—even though many were opposed to Lila Jimerson's and Nancy Bowen's behavior, and some even thought them "crazy"—rose to their defense and used the "disgraceful" trial not to hide shame, but to attack racist white justice. Direct Iroquois involvement in the case was completely unexpected, and could not be explained by the prevailing stereotypes. Chief Clinton

Rickard of the Tuscaroras reported that some Tuscaroras did not want to defend Lila and Nancy because they were Cayugas, but the majority of the tribe took the position that Native Americans must stand together and fight for their rights. Individual Iroquois, stopped in Cattaraugus by newspaper reporters and asked about the trial, criticized white justice.[34]

Visibly moving were the daily demonstrations of support by dozens of Seneca and Cayuga men and women who stood about in the courthouse hallways. The courtroom was full of white officials, reporters, telegraph operators with silent instruments, and security guards unable to comprehend the social context of the event, while the hallway was full of quiet Iroquois.

Though the presence of ordinary Iroquois was significant, the Iroquois leadership also rallied to the cause. Chief Ray Jimerson of the Seneca and Chief Clinton Rickard of the Tuscarora were instrumental in mobilizing federal intervention. Alice Lee Jimison, a writer and Indian reformer, worked closely with Rickard and Ray Jimerson to combat the racist flow of public opinion surrounding the case.[35]

The growing Iroquois boldness on political matters and the willingness to defend two Iroquois charged with a witch murder were positive developments in the politicization of the Iroquois people. However, some uncertainty was left as to how to deal with the witchcraft issue in Lila's and Nancy's defense. Much of the Iroquois nationalism that was beginning to mobilize was deeply rooted in the traditional religion of the longhouse. As the trial progressed, the press confused religion with the Iroquois belief in witchcraft, a side effect regretted by many Iroquois who wanted to protect the integrity of their two traditional belief systems. Apparently the defense chose deliberately to underplay witchcraft at the behest of those Iroquois actively involved in the trial strategy. It is not surprising that the Iroquois should want to protect their traditional belief system and also defend Jimerson and Bowen. They were already facing a strong drive by New York State to govern the reservations, they lacked control of their educational system, and they confronted continuing pressure from Christian missionaries. In the face of this onslaught, their decision to defend Lila and Nancy was even more remarkable. . . .

A criminal trial often transcends its status as a legal event because of the popular attention such trials receive and because of the distinct historical data they generate—sometimes in the form of legal documents and transcripts, sometimes from sources outside the courtroom. This allows the historian to see beyond the legal history made by judges and legislators to the legal history made by ordinary people. The

Jimerson/Bowen trial contained a number of episodes that reveal the role of Native Americans in shaping Indian law. Although Clarence Darrow had not seen it, the Iroquois recognized that the great legal issue at stake in the Jimerson/Bowen trial was their sovereignty. While few Iroquois would have chosen to use a witch murder trial as an occasion to assert basic rights, because of the complex and contradictory messages about Iroquois society that the issues exposed, this was the arena available to them, and they succeeded in using it well. Although the trial early asserted strong anti-Iroquois sentiment, Iroquois action carefully and steadily brought the trial around to a victory for Native Americans.

Lila and Nancy were returned to Cattaraugus as free women after their year-long ordeal.[36] But the scope of the victory went further. The Iroquois opposition to New York State control over Indian affairs was strengthened by federal intervention in the case. The Snell Bill became intermeshed with the trial and was defeated.* While the state tried to use the trial to show that federal supervision of Indian affairs had not civilized the Iroquois, and that jurisdictional confusion undermined legal authority, the trial actually proved how essential federal intervention was. The trial also provided another opportunity for the Iroquois to develop their political skills and to consolidate political alliances. When representatives of the Iroquois Nation went to Washington to testify against the Snell Bill, they loudly and effectively protested that they had not been consulted on the question of state control over Indian affairs.

Prior to the late 1920s the Iroquois of New York State were relegated to the margins of social, economic, and political life. They could safely be ignored in policy matters. The roots of change in their status had been laid before the Jimerson/Bowen trial, but in no situation was contemporary reservation life more visible to white society. By the end of the trial it was clear that the Iroquois constituted a distinct cultural, religious, and politically articulate nation.

Anthropologists of law who have studied the interaction between witchcraft and social change see witchcraft and witch killings as evidence of the survival of a minority culture in the face of oppressive domination. But a witch murder trial may say as much about the society that holds the trial: First, how much force is the dominant society willing to exert to destroy the integrity of the vanquished? By 1930,

*The Snell Bill, introduced in 1930 by a New York congressman, was the last attempt to give the state of New York full authority over the Iroquois. Similar measures to challenge Iroquois sovereignty had been sought in 1888, 1906, and 1915.

the overt genocide of the "Indian Wars" was over, but Indians could still be electrocuted for their crimes. Second, how does the law reflect culturally relativist values? The Jimerson/Bowen case was a sensation when it concerned "Indian witches," but when it turned to adultery and murder, the case quickly lost momentum. Finally, holding a witch murder trial showed that the dominant culture assumed both assimilation and acquiescence by the Iroquois, when in actuality their traditional belief systems had not been penetrated.

While the traditional practices of Bowen and Jimerson were vestigial and marginal to the reservation, they were sufficiently significant to generate powerful support. An understanding of the witchcraft element is essential to an understanding of the murder, the trial, or Iroquois and white society in western New York in 1930.

The core of this story is a murder trial, so it is not inappropriate to end with the query: Who killed Clothilde Marchand? The Iroquois version never changed: White people did. Chief Rickard accepted the suggestion that Marchand and a friend had done the killing and had paid Lila Jimerson and Nancy Bowen to take the blame.[37] Another scenario that was circulated at the time of the trials is that Nancy and Lila killed Clothilde but that Henri manipulated their belief system into a murder weapon. His knowledge of Iroquois society, his assistant Burmeister's expertise in witchcraft, and his friendship with the most traditional Iroquois people would supposedly have enabled him to set up the tragic chain of events. If this speculation is accurate, then Marchand's reaction upon hearing that Lila had been acquitted is the ultimate insult. He said, "It was a terrible injustice."

Notes

1. See Rennard Strickland, ed., *Felix S. Cohen's Handbook of Federal Indian Law* (Charlottesville: Michie Bobbs-Merrill, 1982), 62–180, which contains a complete list of sources. On the policy of assimilation, see Frederick E. Hoxie, *A Final Promise: The Campaign to Assimilate the Indians, 1880–1920* (Lincoln: University of Nebraska Press, 1984); Francis Paul Prucha, *The Great Father: The United States Government and the American Indians* (Lincoln: University of Nebraska Press, 1984), especially chaps. 24–35; Francis Paul Prucha, *Americanizing the American Indians: Writings of the Friends of the Indian, 1880–1900* (Lincoln: University of Nebraska Press, 1973).

2. The best summary of the unique character of New York State Indian law in historical context is Gerald Gunther, "Governmental Power and New York Indian Lands—A Reassessment of a Persistent Problem of Federal State Relations," *Buffalo Law Review* 8 (1958), 1. A more detailed discussion of the critical period of the late 19th and early 20th centuries is Judge Cuthbert Pound, "Na-

tionals Without a Nation: The New York State Tribal Indians," *Columbia Law Review* 29 (1922), 97. The quotation on modern Iroquois life is at p. 97. A general historical overview of New York State Indian policy is in Helen M. Upton, *The Everett Report in Historical Perspective* (Albany: New York State Bicentennial Commission, 1980), chaps. 2–4.

3. Buffalo *Evening News*, March 7, 1930; Buffalo *Courier Express*, March 7, 1930. No transcript of the trial exists. However, we can study the trial in great detail because it was extensively covered by the news media. More than twenty reporters covered the entire trial, sending "live" Morse Code transmissions from the courtroom, using special silent telegraph instruments. All three of Buffalo's major daily newspapers ran detailed daily accounts, including long segments of transcripts of trial testimony. We are relying on three independent versions, the Buffalo *Courier Express*, the Buffalo *Times*, and the Buffalo *Evening News*.

4. *Courier Express*, March 7–8, 1930; *Evening News*, March 7–8, 1930.

5. This represents the final version of the murder story as it came out at the trial, primarily in the testimony of Nancy Bowen. During the two weeks before the trial, elements of the story were reported as they were "discovered" by the press, through leaks by the police or defense lawyers. *Evening News*, March 26, 1930; *Courier Express*, March, 8, 9, 19, 1930.

6. This account is based entirely on the two confessions of Lila and Nancy, taken by the Buffalo police on March 8, the day after the murder. *Courier Express*, March 8–9, 1930, *Evening News*, March 8–9, 1930.

7. *Evening News*, March 14, 1930.

8. *Courier Express*, March 12–14, 1930; *Times*, March 14, 1930.

9. *Times*, March 16, 1930. The publication of the love letters, Marchand's arrest, and a tour of witchcraft rites at Cattaraugus grave sites threw the opening of the trial on March 19 into a state of complete confusion. It also exposed how the state had followed up only on the evidence that supported its own case.

10. *Courier Express*, March 20–21, 24–25, 1930.

11. *Courier Express*, March 20–21, 24–25, 1930.

12. *Evening News*, March 25–26, 1930; *Courier Express*, March 26, 1930.

13. First mention of the Dooley letters appeared in the *Courier Express* on March 22, 1930.

14. *Courier Express*, March 30–31; April 1, 1930.

15. *Evening News*, April 1–3, 1930.

16. *Courier Express*, April 16–18, 1930.

17. *Courier Express*, April 30, 1930; February 21–March 1, 1931.

18. *Courier Express*, March 13–14, 1930.

19. There is a substantial literature on law and witchcraft that develops these themes. The major article initiating the discussion is Robert B. Seidman, "Witch Murder and Mens Rea: A Problem of Society under Radical Social Change," *Modern Law Review* 28 (1965), 46. See also Isaac Shapera, "Sorcery and Witchcraft in Bechuanaland," in 51 *African Affairs* 44; T.W. Bennett, "Witchcraft: A Problem in Fault and Causation," *Comparative and International Law Journal of South Africa* 12 (1979), 293; Adrienne van Blerk, "Sorcery and Crime," *Comparative and International Law Journal of South Africa* II (1978), 336; Law Reform Commission of Papua New Guinea, "Sorcery among the Sepiks," Occasional Paper No. 10 (October 1978); Martin Zelenietz, "The Effects of Sorcery in Kilenge, West New Britain Province," *Law Reform Commission of Papua New Guinea, Occasional Paper* No. II (August 1979); Mathole Motshekge, "The Ideology behind Witchcraft and the Principle of Fault in Criminal Law, " paper

presented at a workshop on "Conflict, Accommodation and Conflict Management" in South Africa, Cape Town, August 1984.

Beyond this legal analysis of the phenomenon of witchcraft, there is literature broader in its historical and sociological coverage that is important in locating witchcraft in its social context. Two examples are John Putnam Demos, *Entertaining Satan: Witchcraft and the Culture of Early New England* (New York: Oxford University Press, 1982), 82; Paul Boyer and Stephen Nissenbaum, *Salem Possessed: The Social Origins of Witchcraft* (Cambridge, Mass.: Harvard University Press, 1974).

Two general surveys of the range of anthropological explanations of witchcraft are Max Marwick, *Witchcraft and Sorcery* (London: Penguin Books, 1970); John Middleton and E. H. Winter, *Witchcraft and Sorcery in East Africa* (London: Routledge and Kegan Paul, Ltd., 1963); John Middleton, *Magic, Witchcraft, and Curing* (Austin: University of Texas Press, 1976).

20. Sandra Burman and Barbara Harrell-Bond, *The Imposition of Law* (London: Academic Press, 1979); Michael B. Hooker, *Legal Pluralism* (Oxford: Oxford University Press, 1972); Robert Seidman, "Mens Rea and the Reasonable African: The Pre-Scientific World-View and Mistake of Fact," *International and Comparative Law Quarterly* 15 (1966), 1135.

21. Robert Berkhoffer, *The White Man's Indian* (New York: Alfred A. Knopf, 1978), 3. Berkhoffer's central thesis is that while the Native American is real, the Indian was "invented" by whites. The term "Indian" refers to the white "image" and not to Native Americans.

22. *Courier Express*, March 16, 1930; *Times*, March 8, 1930.

23. The daily papers printed numerous accounts of Iroquois spectators in the unfamiliar setting of the trial. See, for example, *Courier Express*, March 16, 21, 23, 25, 29, 30, 1930; April 1, 1930.

24. *Courier Express*, March 13, 20, 1930.

25. *Courier Express*, March 11, 17, 1930; *Evening News*, March 21, 1930.

26. Buffalo *Evening News*, March 27, 1930, from an interview with Wilson Stevens, described in the *Evening News* as a "Seneca Medicine Man" and "one of the [longhouse] cult's leaders."

27. Anthony F. C. Wallace, *The Death and Rebirth of the Seneca* (New York: Alfred A. Knopf, 1970), 235–236.

28. Arthur C. Parker, "Seneca Belief in Witchcraft," in *Seneca Myths and Legends*, Buffalo and Erie County Historical Society Publications 23 (1925), 365. Five years before the Marchand murder, Parker had noted that "[t]his belief in witches and sorcerers has not been entirely eliminated."

The most complete account of the Tommy Jemmy incident is found in William L. Stone, *The Life and Times of Sa-Go-Ye-Wa-Ha or Red Jacket* (Albany: J. Munsell, 1866), 383–387. Another account is Robert W. Bingham, *The Cradle of the Queen City: A History of Buffalo* (Buffalo: Buffalo Historical Society, 1931), 386–388.

29. Lewis Henry Morgan, *The League of the Iroquois* (Secaucus, N.J.: Citadel Press, 1962; originally published 1851), 164–166.

30. Although Parker agreed to testify to these conclusions, when he took the stand he was not asked about witchcraft. This may reflect second thoughts about strategy, because the publicity over witchcraft reflected negatively on traditional Iroquois. Parker's testimony went only to Nancy's *mens rea*. She was not facing the same serious threat of death as Lila was. *Courier Express*, March 25, 27, 1930.

31. This story can be found in considerably more detail on the front page of the *Courier Express* for March 17, 1930, under the headline: "Graves Link Witchery, Murder."

32. *Courier Express*, March 20, 22, 27, 1930.

33. See, for example, Donald Parman, "The 'Big Stick' in Indian Affairs: The Bai-a-lil-le Incident in 1909," *Arizona and the West* 20 (Winter 1978), 343–360; J. Lee Correll, "Bai-a-lil-le: Medicine Man—or Witch?" (Window Rock, Arizona: Navajo Parks and Recreation, Research Section, 1970); Clyde Kluckhohn, *Navajo Witchcraft*, Papers of the Peabody Museum of American Archaeology and Ethnology, vol. 23 (1944).

34. *Courier Express*, March 10, 24, 1930; Clinton Rickard, *Fighting Tuscarora: The Autobiography of Chief Clinton Rickard*, ed. Barbara Graymont (Syracuse: Syracuse University Press, 1973), 98–100.

35. Rickard, *Fighting Tuscarora*, 69–89.

36. Sometime after the trial, Lila Jimerson married Wallace Hilliker and lived near Perrysburg, N.Y., in Cattaraugus County where she died in 1972. Nancy Bowen died many years earlier. Henri Marchand, who had sculpted several of the figures in the exhibit of Iroquois Indian Groups at the New York State Museum, returned to the Albany area. He died in Troy, N.Y., in 1951. The author is grateful to Lisa Seivert, librarian and archivist at the Buffalo Museum of Science, for her assistance. See also Rickard, *Fighting Tuscarora*, 175 n.4; David C. Lithgow, "History of the Indian Groups with a Description of the Technic," and Noah T. Clarke, "The Indian Groups of the New York State Museum and a Description of the Technic," in *New York State Museum Bulletin* 310 (Albany: The University of the State of New York, 1937), 83, 104.

37. Rickard, *Fighting Tuscarora*, 100.

10

Witchcraft as Goddess Religion

~

Starhawk

This introductory chapter from Starhawk's path-breaking book on witchcraft is intended to initiate readers to the history, philosophy, and practices of the craft. Starhawk sees witchcraft as the revival of an ancient tradition that predates patriarchal religion; in her telling of the story, Christianity sought to extinguish practitioners of the ancient way, and thus witches went underground, continuing to worship their goddesses and gods and practicing their rituals in secrecy. Witchcraft is a religion that reveres nature; according to Starhawk, "Love for life in all its forms is the basic ethic of Witchcraft." Witchcraft empowers women; it not only frees them from a patriarchal understanding of God the father, but, they believe, the positive energy they raise through magical rituals allows them to play an active role in shaping their lives as well.

Starhawk embraces the label of "witchcraft" for the Goddess-oriented spirituality that defines this revived feminist religion. To rehabilitate the word "witch," despite its many negative connotations, she argues, is to reclaim the right to be powerful women and to identify with and remember the countless victims of fear and hatred during the European and American witch-hunts. Starhawk's assertions raise several questions about the crafting of a usable past. As readers of this anthology will understand, for example, the seventeenth-century "witches" of Salem had little in common with contemporary witches. While Starhawk suggests the

From Starhawk, *The Spiral Dance: A Rebirth of the Ancient Religion of the Great Goddess*, revised edition (San Francisco: Harper and Row, 1989), 15–30, 213–15.

possibility "that a genuine coven was meeting in the woods of Salem before the trials," no proof of such activity has ever surfaced. Nonetheless, Starhawk's larger point is well taken: Women have been demonized historically, particularly women who are perceived to live their lives outside the bounds of acceptable womanhood.

Between the Worlds

THE MOON IS FULL. We meet on a hilltop that looks out over the bay. Below us, lights spread out like a field of jewels, and faraway skyscrapers pierce the swirling fog like the spires of fairytale towers. The night is enchanted.

Our candles have been blown out, and our makeshift altar cannot stand up under the force of the wind, as it sings through the branches of tall eucalyptus. We hold up our arms and let it hurl against our faces. We are exhilarated, hair and eyes streaming. The tools are unimportant; we have all we need to make magic: our bodies, our breath, our voices, each other.

The circle has been cast. The invocations begin:

All-dewy, sky-sailing pregnant moon,
Who shines for all.
Who flows through all . . .
Aradia, Diana, Cybele, Mah . . .

Sailor of the last sea,
Guardian of the gate,
Ever-dying, ever-living radiance . . .
Dionysus, Osiris, Pan, Arthur, Hu . . .

The moon clears the treetops and shines on the circle. We huddle closer for warmth. A woman moves into the center of the circle. We begin to chant her name:

"Diana . . ."

"Dee-ah-nah . . ."

"Aaaah . . ."

The chant builds, spiraling upward. Voices merge into one endlessly modulated harmony. The circle is enveloped in a cone of light.

Then, in a breath—silence.

"You are Goddess," we say to Diana, and kiss her as she steps back into the outer ring. She is smiling.

She remembers who she is.

One by one, we will step into the center of the circle. We will hear our names chanted, feel the cone rise around us. We will receive the gift, and remember:

"I am Goddess. You are God, Goddess. All that lives, breathes, loves, sings in the unending harmony of being is divine."

In the circle, we will take hands and dance under the moon.

"To disbelieve in Witchcraft is The greatest of all heresies."

Malleus Maleficarum (1486)

On every full moon, rituals such as the one described above take place on hilltops, beaches, in open fields and in ordinary houses. Writers, teachers, nurses, computer programmers, artists, lawyers, poets, plumbers, and auto mechanics—women and men from many backgrounds come together to celebrate the mysteries of the Triple Goddess of birth, love, and death, and of her Consort, the Hunter, who is Lord of the Dance of life. The religion they practice is called *Witchcraft.**

Witchcraft is a word that frightens many people and confuses many others. In the popular imagination, Witches are ugly, old hags riding broomsticks, or evil Satanists performing obscene rites. Modern Witches are thought to be members of a kooky cult, primarily concerned with cursing enemies by jabbing wax images with pins, and lacking the depth, the dignity and seriousness of purpose of a true religion.

But Witchcraft is a religion, perhaps the oldest religion extant in the West. Its origins go back before Christianity, Judaism, Islam—before Buddhism and Hinduism, as well, and it is very different from all the so-called great religions. The Old Religion, as we call it, is closer in spirit to Native American traditions or to the shamanism of the Arctic. It is not based on dogma or a set of beliefs, nor on scriptures or a sacred book revealed by a great man. Witchcraft takes its

*When I originally wrote *The Spiral Dance*, my covens always invoked both the Goddess and the God. In the intervening decade, the covens I work with have become more fluid in our interpretation of our relationship to images of divinity, or perhaps more frank in our understanding that these things are mysteries that we cannot ever fully understand. Now we invoke whatever aspects of deity we feel are appropriate or hovering around us at any given time. Almost always we invoke some form of the Goddess, although not always as a specific named aspect. For example, if we are doing a ritual with people who are not Pagans, perhaps during a political action, we might simply invoke the elements or all the God(dess) by the names of people present. If we feel some aspect of the God demanding our attention, we invoke him.

teachings from nature, and reads inspiration in the movements of the sun, moon, and stars, the flight of birds, the slow growth of trees, and the cycles of the seasons.*

According to our legends, Witchcraft began more than 35 thousand years ago, when the temperature of Europe began to drop and the great sheets of ice crept slowly south in their last advance. Across the rich tundra, teeming with animal life, small groups of hunters followed the free-running reindeer and the thundering bison. They were armed with only the most primitive of weapons, but some among the clans were gifted, could "call" the herds to a cliffside or a pit, where a few beasts, in willing sacrifice, would let themselves be trapped. These gifted shamans could attune themselves to the spirits of the herds, and in so doing they became aware of the pulsating rhythm that infuses all life, the dance of the double spiral, of whirling into being, and whirling out again. They did not phrase this insight intellectually, but in images: the Mother Goddess, the birthgiver, who brings into existence all life; and the Horned God, hunter and hunted, who eternally passes through the gates of death that new life may go on.

Male shamans dressed in skins and horns in identification with the God and the herds; but female priestesses presided naked, embodying the fertility of the Goddess.[1] Life and death were a continuous stream; the dead were buried as if sleeping in a womb, surrounded by their tools and ornaments, so that they might awaken to a new life.[2] In the caves of the Alps, skulls of the great bears were mounted in niches, where they pronounced oracles that guided the clans to game.[3] In lowland pools, reindeer does, their bellies filled with stones that embodied the souls of deer, were submerged in the waters of the Mother's womb, so that victims of the hunt would be reborn.[4]

*The history presented here is a mixture of oral tradition, interpretations of physical evidence, and standard scholarship. A complete, documented, and footnoted presentation of this material would require volumes—many of which have already been written by other people. In *Truth or Dare*, I explored more fully the history of the Middle East and the transition to patriarchy. In the Appendix to *Dreaming the Dark*, I give a much more developed account of the European Witch persecutions. A wealth of Goddess scholarship is available today that was not yet published ten years ago. See the Updated Bibliography for references.

Rereading this history, I am struck by its Eurocentric character. Of course, I am tracing the history of a European tradition; however, it is important to know that matrifocal, Goddess-centered traditions also underlie the rich cultures of Asia, the Americas, Africa, and Polynesia. African and Asian roots also fed the European tradition. In many areas these traditions survive today. The works of Paula Gunn Allen and Luisa Teish, as well as Carl Olsen's anthology, are good starting points for exploring other traditions.

In the East—Siberia and the Ukraine—the Goddess was Lady of the Mammoths; she was carved from stone in great swelling curves that embodied her gifts of abundance.[5] In the West, in the great cave temples of southern France and Spain, her rites were performed deep in the secret wombs of the earth, where the great polar force were painted as bison and horses, superimposed, emerging from the cave walls like spirits out of a dream.[6]

The spiral dance was seen also in the sky: in the moon, who monthly dies and is reborn; in the sun, whose waxing light brings summer's warmth and whose waning brings the chill of winter. Records of the moon's passing were scratched on bone,[7] and the Goddess was shown holding the bison horn, which is also the crescent moon.[8]

The ice retreated. Some clans followed the bison and the reindeer into the far north. Some passed over the Alaskan land bridge to the Americas. Those who remained in Europe turned to fishing and gathering wild plants and shellfish. Dogs guarded their campsites, and new tools were refined. Those who had the inner power learned that it increased when they worked together. As isolated settlements grew into villages, shamans and priestesses linked forces and shared knowledge. The first covens were formed. Deeply attuned to plant and animal life, they tamed where once they had hunted, and they bred sheep, goats, cows, and pigs from their wild cousins. Seeds were no longer only gathered; they were planted, to grow where they were set. The Hunter became Lord of the Grain, sacrificed when it is cut in autumn, buried in the womb of the Goddess and reborn in the spring. The Lady of the Wild Things became the Barley Mother, and the cycles of moon and

---

Shamanism has become a trendy word over the past ten years. The interest in spiritual traditions that offer direct encounters with dimensions beyond the everyday has grown enormously, spawning a minor industry in workshops and exotic tours. But real spiritual growth takes place in the context of a culture. People of European heritage, out of hunger for what the culture lacks, may unwittingly become spiritual strip miners, damaging other cultures in superficial attempts to uncover their mystical treasures.

Understanding the suppression and grounding ourselves in the surviving knowledge of the European traditions can help people with European ancestors avoid flocking to the sad tribe of "Wannabees"—want to be Indians, want to be Africans, want to be anything but what we are. And, or course, any real spiritual power we gain from any tradition carries with it responsibility. If we learn from African drum rhythms or the Lakota sweat lodge, we have incurred an obligation not to romanticize the people we have learned from but to participate in the very real struggles being waged for liberation, land, and cultural survival.

Readers whose own heritage preserves a living, earth-based spirituality may find here interesting parallels and comparisons.

sun marked the times for sowing and reaping and letting out to pasture.

Villages grew into the first towns and cities. The Goddess was painted on the plastered walls of shrines, giving birth to the Divine Child—her consort, son, and seed.[9] Far-flung trade brought contact with the mysteries of Africa and West Asia.

In the lands once covered with ice, a new power was discovered, a force that runs like springs of water through the earth Herself. Barefoot priestesses trace out "ley" lines on the new grass.* It was found that certain stones increase the flow of power. They were set at the proper points in great marching rows and circles that mark the cycles of time. The year became a great wheel divided into eight parts: the solstices and equinoxes and the cross-quarter days between, when great feasts were held and fires lit. With each ritual, with each ray of the sun and beam of the moon that struck the stones at the times of power, the force increased. They became great reservoirs of subtle energy, gateways between the worlds of the seen and the unseen. Within the circles, beside the menhirs and dolmens and passage graves, priestesses could probe the secrets of time, and the hidden structure of the cosmos. Mathematics, astronomy, poetry, music, medicine, and the understanding of the workings of the human mind developed side by side with the lore of the deeper mysteries.[10]

But later, cultures developed that devoted themselves to the arts of war. Wave after wave of Indo-European invasions swept over Europe from the Bronze Age on. Warrior Gods drove the Goddess peoples out from the fertile lowlands and fine temples, into the hills and high mountains where they became known as the Sidhe, the Picts or Pixies, the Fair Folk or Faeries.[11] The mythological cycle of Goddess and Consort, Mother and Divine Child, which had held sway for 30 thousand years, was changed to conform to the values of the conquering patriarchies. In Greece, the Goddess, in her many guises, "married" the new gods—the result was the Olympian Pantheon. In the British Isles, the victorious Celts adopted many features of the Old Religion, incorporating them into the Druidic mysteries.

The Faeries, breeding cattle in the stony hills and living in turf-covered, round huts, preserved the Old Religion. Clan mothers, called

*"In the lands once covered . . ." The power of the ley lines and standing stones was perhaps not newly discovered, nor was Northern Europe necessarily its place of discovery. Similar stones and alignments are found all around the world, from the medicine wheels of North America to the monoliths of Easter Island.

"Queen of Elphame," which means Elfland, led the covens, together with the priest, the Sacred King, who embodied the dying God, and underwent a ritualized mock death at the end of his term of office. They celebrated the eight feasts of the Wheel with wild processions on horseback, singing, chanting, and the lighting of ritual fires. The invading people often joined in; there were mingling and intermarriage, and many rural families were said to have "Faery blood." The Colleges of the Druids, and the Poetic Colleges of Ireland and Wales, preserved many of the old mysteries.

Christianity, at first, brought little change. Peasants saw in the story of Christ only a new version of their own ancient tales of the Mother Goddess and her Divine Child who is sacrificed and reborn. Country priests often led the dance at the Sabbats, or great festivals.[12] The covens, who preserved the knowledge of the subtle forces, were called *Wicca* or *Wicce*, from the Anglo-Saxon root word meaning "to bend or shape." They were those who could shape the unseen to their will. Healers, teachers, poets, and midwives, they were central figures in every community.

Persecution began slowly. The twelfth and thirteenth centuries saw a revival of aspect of the Old Religion by the troubadours, who wrote love poems to the Goddess under the guise of living noble ladies of their times. The magnificent cathedrals were built in honor of Mary, who had taken over many of the aspects of the ancient Goddess. Witchcraft was declared a heretical act, and in 1324 an Irish coven led by Dame Alice Kyteler was tried by the Bishop of Ossory for worshiping a non-Christian god. Dame Kyteler was saved by her rank, but her followers were burned.

Wars, Crusades, plagues, and peasant revolts raged over Europe in the next centuries. Joan of Arc, the "Maid of Orleans," led the armies of France to victory, but was burned as a Witch by the English. "Maiden" is a term of high respect in Witchcraft, and it has been suggested that the French peasantry loved Joan so greatly because she was, in truth, a leader of the Old Religion.[13] The stability of the medieval Church was shaken, and the feudal system began to break down. The Christian world was swept by messianic movements and religious revolts, and the Church could no longer calmly tolerate rivals.

In 1484, the Papal Bull of Innocent VIII unleashed the power of the Inquisition against the Old Religion. With the publication of the *Malleus Maleficarum*, "The Hammer of the Witches," by the Dominicans Kramer and Sprenger in 1486, the groundwork was laid for a reign of terror that was to hold all of Europe in its grip until well into the seventeenth century. The persecution was most strongly directed against women: Of an estimated nine million Witches executed,* eighty percent were women, including children and young girls, who were believed to inherit the "evil" from their mothers. The ascetism of early Christianity, which turned its back on the world of the flesh, had degenerated, in some quarters of the Church, into hatred of those who brought that flesh into being. Misogyny, the hatred of women, had become a strong element in medieval Christianity. Women, who menstruate and give birth, were identified with sexuality and therefore with evil. "All witchcraft stems from carnal lust, which is in women insatiable," stated the *Malleus Maleficarum.*

The terror was indescribable. Once denounced, by anyone from a spiteful neighbor to a fretful child, a suspected Witch was arrested suddenly, without warning, and not allowed to return home again. She was considered guilty until proven innocent. Common practice was to strip the suspect naked, shave her completely in hopes of finding the Devil's "marks," which might be moles or freckles. Often the accused were pricked all over their bodies with long, sharp needles; spots the Devil had touched were said to feel no pain. In England, "legal torture" was not allowed, but suspects were deprived of sleep and subjected to slow starvation, before hanging. On the continent, every imaginable atrocity was practiced—the rack, the thumbscrew, "boots" that broke the bones in the legs, vicious beatings—the full roster of the Inquisition's horrors. The accused were tortured until they signed confessions prepared by the Inquisitors, until they admitted to consorting with Satan, to dark and obscene practices that were never part of true Witchcraft. Most cruelly, they were tortured until they named others, until a full coven quota of thirteen were taken. Confession earned a merciful death: strangulation before the stake. Recalcitrant suspects, who maintained their innocence, were burned alive.

Witch hunters and informers were paid for convictions, and many found it a profitable career. The rising male medical establishment welcomed the chance to stamp out midwives and village herbalists, their major economic competitors. For others, the Witch trials offered opportunities to rid themselves of "uppity women" and disliked neigh-

*". . . an estimated nine million Witches . . ." Actually, estimates range between a low of one hundred thousand and this figure, which is probably high. The truth, clearly, is that nobody knows exactly how many people died in the persecutions. Many died in prison who were not counted in the executioners' tallies. But the effect of the persecutions on the psyche of Europe, and especially on women, was that of a collective trauma. In the appendix of *Dreaming the Dark*, I explore this whole question more fully than I can here.

bors. Witches themselves say that few of those tried during the Burning Times actually belonged to covens or were members of the Craft. The victims were the elderly, the senile, the mentally ill, women whose looks weren't pleasing or who suffered from some handicap, village beauties who bruised the wrong egos by rejecting advances, or who had roused lust in a celibate priest or married man. Homosexuals and freethinkers were caught in the same net. At times, hundreds of victims were put to death in a day. In the Bishopric of Trier, in Germany, two villages were left with only a single female inhabitant apiece after the trials of 1585.

The Witches and Faeries who could do so escaped to lands where the Inquisition did not reach. Some may have come to America. It is possible that a genuine coven was meeting in the woods of Salem before the trials, which actually marked the end of active persecution in this country. Some scholars believe that the family of Samuel and John Quincy Adams were members of the megalithic "Dragon" cult, which kept alive the knowledge of the power of the stone circles.[14] Certainly, the independent spirit of Witchcraft is very much akin to many of the ideals of the "Founding Fathers": for example, freedom of speech and worship, decentralized government, and the rights of the individual rather than the divine right of kings.

This period was also the time when the African slave trade reached its height and the conquest of the Americas took place. The same charges leveled against the Witches—charges of savagery and devil worship—were used to justify the enslavement of the Africans (who were brought to the New World, supposedly, to Christianize them) and the destruction of cultures and wholesale genocide of Native Americans. African religions took on a protective cloak of Catholic nomenclature, calling their orishas saints, and survived as the traditions of Macumba, Santeria, Lucumi, and Voudoun, religions that have been as unfairly maligned as the Craft.

Oral tradition tells us that some European Pagans, brought over as indentured servants or convict labor, fled to join the Indians whose traditions were similar in spirit to their own. In some areas, such as the American South, black, white Pagan, and Native American elements combined.

In America, as in Europe, the Craft went underground, and became the most secret of religions. Traditions were passed down only to those who could be trusted absolutely, usually to members of the same family. Communications between covens were severed; no longer could they meet on the Great Festivals to share knowledge and exchange the results of spells or rituals. Parts of the tradition became lost or forgotten. Yet somehow, in secret, in silence, over glowing coals, behind closed shutters, encoded as fairytales and folksongs, or hidden in subconscious memories, the seed was passed on.

After the persecutions ended, in the eighteenth century, came the age of disbelief. Memory of the true Craft had faded; the hideous stereotypes that remained seemed ludicrous, laughable, or tragic. Only in this century have Witches been able to "come out of the broom closet," so to speak, and counter the imagery of evil with truth. The word "Witch" carries so many negative connotations that many people wonder why we use the word at all. Yet to reclaim the word "Witch" is to reclaim our right, as women, to be powerful; as men, to know the feminine within as divine. To be a Witch is to identify with nine million victims of bigotry and hatred and to take responsibility for shaping a world in which prejudice claims no more victims. A Witch is a "shaper," a creator who bends the unseen into form, and so becomes one of the Wise, one whose life is infused with magic.

Witchcraft has always been a religion of poetry, not theology. The myths, legends, and teachings are recognized as metaphors for "That-Which-Cannot-Be-Told," the absolute reality our limited minds can never completely know. The mysteries of the absolute can never be explained—only felt or intuited. Symbols and ritual acts are used to trigger altered states of awareness, in which insights that go beyond words are revealed. When we speak of "the secrets that cannot be told," we do not mean merely that rules prevent us from speaking freely. We mean that the inner knowledge literally *cannot* be expressed in words. It can only be conveyed by experience, and no one can legislate what insight another person may draw from any given experience. For example, after the ritual described at the opening of this chapter, one woman said, "As we were chanting, I felt that we blended together and became one voice; I sensed the oneness of everybody." Another woman said, "I became aware of how different the chant sounded for each of us, of how unique each person is." A man said simply, "I felt loved." To a Witch, all of these statements are equally true and valid. They are no more contradictory than the statements, "Your eyes are as bright as stars" and "Your eyes are as blue as the sea."

The primary symbol for "That-Which-Cannot-Be-Told" is the Goddess. The Goddess has infinite aspects and thousands of names—She is the reality behind many metaphors. She is reality, the manifest deity, omnipresent in all of life, in each of us. The Goddess is not separate from the world—She is the world, and all things in it: moon, sun, earth, star, stone, seed, flowing river, wind, wave, leaf and branch, bud and blossom, fang and claw, woman and man. In Witchcraft, flesh and spirit are one.

As we have seen, Goddess religion is unimaginably old, but contemporary Witchcraft could just as accurately be called the New Religion. The Craft, today, is undergoing more than a revival, it is experiencing a renaissance, a re-creation. Women are spurring this renewal, and actively reawakening the Goddess, the image of "the legitimacy and beneficence of female power." [15]

Since the decline of the Goddess religions, women have lacked religious models and spiritual systems that speak to female needs and experience. Male images of divinity characterize both Western and Eastern religions. Regardless of how abstract the underlying concept of God may be, the symbols, avatars, preachers, prophets, gurus, and Buddhas are overwhelmingly male. Women are not encouraged to explore their own strengths and realizations; they are taught to submit to male authority, to identify masculine perceptions as their spiritual ideals, to deny their bodies and sexuality, to fit their insights into a male mold.

Mary Daly, author of *Beyond God the Father*, points out that the model of the universe in which a male God rules the cosmos from outside serves to legitimize male control of social institutions. "The symbol of the Father God, spawned in the human imagination and sustained as plausible by patriarchy, has in turn rendered service to this type of society by making its mechanisms for the oppression of women appear right and fitting." [16] The unconscious model continues to shape the perceptions even of those who have consciously rejected religious teachings. The details of one dogma are rejected, but the underlying structure of belief is imbibed at so deep a level it is rarely questioned. Instead, a new dogma, a parallel structure, replaces the old. For example, many people have rejected the "revealed truth" of Christianity without ever questioning the underlying concept that truth is a set of beliefs revealed through the agency of a "Great Man," possessed of powers or intelligence beyond the ordinary human scope. Christ, as the "Great Man," may be replaced by Buddha, Freud, Marx, Jung, Werner Erhard, or the Maharaj Ji in their theology, but truth is always seen as coming from someone else, as only knowable secondhand. As feminist scholar Carol Christ points out, "Symbol systems cannot simply be rejected, they must be replaced. Where there is no replacement, the mind will revert to familiar structures at times of crisis, bafflement, or defeat." [17]

The symbolism of the Goddess is not a parallel structure to the symbolism of God the Father. The Goddess does not rule the world;

She is the world. Manifest in each of us, She can be known internally by every individual, in all her magnificent diversity. She does not legitimize the rule of either sex by the other and lends no authority to rulers of temporal hierarchies. In Witchcraft, each of us must reveal our own truth. Deity is seen in our own forms, whether female or male, because the Goddess has her male aspect. Sexuality is a sacrament. Religion is a matter of relinking, with the divine within and with her outer manifestations in all of the human and natural world.

The symbol of the Goddess is *poemagogic*, a term coined by Anton Ehrenzweig to "describe its special function of inducing and symbolizing the ego's creativity."[18] It has a dreamlike, "slippery" quality. One aspect slips into another: She is constantly changing form and changing face. Her images do not define or pin down a set of attributes; they spark inspiration, creation, fertility of mind and spirit: "One thing becomes another,/In the other . . .In the Mother . . ." (ritual chant for the Winter Solstice).

The importance of the Goddess symbol for women cannot be overstressed. The image of the Goddess inspires women to see ourselves as divine, our bodies as sacred, the changing phases of our lives as holy, our aggression as healthy, our anger as purifying, and our power to nurture and create, but also to limit and destroy when necessary, as the very force that sustains all life. Through the Goddess, we can discover our strength, enlighten our minds, own our bodies, and celebrate our emotions. We can move beyond narrow, constricting roles and become whole.

The Goddess is also important for men. The oppression of men in Father God-ruled patriarchy is perhaps less obvious but no less tragic than that of women. Men are encouraged to identify with a model no human being can successfully emulate: to be minirulers of narrow universes. They are internally split, into a "spiritual" self that is supposed to conquer their baser animal and emotional natures. They are at war with themselves: in the West, to "conquer" sin; in the East, to "conquer" desire or ego. Few escape from these wars undamaged. Men lose touch with their feelings and their bodies, becoming the "successful male zombies" described by Herb Goldberg in *The Hazards of Being Male*: "Oppressed by the cultural pressures that have denied him his feelings, by the mythology of the woman and the distorted and self-destructive way he sees and relates to her, by the urgency for him to 'act like a man,' which blocks his ability to respond to his inner promptings both emotionally and physiologically, and by a generalized self-hate that causes him to feel comfortable only when he is functioning well in harness, not when he lives for joy and personal growth."[19]

Because women give birth to males,* nurture them at the breast, and in our culture are primarily responsible for their care as children, "every male brought up in a traditional home develops an intense early identification with his mother and therefore carries within him a strong feminine imprint."[20] The symbol of the Goddess allows men to experience and integrate the feminine side of their nature, which is often felt to be the deepest and most sensitive aspect of self. The Goddess does not exclude the male; She contains him, as a pregnant woman contains a male child. Her own male aspect embodies both the solar light of the intellect and wild, untamed animal energy.

Our relationship to the earth and the other species that share it has also been conditioned by our religious models. The image of God as outside of nature has given us a rationale for our own destruction of the natural order, and justified our plunder of the earth's resources. We have attempted to "conquer" nature as we have tried to conquer sin. Only as the results of pollution and ecological destruction become severe enough to threaten even urban humanity's adaptability have we come to recognize the importance of ecological balance and the interdependence of all life. The model of the Goddess, who is immanent in nature, fosters respect for the sacredness of all living things. Witchcraft can be seen as a religion of ecology. Its goal is harmony with nature, so that life may not just survive, but thrive.

The rise of Goddess religion makes some politically oriented feminists uneasy. They fear it will sidetrack energy away from action to bring about social change. But in areas as deeply rooted as the relations between the sexes, true social change can only come about when the myths and symbols of our culture are themselves changed. The symbol of the Goddess conveys the spiritual power both to challenge systems of oppression and to create new, life-oriented cultures.

Modern Witchcraft† is a rich kaleidoscope of traditions and orientations. Covens, the small, closely knit groups that form the congregations of Witchcraft, are autonomous; there is no central authority that determines liturgy or rites. Some covens follow practices that have been handed down in an unbroken line since before the Burning Times.

*"Because women give birth to males . . ." I am no longer so sure that there is a "feminine side" to a man's nature or a "masculine side" to a woman's nature. Today I find it more useful to think of the whole range of human possibilities—aggression, nurture, compassion, cruelty, creativity, passivity, etc.—as available to us all, not divided by gender, either outer or inner

†"Modern Witchcraft . . ." The Craft has grown enormously in the last ten years, and probably its greatest growth has been among groups that are self-started, cooperatively run, mostly self-trained, and eclectic.

Others derive their rituals from leaders of modern revivals of the Craft—the two whose followers are most widespread are Gerald Gardner and Alex Sanders, both British. Feminist covens are probably the fastest-growing arm of the Craft. Many are Dianic: a sect of Witchcraft that gives far more prominence to the female principle than the male. Other covens are openly eclectic, creating their own traditions from many sources. My own covens are based on the Faery tradition, which goes back to the Little People of Stone Age Britain, but we believe in creating our own rituals, which reflect our needs and insights of today.

The myths underlying philosophy and "thealogy" (a word coined by religious scholar Naomi Goldenburg from "thea,"the Greek word for Goddess) in this book are based on the Faery tradition. Other Witches may disagree with details, but the overall values and attitudes expressed are common to all of the Craft. Much of the Faery material is still held secret, so many of the rituals, chants, and invocations come from our creative tradition. In Witchcraft, a chant is not necessarily better because it is older. The Goddess is continually revealing Herself, and each of us is potentially capable of writing our own liturgy.

In spite of diversity, there are ethics and values that are common to all traditions of Witchcraft. They are based on the concept of the Goddess as immanent in the world and in all forms of life, including human beings.

Theologians familiar with Judeo-Christian concepts sometimes have trouble understanding how a religion such as Witchcraft can develop a system of ethics and a concept of justice. If there is no split between spirit and nature, no concept of sin, no covenant or commandments against which one can sin, how can people be ethical? By what standards can they judge their actions, when the external judge is removed from his place as ruler of the cosmos? And if the Goddess is immanent in the world, why work for change or strive toward an ideal? Why not bask in the perfection of divinity?

Love for life in all its forms is the basic ethic of Witchcraft. Witches are bound to honor and respect all living things, and to serve the life force. While the Craft recognizes that life feeds on life and that we must kill in order to survive, life is never taken needlessly, never squandered or wasted. Serving the life force means working to preserve the diversity of natural life, to prevent the poisoning of the environment and the destruction of species.

The world is the manifestation of the Goddess, but nothing in that concept need foster passivity. Many Eastern religions encourage quietism not because they believe the divine is truly immanent, but because they believe she/he is not. For them, the world is Maya, Illusion, masking the perfection of the Divine Reality. What happens in such a world is not really important; it is only a shadow play obscuring the Infinite Light. In Witchcraft, however, what happens in the world is vitally important. The Goddess is immanent, but she needs human help to realize her fullest beauty. The harmonious balance of plant/animal/human/divine awareness is not automatic; it must constantly be renewed, and this is the true function of Craft rituals. Inner work, spiritual work, is most effective when it proceeds hand in hand with outer work. Meditation on the balance of nature might be considered a spiritual act in Witchcraft, but not as much as would cleaning up garbage left at a campsite or marching to protest an unsafe nuclear plant.

Witches do not see justice as administered by some external authority, based on a written code or set of rules imposed from without. Instead, justice is an inner sense that each act brings about consequences that must be faced responsibly. The Craft does not foster guilt, the stern, admonishing, self-hating inner voice that cripples action. Instead, it demands responsibility. "What you send, returns three times over" is the saying—an amplified version of "Do unto others as you would have them do unto you." For example, a Witch does not steal, not because of an admonition in a sacred book, but because the threefold harm far outweighs any small material gain. Stealing diminishes the thief's self-respect and sense of honor; it is an admission that one is incapable of providing honestly for one's own needs and desires. Stealing creates a climate of suspicion and fear, in which even thieves have to live. And, because we are all linked in the same social fabric, those who steal also pay higher prices for groceries, insurance, taxes. Witchcraft strongly imbues the view that all things are interdependent and interrelated and therefore mutually responsible. An act that harms anyone harms us all.

Honor is a guiding principle in the Craft. This is not a need to take offense at imagined slights against one's virility—it is an inner sense of pride and self-respect. The Goddess is honored in oneself, and in others. Women, who embody the Goddess, are respected, not placed on pedestals or etherealized but valued for all their human qualities. The self, one's individuality and unique way of being in the world, is highly valued. The Goddess, like nature, loves diversity. Oneness is attained not through losing the self, but through realizing it fully. "Honor the Goddess in yourself, celebrate your self, and you will see that Self is everywhere," says Faery priest Victor Anderson.

In Witchcraft, "All acts of love and pleasure are My rituals." Sexuality, as a direct expression of the life force, is seen as numinous and sacred. It can be expressed freely, so long as the guiding principle is love. Marriage is a deep commitment, a magical, spiritual, and psychic bond. But it is only one possibility out of many for loving, sexual expression.

Misuse of sexuality, however, is heinous. Rape, for example, is an intolerable crime because it dishonors the life force by turning sexuality to the expression of violence and hostility instead of love. A woman has the sacred right to control her own body, as does a man. No one has the right to force or coerce another.

Life is valued in Witchcraft, and it is approached with an attitude of joy and wonder, as well as a sense of humor. Life is seen as the gift of the Goddess. If suffering exists, it is not our task to reconcile ourselves to it, but to work for change.

Magic, the art of sensing and shaping the subtle, unseen forces that flow through the world, of awakening deeper levels of consciousness beyond the rational, is an element common to all traditions of Witchcraft. Craft rituals are magical rites: They stimulate an awareness of the hidden side of reality, and awaken long-forgotten powers of the human mind.

The magical element in Witchcraft is disconcerting to many people. . . . I would like to speak to the fear I have heard expressed that Witchcraft and occultism harbor fascist tendencies or are linked to Nazism. There does seem to be evidence that Hitler and other Nazis were occultists—that is, they may have practiced some of the same techniques as others who seek to expand the horizons of the mind. Magic, like chemistry, is a set of techniques that can be put to the service of any philosophy. The rise of the Third Reich played on the civilized Germans' disillusionment with rationalism and tapped a deep longing to recover modes of experience Western culture had too long ignored. It is as if we had been trained, since infancy, never to use our left arms: The muscles have partly atrophied, but they cry out to be used. But Hitler perverted this longing and twisted it into cruelty and horror. The Nazis were not Goddess worshipers; they denigrated women, relegating them to the position of breeding animals whose role was to produce more Aryan warriors. They were the perfect patriarchy, the ultimate warrior cult—not servants of the life force. Witchcraft has no ideal of a "superman" to be created at the expense of inferior races. In the Craft, all people are already seen as manifest gods, and differences in color, race, and customs are welcomed as signs of the myriad beauty of the Goddess. To equate Witches with Nazis because neither are Judeo-Christians and both share magical elements is like saying that swans are really scorpions because neither are horses and both have tails.

Witchcraft is not a religion of masses—of any sort.* Its structure is cellular, based on covens, small groups of up to thirteen members that allow for both communal sharing and individual independence. "Solitaries," Witches who prefer to worship alone, are the exception. Covens are autonomous, free to use whatever rituals, chants and invocations they prefer. There is no set prayer book or liturgy.

Elements may change, but Craft rituals inevitably follow the same underlying patterns. The techniques of magic, which has been termed by occultist Dion Fortune "the art of changing consciousness at will," are used to create states of ecstasy, of union with the divine. They may also be used to achieve material results, such as healings, since in the Craft there is no split between spirit and matter.

Each ritual begins with the creation of a sacred space, the "casting of a circle," which establishes a temple in the heart of the forest or the center of a covener's room. Goddess and God are then invoked or awakened within each participant and are considered to be physically present within the circle and the bodies of the worshipers. Power, the subtle force that shapes reality, is raised through chanting or dancing and may be directed through a symbol or visualization. With the raising of the cone of power comes ecstasy, which may then lead to a trance state in which visions are seen and insights gained. Food and drink are shared, and coveners "earth the power" and relax, enjoying a time of socializing. At the end, the powers invoked are dismissed, the circle is opened, and a formal return to ordinary consciousness is made.

Entrance to a coven is through an initiation, a ritual experience in which teachings are transmitted and personal growth takes place. Every initiate is considered a priestess or priest; Witchcraft is a religion of clergy. . . .

Interest in Witchcraft is growing rapidly. Colleges and universities are beginning to feature courses in the Craft in their religious studies departments. Women in ever greater numbers are turning to the Goddess. There is a desperate need for material that will intelligently explain Witchcraft to non-Witches in enough depth so that both the practices and philosophy can be understood. Because entrance to a coven is a slow and delicate process, there are many more people who want to practice the Craft than there are covens to accommodate them. So this book also contains exercises and practical suggestions that can lead to a personal Craft practice. A person blessed with imagination

*"Witchcraft is not a religion of masses . . ." Besides covens, there are many Witches who are solitaries, who choose to practice alone, either because they cannot find companions in their area or because they prefer it that way, just as some people prefer to live alone.

and a moderate amount of daring could also use it as a manual to start her or his own coven. It is not, however, meant to be followed slavishly; it is more like a basic musical score, on which you can improvise.

Mother Goddess is reawakening, and we can begin to recover our primal birthright, the sheer, intoxicating joy of being alive. We can open new eyes and see that there is nothing to be saved *from*, no struggle of life *against* the universe, no God outside the world to be feared and obeyed; only the Goddess, the Mother, the turning spiral that whirls us in and out of existence, whose winking eye is the pulse of being—birth, death, rebirth—whose laughter bubbles and courses through all things and who is found only through love: love of trees, of stones, of sky and clouds, of scented blossoms and thundering waves; of all that runs and flies and swims and crawls on her face; through love of ourselves; life-dissolving world-creating orgasmic love of each other; each of us unique and natural as a snowflake, each of us our own star, her Child, her lover, her beloved, her Self.

Notes

1. The female figure is almost always shown naked in Paleolithic art. Examples include: the bas-reliefs of Laussel, Dordogne, France—see Johannes Maringer and Hans-George Bandi, *Art in the Ice Age* (New York: Frederick A. Praeger, 1953), pp. 84–85 for photograph; nude figures in La Magdaleine and Angles-Sur-Anglin, Dordogne, France, described by Philip Van Doren Stern in *Prehistoric Europe: From Stone Age Man to the Early Greeks* (New York: W. W. Norton, 1969), p. 162; engraved figures in the underground sanctuary of Pech-merle, France, described by Stern, pp. 174–75; and the Aurignacian sculptured "fat Venuses" such as that of Willendorf, shown by Maringer and Bandi on p. 28, and Lespugue, see Maringer and Bandi, p. 29.

Examples of male "sorcerers" are found painted in the cave of Les Trois Frères, Dordogne, France (Stern, p. 115), and the chamois-headed figures of Abu Mege, Teyjat, France (Stern, p. 166), among many other examples.

References are given for the purpose of indicating description and illustration of archaeological and anthropological finds that corroborate Craft oral tradition. The interpretations given here of the meanings of finds and customs illustrate Craft traditions of our history, and are by no means meant to be taken as academically accepted or proven. If scholars agree on anything, it is that they don't know what many of these figures meant, or how they were used.

2. See descriptions of La Ferassie, Dordogne, France, in Stern, pp. 85, 95; also La Barma Grande, France, in Grahame Clark and Stuart Piggott, *Prehistoric Societies* (London: Hutchinson & Co., 1967), pp. 77–79; and Grimaldi, Calabria, Italy, in Clark and Piggott, pp. 77–79.

3. As at Drachenloch, Switzerland, described by Stern, p. 89.

4. At Meindorf and Stellmoor, Germany; see Alberto C. Blanc, "Some Evidence for the Ideologies of Early Man," in Sherwood L. Washburn, ed., *The Social Life of Early Man* (Chicago: Aldine Publications, 1961), p. 124.

5. Finds of the Mammoth Goddess near the Desna River in the Ukraine are described by Joseph Campbell, *The Masks of God: Primitive Mythology* (New York: Penguin Books, 1976), p. 327.

6. Annette Laming, *Lascaux*, trans. by Eleanor Frances Armstrong (Harmondsworth, Middlesex: Penguin Books, 1959); André Leroi-Gourhan, "The Evolution of Paleolithic Art," in *Scientific American*, Vol. 218, No. 17, 1968, pp. 58–68.

7. Gerald S. Hawkins, *Beyond Stonehenge* (New York: Harper & Row, 1973), see descriptions of engraved mammoth tusks (15,000 B.C.) from Gontzi in the Ukraine, Russia, pp. 263–67; red ochre markings at Abri de las Vinas, Spain (8000–6000 B.C.), pp. 232–33; and wall paintings at Canchal de Mahoma, Spain (7000 B.C.), pp. 230–31.

8. Laussel, Dordogne, France: see Maringer and Bandi, pp. 81–85.

9. James Mellaart, *Catal Húyük, a Neolithic Town in Anatolia* (New York: McGraw-Hill, 1967).

10. Alexander Thom, "Megaliths and Mathematics," *Antiquity*, 1966, 40, 121–28.

11. Margaret A. Murray, *The Witch-Cult in Western Europe* (New York: Oxford University Press, 1971), pp. 238–46.

12. Murray, p. 49

13. Murray, pp. 270–76.

14. Andrew E. Rothovius, "The Adams Family and the Grail Tradition: The Untold Story of the Dragon Persecution," *East-West* 1977, 7(5), 24–30; Andrew E. Rothovius, "The Dragon Tradition in the New World," *East-West* 1977, 7(8), 42–54.

15. Carol P. Christ, "Why Women Need the Goddess," in Carol P. Christ and Judith Plaskow, *Woman Spirit Rising: A Feminist Reader in Religion* (San Francisco: Harper & Row, 1979), p. 278.

16. Mary Daly, *Beyond God the Father* (Boston: Beacon Press, 1973), p. 13.

17. Christ, p. 275.

18. Anton Ehrenzweig, *The Hidden Order of Art* (London: Paladin, 1967), p. 190.

19. Herb Goldberg, *The Hazards of Being Male* (New York: Signet, 1977), p. 4.

20. Goldberg, p. 39.

11

Affinities and Appropriations in Feminist Spirituality

~

Cynthia Eller

This chapter from Cynthia Eller's book Living in the Lap of the Goddess: The Feminist Spirituality Movement in America *raises important issues about the direction in which feminist spirituality is headed. As we have just seen in Starhawk's chapter, Goddess worship's correspondence to neopaganism is not exact because not all neopagans are feminist, and the two groups often practice and employ goddess symbolism in different ways. Eller's work suggests that contemporary spiritual feminists, some of whom call themselves witches and some of whom do not, range much more widely in their search for meaningful symbols and rituals that empower women. While some continue to look to neopaganism as their guide, others turn to various elements of the New Age movement: astrology,* I Ching, *yoga, meditation. Spiritual feminists borrow also from non-European religious traditions, including Eastern, African, and Native American religions.*

Cultural borrowing introduces ethical questions. Do outsiders have the right to use religious symbols and traditions indigenous to another group? When spiritual feminists incorporate the Native American sweat lodge into their panoply of religious action, for example, does that violate the sanctity of that ritual? When white Euro-American feminist healers begin to call themselves shamans, and perhaps make a profit from doing so, does such action

From Cynthia Eller, *Living in the Lap of the Goddess: The Feminist Spirituality Movement in America* (Boston: Beacon Press, 1995), 62–82, 242–45.

constitute expropriation, cultural property theft, or desecration? Eller examines these concerns and explores the ways in which various spiritual feminists have dealt with the issue of cross-cultural borrowings. Not surprisingly, their responses are as diverse as the traditions from which they draw; some believe that any and all borrowing, if done respectfully, is legitimate; those who would rather avoid this controversy limit their religious symbolism to their own particular ethnic background, and they encourage women to find something meaningful and empowering in the Euro-American heritage.

We might ask, in empowering themselves as marginalized people, can spiritual feminists/witches, through their appropriation, disempower others on the margins, such as Native Americans? In their opposition to mainstream, patriarchal traditions, can these women unwittingly imitate the behavior of their perceived oppressors?

WITH SOME FEMINISTS HAVING ESTABLISHED a beachhead in the neopagan community in the early 1970s, women felt increasingly free to fan out into the alternative religious tradition in their quest for a truly feminist spirituality. The alliances they formed there greatly expanded feminist spirituality's religious repertoire, setting the stage for the religious diversity that characterizes feminist spirituality today.

The influx of feminists into alternative religions in the early 1970s was not entirely without precedent. The emergent religious tradition has long been sympathetic toward women, and to at least a variant of feminist politics, in ways that the established tradition has not. One of the main symbols of alternative religion that Robert Ellwood notes appearing throughout American religious history is that of women's leadership and "feminine identity in the divine."[1] In this sense, feminist spirituality is not radically, but only relatively, new. The alternative religious tradition has long provided a refuge for women (and men) to incorporate femaleness into divinity, to experience gender religiously, and to offer women special religious roles. But the emergent religious tradition feminist spirituality entered in the early 1970s was in a state of great agitation and flux. While it had not disavowed any of its traditional openness toward women and the female, it had been revivified, expanded, and seen its foci shift into new territories through the agency of the countercultural movements of the 1960s. There was considerable overlap between feminist interests and countercultural ones, in part because many of the individuals who made up the developing feminist spirituality movement already had a charter membership in the counterculture. Some of the key elements of the counterculture were taken up by women and given a feminist spin: The alternative forms of healing that the counterculture advocated resonated with the feminist desire to take women's bodies out from under the control of a patriarchal medical establishment. The back-to-nature movement and concerns with ecology became in feminist hands an analysis of the similarities between the patriarchy's treatment of nature and its treatment of women, and a demand for new models. Countercultural enthusiasm for bodily pleasure translated into the rescue of women from the constrictive sexual options of madonna and whore, and a potential sanctification of women's sexuality.

With common ground like this, the path to a feminist spirituality was greatly smoothed. Spiritual feminists came into contention with certain aspects of the counterculture (and the emergent religious tradition of which it was a part), but in the main they were given a forum in which they had sufficient freedom to meld their feminist insights with religious practices. With a whole religious world at their fingertips and the permission to pick and choose, feminists set about claiming religious images and practices that enhanced women's power. In 1975, Susan Rennie and Kirsten Grimstad reported that this process of feminist religious syncretism was already well under way: Rennie and Grimstad traveled throughout the United States acquiring material for *The New Woman's Survival Catalog*, and this is what they found:

> Wherever there are feminist communities, women are exploring psychic and non-material phenomena; reinterpreting astrology; creating and celebrating feminist rituals around birth, death, menstruation; reading the Tarot; studying pre-patriarchal forms of religion; reviving and exploring esoteric goddess-centered philosophies such as Wicce; developing and cultivating dream-analysis, ESP, astral projection, precognition; learning psychic and homeopathic healing; rescuing the holistic perspective of the right hemisphere of the brain from the contempt of left-brained linear-mindedness; practicing meditation and yoga, rewriting the *I Ching*; revolutionizing our food and natural resource consciousness of our connectedness with the rest of the biosphere.[2]

From the length of his list, it would seem that when feminists turned themselves loose in the world of alternative religions to choose religious practices empowering for women, they decided to pick everything. There is a lot of truth in this observation. For almost every religious artifact in the emergent religious tradition today, there is a feminist counterpart: There are many books on astrology, and a few on feminist astrology; many guides to homeopathic healing, and a few on women's homeopathic healing; many Buddhist sanghas (communities), and a few for women exclusively; and so on. Feminist spirituality cuts across the emergent religious milieu, giving a feminist echo for every shout, and sometimes shouting loud enough itself to provoke the rest of the alternative religious tradition to echo with new ideas.

Affinities

The New Age Movement

Apart from neopaganism, the most significant source for spiritual feminist ideas and practices has been the New Age movement. An obvious reason for this is not only the prominence of the New Age movement in the past ten to twenty years, but its breadth. In a sense, "New Age" has taken over where "counterculture" left off, setting a name to the impulse to explore non-Western religions, occult practices, and innovative forms of psychotherapy freely and indiscriminately, apart from any commitment to a single religious institution. In a journalistic account of the New Age movement, Russell Chandler, religion writer for the *Los Angeles Times*, traces the movement's roots to sources as various as Hinduism, Buddhism, Western occultism, the oracles of ancient Greece and Egypt, Abraham Maslow's theory of self-actualization, transcendental meditation, and Werner Erhard's "est" seminars. The subjects he chooses to treat as properly New Age include crystals and pyramids, Native Americans and shamans, goddesses and neopagans, holistic health and healing, and general principles of mind over matter. He cites J. Gordon Melton as dating the movement's beginnings to 1971, when the *East-West Journal* was first published and when Baba Ram Dass (formerly Richard Alpert) released his first book.[3] "New Age" in this account begins to sound like the counterculture with less drugs, less music, and more religion.

The attentive reader will have noticed that Chandler includes "goddesses and neopagans" among those things he calls New Age, and he specifically mentions feminist spirituality as belonging in this category. Certainly the feminist spirituality movement and the New Age movement rub up against one another frequently enough. Classes and workshops in feminist spirituality are offered through New Age centers; spiritual feminists patronize New Age shops in their area to purchase incense, jewelry, and books; articles on women's spirituality make their way into New Age journals.[4] Because there is so much overlap between the two movements—and because the New Age is the larger of the two—it sometimes seems as though feminist spirituality is merely the women's auxiliary of the New Age movement, occupying a position similar to that held by the women's mission society or ladies' prayer breakfast in a Protestant church. This implies that the New Age movement came first, and that feminist spirituality sent branches off of it when there were a sufficient number of women interested in developing their New Age spirituality in a particularly feminist or female way. It is true that many women first involved themselves in countercultural or New Age spiritualities, and only later came to experience them as feminist, but there is also a contingent of women who came into these spiritualities for specifically feminist reasons. Also, it is important to remember that if the dating system Melton advocates is accepted, the New Age movement and feminist spirituality were started at essentially the same time. It would seem more reasonable then to think of feminist spirituality and the New Age movement as following related, but not identical, paths.

Nevertheless, it is also impressive to note the influence of the New Age on feminist spirituality, because it is ubiquitous. Throughout spiritual feminist literature, there is discussion of crystals, chakras, channeling, past life regressions, astrology, and other topics usually taken to be New Age in provenance. (There are also interesting echoes of earlier alternative religions: references to astral bodies and etheric doubles that are reminiscent of Theosophy.) Spiritual feminists report having their astrological charts analyzed, going to rebirthing seminars, consulting with healers, and so forth, sometimes through other spiritual feminists who are taking a feminist approach to these activities, but often through the broader New Age network.[5]

Therapy as Religion

Feminist spirituality has also been influenced by the presence of therapeutic groups in the emergent religious tradition, particularly by the 12-step programs first developed through Alcoholics Anonymous. Some of the rhetoric of these programs ("Higher Power," "working the steps") is heard at spiritual feminist retreats, and meetings and workshops with therapeutic foci are offered for those who wish to attend. For example, at the 1990 Womongathering retreat, a workshop titled "Bodywork for Adult Children of Alcoholics" was on the program, and the description of the workshop made no mention of feminism, women's experience, goddesses, or anything else that made a direct tie back to the feminist spirituality movement. There is also a move afoot to take the 12-step programs many women have found helpful and interpret them in a manner more in accord with feminist spirituality's thealogy.[6]

Vicki Noble, known among spiritual feminists for her design of a new feminist Tarot deck, describes women's involvement in therapeutic programs:

> All over the United States, women are in "recovery." We are seeing private therapists and joining groups to talk about our pain and helplessness around incest, rape, pregnancy, "loving too much," overeating, being abused by our husbands, and all the addictions to the various substances our culture offers for the dulling of pain and awareness, and the escape into denial that has characterized our lives. It is time we name this "recovery movement" and see it in the broadest sense possible, so that we include all the women who are choosing to get well. Women are choosing to heal ourselves from the world illness of Patriarchy.[7]

Noble here works to claim all types of therapy, traditional and alternative, individual and collective, as part of a spiritual feminist project. Indeed, concerns that are generally labeled therapeutic—recovering from childhood trauma, for example—are a common focus of spiritual feminist thought and ritual action.

Jungianism

Another resource for feminist spirituality, one that emerged early in the history of the movement, is Jungianism. For a movement interested in experimenting with different images of women, Carl Jung had much to offer. Not only did he elevate femaleness and female power to a degree that mainstream society did not, he also give spiritual feminists a theoretical structure through which they could validate their personal experiences of goddesses as legitimate knowledge. Through the theory of archetypes and the collective unconscious, women could conceive of goddess images as something more than merely modern inventions (an important contribution to the movement in the days before archaeological evidence of alleged ancient goddess worship had been widely disseminated). Spiritual feminists often employ the theory of archetypes in their spirituality, whether they mention Jung explicitly or not. As one woman explains in the spiritual feminist newsletter *Of a Like Mind*: "These [goddess-inspired] images represent archetypes that dwell, slumbering, in the deepest parts of our souls. Awaken their presence in your life through meditation, visualization, and interior dialogue. . . .The Goddesses have much to say to us if we can be still and . . . listen."[8]

What the New Age movement, therapeutic programs, and Jungianism have in common is that they are all European-American and modern in orientation and thus draw on the "home" tradition of the predominantly white adherents of feminist spirituality. But much of feminist spirituality's borrowing is from other cultural and religious traditions—including Eastern, ancient Greek, Native American, and African religions—and these materials must be appropriated.

Appropriations

Ancient Religions

Probably the greatest area of feminist borrowing is from ancient cultures. It is not the intent of spiritual feminists to reconstruct and replicate ancient goddess worship, but to find images and myths they can use today in their own feminist way. Carol Christ describes this relationship of spiritual feminists to ancient goddess symbols in her book *Laughter of Aphrodite: Reflections on a Journey to the Goddess*:

> Though nourished by ancient symbols of Goddesses from around the world, women's imagination is by no means subject to the authority of the past. Instead, modern women joyfully discover what is useful to us in the past and reject what is not. We understand that many symbols of the Goddess have come down to us from patriarchal cultures, and, using feminism as a principle of selection, we reject those aspects of ancient mythologies that picture Goddesses as legitimizers of the power of men.[9]

Myths featuring goddesses that come down to us from cultures all over the globe are lovingly retold—sometimes reinterpreted—by spiritual feminists. They are often a part of ritual, and certainly a favorite reading subject. Artistic reproductions of female statuettes recovered from archaeological sites (particularly European and Middle Eastern ones) are printed in books and calendars, placed on altars, or worn in the form of jewelry. Such images are often the subject of meditation or group discussion, and they play an important role in the movement's reconstruction of Western history.

Eastern Religions

Another fertile field spiritual feminists harvest is that of Eastern religions (here taken to mean religions found east of Europe and south of Russia). Spiritual feminists have encountered Eastern religions mostly in the context of their presence within the emergent religious tradition in the United States,[10] though occasionally through individual pilgrimage to Eastern centers of religious practice and learning. They have found much to like about Eastern religions, including meditation and chanting rituals as taught by Buddhists and Hindus of all stripes; alternative forms of healing such as acupuncture; dietary programs such as macrobiotics; and movement traditions such as hatha yoga, taiji, sufi dancing, traditional Indian dance, and Soaring Crane Qigong. In addition to adopting specific practices, many spiritual feminists have been drawn toward the East for more general qualities they find in Eastern religions. They condemn Western religions and Western gods as punitive and guilt-producing, while praising Eastern religions as spiritualities of growth, holism, and integration that allow the believer to pursue spiritual growth over many lifetimes. [11]

But of the many things that spiritual feminists find to love in Eastern religions, it is above all their goddesses that attract the attention of spiritual feminists. In Eastern religions spiritual feminists discover the living remnants of what they believe was once a worldwide phenomenon of goddess worship. Where Western cultures have virtually rubbed out any female presence in the divinity, they argue, Eastern cultures have retained it. As Sharon Logan asserts, "The real lineages are still Eastern religions: Hinduism, Tibetan Buddhism, and Tantra." Even women whose natural inclination is not toward the East have nevertheless been moved to embrace its goddesses. Luisah Teish, who in the late 1960s and early 1970s rejected Eastern religions as distractions from Western politics, has since become interested in Eastern goddesses. She explains, "It was feminism that made me cast my eyes eastward. The Eastern Goddesses Sarasvati, Quan Yin, and the Green Tara took their places on my altars." Some Eastern goddesses have been so thoroughly incorporated into feminist spirituality that their specific origins have been lost altogether. For example, one spiritual feminist listed her favorite goddesses for me: Kali, Tara, Artemis, Aphrodite, Isis. She keeps a statue of Tara on her altar, and uses this image in her meditation practice. However, when I asked her what tradition Tara came from, she was unsure, saying it was either Hindu or Buddhist; something Eastern, at any rate. [12]

Overall, spiritual feminists are enthusiastic about the adoption of the goddesses of Eastern religions, but there are some dissenting, or at least uncertain, voices. Spiritual feminists who actively dissent from the consensus excoriate Eastern religions for their demand that women sacrifice their egos—which are poorly enough developed as it is—and for their hostility toward life in the body and in the world. Monica Sjöö and Barbara Mor, in a comprehensive work titled *The Great Cosmic Mother*, castigate Buddhism in this way: "The sexual misers and misogynists of Buddhism, practicing a secret and dangerous self-indulgence in the form of spiritual nihilism, leading to institutionalized sadism, neglect, and hatred of their fellow creatures, are very similar to the patriarchal monastic Christian world of the European Middle Ages." Several women interviewed were more moderate in their criticisms, saying they were happy to bring Eastern goddesses into feminist spiritual practice, but disturbed by the patriarchal nature of the religions and cultures from which these goddesses have been taken. They note an uncomfortable discrepancy between the powerful goddess images of these cultures and the treatment of women in the same cultures, and conclude, as does Rosemary Sackner, "You can pull stuff out of [the religions of India, China, and Japan], but you can't just accept the whole thing any more than you could Christianity." Marguerite Keane, who is herself involved with Hindu and Buddhist meditation in addition to and as part of her feminist spiritual practice, remarks, "Everything has the overlay, the accretion of patriarchy."[13]

Others feel a real affection for Eastern religions, and want to continue to practice them in some form, but have experienced despair in the course of their efforts to relate to the organized manifestations of the religions in the United States. They say that they have been disappointed by the hierarchical nature of their leadership, by some of the traditional texts and liturgies that are antifemale, and especially by the sexual improprieties of male leaders, gurus, and masters. Such experiences have, in a backward way, strengthened feminist spirituality: Women who might otherwise have stuck to an early, exclusive commitment to a particular Eastern tradition have been cast back on their feminist sisters for a sense of community. They have begun to search out other, non-Eastern religious traditions to complement and "feminize" their Buddhist or Hindu practice.[14] Though such women may still describe themselves first as Buddhist or Hindu, the combination of their syncretistic mood and their feminist hermeneutic brings them closely into the orbit of the feminist spirituality movement.

Native American Religions

The most popular source for feminist religious borrowing over the last decade has been Native American religions. These days at feminist spirituality workshops and retreats, one is as likely to run across the symbols and rituals of Native American religions as those of wicca. (This dissemination of Native American spirituality is not limited to feminist spirituality, but is permeating the entire emergent religious culture.) A key figure in the growing connection between women and Native American religions is Lynn Andrews. In 1981, Andrews adopted a Native American mentor and began a series of books lauding Native

American connection to nature. These books also revealed the existence of a secret sorority of spiritual women from tribal cultures, adding gender to the old brew of vision quests and medicine bundles.[15] Like Carlos Castaneda before her, Andrews is widely suspected of creating her Native American mentors and their marvelous experiences in the privacy of her own home, though she has always insisted that her books and the characters in them are not fictional. Lynn Andrews is rarely praised very highly by spiritual feminists, but some say they have enjoyed her books; it is certainly true that she has been largely responsible for precipitating and feeding an interest in Native American spirituality among white women.

The title "medicine woman," like "witch" before it, has now found its way into the spiritual feminist vocabulary (though it lacks the common currency in the feminist movement as a whole that "witch" has enjoyed). In her flyer "The Modern Medicine Woman," Shirley Schnirel of Rising Signs, an organization in Utah, reassures women that "either you already are, or have the potential to be, a modern Medicine Woman," regardless of ethnic ancestry. She describes a medicine woman as "a woman who works with natural healing energies of her own mind and hands, a teacher, a listener, a caretaker of the earth (including water and air), and a protector of earth's children, including the two-footed, the four-footed, the winged, and the water creatures." The annual Medicine Woman Retreat offered by Rising Signs with the multiple subtitles "Exploring Your Shamanic Path, Reconnecting with the Ancient Mother, Meeting your Personal Power Animal, Creating a Sacred Sisterhood" is a potpourri of what happens when feminist spirituality meets Native American religions.[16]

Those spiritual feminists who adopt Native American religions (or pieces of them) are mostly European-American women, but there is a core of Native American women who act as teachers and leaders and grant a certain legitimacy to the project. Among the most prominent of these Native American teachers are Brooke Medicine Eagle and Dhyani Ywahoo. They and others like them say that they have been instructed by their elders or spirit guides to release formerly secret teachings to outsiders so that they may be of use in the present perilous age. Though their teachings are predominantly Native American, they are also eclectic: Dhyani Ywahoo is the director of the Sunray Meditation Society in Vermont, which combines Native American spirituality with Tibetan Buddhism; Brooke Medicine Eagle receives guidance from "the Masters of Light" (her Native spiritual guides), but also draws on Feldenkrais practice and Neurolinguistic Programming.[17]

Spiritual feminist interest is focused less on living Native American cultures and more on what is reported about preconquest Native

American cultures. A seminal work in this area is *Daughters of Copper Woman*, by Anne Cameron, in which a series of origin tales—all of them featuring strong female characters—are transcribed from the oral tradition of the Native Americans from Vancouver Island. In addition, Cameron includes stories of the coming of Europeans to the island, and the dreadful events that ensued, not the least of which was the subjection of women. Cameron asserts that these tales come from women "who are members of a secret society whose roots go back beyond recorded history to the dawn of Time itself. . . . A few dedicated women [who] belong to a matriarchal, matrilineal society." Just as spiritual feminists are drawn to Eastern goddesses as remnants of an earlier matriarchal, goddess-worshiping culture, they are drawn to Native American mythology and culture (and Native American women themselves, as mythic stand-ins) as remnants of a more recent matriarchy. In a workshop titled "Sharing the Medicine Bundle: A Giveaway from the Grandmothers," the leader, Amy Lee, made casual reference to her heritage in "the Iroquois matriarchy"; in an article titled "Cultural Robbery: Imperialism, Voices of Native Women," Jeanette C. Armstrong explains that in her own Okanogan culture—precontact—there was no rape, the dignity of women was protected, and their language contained nothing corresponding to male and female pronouns.[18] Native American culture is further admired for the institution of the menstrual hut in which women were secluded each month during their menstruation.* As Paula Gunn Allen explains in her article "Grandmother of the Sun":

> The water of life, menstrual or postpartum blood, was held sacred [in preconquest American Indian culture]. Sacred often means taboo; that is, what is empowered in a ritual sense is not to be touched or approached by any who are weaker than the power itself, lest they suffer negative consequences from contact. The blood of woman was in and of itself infused with the power of Supreme Mind, and so women were held in awe and respect.[19]

Other Native Americans and spiritual feminists stress that in addition to the prominent place given to women in Native American religions and cultures, it is also important to recognize that these religions developed on American soil, and were not imported from other lands as were Christianity, Judaism, Buddhism, Islam, and even witchcraft, whose roots are European. They argue that there is something special about the relationship between spirituality and land, and that if Americans are to restore a sense of sacredness to the earth, they need to take

*This is somewhat ironic, given that early feminists used this same institution as a particularly heinous example of the subordination of women.

their cues from Native Americans who are already expert in relating to the "energies" of this continent. Carol Lee Sanchez recommends that "non-Tribal Americans . . . acknowledge their own connections to *this* land (through birth or adoption) and to revere this land base more than they revere an abstract notion of freedom symbolized by their Declaration of Independence, their Constitution, and the flag that flew over their conquest and disenfranchisement of approximately forty million native peoples."[20]

The spiritual feminist reverence toward and appropriation of Native American religions is frequently extended to encompass all indigenous or tribal religions in whatever part of the world. Though these are not specially connected to the North American continent, tribal religions generally are beloved by spiritual feminists for the same reasons that Native American religions are. They "live close to the land," they respect women and women's special powers, and are held to be the living fragments of a global culture that was nonsexist. Fascination with tribal cultures is often captured in the term "shamanism." Shamanism is very au courant, occupying a place in the emergent religious tradition that witchcraft and paganism only approach. It has succeeded in making great inroads in the feminist spirituality population as well, where many women aspire to being "shamans" (or less often, "shamanesses"), instead of "wise women," "witches," "pagans," "crones," "medicine women," or any of the other honorifics available to them. The shaman is described as one who can transform both the seen and the unseen, who can journey to other realms, who experiences trances and visions and can predict the future, and who can move between this world and a less substantial—though ultimately more "real"— world for the benefit of others as well as herself. It is not a description that is markedly different from that of the nineteenth-century spiritualists, but it conjures up a different set of associations, ones that exert a greater appeal to late twentieth-century feminists. Rather than associating to crystal balls, gypsies, and darkened rooms, as does spiritualism, shamanism associates to ritual masks, tribal peoples, and ecstatic dancing under the open sky.

African Religions

Spiritual feminists are also interested in African religions for some of the same reasons they find Native American religions attractive. Again, there is a population of women who are African-American, and who explore African religions in search of their distant heritage, or as the proper lineage of the voodoo practices or black folk Catholicism they learned as children. Much larger is the group of European-American fellow travelers in search of feminine symbols, "authentic" spirituality, and a form of religion that makes room for women. Study and practice of African religions is usually limited to West Africa, to the ancestral homelands of those who were taken to the Americas during the slave trade. Use of African symbols and goddesses was not common in the early days of feminist spirituality, but is more so now, mostly owing to the efforts of black spiritual feminists. In 1982, Sabrina Sojourner complained: "The lack of information about black Goddesses in most works on Goddess worship might lead one to believe that such information does not exist. That simply is not so! We of African descent have a rich Goddess and matrifocal heritage." In 1985, with the publication of *Jambalaya* by voodoo priestess Luisah Teish, African religions were made more available to the general feminist spirituality movement. Teish claims that voodoo has much to offer women: As the "child of matristic tradition, it recognizes spiritual kinship; encourages personal growth; respects the earth; and utilizes the power of sexuality and women's menstrual blood." [21]

Interest in African religions among white women is largely due to the fact that African religions have goddesses, and spiritual feminists are always eager to discover new goddess images and new goddess names. But there is also interest in African or African-influenced religions because they have had several hundred years in the Americas to develop into an alternative tradition, and thus have a more visible history behind them than has European witchcraft, for example. Also, there is some sentiment among spiritual feminists that Africa is the motherland, the cradle of humanity, and thus the source of the earliest goddess-worship humanity has known. Finally, from the beginning, an important policy of spiritual feminists has been to locate the most negative images of women available and to find in them instead the very best of what the human race has to offer. Just as "woman" and "witch," "dyke" and "crone" are rescued from patriarchal disapprobation, so is blackness. Liturgically, spiritual feminists often talk about "going into the dark," "going underground," "entering the night," as a pointed contrast to the New Age or Eastern call for "enlightenment." Adopting African religions and black goddesses is another way of reversing traditional symbol structures, siding with the oppressed and making them the real heroines of spiritual feminist culture. For example, Monica Sjöö and Barbara Mor, in *The Great Cosmic Mother*, construct the spiritual feminist role model like this: "The original witch was undoubtedly black, bisexual, a warrior, a wise and strong woman, also a midwife, also a leader of her tribe." [22]

Judaism and Christianity

In the main, feminist spirituality has been little interested in adopting images or practices from the dominant established religions of America. However, there have been some small-scale incorporations of Jewish and Christian elements into feminist spirituality. These mostly occur in individual rather than group practice, except in those cases where a group of women is meeting specifically to experiment with linking feminist spirituality and traditional religions. When aspects of Judaism and Christianity become a part of feminist spirituality, they usually change so drastically (in context, if nothing else) that they would not be recognized by practitioners of these traditional religions. Judaism and Christianity, though native to most spiritual feminists, have had to be appropriated for spiritual feminist use.

Feminist spirituality, particularly in its early days, spoke of the Shekhinah of Judaism as another in its list of goddesses, and it interpreted some women of the Hebrew Bible to be early feminist role models. Joan Maddox, for example, hails Judith as a woman "you can want to be like in terms of how you live your life with integrity, how you kill some fucker who's gonna destroy your tribe; you know, if you can do it, you go and do it." I have also heard of a few spiritual feminist groups, composed mainly of women of Christian extraction, that have experimented with holding greatly modified Passover seders, and I attended one ritual that included the Hebrew blessings over wine and bread (immediately after an invocation to "the grandmothers of Turtle Island" [a Native American term for the North American continent]).[23]

The use of Christian images in feminist spirituality has been slower in coming, and is still practically invisible. A few women interviewed mentioned that they include female Christian figures in their spiritual practice, but they justify this inclusion by stressing these figures' pagan roots. For example, Barbara Otto has an extensive collection of icons and photographs of Our Lady of Guadalupe, and has made several trips to Mexico to visit her sacred sites. She explains: "[Guadalupe] is the old Aztec moon goddess, really. Now, of course, the Church has taken her over. . . . But she is God, she is God in Mexico. . . . You go into Catholic churches and there's no Jesus and there's no crucifix. She's right there on the altar."[24] More rare is adoption of Christian symbols or personages without any such appeal to pagan roots, as seen in Helen Littlefield's desire to include Jesus in her spirituality:

> For the first time in my life, over the last couple months, it's occurred to me that I might be able to develop some sort of relationship with Christ. . . . Now I'm not saying I'm interested in developing

> this relationship with Christ exclusive of any other relationship. I'm not exclusive. But I've had some very interesting experiences over the last couple of months that lead me to believe that that might be possible.[25]

Littlefield's hopes for her own spiritual life notwithstanding, Jewish and Christian elements are still handled very gingerly in feminist spirituality, if at all.

The Ethics of Cross-Cultural Borrowing

The joy of feminist religious syncretism is marred somewhat by the fact that when one borrows religiously, one is borrowing *from* someone (or some culture), and often without their permission. This is a problem that has troubled spiritual feminists, though not ultimately prevented them from lifting myths and images that suit their purposes from almost any place they can be found. Still, there is a tremendous variety of opinion among spiritual feminists as they try to decide what entitles them to borrow elements from other cultures and just what they are permitted to take. At one end of the spectrum, women feel comfortable taking anything they like from wherever they find it, while at the other end, women agonize over how to be ever more circumspect in sticking to those things that are uncontestably theirs by birthright.

Those who love to dabble in other religions and see no reason not to, often speak in glowing terms about the family of humankind or the global community. That vastly different cultures separated in time and space have come up with similar religious elements is in itself an epiphany for them. Spiritual truth is more likely to be true, they reason, if it surfaces repeatedly over the course of history and across the face of the earth. Barbara Otto likes to put together rituals that draw on many different religious traditions as a way of focusing on what is most universally human. Oceana Woods calls herself a "rainbow witch," because she feels that in a global age, it's important to include materials from all over the world. Even Zsuzsanna Budapest, who is usually quite adamant about sticking to her own European tradition, says in the preface to *The Grandmother of Time*: "The focus of this book is the lost traditions and holydays of the ancient Europeans before they were Christianized by force, but I could not resist the rich culture of Asia, Africa, and North and South America to show the unity of spirit."[26]

Women enamored of the grab-bag approach to feminist spirituality have little patience for those who wring their hands when a spiritual feast is laid before them. At one retreat I attended, there was quite a lot of informal (and some formal) discussion of the problems associated with religious borrowing. Several women were clearly annoyed that the matter even came up, saying that if they chose to use another culture's spirituality, they were paying them a compliment, and it should be taken as such.[27] But some women aren't receiving the compliment; they are taking it as more of an insult. At the National Women's Studies Association meeting in 1990, Andrea Smith circulated a paper titled "Indian Spiritual Abuse" to encourage women to boycott workshops, retreats, books, and records about Native American spirituality that were led or authored by white women. Smith states:

> The New Age movement has sparked a new interest in Native American traditional spirituality among white feminists. . . . Not surprisingly, many white "feminists" see the opportunity to make a great profit from this new craze. They sell sweat lodges or sacred pipe ceremonies which promise to bring individual and global healing. Or, they sell books and records which supposedly describe Indian traditional practices so that you, too, can be Indian. . . . While it may appear that this new craze is based on a respect for Indian spirituality, in reality, these white feminists are continuing the same exploitative and genocidal practices of their forefathers/mothers. Despite the fact that there does not seem to be any desire amongst these writers to really understand Indian spirituality on its own terms and to respect its integrity, these white so-called feminists, unwilling to give up their romanticized view of Indians, and despite the protestations from the Indian community, continue to buy what they see as Indian spirituality.[28]

The only "white New Age feminist" Smith accuses by name is Lynn Andrews, and the accusation is understandable. For if Andrews is a contemporary of Carlos Castaneda, it is with a heavy dose of Jackie Collins: In her early books particularly, she portrays herself as a fashionable, wealthy Beverly Hills socialite who through her naive interest in Native American art finds herself off on an adventure she is ill equipped to handle. In her first book, *Medicine Woman*, she peppers her prose with references to her "Jaguar sedan," "Gucci bag," and "Sassoon jeans"; she eats out at La Famiglia, where she is a regular customer who is allowed "long hours for talk over dinner." When her Native American quest leaves her frustrated, she drops in on dinner parties at the homes of her famous producer friends. Among the tragedies that befall her when she is in Manitoba, where her mentor, Agnes Whistling Elk, is waiting for her, are a flat tire, a broken fingernail, and the forced purchase of three packages of Twinkies. In an especially comical passage, she relates her frustration over being unable to find a photograph of a Native American marriage basket that she is sure she has seen at a gallery showing. She concludes: "I needed a dose of reality. I decided to go to Elizabeth Arden's and have a pedicure."[29] By 1987, in her fifth book, *Crystal Woman*, Lynn Andrews is no longer from Beverly Hills: She now hails from Los Angeles. There are no more references to Elizabeth Arden or Gucci, and she is now no spoiled socialite, but an earnest apprentice questing after spiritual truth under the tutelage of her faithful Indian guides.

Although Andrews had adopted a new image for herself, she has retained the same image of her Native American mentors and sisters: They are "ancient" and "primitive" women who lack all ordinary signs of intelligence or civilized values, but who nevertheless exude an inner wisdom and almost surreal nobility. As Andrews says of Agnes Whistling Elk, she "had difficulty expressing the simplest thought in English" but "she was erudite as anyone I have ever known, and she had great dignity." Andrews's native guides are living icons of what Andrews and other spiritual feminists celebrate spiritually. She describes one of her guides, an Australian aboriginal woman, in these words: "Her elderly dark face was creased and withered like the crusty earth from which she was born." The portrait is consistent with a general romanticism in feminist spirituality toward "primal peoples," "aboriginal peoples," or "Third World peoples," who are felt, despite all their cultural and religious differences, to share spiritual insights that are undisclosed to First World peoples.[30] Some Native Americans object to being white women's icons, and resent the implication that all Native American cultures (or all aboriginal cultures) are the same, that anything like a generic Native American spirituality exists.[31]

Similar complaints have come from African-American women. This fragment from Lorraine Bethel's poem "What Chou Mean *We*, White Girl" puts a fine point on their anger:

> So this is an open letter to movement white girls:
> Dear Ms Ann Glad Cosmic Womoon,
> We're not doing that kind of work anymore
> educating white women
> teaching Colored Herstory 101.[32]

These are probably the sorest points in the feminist spirituality community. Though women occasionally fret over worshiping a Buddhist goddess, this is rare. The people spiritual feminists worry about offending are the people that white culture has already offended very deeply: Native Americans and African-Americans. The concern is that European-Americans have destroyed or appropriated nearly everything about these oppressed cultures, and are now scouring around to collect the last shred of precious spirituality they have left. In her article "New Age or Armageddon?" Monica Sjöö launches this blistering attack: "New Age shamanism is left out of the context of tribal life and the struggle for survival and sacred communication with the Earth and Cosmos, and is used by wealthy privileged white people. White culture rips off a people's land and leaves them dying in poverty, and enriches itself on their spiritual teachings."[33] European-Americans are accused of practicing what Renato Rosaldo calls an "imperialist nostalgia," initiating the imperialist culture contact that leads to the destruction of whole cultures, and then mourning over the loss of these same cultures, and hungrily collecting their myths, rituals, and traditional crafts for use or preservation.[34]

Navigating in these rough seas is a challenge for all those spiritual feminists who are eager to have a female-oriented spirituality that their own mainstream culture does not offer them but are reluctant to trample over other people's "property" to get it. Compromises and rationalizations scatter all across the spectrum. Those of the Jungian persuasion are inclined to believe that if they see a goddess from another culture in a dream or a vision, it is as much their property as anyone else's, having arisen from the collective unconscious.[35] Others suggest that if one is careful to say that what one is practicing is not the religion itself, but simply some element from it, it is permissible to borrow. So, for example, it is all right for white women to smudge with cedar and sage as Native American peoples have, if the proper source is credited and participants are clear about the fact that they are not practicing a Native American religion—because they are not, by virtue of ethnic identity, qualified to define what Native American religion is.[36]

Still others stress the importance of borrowing judiciously and with respect, avoiding the temptation to, as Angela Price says, "feel that we are entitled to the cream off the top once again."[37] Portia Cornell, who has participated in a number of sweat lodges with other white women in Connecticut, attempts to embody this type of respect:

> We have been asked how we feel about borrowing from a ceremony that is sacred to Native Americans. We have respect and gratitude to Native Americans for showing us a form that works so well. We feel drawn to using the sacred rites of Turtle Island to heal her of the havoc she is wreaking worldwide. We hope it offends no one that we use this form to empower us to continue our work of healing the Earth Mother.[38]

In part though, spiritual feminists advise respect not in consideration of those they are borrowing from, but in a concern for the integrity of their own spiritual practice. They describe the spiritual pastiche approach as "dangerous" and "flaky," and caution that one may accidentally invoke energies or powers that can't be readily controlled by the uninitiated.[39]

A number of white spiritual feminists seek to avoid the whole issue by staying within that spirituality that they believe is properly theirs. They speak of the need for religions to come organically out of cultures if they are to have power and meaning. Sal Frankel notes a tendency on the part of Americans, "because we're such a polyglot society," to "think everything's much more interesting than our own culture." She recommends looking at other cultures but remembering to come back home. Those who have centered their practice on feminist witchcraft are most outspoken about this position, saying, "Let's not overlook the rich tradition which exists in our own backyard," and "Let's look at our own heritage." Zsuzsanna Budapest enthuses (to what she assumes is an exclusively white audience): "We know more about Native American shamanism than our own. We have honorable spiritual roots, so let's reclaim them! White people worshiped Life and the elements of nature; they prophesied by the birds and the winds; they practiced rune magic. Most significantly, they used song and dance as magical tools."[40] Angela Price similarly finds a real strength and redemption from white liberal guilt by practicing a European-American spirituality:

> We need to look at what there is that's positive in the white Anglo-Saxon tradition. We hate ourselves so much, we hate our whiteness in ourselves as a result of the cumulative guilt so much that there really is something to be said for looking at what in our own tradition is real positive. . . . European Witchcraft is a white, Anglo-Saxon tradition, and for somebody who is a white Anglo-Saxon person, there's something to be said about owning that.[41]

But some white spiritual feminists, however anxious they are not to offend, just cannot walk away from religious traditions not their own. These traditions speak to them too powerfully. Such women offer a variety of rationalizations for their decision to continue to use what works for them. Those who practice feminist versions of Native American religions will refer to the fact that Native American teachers have been instructed by elders or spirit guides to reveal this spiritual information to white women. Others say that though they may not be entitled by blood to use Native American religions, they are entitled by residence upon this continent. Some employ the doctrine of reincarnation, suggesting that they have had former lives as indigenous persons. Lynn Andrews, for example, says that according to her mentors, she has "walked the moccasin path as a shamaness in previous lifetimes." Helen Littlefield assured me that her friends say her aura is Native American.[42]

Another way spiritual feminists justify interest in the religions of other cultures is to expand the territory of what they consider to be their own tradition. Rosemary Sackner, who after exploring wicca for several years returned to a previous love for voodoo, tells her story like this:

> I feel like for a long time I tried to force myself into this Anglo-Saxon thing, because I felt like I'm white and this is my tradition, or whatever. But I guess recently the way I've sort of come to think is that that's not exactly true. Because I grew up in the South, and I just feel like the South is profoundly African in this kind of way that I'd say about ninety percent of white people would not acknowledge because of racism. So I grew up in a culture that is African in a lot of ways, so that it does feel familiar to me, it does feel like it's some part of my culture.[43]

One final solution to the problem of religious borrowing suggested by some spiritual feminists is that it is permissible to borrow from another culture, but only if one contributes something back to that culture in return. In *The Heart of the Goddess*, Hallie Iglehart Austen instructs her readers: "If you receive great inspiration from the Goddess Tara, send aid to Tibetan refugees and/or write letters to world leaders in support of human rights in Tibet. If you experience Spider Grandmother guiding you, work for Native Americans' rights to regain and keep their lands."[44]

The problematics of cross-cultural borrowing have deeply impacted the feminist spirituality movement. If a spiritual feminist feels she has been born into a religiously impoverished culture, is she doomed to remain there the rest of her life in deference to the sanctity of ethnic and cultural borders? If feminist wicca is a terrific way to experience one's whiteness positively, does this mean that black women are not welcome? If they are, then are there reasons why white women should not study and worship African goddesses? These questions continue to be debated, and even before they are answered, they tend to sway the movement in certain directions. West African goddesses, though more common now than they were in the early days of the movement, are still far down the list after Greek, Mesopotamian, Hindu, Egyptian, Celtic, Buddhist, Norwegian, Hawaiian, and Native American goddesses. The probability is that this lapse is due to the fact that the predominantly white population of the feminist spirituality movement is afraid of offending African-American women. Indeed, there are a lot more African-American women around to offend than there are Tibetans, Japanese, ancient Sumerians, medieval Celts, or even Native Americans.

The fate of Jewish religious elements in feminist spirituality lends credence to this theory. In early issues of *Womanspirit*, Jewish women sometimes contributed feminist versions of Jewish myth and ritual, and meditations on the Shekhinah, which they reinterpreted to be "the female half of the deity." But when non-Jewish women tried to use Jewish religious elements in a positive way (or rejected Judaism with the same breath they used to dispose of Christianity), their Jewish sisters called them on the carpet for their misinterpretations and distortions.[45] Jewish feminists continue to use Jewish symbols, even while in their capacity as members of the feminist spirituality movement, but Jewish symbols have not earned the seal of approval for inclusion in feminist spirituality liturgies. When there is a possibility of alienating a living, breathing, Jewish feminist who is there in the same room by invoking Lilith or the Shekhinah, it seems the better part of wisdom to call on Sarasvati or Cerridwen. The same is also true of Christian religious elements, though there seems to be less desire on the part of spiritual feminists to include them in the first place. Rather than risk offending the Christian—or anti-Christian sensibilities of participants (and even those not present), feminist spirituality typically dispenses with Christianity altogether.

If all this politeness begins to feel too constraining, there is always another option: imaginative invention. Morgan Grey and Julia Penelope have done just that in *Found Goddesses*, a collection of brand-new goddesses tailor-made for the needs of the current day. Their first and most famous new goddess was Asphalta, the parking goddess. As they reasoned, "Why, after all, would Artemis or Demeter wander so far from their ancient spheres of influence to materialize parking spaces?" Grey and Penelope describe Asphalta as follows:

> Asphalta, goddess of all roads, streets, and highways, and guardian of those who travel on them, is best known for Her miraculous powers of finding parking places. The formal Parking Place Invocation to Asphalta, chanted by Her devotees around the world, and never known to fail when sincerely uttered, even in impossible-to-park-in cities like New York and Montreal, is:
>
> Hail, Asphalta, full of grace:
> Help me find a parking place.
>
> This invocation should be intoned at least two blocks before you want to park, although it has been known to work on very short notice. . . . Asphalta is one of the most widely-worshiped of all

> modern Found Goddesses. Her major temples are located wherever road construction is underway, and are attended by Her High Priestesses, who usually wear jeans or overalls, boots, hardhats, and colorful scarves or handkerchiefs about their necks or heads, as well as vestments of Her sacred color, Day-Glo orange.[46]

The pantheon of *Found Goddesses* obviously started in fun, but its authors note that invoking these goddesses has also worked, bringing them parking spaces and money when these are needed. This is perhaps truly the oldest religious tradition: taking old things and making them unrecognizable, because they are so new. It is here where feminist spirituality has shown its true brilliance: Wherever spiritual feminists have gone for inspiration, when they have brought it back home, religion has become something new in their hands. This imaginative and often contradictory mixture of religious elements is being molded into a spirituality for those women who are willing to enter the fray and see what it can do for them.

Notes

1. Robert S. Ellwood, Jr., *Alternative Altars: Unconventional and Eastern Spirituality in America*, Chicago History of American Religion Series, ed. Martin E. Marty (Chicago: University of Chicago Press, 1979), 40. See also Mary Farrell Bednarowski, "Women in Occult America," in *The Occult in America: New Historical Perspectives*, ed. Howard Kerr and C. L. Crow (Urbana: University of Illinois Press, 1983), 178.

2. Susan Rennie and Kirsten Grimstad, "Spiritual Explorations Cross-Country," *Quest* 1/4 (Spring 1975): 49–50.

3. Russell Chandler, *Understanding the New Age* (Dallas: Word Publications, 1988), 17–18, 48.

4. Logan; Hoffman. For example, the New Age journal *Creation*, the brainchild of Matthew Fox, includes articles by Charlene Spretnak and Deena Metzger, both of whom are writers in the feminist spirituality movement.

5. Diane Stein, *The Women's Spirituality Book* (St. Paul: Llewellyn Publications, 1987), 154–55; Diane Mariechild, *Mother Wit: A Guide to Healing and Psychic Development*, rev. ed. (Freedom, Calif.: Crossing Press, 1988); Luisah Teish, *Jambalaya: The Natural Woman's Book of Personal Charms and Practical Rituals* (San Francisco: Harper and Row, 1985), 217. Also Littlefield; Landau.

6. Marion Garbo Todd, "Bodywork for Adult Children of Alcoholics" (workshop at Womongathering, May 1990); Hoffman. See also Christina Robb, "In Goddess They Trust: Feminists Eschew Tradition in Pursuit of 'Deeper' Worship," *Boston Globe*, July 9, 1990, Living/Arts section.

7. Vicki Noble, "The Shakti Woman," *Snake Power* (Hallowmas 1989): 27.

8. Stone, "Return of the Goddess"; Littlefield; Veracruz; Bjorkman; *Of a Like Mind* 6/1 (May Day/Summer Solstice 9989 [1989]): 1.

9. Carol P. Christ, *Laughter of Aphrodite: Reflections on a Journey to the Goddess* (San Francisco: Harper and Row, 1987), 154.

10. Ellwood, *Alternative Altars*, 105–106.

11. Garawitz; Littlefield; Sharp; Logan; Keane; Mendel; Foster; Veracruz; Copeland; Landau; Washington; Charlene Spretnak, "Introduction," in *Politics of Women's Spirituality: Essays on the Rise of Spiritual Power within the Feminist Movement*, ed. Charlene Spretnak (Garden City, N.Y.: Anchor Books, 1982), xvi.

12. Logan. See also Monica Sjöö and Barbara Mor, *The Great Cosmic Mother: Rediscovering the Religion of the Earth* (San Francisco: Harper and Row, 1987), 219; Teish, *Jambalaya*, 150; also Woods.

13. Sjöö and Mor, *Great Cosmic Mother*, 221; Sackner; Keane. See also Starhawk, *The Spiral Dance: A Rebirth of the Ancient Religion of the Great Goddess*, 1st ed. (San Francisco: Harper and Row, 1989), 193; also Robison, Gordon, Veracruz.

14. Logan; Engler; Mendel; Sandy Boucher, "Daughters of the Theris: American Women's Transformation of Buddhism," *woman of power* 12 (Winter 1989): 35.

15. Lynn Andrews, *Medicine Woman* (San Francisco: Harper and Row, 1981); Lynn Andrews, *Flight of the Seventh Moon* (San Francisco: Harper and Row, 1984); Lynn Andrews, *Jaguar Woman* (San Francisco: Harper and Row, 1985); Lynn Andrews, *Star Woman* (New York: Warner Books, 1986); Lynn Andrews, *Crystal Woman* (New York: Warner Books, 1987).

16. Shirley Schnirel, "The Modern Medicine Woman" (flyer from Rising Signs, Summit Park, Utah).

17. Michele Jamal, *Shape Shifters: Shaman Women in Contemporary Society* (New York and London: Arkana, 1988), 159; Sunray Meditation Society, "The Peacekeeper Mission" (flyer, Bristol, Vermont); Melissa Moore, "One Road of Beauty: Dhyani Ywahoo Speaks on Native American and Buddhist Teachings," *The Vajradhatu Sun* 6/6 (Aug.–Sept. 1984): n.p.

18. Anne Cameron, *Daughters of Copper Woman* (Vancouver: Press Gang Publishers, 1981), 7; Amy Lee, workshop in "Sharing the Medicine Bundle: A Giveaway from the Grandmothers" (workshop at Womongathering, May 1990); Jeanette C. Armstrong, "Cultural Robbery: Imperialism, Voices of Native Women," *Trivia* 14 (Spring 1989): 23.

19. Paula Gunn Allen, "Grandmother of the Sun: The Power of Woman in Native America," in *Weaving the Visions: New Patterns in Feminist Spirituality*, ed. Judith Plaskow and Carol P. Christ (San Francisco: Harper and Row, 1989), 27.

20. Carol Lee Sanchez, "New World Tribal Communities: An Alternative Approach for Recreating Egalitarian Societies," in *Weaving the Visions*, ed. Plaskow and Christ, 346. See also Jade, *To Know: A Guide to Women's Magic and Spirituality* (Oak Park, Ill.: Delphi Press, 1991), 70; Christ, *Laughter of Aphrodite*, 110.

21. Micol Seigel, "Womanspirit Magazine: (Re-)Incarnating the Goddess" (sr. essay, Yale University, 1990), 1:8; Sabrina Sojourner, "From the House of Yemanja: The Goddess Heritage of Black Women," in *Politics of Women's Spirituality*, ed. Spretnak, 58: Teish, *Jambalaya*, xi, 171. Serious researchers and practitioners of African religions have been hindered somewhat by what they call "contemporary patriarchs of the Yoruban [West African] culture," who they say have twisted an originally female-oriented religion into a patriarchal one; it turns out that African religions too have had to be reclaimed. Black intellectuals of the 1960s sought out African religions, but it has been left to women of the 1980s and 1990s to rescue them for women. Sabrina Sojourner explains that these women

believe "that half-truths and false taboos have been imposed on them [as women] and the Yoruban manifestations of the goddess, that undue power has been placed in the hands of men, and that it is their duty as the daughters of Yemanja, Oshun, and Oya to restore their mothers as the heads of the House and regain respect for women" (Sojourner, "From the House of Yemanja," 60).

22. Sjöö and Mor, *Great Cosmic Mother*, 210. See also Teish, *Jambalaya*, 33; also Sackner.

23. Maddox; Laura. Most feminist revisions of Jewish rituals take place in groups that are dominantly or totally Jewish, and thus would, in my construction of feminist spirituality, be limited to the movement's margins where Jewish and Christian feminism meet feminist spirituality. For resources on Jewish feminist spirituality, see Penina Adelman, *Miriam's Well: Rituals for Jewish Women Around the Year* (Sunnyside, N.Y.: Biblio Press, 1986); E. M. Broner, "Honor and Ceremony in Women's Rituals," in *Politics of Women's Spirituality*, ed. Spretnak, 236; Maureen Murdock, "Changing Woman: Contemporary Faces of the Goddess," *woman of power* 12 (Winter 1989): 42 (description of Naomi Newman's performances with the Traveling Jewish Theater).

24. Otto. See also Rose Romano, "In Praise of Santa Lucia," *SageWoman* (Spring 9989 [1989]): 23; also Miw.

25. Littlefield. Also Whiting; Keane.

26. Otto; Woods; Zsuzsanna E. Budapest, *The Grandmother of Time: A Women's Book of Celebrations, Spells, and Sacred Objects for Every Month of the Year* (San Francisco: Harper and Row, 1989), xv. See also Lynn Andrews, quoted in Jamal, *Shape Shifters*, 26; Garawitz; Hoffman.

27. FSC Retreat, June 1990.

28. Andrea Smith, "Indian Spiritual Abuse" (handout at the annual meeting of the National Women's Studies Association, 1990).

29. Andrews, *Medicine Woman*, 5, 14, 29, 30, 35, 77.

30. Andrews, *Crystal Woman*, xv, 3; Andrews, *Medicine Woman*, ix, 37, 50; Elinor W. Gadon, *The Once and Future Goddess: A Sweeping Visual Chronicle of the Sacred Female and Her Reemergence in the Cultural Mythology of Our Time* (San Francisco: Harper and Row, 1989), 352; Sjöö and Mor, *Great Cosmic Mother*, 43, 210; Brian Swimme, "How to Heal a Lobotomy," in *Reweaving the World: The Emergence of Ecofeminism*, ed. Irene Diamond and Gloria Feman Orenstein (San Francisco: Sierra Club Books, 1990), 17; Budapest, *Grandmother of Time*, 58.

31. Seigel, "(Re-)Incarnating the Goddess," 1:3. For differing opinions on the existence or lack thereof of a pan-Indian spirituality, see Sam D. Gill, *Mother Earth: An American Story* (Chicago: University of Chicago Press, 1987); and Ake Hultkrantz, "The Religion of the Goddess in America," in *The Book of the Goddess, Past and Present*, ed. Carl Olson (New York: Crossroad, 1983).

32. Lorraine Bethel, "What Chou Mean *We*, White Girl," in *Conditions: Five—The Black Women's Issue*, ed. Lorraine Bethel and Barbara Smith (New York: Conditions, 1979), 88. See also Blanche Jackson, "Sakti-Root" (workshop at Womongathering, May 1990).

33. Monica Sjöö, "New Age or Armageddon?" *woman of power* 16 (Spring 1990): 65.

34. Renato Rosaldo, *Culture and Truth: The Remaking of Social Analysis* (Boston: Beacon Press, 1989), 68–87.

35. Veracruz; Whiting.

36. Keane; Sharp.

37. Price. See also Shuli Goodman and Diane Mariechild, "Keepers of the Flame" (workshop at Womongathering, May 1990); also Mendel.

38. Portia Cornell, quoted in Patrice Wynne, *The Womanspirit Sourcebook* (San Francisco: Harper and Row, 1988), 187.

39. Landau; Logan; Robison.

40. Frankel; Marion Weinstein, *Positive Magic: Occult Self-Help*, rev. ed. (Custer, Wash.: Phoenix Publishing, 1981), xxiv; Zsuzsanna E. Budapest, *The Holy Book of Women's Mysteries: Feminist Witchcraft, Goddess Rituals, Spell-casting, and Other Womanly Arts . . . , complete in one vol.* (Berkeley: Wingbow Press, 1989), 239. See also Delores Cole, "Feminist Wicca Philosophy" (workshop presented at FSC Retreat, June 1990); Budapest, *Grandmother of Time*, 58–59.

41. Price.

42. Garawitz; Engler; Washington; Littlefield; Andrews, *Crystal Woman*, xv–xvi.

42. Sackner.

44. Hallie Iglehart Austen, *The Heart of the Goddess: Art, Myth, and Meditations of the World's Sacred Feminine* (Berkeley: Wingbow Press, 1990), xxiii. (Austen's earlier works can be found under the name Hallie Iglehart.) See also Starhawk, *Truth or Dare: Power, Authority, and Magic* (San Francisco: Harper and Row, 1987), 136.

45. Seigel, "(Re-)Incarnating the Goddess," 1:14.

46. Morgan Grey and Julia Penelope, *Found Goddesses: Asphalta to Viscera* (Norwich, Vt.: New Victoria Publishers, 1988), 1, 18–19.

12

In Whose Image? Misogynist Trends in the Construction of Goddess and Woman

~

Linda Jencson

Linda Jencson's article examines the underside of Goddess worship. She has interviewed pagans for whom feminism is not a priority, or even a necessary condition, of their rituals. She encounters misogynist men who use the Goddess and the women they can lure into their covens as vehicles for their own sexual pleasure. For them, the Goddess is healing or transformative only insofar as the worship of her enhances their magical/sexual performance. Jencson suggests that this alternative reading of the Goddess, while anathema to feminists, goes largely unchecked. Perhaps because they fear a broader witch hunt if paganism were targeted, spiritual feminists have not wanted to call attention to the misogynist uses of their revered religious symbol.

According to Jencson, Goddess misogynists define themselves against mainstream Christianity in several ways, most notably in their interpretation of female sexuality. If a good Christian woman abstains from sexual relations outside of marriage, a good pagan woman should be willing and eager to have sex with any man who desires it. Clearly this view, emphasizing only male pleasure, runs counter to feminist versions of female sexuality as well. Neopagan women who do not wish to conform are seen as nothing short of heretics, inappropriately and unfortunately bound to mainstream Christianity. In fact, many women who join these covens are rebelling against strict Christian upbringings; as Jencson suggests, they may be naively trading one perceived form of religious oppression for another.

THE INCREASED ATTENTION PAID TO the Goddess and Her magic in contemporary America is an extremely varied cultural phenomenon. On the one hand there are feminists who view Her emergence as a positive step, a resource for women's self-esteem and liberation. Reconstructions of Goddess-worshiping religions of the past are put forth as role models for the future. Yet some feminists denounce Her worship as a diversion from genuine social change. Other groups, notably right-wing Christians and certain law enforcement personnel, include Her rites as part of the "occult" threat to the well-being of society, particularly to the women and children that the feminists say She benefits the most. Why the confusion? Can all these perspectives contain a grain of truth? Indeed they can.

"The Goddess" represents the idealized projections of a disputed womanhood put forth by a surprisingly diverse array of women and men. At one extreme we find the empowering creator-healer Goddess of the feminists. At the other we find a subservient whore-Goddess, based on the most demeaning of male fears and fantasies. Most significantly, we also find flesh-and-blood women living out the mythologies of both extremes (and everything in between), not only in ritual but also in their daily lives, given form and meaning by their religious cosmology.

Because feminist scholars have done an excellent job of describing and promoting the feminist Goddess elsewhere,[1] I shall focus on describing Her divine Sister whose persona has yet to garner much attention in the scholarly literature—the Goddess of the misogynists. She and Her rites shall be contrasted with those of the better publicized feminists. In order to understand Her, I shall employ a variation on the guidelines for unraveling the meaning of a symbol first laid out by Victor Turner.[2] I shall let those who use and worship the Goddess speak for themselves in exegesis. I shall study Her positional aspects, Her relationship to other deities and other symbols in mythology and ritual. And, because I am most interested in the relationship between the Goddess symbol and the symbolic representation of ideal womanhood, I shall seek to determine Her *use*, both in ritual and in daily life, to both explain and determine the gender roles of Her worshipers. Or, in Geertzian terms, I shall seek to uncover the "moods and motivations"[3] that Her worship instills, as well as investigating the prior motivations of those who come to approach Her worship in so great a variety of ways.[4]

We have come to speak of "the Goddess," but the fact is that there are many Goddesses, each with Her own complex of myths, rites, and object lessons to be learned through Her worship.[5] Each of the many Goddesses comes with Her own political agenda, political in the sense that Her various forms represent different role models for power relationships between the sexes, both in the public and private realm of daily life. The dynamic symbol-sets of the many Goddesses have been, and continue to be, constructed to suit the needs, desires, and limitations of those who construct them. As such "the Goddess" is used as a metaphor and a role model for defining the essence and societal place of "Woman."

The people of the Goddess refer to their own variations in Goddess symbol sets as different "traditions." Tradition need not mean an ongoing corporate group of worshipers, passing their tradition from one generation to the next. It refers rather to a symbol cluster, often (but not always) based on modern reinterpretations of ancient or tribal pagan religions. Thus, among others, there is a Celtic tradition, a Norse, an Egyptian. Pagan religions may be combined to form modern composites, such as the Huna tradition, which unites Hawaiian shamanism with the worship of the Egyptian Goddess Isis. New traditions are constructed—synthesized from books, personal experience, group ritual—with great rapidity. For example, the Gardnerian Witchcraft (or Wiccan) tradition claims in its historical origin myth to be a survival of the ancient pagan religions of tribal Europe, but it is admitted by many Wiccans to be a synthesis created by Gerald Gardner in the 1940s.

The phenomenon of modern Goddess worship is difficult to categorize. The religions of the many Goddesses fall loosely into several categories: "occult," "New Age," "Neopagan," "nature religion," all of which have contested definitions among social scientists and even more divergent definitions among the general populace.[6] Neopaganism is defined by Margot Adler as being those spiritualities based on a shamanic, experiential, magical polytheism, often drawing mythology and symbolism from classical antiquity or non-Christian paganism.[7] The Goddess religions most certainly fulfill this criteria, but Mary Jo Neitz distinguishes between Neopagans and feminists, claiming that feminist Goddess worship is outside the Neopagan tradition because it is less hierarchical, has a political agenda, and is less oriented toward play.[8] Neitz makes a very significant point: The worship of the Goddess is not synonymous with feminism. That a female rules some facet of one's spirit-world has scant connection with the reign (or equality) of women on earth.

Take for example, the following incident, observed during my ten years of fieldwork, an incident that at first seemed surprising in light of the feminist claims that Goddess worship elevates the status of women. There was a certain male Goddess worshiper who had a habit of seducing female newcomers after rituals. He would make great promises of ongoing worship and adoration, use them for sex once, and shun them afterward. The sexual symbolism inherent in the Wiccan Goddess tradition seemed to facilitate the immediate, willing compliance of his targets, enhanced by performance of arousing rituals with sexual symbolism.

I was present when two women who had been seduced and abandoned by this man met and began comparing notes. I was also present to witness his seductive style firsthand when one of these two women was his target. She had gone to great lengths to continue calling him and trying to pursue a relationship. She had given him oral sexual pleasure while denying herself similar stimulation in return: It was all for him. The other had caught on sooner (in about a week) that one night was all he wanted her for. Both felt used, deceived, rejected, and suffered a loss of self-esteem. Each was angry when she learned that she was not the only victim. Others present added that the same man shunned them from the beginning: They were apparently not sexually attractive to him, and the consensus was that he wasted conversation only on women he hoped to bed.

Worship of a Goddess at the head of his pantheon in no way created a respect or reverence for women. In fact, his participation in Goddess rituals facilitated his use of women as discardable sex objects. The sexual symbolism of the rituals, and the easy access to the women's trust gained through his "hey, baby, wanna be worshiped?" line of approach served him well. In light of such examples of behavior, the equation of Goddess worship and elevated status for women seems to be simplistic, and perhaps just false, wishful thinking. One must ask if such incidents are aberrant exceptions to the rule or symptomatic of a regular, pervasive pattern in some Goddess-worshiping contexts. Field observation as well as decades of written evidence indicate that they are part of a regular pattern.

A major chapter in the story of the misogynist's Goddess in the twentieth cent[illegible] begins with Aleister Crowley, "an adept whose vast knowledge o[illegible]ltism was unsurpassed by any previous Western authority."[9] [illegible]n 1873, he died in 1947 of complications resulting from decad[illegible] alcoholism and heroin addiction. His prolific writings on m[illegible] (as well as violently pornographic poetry and prose) have ens[illegible]hat his influence will live on among serious practitioners of [illegible] magic well into the next century. He is so popular among those i[illegible]ted in serious modern magic that more of his books are in pr[illegible]an are the books of Rudyard Kipling and Mark Twain com[illegible].

[illegible]ley's primary image of the Goddess was a combination of th[illegible]ptian creator-sky Goddess Nut (Nuit) and the Christian Whore of Babylon. Believing himself to be the Anti-Christ, or The Beast-666, he spent his life searching for the earthly incarnation of The Whore. His supernatural goal was to breed human children with unprecedented magical abilities, and spirit entities to control as slaves, through sadomasochistic ritual sex with The Whore, or "Scarlet Woman," and to found a secret magical order through which to rule the world.

The base commandment of his religious ethics was "Do what thou wilt shall be the whole of the law."[10] Through his writings, the Goddess Nuit tells her worshipers, "My sole word of sin is restriction."[11] Its meaning is debated, but one way to discover Crowley's intent is to examine how he applied it in his own life. His biography reveals that he essentially meant that whatever one can get away with is "moral." It was a religion in which the strong were to dominate the weak, without compassion, as he did. In his quintessential *Book of the Law*, the role of the Goddess (as well as the ideal woman) is defined:

> Let the Scarlet Woman beware! If pity and compassion and tenderness visit her heart; if she leave my work to toy with old sweetnesses; then shall my vengeance be known. . . . But let her raise herself in pride! Let her follow me in my way! Let her work be the work of wickedness! Let her kill her heart! Let her be loud and adulterous! Let her be covered with jewels, and rich garments, and let her be shameless before all men! Then will I lift her to the pinnacles of power: then will I breed from her a child mightier than all the kings of the earth.[12]

Nothing could be further from the feminist ideal of Goddess and woman! This holy woman is to be a nonsentient, unfeeling object of male lust, no longer capable of love or compassion, no longer capable of deciding for herself when to say "yes" or "no" to sexual advances, ready to be bred by men, like an animal, and only through a man's child shall she have "power."

Elsewhere Crowley speaks often of love, as in the lesser commandment, "Love is the law: love under will," still used by many of his followers as a closing to personal letters. His actions reveal, however, that he means "love" in the traditional misogynist sense, well expressed in Country Western songs in which the drunken cowboy picks up a "honky tonk 'angel' " to "love" for the night.

Inquiry as to the meaning of "love is the law," solicited from modern Crowleyites,[13] elicits exegesis by example. Answers often refer to ritual masturbation wherein one "wills" an erotic or magical image to remain in one's mind while eliciting or delaying orgasm in order to obtain magical power. This, to Crowley's whore-Goddess and Her worshipers, is the essence of "love": sex and control.[14] This attitude is further revealed in another common Crowleyite ending to letters and communications: "sex is peace"—sex, not love.

Crowley's "peaceful," "loving" intent is most obvious from his treatment of the real women who fell for his charisma and tried to be his Scarlet Woman. They found themselves living symbols of the Goddess Nuit, and therefore their lives can be examined to understand the meaning of the symbol they themselves symbolized. He attracted many. He used them in (sometimes group) sex rituals, often with violent sadomasochistic content involving beating, biting, kicking, and cutting with ritual knives and penetration by animals that were then ritually killed. Outside the ritual context he stabbed, beat, and drugged women, left them bound and gagged naked on the floor, or stored his women hanging upside down in a closet. Many went mad under this type of "worship," and several killed themselves. Medical sedation, forced drugging, mental hospitalization, and suicides were the statistical norm among Crowley's Scarlet Women.[15]

Crowley fathered children with them as well. One little girl died when he abandoned her and her mother on a trip through the Far East. Another died of "influenza" at his retreat in Italy, where adults and at least one small, purchased orphan were subjected to a combination of psychoactive drugs, rigorous asceticism, scourging, and ritual sex in an environment without adequate food or sanitation. At the birth of a third daughter he drew up a horoscope, summarizing it with the words "She will become a fairly ordinary little whore."[16] It was not that his daughter might be bought and sold by men for use as a sex object that disappointed him, only that it would take place in an unextraordinary manner.

Amazingly, feminist writers on the history of Neopagan magic and the Goddess describe Crowley's power and authority without mention of his sexist brutality. Male occult/pagan authors are far more likely to describe these biographical facts. These male authors show little, if any, disapproval. Where he is not admired openly, Crowley is excused in the context of "school boy prankster." Occult historian Colin Wilson goes so far as to express sympathy for Crowley as a man plagued by "weak women" who could not live up to his high ideals. According to Wilson, these "weak women" were drawn by Crowley's alleged "strength"![17]

Margot Adler and Mary Jo Neitz describe a brief flurry of debate on Neopagan sexism that took place in Neopagan journals in the late 1970s. These included antifeminist women and vocally feminist men.[18] Arguments centered on the coercive nature of "love magic," whether

High Priestesses should be true leaders or mere figureheads, and whether or not women are essentially sex objects. Published in journals with small circulations, the arguments are largely over. Popular books on women's spirituality in wide circulation make no mention of any misogyny in the Neopagan community. Feminist traditions have gained some respect within Neopaganism, while nonfeminist traditions are less likely to receive feminist criticism: "Live and let live" seems to be the order of the day.[19]

We could accept Adler's Neopagan peace pact, and Crowley could be dismissed as just another dead sociopath, were it not for his popularity among Neopagans and occultists today, as observed in my field research. "So he used his magic to score with a lot of women—what's wrong with that!" exclaimed one modern Crowley disciple. Another who overheard his statement concurred and joined the conversation. Both men were acquaintances with a number of personal and religious animosities toward one another, but they joined forces against my feminist position on this particular point. Crowley was a hero—a man to be emulated; his use of women was admirable, they told me. They went to great lengths to convince me.

At another time, a modern Crowleyite phoned to remind me it was Aleister's birthday, and to tell me one of the legends about Crowley in circulation among his admirers today. The story tells how the heroic Crowley had such great mental control that he beat a chess grand master while a woman under the table performed oral sex on Crowley's erect penis. "What a guy!" My caller could not understand my concern for the woman. Who was she? What were her magical accomplishments? How did she feel about her role in the event? Was she one of the many who went mad or killed herself? None of these questions had occurred to my contemporary Goddess worshiper on the other end of the line, even though his personal pantheon incorporated the goddesses of two other traditions in addition to Crowley's. To him the nameless woman under the table was a pawn for displaying Crowley's admirable power, like the chess pieces, nothing more.

Some of Crowley's sex magic involves masturbation or homosexual sodomy, but his most powerful rituals require a female partner. A woman's presence is believed to create greater sexual excitement, especially if she is treated sadistically, hence more magical power is raised in the male this way than in masturbatory rituals that employ a jar or other inanimate object to receive his semen. A woman is simply seen as a better jar: The goals of the ritual fail to recognize her personhood, let alone address the question of *her* empowerment through magic. Sex is essential to Crowley's system of magic, and since his magic is concerned with power over others, sadistic sex is naturally viewed as most powerful.

In emulation of their hero-teacher, some of Crowley's male admirers who collect his books and perform their rites still make efforts to acquire women's participation. They bemoan the great number of unwilling Neopagan women. (Because of my interest and frequent questions I was often viewed by male participants in my study as a potential recruit, and I can attest to the degree of verbal coercion these men employ, as well as their anger when a firm "no" remains no.)

For their part, many Neopagan women express fear of their male partners' consumption of Crowley's literature. Such men needn't be initiates in one of the many magical secret societies that trace their origins to Crowley: Crowley's theories on magic permeate modern Neopaganism, and people from many traditions read his works. Both men and women in Neopaganism tell me that male demands and female reluctance to submit to Crowley's sadomasochistic sex magic have contributed to the breakup of long-term relationships. When I asked one female Neopagan why she did not like Crowley, she tersely exclaimed the obvious, "I'm female!" while other Goddess worshiping women accept the role of masochist as "natural" and "feminine."

In many of the traditions inspired or directly founded by Crowley, violent sexual urges and actions are projected by men onto women. Certain Crowleyite newsletters and computer net newsgroups continue to produce violent pornography in imitation of Crowley's own. For example, in one story Priestesses of Nuit rape men in order to produce magical children, and mothers collude in the rape of their own sons.[20] Of course, the pornography is largely about violent sexual acts that men commit against women, but in their literature they let their imaginary women rape too! "How can such 'equal time' be sexist?" they demand angrily.

The feminists, in their devotion to The Goddess, view sexuality as natural, beautiful, life-giving and healing, the expression of a compassionate, nurturing love. Goddess feminists might, for instance, employ menstrual blood in ritual to celebrate life, the natural life cycle, and the sacredness of the female body. Crowley's meaning of this same symbol can best be understood by its use—for example, in a recipe for power-giving cakes to be consumed by Crowleyite magicians: "The best blood is of the moon, monthly: then the fresh blood of a child, or dropping from the host of heaven; then of enemies; [etc., etc.]"[21]

Worshipers of the misogynist's Goddess view sex and sexual symbols as a means to domination, as in taking the blood of an enemy, or bleeding a helpless child. The feminists yearn for empowerment—a chance to run their own lives. The misogynists crave and take power—power over others. This is one of the greatest contrasts between feminist and misogynist magical philosophy. Feminist authors devote considerable attention to defining what they term to be the difference between "power from within" (also called "power to") and "power over": "power to" liberates people to do their own will, while "power over" enslaves others to do it for them.[22] Feminists denounce the latter type of power as the essence of patriarchy. In feminism, menstrual blood is a symbol of life; to Crowley, it stood for death, war, and sexual conquest. Crowley's magic (exemplified by Crowley's life) is entirely based on acquiring the latter type of power over subjugated others.

While Crowleyites remain somewhat underground and probably undercounted, Wiccans compose a public majority within Neopagan traditions.[23] Wicca was founded by Gerald Gardner, a friend and student of Aleister Crowley. Wiccans admit Crowley's influence to varying degrees. Some claim that Gardner hired Crowley to write all the early Wiccan liturgy, while others believe that Gardner found some remnants of ancient covens and merely spiced their stuff up with more sex by imitating Crowley's style when he published it.[24]

Gardner was first to promote and publicize a magical-religious pantheon *headed* by the Goddess, an idea which he seems to have gotten in part from the writings of C. G. Leland, a folklorist who described late-nineteenth-century witch cults in Italy. Although the Goddess reigned in heaven, and women could attain the title of High Priestess in every coven, Gardner's cosmology and liturgy had a number of Crowleylike aspects: Rituals were to be done in the nude; sexual arousal was a source of magical power; the High Priestess was to perform ritual sex acts with the High Priest (if not the whole of the male congregation); flogging and brandishment of knives went hand in hand with a mythology of ritual incest (mother/son) and human sacrifice. There is evidence that rape was (and may still be) viewed as a legitimate exercise of power by High Priests seeking to discipline female coveners in some Gardnerian covens.[25] And T. M. Luhrmann states plainly that few British Gardnerian covens (far more "conservative" than American offshoots) would entertain ideas such as feminism.[26]

There are nearly as many Wiccan traditions as there are Wiccan covens (and circles) today, and, perhaps surprisingly, many have evolved a close proximity to the feminist Goddess and feminist ethics described by Starhawk, Carol Christ, Margot Adler, and others. My initial training in the witches' Craft was in one such coven. I was led to believe that "real" Wiccan covens are supposed to be feminist. I observed women taking real positions of leadership, and men who were willing to follow and admire them. But the coven evolved into something else after the feminist-leaning High Priestess who led us moved to another town and membership rapidly changed.

The new High Priest and Priestess of the group reintroduced more Gardnerian rites. As each covener entered the consecrated space for the premiere ritual performance of the new leadership, we were greeted by a man who held a knife at our throats, bent us backward, and demanded, "With what do you enter?" The proper Gardnerian reply is "With perfect love and trust." (I was glad to have done my homework on this—to me—"other" tradition! Failure to respond correctly would have resulted in my expulsion, at the very least.) The High Priest danced about the altar brandishing a scourge, playfully whipping it in the air at those who danced around him. Although a standard Gardnerian ritual tool, this sadomasochistic item was a new addition to the altar of our group.

Whereas after-ritual parties had once been times to tell one another inspiring tales of the magic of the Goddess, they increasingly became times for pairs (or groups) of men and women to "make out," while the new High Priest made statements such as, "This group is going to become a force to be reckoned with!"—phrasing with strong connotations of "power over" rather than "power to." As the anthropologist, I was eventually purged, as was another woman covener who objected to taking off her clothes because of a physical disability. Most feminist covens, with their focus on nurturance and healing, would have been shocked to find that nudity was mandatory, despite personal boundaries dealing with a disabling physical condition.

Even among misogynist Goddess worshipers where violence is not the norm, sexist attitudes are common. "Lots of guys become witches just to get laid!" according to one male Goddess worshiper. This bold statement condensed considerable truth that many female Neopagans would rather not acknowledge. The males of the misogynist Goddess see no reason to hide it. They know who is really in charge and they know that might makes right. At the same time that they cheat on female partners and seek to score the sexual services of underage teens, they also write lovely poetry expressing their yearning for "Her." Needless to say, some of their poetry describes Her heavenly body and all of its orifices in fine, arousing detail, but one cannot deny that it also praises the Goddess and expresses admiration of Her. As Neitz describes, most (but not all) male Neopagans have little use for the Wise Old Crone, the Lesbian, or the Virgin aspects of the feminist Goddess, and not much recognition of the Great Mother aspect in any way that involves birth-labor, creation, or childrearing.[27] The Goddess so yearned for is primarily a Goddess of sex:

young, busty, and ready to roll. She opposes the conservative Christian ideal of womanhood, not by being powerful and self-determined, but because instead of feeling Christian shame at her sexual servitude, she is expected to glory in it, the better to be of service to the males who make frequent use of it.

Both feminist and misogynist Neopagans speak of a new era of sexual freedom. The feminists envision a world in which sex is a loving act performed between persons concerned with one another's well-being, celebrating the forces that gave them life, without traces of Christian guilt or fear.[28] The misogynists have something rather different in mind, and in practice it has little to do with the advancement of female freedom. If the imposition of fear can get one laid, so be it, and sadistic sex, with its obvious expression of domination, is believed by many to be more magically potent than loving sex.

In the Neopagan community there is open exploration of sexual arrangements that violate mainstream Christian and secular norms. Polygamy is one. Although in theory women are as entitled to multiple mates as are men, it usually works the other way around. Women who seek to acquire a number of men are likely to find themselves in revolving door relationships with nothing resembling a marital commitment. Men on the other hand often acquire two (or more) committed co-wives who stay for years. In my fieldwork I encountered four families with multiple wives. There were no families with multiple husbands. Two women who had tried to add a new mate to a preexisting marriage lost their husbands, both within a month of initiating the experiment.

In one of the two cases, the woman began having a sexual relationship with a new man, while attempting to keep her old husband in the same household. The old mate grew jealous of the new within a month of the experiment's beginning. He did not leave quietly, however. He demanded cash compensation for his loss. Her new mate readily complied. It is difficult to say that under such circumstances the woman retained much power. The men involved turned this woman's bid for "nineties" liberation into a sort of "retro-patriarchy," in which they became the ultimate arbiters of her sexuality through the exchange of cash. Under the guise of Neopagan sexual freedom, the biblical role of woman as chattel property has been revived, with a modern twist.

The instance above illustrates a complex (superficially oppositional) relationship between Christianity and Neopaganism. Both feminist and misogynist magic places itself in opposition to Christianity, but in utterly opposite ways. Whereas the feminists see Christianity as the root of all patriarchy, citing centuries of witch burnings, misogynist biblical texts, and misogynist preachings from the Christian pulpit, the misogynists see Christ's pacificism, celibacy, and forgiveness as evidence of Christianity's "effeminate" weakness and unnatural repression of manly sexual conquest.[29]

Hence, in addition to polygyny and the occasional cash sale of women, teen and child sexuality is explored by Goddess misogynists. Some Wiccan groups and other Neopagan traditions see nothing at all wrong with men aged thirty-five seducing fourteen-year-old girls, and younger. They argue for the nobility of such actions precisely because of mainstream Christian disapproval. Discussions of the power imbalance between inexperienced near-children and grown men in such relationships is forbidden territory, usually silenced with the familiar, traditional Neopagan accusation of "Christian repression."

Neopagan misogynists' verbal coercion of women incorporates anti-Christian arguments in devious ways. One of these is the assertion that the abuse and disrespect is actually worship and liberation. This assertion "makes sense" because Goddess misogyny exists as a subculture in a cultural milieu overshadowed by the misogyny of dominant Christian religions. Much Christian dogma defines women as sex objects, "unholy vessels," "temptresses of the Devil," and less than persons in connection with the essential sexual nature that Christianity ascribes to them. The Bible is replete with the incrimination of females, from Eve through a vast variety of female enemies of the Christian God who "seduce" men away from true religion through their uncontrollable sexual nature.[30] Goddess misogynists have no argument with the biblical idea that women are essentially sex objects. To make matters worse, they downplay the motherhood and homemaker roles allowed women in the most conservatively misogynist Christian literature, limiting women even further to a purely sexual role. But, unlike their Christian counterparts, Goddess misogynists praise women for being nothing but sexual bodies, and there is an attitude of "put out or get out" in many misogynist Goddess subcultures. Eager to scoff at the recent media barrage of news stories about child-molestations by Christian clergy, devotees of the misogynist Goddess disapprove only of the hypocrisy inherent in such acts among those who preach abstinence. As long as one preaches sex and acts out sex, whatever sex takes place, they approve.

Women raised in strict Christian homes often speak of the terrible shame and self-hatred experienced there because of their imputed sexual essence. Sadly, they are not permitted any other aspects of personhood—denied them by Christian and Goddess misogynists alike—but at least in Goddess misogyny they are allowed to stop hating themselves for being the subhuman temptresses that both religions teach them they will always be. To many of the most abused survivors of Christian misogyny, this at first appears liberating.[31] An eagerness to be as un-Christian as possible becomes a trap for many Neopagans who do not think through the implications of simply turning Christian codes of behavior upside down. Alas, the flip side of the patriarchal coin is still patriarchy.

A related control tactic is the use of derisive humor. While feminist Goddess worshipers interpret nude images of women in their religious art as representing a new pride and respect for the female body, misogynist male Neopagans view them in much the same way that sexist males view pornography. As one Goddess-worshiping male exclaimed upon drawing a card from a contemporary Tarot deck, "I got a naked blonde bimbo!" Hardly a statement of growing reverence for the female body, or the spiritual power of woman. "It's a joke, what's the big deal!" he explained, adding further that the statement would offend a good Christian church matron, so it ought *not* to offend a Neopagan.

Criticism from a feminist or humanitarian perspective of the types of words and actions described above generally brings on the standard misogynist attack, claiming that feminists have no sense of humor. But humor can bite, and humor is recognized by anthropologists as a mechanism of social control. No one likes to be laughed at with scorn, or trivialized when making a serious point. People conform to group pressures when derisive laughter is used as punishment for nonconformity. Hence misogynist Neopagans make use of humor to coerce conformity from Neopagan women, as exemplified in the following two-part joke. Its double punch line criticizes both Crowleyites and feminists, promoting the "proper" misogynist Neopagan values of sex, sex with human females, sexually compliant females, trivialization of feminist concerns, and antifeminism. It is clearly stated from a male perspective. It is anti-Crowley only because outsiders to Crowley traditions believe they use animals for ritual sex and object to it, not because Crowleyites may also use women and children:

"How many Crowleyites does it take to screw in a lightbulb? None: They prefer the dark side, and besides, they're too busy screwing the goat."

"How many feminist pagans does it take to screw in a lightbulb? (Mocking a pouty, feminine whine) 'That's not funny!' "

Some Crowleyites also believe this joke to be funny because they enjoy having a "more sinfully un-Christian than thou" image. To them, it's cool to have a reputation for "screwing goats" in addition to women. Women who object to the implication that they have a purpose similar to that of goats, and who wish to assert their personhood, are commonly silenced by the "no sense of humor" charge. Women in the misogynist Goddess traditions are expected to learn to laugh on cue at the male humor designed to control them through derision.

Control through humor and the desire to be un-Christian merge well with the third control tactic—use of Christian misogyny as a threat. If all else fails to control them, wayward Neopagan women may find themselves with a "gift" membership in Jerry Falwell's Moral Majority, with frequent postal reminders from Jerry of the misogynist tradition's world view: Submit to playing the Scarlet Woman, or find yourself a right-wing Christian husband and submit yourself to him. In misogynist Neopagan teachings, there is *no* other choice. Many women in the whore-Goddess traditions believe this—they are told it so often—they stay where they are, fearing that the sole alternative may be even worse. Many of these women report physical, emotional, and sexual childhood abuse at the hands of Christian parents, guardians, and clergy.[32] They know Christian misogyny firsthand and are not willing to go back to it. Their Christian background was the ultimate origin of their belief that a woman's only choice is between that of submissive wife or submissive whore, and Goddess misogynists happily capitalize on this Christian indoctrination. (One young Neopagan woman was allegedly gang-raped by family friends while growing up in her middle-American Christian family household, and another abused by her own father, a clergyman. In both "Christian" households it was "inappropriate" for the girls to speak of such things, but not for the incidents to happen and be hidden.) I assert that Christian and un-Christian misogyny need one another to exist. If either were a genuine haven for liberated women, it would be difficult to maintain the long-term, unmodified survival of its opponent.

Why do feminist spirituality spokespersons remain silent about Neopagan abuses of women and children? One reason is a pan-Neopagan loyalty: They fear that public criticism of any Neopagans will contribute to a witch-hunt against them all. "The Burning Times" when millions of witches were tortured and killed by Christians is a prominent part of their historical world view of their relationship to the Christian majority. Hence, Neopagan men who rape are less a threat than Neopagan women who would seek justice and empowerment by reporting it to outsiders.

The Neopagan response to sexual abuse within Neopagan communities may be exemplified by data that have recently come to light as a result of a murder investigation. In the spring of 1997, Duane Rostoker, better known by his pagan name, Adam Walks Between Worlds, was found shot to death in the apartment that he shared with friends. Looking for a motive, police discovered that he had been ejected from the national pagan Church of All Worlds because of no fewer than fourteen written and nine oral complaints of sexual harassment and rape, from both minor and adult females, although it is unclear that the rapes relate to the murder. Why did it take twenty-three complaints before he was "excommunicated"? And why were all victims successfully discouraged from reporting crimes to the police? According to a pagan friend of Walks Between Worlds, "In the pagan world, that is not how we settle things. We tend to keep it among ourselves."[33] But in keeping it among themselves it appears that sexual predators are harbored safely, little is done until victims number in the dozens, and consequences amount only to ejection from an organization that the vast majority of Neopagans do not view highly enough to join anyway!

Some Neopagans, including Parris McBride (manager of Walks Between Worlds's aborted musical career) criticize the Covenant of the Goddess for his excommunication. McBride has stated publicly that the twenty-three complainants were wrong, relying on the usual misogynist implications that great numbers of women make false accusations, women are too stupid to interpret tender sexual advances, women ought to be happy to fulfill a man's desires, and women just plain lie. McBride believes that only a "hidden agenda" would have led the leadership of the Church of All Worlds to excommunicate a man for something so trivial as twenty-three complaints of rape and harassment.[34] No one in the Neopagan community shows signs of organizing a response aimed to reduce the number of rape and harassment victims by examining the sexism within, but many speak of a need to increase internal secrecy and suspicion of outsiders. The general response within Neopaganism has been a strong wish that the Goddess's dirty laundry had remained hidden, combined with finger pointing to the sexism and sexual abuse committed by nonpagans.

Another reason why feminist pagans turn their back on the sexism and sexual abuse within seems to be a subconscious borrowing from Christian dogma itself. Primary to the mainstream American religious world view is the notion of dualism: one great Good versus one great Evil, with little if anything in between. However much they claim to be opposed to dualism, many Neopagans see fellow pagans as Good, and Christians as the source of Evil. Open perception of Neopagans causing harm to one another in anything but occasional, easily dismissed accidents, is anathema to this covert Neopagan dualism and overt Neopagan loyalty. Negative reaction against Christian dogma has created a poorly examined counterdogma among many Neopagans, including the feminists. Since sex is seen as Evil in the Christian dualistic universe, then it must be made out to be Good in Neopaganism.

Too much effort is made to do and be the opposite of the Christians, and too little effort is made to think ethical questions through for themselves. Hence, no effort is made to distinguish between those who may have been gang-raped on the altar when they had hoped to be worshiped, and those who understood all implications, were in total control of their own participation, and truly felt worshiped in a ritual with sexual content.

Adler, Luhrmann, and Neitz describe Wiccan women as taking flamboyant positions of ritual leadership, commanding deities and spirits and briefly commanding coveners as well. These same women are then described as going home to domineering Neopagan and nonpagan mates, and working as exploited drudges in the job market. Scholars acknowledge both a feminist and a nonfeminist Goddess movement, but they never get beyond implying that nonfeminist means neutral, simply not forwarding women's cause. They do not entertain the possibility that some of the creative, freedom-loving, playful nonfeminists they describe might be doing women serious harm. And they never describe what happens in the confusing maze of many Goddess traditions when women go in search of the feminist Goddess and find the misogynist Goddess instead.

One such woman was harmed greatly. When we first met, she was trapped in an abusive marriage. Her husband threatened her often with a gun, and was obsessed by the suicide of his own parent. She described waking from a sound sleep on more than one occasion with her husband's rifle pointed at her head. "Don't move or I'll kill you"; she'd lie still until morning. She described his use of pornography, followed by demands for sex, followed by brutality: "I felt like a toilet, a human toilet." She sought the liberation of the feminist Goddess, and went to a leading reader-adviser-healer in the feminist Goddess tradition, who read the cards for her and told her all would be well for both her and her husband if she left him as soon as possible. The woman packed up and went to a local shelter for battered women. A year later she was doing better in college, had a new wardrobe to show the world a new-found pride in her body, and was exploring Goddess spirituality with avid interest. But she met up with a Neopagan man and his two "wives," and they soon invited her to leave her home and school and move to their farm. She was given the use of a cabin. Here she was to work and grow in spiritual strength, using her extensive gardening skills to plant and tend an orchard for her Neopagan hosts. Isolated on the farm, her labor went unpaid. She was castigated for her reluctance to act as innkeeper and sexual hostess for visitors to the farm.

When last I saw her, her clothing was ragged. She raved almost incoherently, shouting the final intimate details of this personal tragedy to me on a public bus. Through attrition and coerced contributions "for the sake of the Goddess and Her land," she had even lost a house she owned to the Neopagan "liberator" and his two wives. Her exploitation went far beyond the sexual. It was a near-classic case of the media image of "cult" abuse, but her story and many others like it never make the mass media. There is little sympathy for deceived women who do not mend their ways by completing the media-construction of the "right" story—by turning to the mainstream patriarchal God. Not recounting the story that Christians want to hear, she does not tell the "right" Goddess story, either. Her encounter with the Goddess, work on Mother Earth, release from mainstream monogamy to explore "free" sex, and life in the Goddess community should have caused her to live happily ever after. She did not, and speaking of the fact and form of her exploitation is as unacceptable in the Goddess communities as it is in right-wing Christian groups.[35]

The complex intricacies of interactions and overlaps between the symbol-sets of the many Goddesses make for a confusing spiritual terrain, one in which all sides seek to promote faulty, partial road maps. The Goddess feminists would like to believe that they alone construct the Goddess. She will set us all free if only we envision Her strongly enough. Sex is dogmatically defined as "good" because it is believed that the patriarchy dogmatically defines it as "bad." Too little is done to distinguish good from bad sex, and Christian patriarchy is perceived as the only patriarchal obstacle on the road to women's freedom and safety, while other patriarchies are ignored.

The feminist Goddess is a creator and nurturer of life with a variety of aspects supposedly relating to mortal female potentialities. Yet to feminist critics of Goddess spirituality, She and the women modeling Her image are still predominantly defined by the same limiting bodily functions that the Bible uses to define and limit womankind.[36]

For promoters of the misogynist Goddess, what women want or need is of little consequence. The Goddess is a sex Goddess, existing to breed and to be bred. She creates nothing but that which males create through Her body. Her sole raison d'être is the sexual service of men and gods in order to enhance their power. Women must worship her through emulation. The misogynist men who construct this Goddess want to express a sexuality of dominance, and female vessels for their power-lust must be obtained and controlled. In the misogynist cosmology, the only alternative for women is life under Christian patriarchy, which, as a rival group seeking control over female sexuality in its own way, is defined by Goddess misogynists as the enemy. Fear of the Christian variety of patriarchy is used as a threat to keep female devotees of the misogynist Goddess in line.

Meanwhile, activists within the Christian patriarchy make much of the "occult threat" to modern society. They play up the danger to women and children, labeling the occult enemy as "Satanic," allies of the enemy of their own patriarchal God, and thus a threat to the continued hegemony of His devotees, the Satan hunters. The real needs of women and children get lost in the fray. The Satan hunters attack the sadistic fantasies, appetites, and actions of the devotees of the misogynist Goddess, as well as feminist institutions such as day-care facilities, birth control, career women—all that is perceived as a threat to male-dominated, right-wing Christianity. Fearful depictions of Satan's witches (incorporating some of the genuine abuses encountered in misogynist Goddess traditions plus a whole lot of fantasy) are used to keep Christian women from turning to the feminist Goddess. The Satan hunter's image of the Goddess is that of a front for the male anti-God.

In either Christian or Neopagan systems of misogyny, Goddesses are pawns in male contests for dominion over one another, as are mortal females. The majority of Americans are concerned but understandably confounded by the debates. Until issues of sexism are addressed and realistically confronted, most Americans will remain confused. Sexual politics are played out in the heavens ad infinitum with contenders on many sides. Each side obscures the picture by promoting a dualistic view in which only two sides exist, but there are many (and each has dozens, if not hundreds of manifestations, all with their own complex web of varieties and interrelationships). The stakes are the control of women's bodies, hearts, minds, and souls. The confusion in the skies (and within the womb of "Mother Earth") reflects, but also serves to maintain, the confusion of the living. A goddess and her magic can be constructed so as to liberate, or to enslave, female mortals. Spiritual feminists make a grave, dogmatic mistake in assuming that the worship of Goddesses has a direct correlation with the empowerment of women. It does not. Only by studying the nature of diverse goddesses and their associated symbol-sets can we understand how one is used as the role model of a slave, while another becomes a genuine role model for liberation.

Notes

1. See the fine insider descriptions of feminist spirituality by Carol P. Christ, "Why Women Need the Goddess: Phenomenological, Psychological, and Political Reflections," in *The Politics of Women's Spirituality*, ed. Charlene Spretnak

(Garden City, N.Y.: Doubleday, 1982), 71–86; Mary Daly, *Gyn/Ecology: The Metaethics of Radical Feminism* (Boston: Beacon Press, 1978); Naomi Goldenberg, *Changing of the Gods: Feminism and the End of Traditional Religions* (Boston: Beacon Press, 1979); Sheila Ruth, *Take Back the Light: A Feminist Reclamation of Spirituality and Religion* (Lanham, MD: Littlefield Adams Quality Paperbacks, 1993); Starhawk, *The Spiral Dance: A Rebirth of the Ancient Religion of the Great Goddess* (San Francisco: Harper and Row, 1979); and *Dreaming the Dark: Magic, Sex and Politics*, 2nd ed. (Boston: Beacon Press, 1988); as well as the ethnography by Cynthia Eller, *Living in the Lap of the Goddess: The Feminist Spirituality Movement in America* (New York: Crossroad, 1993).

2. Turner believed in a threefold method for determining the total meaning of a symbol: Ask for an exegesis from native informants, observe its use in ritual and daily life, and observe the pattern of its appearance with other symbols. Victor Turner, *The Forest of Symbols* (Ithaca, N.Y.: Cornell University Press, 1967), 50–52.

3. Geertz's anthropological definition of religion had a profound effect on many disciplines by removing the essence of religion from the realm of belief, to an essence of deeply felt emotions and the actions those emotions inspired. Clifford Geertz, "Religion as a Cultural System," *Anthropological Approaches to the Study of Religion*, ASA Monographs, 3 (London: Tavestock, 1966).

4. Research was conducted over a ten-year period of participant observation both on the West Coast and the northern Midwest. I initially had three teachers, two specialists in Women's Spirituality and one Wiccan. By joining their groups in study and ritual, I eventually learned enough to prove my competence in their traditions by leading a ritual of my own. I conducted few structured interviews. The most useful information has come from ritual participation and hundreds of informal conversations with the Goddess's people, some of whom I have come to consider close friends; others I have come to fear. I have come in contact with some two hundred Neopagans who recognize various manifestations of the Goddess in over two dozen "traditions."

5. There is some debate about this among Goddess worshipers themselves, but for the most part the many Goddesses are viewed as aspects of the One. Any and all Goddesses worshiped in the past may be worshiped as the Goddess today. Differences are usually ignored in theoretical/dogmatic statements, although in practice differing views of the Goddess contribute to the small size of practicing groups and the exclusion of those with overly divergent images of Her from participation in groups with dissimilar views.

6. For a taste of the controversy over classification of Neopaganism, the occult, and the Goddess, see Eller, *Living in the Lap of the Goddess*; James Webb, *The Occult Establishment* (La Salle, Ill.: Open Court, 1976); Marcello Truzzi, "The Occult Revival as Popular Culture: Some Random Observations on the Old and the Nouveau Witch," in *Anthropology and American Life*, ed. Joseph G. Jorgensen and Marcello Truzzi (Englewood Cliffs, N.J.: Prentice-Hall, 1974), 225–50; Colin Wilson, *The Occult: A History* (New York: Random House, 1971); Catherine Albanese, *Nature Religion in America: From the Algonkian Indians to the New Age* (Chicago: University of Chicago Press, 1990); Margot Adler, *Drawing down the Moon*, 2nd ed. (Boston: Beacon Press, 1986).

7. Adler, *Drawing down the Moon*, 24–38.

8. Mary Jo Neitz, "In Goddess We Trust," in *In Gods We Trust: New Patterns of Religious Freedom in America*, ed. Thomas Robbins and Dick Anthony, 2nd ed. (New Brunswick, N.J.: Transaction), 353–72.

9. Kenneth Grant, *Aleister Crowley and the Hidden God* (New York: Samuel Weiser, 1974), 30.

10. This phrase is so often repeated in writings by and about Crowley that citing a specific location belies its significance to Crowley's world view. He even used it to preface personal letters, as he used the lesser commandment, "Love is the law, love under will," to close them. Francis King, *The Magical World of Aleister Crowley* (New York: Coward, McCann, and Geoghegan, 1977), and Wilson, *The Occult*, give useful descriptions of its meaning and use.

11. Internet communication by the Crowleyite "Thelemoid Clique," an Ordo Templis Orientis offshoot.

12. Aleister Crowley, *Book of the Law*, ed. James Wasserman (New York: Magickal Childe, 1990), part II, passages 43–45. *Book of the Law* has been published in numerous editions, including hand-typed photocopies and Internet versions. Its passages are conveniently numbered, in imitation of the Bible.

13. The term Crowleyite is used specifically in reference to my informants who identified themselves as such to me, all but one of whom were unaffiliated with any ongoing corporate group. Despite lack of formal membership, they were no mere dabblers but serious students of his teachings, having spent years in study and practice. I was surprised to find such individuals so willing to exemplify before my eyes what I had once believed was an undeservedly bad reputation. One must remember that, as with most Neopagan "denominations," there is great variety among those who identify themselves as practitioners of Crowley's magick; some, especially some of the groups that have been functioning for decades, seem to interpret the meaning of his writings in a more benign manner. One must guard against assuming all are guilty of the actions of some.

14. Compare this with the hypothesis of radical feminists, in which the essence of masculine, heterosexual sex (sex with the "other") is shown to be increasingly defined by subjugation of the "love" object through coercion, degradation, and violence. It appears as no accident that Crowley's popularity has soared since the "sexual revolution," a revolution, some would argue, waged by different groups of misogynist men against one another to determine the form and style of female subjugation. See Sheila Jeffreys, *Anticlimax: A Feminist Perspective on the Sexual Revolution* (New York: New York University Press, 1990).

15. Biographical material on Crowley was obtained from John Symonds, *The Great Beast* (London: Mayflower, 1973); Francis King, *The Magical World of Aleister Crowley* (New York: Coward, McCann & Geoghegan, 1974); and *Sexuality, Magic and Perversion* (New York: Citadel Press, 1977); Colin Wilson, *The Occult: A History* (New York: Random House, 1971), 351–77.

16. Wilson, *The Occult*, 371.

17. Ibid., 373.

18. Cf. Adler, *Drawing down the Moon*, 212. "Bonewits, in his short editorship of *Gnostica*, refused any manuscripts of a racist or sexist nature. In one editorial he noted the tendency of Neopagan articles to imply that any woman not interested in homemaking, religious activities, and raising children 'is somehow a psychic cripple; that she is an incomplete and inferior image of the Goddess.' This notion, Bonewits said, was not far from the Nazi conception of woman's purpose: *Kirche, Kuche, und Kinder* (church, kitchen, and children)."

19. Adler, *Drawing down the Moon*, 201–29; Neitz, "In Goddess We Trust," 367–69.

20. One example can be found in a pornographic story entitled "White and Black" serialized in the 1992 newsletter of the Kali Lodge of the Ordo Templis

Orientis, once available through the Internet. The OTO is one of the many groups directly descended from Crowley's attempts to found the ultimate secret magical order.

21. Crowley, *Book of the Law*, part II, passage 24.

22. Starhawk, *Dreaming the Dark*; Ruth, *Take Back the Light.*

23. George R. Kirkpatrick, Rich Rainey, and Kathryn Rubi, "Pagan Renaissance and Wiccan Witchcraft in Industrial Society: A Study of Parasociology and the Sociology of Enchantment," *Iron Mountain* 1, no. 1 (1984): 30–42.

24. Adler, *Drawing down the Moon*, 62–64; an Internet communication from the Ordo Templis Orientis states firmly that in their world view, Wicca is a direct descendant of Crowley's magic, as is Scientology, the "Family" of Charles Manson, and at least two groups of Satanists (The Church of Satan and The Process).

25. Wilson, *The Occult*, 457.

26. T. M. Luhrmann, *Persuasions of the Witch's Craft: Ritual Magic in Contemporary England* (Cambridge, Mass.: Harvard University Press, 1989), 42–54.

27. Neitz, "In Goddess We Trust," 353.

28. Starhawk, *Dreaming the Dark* , 135–53.

29. Wilson, *The Occult*, 417–18.

30. For sample discussions of biblical and Christian misogyny, see Mary Daly, *The Church and the Second Sex* (New York: Harper and Row, 1968); Charlene Spretnak, ed., *The Politics of Women's Spirituality* (Garden City, N.Y.: Anchor, 1982); for specific information on the direct connection between Christian misogyny and sexual abuse, see Annie Imbens and Ineke Jonker, *Christianity and Incest*, trans. Patricia McVay (Minneapolis, Minn.: Fortress, 1992).

31. For a case study of the mechanisms by which Christian misogyny drives some women to "secular" sexual exploitation, see Mary Zeiss Stange, "Jessica Hahn's Strange Odyssey from PTL to Playboy," *Journal of Feminist Studies in Religion* 6, no. 1 (1990): 105–16.

32. Sexual abuse by Christian clergy now appears to be so pervasive that, for example, the Roman Catholic Church has budgeted 1 billion dollars to spend on settlements in sexual abuse litigation by the year 2000; see Marie M. Fortune, "Is Nothing Sacred: The Betrayal of the Ministerial or Teaching Relationship," *Journal of Feminist Studies in Religion* 10, no. 1 (1994): 17–26.

33. Michael Granberry, "Clues Scarce in Slaying of Neopagan," *L.A. Times*, Orange Co. ed., March 16, 1997.

34. Ibid.

35. Laurel Rowe and Gray Cavender, "Cauldrons Bubble, Satan's Trouble, but Witches Are Okay: Media Constructions of Satanism and Witchcraft," in *The Satanism Scare*, ed. James T. Richardson, Joel Best, and David Bromley (New York: Aldine De Gruyter, 1991), 263–75.

36. Jo Ann Hacket, "Can a Sexist Model Liberate Us? Ancient Near Eastern 'Fertility' Goddesses," *Journal of Feminist Studies in Religion* 5, no. 1 (1989): 65–76; Janet Biehl, *Rethinking Ecofeminist Politics* (Boston: South End, 1991).

Suggested Readings

European and British Studies

Anglo, Syndey, ed. *The Damned Art: Essays in the Literature of Witchcraft*. London: Routledge and Kegan Paul, 1977.

Ankarloo, Bengt, and Gustav Henningsen, eds. *Early Modern Witchcraft: Centres and Peripheries*. Oxford: Oxford University Press, 1989.

Barstow, Anne Llewellyn. *Witchcraze: A New History of the European Witch Hunts*. New York: HarperCollins, 1994.

Bovenschen, Silvia. "The Contemporary Witch, the Historical Witch, and the Witch Myth: The Witch, Subject of the Appropriation of Nature and Object of the Domination of Nature." *New German Critique* 15 (Fall 1978): 83–119.

Clark, Stuart. "Inversion, Misrule, and the Meaning of Witchcraft." *Past and Present* 87 (May 1980): 98–127.

Cohn, Norman. *Europe's Inner Demons: An Enquiry Inspired by the Great Witch-Hunt*. New York: Basic Books, 1975.

Garrett, Clarke. "Women and Witches: Patterns of Analysis." *Signs* 3 (Winter 1977): 461–70.

Ginzburg, Carlo. *Ecstasies: Deciphering the Witches' Sabbath*. New York: Pantheon, 1991.

Gregory, Annabel, "Witchcraft, Politics, and 'Good Neighborhood' in Early Seventeenth-Century Rye." *Past and Present* 133 (November 1991): 31–66.

Hester, Marianne. *Lewd Women and Wicked Witches: A Study of the Dynamics of Male Domination*. London: Routledge, 1992.

Holmes, Clive. "Popular Culture? Witches, Magistrates, and Divines in Early Modern England." In *Understanding Popular Culture: Europe from the Middle Ages to the 19th Century*, edited by Steven L. Kaplan, 86–111. Berlin: Mouton, 1984.

Kieckhefer, Richard. *European Witch Trials: Their Foundation in Popular and Learned Culture*. Berkeley: University of California Press, 1976.

———. *Magic in the Middle Ages*. Cambridge: Cambridge University Press, 1990.

Klaits, Joseph. *Servants of Satan: The Age of the Witch Hunts.* Bloomington: University of Indiana, 1985.

Larner, Christina. *Enemies of God: The Witch-Hunt in Scotland.* London: Chatto and Windus, 1981.

———. *Witchcraft and Religion: The Politics of Popular Belief.* Oxford: Basil Blackwell, 1984.

Levack, Brian P. *The Witch-Hunt in Early Modern Europe.* London: Longman, 1987.

Macfarlane, Alan. *Witchcraft in Tudor and Stuart England: A Regional and Comparative Study.* New York: Harper and Row, 1970.

Quaife, G. R. *Godly Zeal and Furious Rage: The Witch in Early Modern Europe.* London: Croom Helm, 1987.

Roper, Lyndal. *Oedipus and the Devil: Witchcraft, Sexuality, and Religion in Early Modern Europe.* New York: Routledge, 1994.

Rosen, Barbara, ed. *Witchcraft in England, 1558–1618.* Amherst: University of Massachusetts Press, 1991.

Russell, Jeffrey Burton. *A History of Witchcraft: Sorcerers, Heretics, and Pagans.* London: Thames and Hudson, 1980.

———. *Lucifer: The Devil in the Middle Ages.* Ithaca, N.Y.: Cornell University Press, 1984.

———. *Witchcraft in the Middle Ages.* Ithaca, N.Y.: Cornell University Press, 1972.

Scarre, Geoffrey. *Witchcraft and Magic in 16th and 17th Century Europe.* Atlantic Highlands, N.J.: Humanities Press, 1987.

Thomas, Keith. *Religion and the Decline of Magic.* New York: Scribner's, 1971.

Trevor-Roper, H. R. *The European Witch-Craze of the Sixteenth and Seventeenth Centuries.* New York: Harper, 1969.

Walker, D. P. *Unclean Spirits: Possession and Exorcism in France and England in the Late Sixteenth and Early Seventeenth Centuries.* Philadelphia: University of Pennsylvania Press, 1981.

Willis, Deborah. *Malevolent Nurture: Witch-Hunting and Maternal Power in Early Modern England.* Ithaca, N.Y.: Cornell University Press, 1995.

Witchcraft in America

Boyer, Paul, and Stephen Nissenbaum. *Salem Possessed: The Social Origins of Witchcraft.* Cambridge: Harvard University Press, 1974.

———, eds. *The Salem Witchcraft Papers: Verbatim Transcripts of the Legal Documents of the Salem Witchcraft Outbreak of 1692.* 3 vols. New York: Da Capo, 1977.

Breslaw, Elaine G. *Tituba, Reluctant Witch of Salem: Devilish Indians and Puritan Fantasies*. New York: New York University Press, 1996.

Burr, George Lincoln, ed. *Narratives of the Witchcraft Cases, 1648–1706*. 1914. Reprint, New York: Barnes & Noble, 1946, 1975.

Butler, Jon. "Magic, Astrology, and the Early American Religious Heritage." *American Historical Review* 84 (April 1979): 317–46.

Demos, John Putnam. *Entertaining Satan: Witchcraft and the Culture of Early New England*. New York: Oxford University Press, 1982.

———. "Underlying Themes in the Witchcraft of Seventeenth-Century New England." *American Historical Review* 75 (1970): 1311–26.

Ehrenrich, Barbara, and Deirdre English. *Witches, Midwives, and Nurses: A History of Women Healers*. New York: Feminist Press, 1973.

Gildrie, Richard P. "Visions of Evil: Popular Culture, Puritanism, and the Massachusetts Witchcraft Crisis of 1692." *Journal of American Culture* 8 (1985): 17–33.

Godbeer, Richard. *The Devil's Dominion: Magic and Religion in Early New England*. Cambridge: Cambridge University Press, 1992.

Hall, David D. "Witchcraft and the Limits of Interpretation." *New England Quarterly* 54 (June 1985): 253–81.

———. *Worlds of Wonder, Days of Judgment: Popular Religious Belief in Early New England*. New York: Knopf, 1989.

———, ed. *Witch-hunting in Seventeenth-Century New England: A Documentary History, 1638–1692*. Boston: Northeastern University Press, 1991.

Harley, David. "Explaining Salem: Calvinist Psychology and the Diagnosis of Possession." *American Historical Review* 101 (April 1996): 307–30.

Heyrman, Christine Leigh. "Spectres of Subversion, Societies of Friends: Dissent and the Devil in Provincial Essex County, Massachusetts." In *Saints and Revolutionaries: Essays on Early American History*, edited by David D. Hall, John M. Murrin, and Thad W. Tate, 38–74. New York: Norton, 1984.

Hoffer, Peter Charles. *The Devil's Disciples: Makers of the Salem Witchcraft Trials*. Baltimore, MD: Johns Hopkins University Press, 1996.

Jacobs, Claude F. "Spirit Guides and Possession in the New Orleans Black Spiritual Churches." *Journal of American Folklore* 102 (January–March 1989): 45–56.

Kamensky, Jane. *Governing the Tongue: The Politics of Speech in Early New England*. New York: Oxford University Press, 1997.

Karlsen, Carol F. *The Devil in the Shape of a Woman: Witchcraft in Colonial New England*. New York: Norton, 1987.

Kibbey, Anne. "Mutations of the Supernatural: Witchcraft, Remarkable Providences, and the Power of Puritan Men." *American Quarterly* 34 (Summer 1982): 125–48.

Perspectives on Witchcraft: Rethinking the Seventeenth-Century New England Experience. A Selection of Papers from the Tenth Salem Conference. Essex Institute Historical Collections 128–29 (October 1992–January 1993).

Reis, Elizabeth. *Damned Women: Sinners and Witches in Puritan New England*. Ithaca, N.Y.: Cornell University Press, 1997.

———. "The Devil, the Body, and the Feminine Soul in Puritan New England." *Journal of American History* 82 (June 1995): 15–36.

Rosenthal, Bernard. *Salem Story: Reading the Witch Trials of 1692*. Cambridge: Cambridge University Press, 1993.

Weisman, Richard. *Witchcraft, Magic, and Religion in Seventeenth-Century Massachusetts*. Amherst: University of Massachusetts Press, 1984.

General Studies of Modern Feminist Spirituality, Witchcraft, and Goddesses

Adler, Margot. *Drawing down the Moon: The Resurgence of Paganism in America*. Boston: Beacon, 1979, 1986.

Bednarowski, Mary Farrell. *New Religions and the Theological Imagination in America*. Bloomington: Indiana University Press, 1989.

Budapest, Zsuzsanna E. *The Grandmother of Time: A Women's Book of Celebrations, Spells, and Sacred Objects for Every Month of the Year*. San Francisco: Harper and Row, 1989.

———. *Holy Book of Women's Mysteries*. Rev. ed. Berkeley, Calif.: Wingbow, 1986.

Christ, Carol. *The Laughter of Aphrodite: Reflections on a Journey to the Goddess*. San Francisco: Harper and Row, 1987.

Culpepper, Emily Erwin. "Contemporary Goddess Thealogy: A Sympathetic Critique." In *Shaping New Vision: Gender and Values in American Culture*, edited by Clarissa W. Atkinson, Constance H. Buchanan, and Margaret R. Miles, 51–71. Ann Arbor: University of Michigan Research Press, 1987.

Eller, Cynthia. *Living in the Lap of the Goddess: The Feminist Spirituality Movement in America*. Boston: Beacon, 1995.

Orenstein, Gloria Feman. *The Reflowering of the Goddess: Contemporary Journeys and Cycles of Empowerment*. New York: Pergamon, 1990.

Orion, Loretta. *Never Again the Burning Times: Paganism Revived.* Prospect Heights, Ill.: Waveland, 1995.

Plaskow, Judith, and Carol Christ, eds. *Weaving the Visions: New Patterns in Feminist Spirituality.* San Francisco: Harper and Row, 1989.

Starhawk. *Dreaming the Dark: Magic, Sex, & Politics.* Boston: Beacon Press, 1982.

———. *The Spiral Dance: A Rebirth of the Ancient Religion of the Great Goddess.* San Francisco: Harper and Row, 1979, 1989.

———. *Truth or Dare: Encounters with Power, Authority, and Mystery.* San Francisco: Harper and Row, 1989.

Stone, Merlin. *When God Was a Woman.* New York: Harcourt, Brace, Jovanovich, 1976.

Teish, Luisah. *Jambalaya: The Natural Woman's Book of Personal Charms and Practical Rituals.* San Francisco: Harper and Row, 1985.

Walker, Barbara. *Women's Encyclopedia of Myths and Secrets.* San Francisco: HarperSanFrancisco, 1983

Weaver, Mary Jo. "Who is the Goddess and Where Does She Get Us?" *Journal of Feminist Studies in Religion* 5 (Spring 1989): 49–64.

About the Contributors

MATTHEW DENNIS is associate professor of history at the University of Oregon and the author of *Cultivating a Landscape of Peace: Iroquois-European Encounters in Seventeenth-Century America* (1993). He is currently writing a book about Seneca witchcraft.

CYNTHIA ELLER is an independent scholar affiliated with the Center for the Study of American Religion at Princeton University. Her most recent book is *Living in the Lap of the Goddess: The Feminist Spirituality Movement in America* (1995), and she is currently working on a book titled *The Myth of Matriarchal Prehistory* (forthcoming).

DAVID C. ESTES has edited *Critical Perspectives on the Fiction of Ernest J. Gaines* (1994). He is associate professor of English at Loyola University in New Orleans.

SIDNEY L. HARRING is professor of law at the City University of New York Law School. He is the author of *Crow Dog's Case: American Indian Sovereignty, Tribal Law, and American Law in the Nineteenth Century* (1994). He has published widely in legal journals and continues to work on indigenous people's relation to the law and the state.

LINDA JENCSON has taught cultural anthropology at Lane Community College and Linfield College in Oregon and Moorhead State University in Minnesota. She is currently an independent scholar doing consulting work.

JANE KAMENSKY is the author of *Governing the Tongue: The Politics of Speech in Early New England* (1997) and is at work on a book about the cultural history of coffee in America. She is assistant professor of history at Brandeis University.

CAROL F. KARLSEN is the author of *The Devil in the Shape of a Woman: Witchcraft in Colonial New England* (1987) and the co-editor of *The Journal of Esther Edwards Burr, 1754–1757* (1984). She is associate professor of history and women's studies at the University of Michigan.

Kenneth P. Minkema is the executive editor of *The Works of Jonathan Edwards* and Lecturer in American Religious History at Yale University. He is the co-editor of *The Sermon Notebook of Samuel Parris* (1993) and *A Jonathan Edwards Reader* (1995), and editor of volume 14 of *The Works of Jonathan Edwards, Sermons and Discourses, 1723–1729* (1997).

Nell Irvin Painter, Edwards Professor of American History at Princeton University, recently published *Sojourner Truth, A Life, A Symbol* (1996). Her current project examines ideals and practices of personal beauty.

Bernard Rosenthal is the author of *Salem Story: Reading the Witch Trials of 1692* (1993). He is professor of English at Binghamton University.

Starhawk is the author of *The Spiral Dance: A Rebirth of the Ancient Religion of the Great Goddess* (1989); *Dreaming the Dark: Magic, Sex, and Politics* (1982); and *Truth or Dare: Encounters with Power, Authority, and Mystery* (1987). Together with Anne Hill and Diane Baker, she is cowriting *Circle Round: Raising Children in the Goddess Tradition* (forthcoming).